Anifeiliaid y Nos

Susan Meredith

Dyluniwyd gan Nicola Butler
a Josephine Thompson

Darluniau gan
Patrizia Donaera ac Adam Larkum

Addasiad Cymraeg: Elin Meek

Ymgynghorydd anifeiliaid y nos: Margaret Rostron

Ymgynghorydd darllen: Alison Kelly, Prifysgol Roehampton

Ffotograff o wiwer hedegog yw hwn.

Cynnwys

- 3 Prysur drwy'r nos
- 4 Bwyta yn y nos
- 6 *Bushbabies*
- 8 Llygaid mawr
- 10 Gwrando a ffroeni
- 12 Tylluanod
- 14 Rhy boeth
- 16 Cysgu drwy'r dydd
- 18 Cuddio
- 20 Ystlumod
- 22 Synau'r nos
- 24 Neges olau
- 26 Draenogod
- 28 Y nos a'r dydd
- 30 Geirfa
- 31 Gwefannau diddorol
- 32 Mynegai

Prysur drwy'r nos

Mae miloedd o anifeiliaid o gwmpas yn y nos. Anifeiliaid nosol yw'r enw arnyn nhw.

Anifeiliaid nosol yw racwniaid. Maen nhw'n effro drwy'r nos.

Bwyta yn y nos

Mae anifeiliaid y nos yn bwyta ac yn chwilio am fwyd yn y tywyllwch. Mae rhai'n teimlo'n fwy diogel.

Mae llewpard yn aros i anifail fynd heibio.

Mae'n neidio i lawr ac yn ei frathu i'w ladd.

Mae'n ei lusgo i goeden i'w fwyta.

Mae mwncïod y nos yn bwyta ffrwythau. Maen nhw'n bachu bwyd tra bydd pawb arall yn cysgu.

Mae adar mawr yn ymosod ar eithr coala. Mae coalas yn cnoi dail yn y nos, pan fydd yr adar yn cysgu.

Bushbabies

Anifeiliaid y nos sy'n byw mewn coed yw *bushbabies*.

Maen nhw'n rhedeg ac yn neidio o gangen i gangen yn y nos.

Gall *bushbaby* symud ei glustiau i ddweud o ble mae sŵn yn dod.

Os yw'n clywed pryfyn, mae'n ei ddal yn yr awyr ac yn ei fwyta.

Gall mam *bushbaby* gario ei baban yn ei cheg.

Bydd hi'n mynd i chwilio am fwyd a'i adael yn cydio wrth frigyn.

Mae cynffon hir *bushbaby*'n ei helpu i gydbwyso yn yr awyr.

Mae'n cribo ei ffwr ag un grafanc fawr.

Llygaid mawr

Mae gan lawer o anifeiliaid y nos lygaid mawr. Maen nhw'n eu helpu i weld yn y tywyllwch.

Tarsierod sydd â'r llygaid mwyaf gan unrhyw anifail o'r un maint.

Mae'r tarsier hwn wedi dal pryfyn enfawr i'w fwyta. Ond mae'n gallu gweld rhai bach hefyd.

Mae'r geco'n agor ei lygaid
led y pen i weld yn
y tywyllwch.

Mae cannwyll llygad anifail y nos yn mynd yn
fach yn y dydd i gadw golau poenus allan.

Mae llygaid rhai
brogaod yn mynd
yn gul yn y dydd.

Mae rhan ddu
llygaid teigr yn
mynd yn fach.

Mae'r geco'n gweld
drwy bedwar twll
bach mewn agen.

Gwrando a ffroeni

Am ei bod hi'n anodd gweld yn y tywyllwch, gall anifeiliaid y nos arogli a chlywed yn dda hefyd.

Mae gan faedd daear glustiau a thrwyn hir. Gall glustfeinio am forgrug a ffroeni am eu nythod.

Mae'n cloddio nythod morgrug â'i grafangau.

Mae'n dal y morgrug ar ei dafod gludiog.

Mae'r gila'n ffroeni ac yn llyfu'r ddaear i weld a oes bwyd o gwmpas.

Corlwynog yw'r llwynog lleiaf yn y byd, ond nhw sydd â'r clustiau mwyaf.

Maen nhw'n gallu clywed llygod, madfallod a phryfed hyd yn oed, o bell.

Tylluanod

Adar lwcus yw tylluanod. Maen nhw'n bwyta llawer o bethau, ond does dim byd eisiau eu bwyta nhw.

Mae gan dylluan adenydd mawr. Does dim rhaid iddi guro'i hadenydd ryw lawer.

Mae ei phlu'n feddal ac yn fflwffog. Dydyn nhw ddim yn gwneud sŵn.

Dydy anifeiliaid eraill ddim yn clywed y dylluan yn dod ac yn glanio arnyn nhw.

Dydy tylluanod ddim yn gallu troi eu llygaid ond gallan nhw droi eu pennau'r holl ffordd i weld y tu cefn iddyn nhw.

Gall tylluanod glywed a gweld yn dda iawn. Mae clustiau'r dylluan hon mewn lle annisgwyl.

Plu

Clust

Rhy boeth

Mae rhai anifeiliaid yn methu dioddef gwres yr haul. Felly maen nhw'n dod allan yn y nos pan fydd hi'n oerach.

Yn y nos, mae hipos yn bwyta gwair.

Yn y dydd maen nhw'n eistedd mewn dŵr i oeri. Maen nhw'n rhoi mwd dros eu hunain i gadw'r haul o'u croen.

Mae gwlithod yn dod allan yn y nos am y bydden nhw'n sychu ac yn marw yn yr haul.

Mae llygod cangarŵ'n byw mewn diffeithwch poeth. Maen nhw'n cloddio twll o dan y tywod â'u traed. Mae hi'n oerach o dan y ddaear.

Yn y nos mae'r llygod yn symud fel cangarŵ.

Maen nhw'n nôl hadau i'w stwffio yn eu cegau.

Maen nhw'n mynd â'r hadau i'r twll i'w bwyta.

Cysgu drwy'r dydd

Mae'r rhan fwyaf o anifeiliaid y nos yn cysgu yn eu cartref yn ystod y dydd.

Mae'r pathew yn gwneud nyth o wair i gysgu ynddo.

Cneuen i'w bwyta.

Mae moch daear yn byw o dan ddaear.

Maen nhw'n cario eu gwely o dan eu gên ac weithiau'n dod ag ef allan i grasu yn yr haul.

Mae'r diogyn yn hongian ben i waered mewn coed. Fel hyn mae'n cysgu hefyd.

Mae'r diogyn mor llonydd, mae planhigion yn tyfu yn ei flew.

Cuddio

Rhaid i anifeiliaid y nos fod yn ddiogel wrth orffwyso yn y dydd. Dydyn nhw ddim eisiau i'w gelynion eu gweld.

Mae gwalchwyfyn yr helyglys yn gorffwyso ar blanhigion pinc a gwyrdd, felly maen nhw'n anodd eu gweld.

Os yw oposwm mewn perygl, mae'n esgus bod yn farw fel bod gelynion yn gadael llonydd iddo.

Mae'r broga llygaid coch yn cuddio ar ddail yn ystod y dydd.

Mae llygaid a choesau llachar y broga'n codi ofn ar y gelyn.

Troellwr llydanbig yw'r aderyn hwn. Mae'n edrych fel cangen oherwydd y marciau ar ei blu.

Ystlumod

Mae ystlumod yn hedfan ond dydyn nhw ddim yn gallu gweld yn dda iawn.

Mae rhai ystlumod yn bwyta pryfed. Maen nhw'n dod o hyd iddyn nhw drwy ddefnyddio'u clustiau mewn ffordd ryfedd.

Mae ystlum yn gwichian yn uchel wrth hedfan.

Mae'r sŵn yn taro pryfyn ac yn bownsio 'nôl.

Mae'r ystlum yn clywed y sŵn ac yn bwyta'r pryfyn.

Mae ystlum ffrwythau'n gallu arogli ffrwyth aeddfed o bell.

Mae'n bwyta'r ffrwyth ben i waered.

Mae rhai ystlumod yn codi pysgod o'r dŵr a'u crafangau i'w bwyta.

Synau'r nos

Pan fydd pobl yn cysgu'n drwm, mae anifeiliaid yn galw ar ei gilydd yn y tywyllwch.

Mae bleiddiaid yn adnabod lleisiau ei gilydd.

Maen nhw'n udo ar fleiddiaid yn eu haid ac i ddweud wrth fleiddiaid eraill am gadw draw.

Dydy teuluoedd mwncïod y nos
ddim yn hoffi gweld eraill yn dod yn agos.
Maen nhw'n parablu nes iddyn nhw fynd.

Mae'r criciedyn gwryw'n canu drwy rwbio'i adenydd.

Mae'r fenyw'n hoffi'r gân ac yn chwilio am y gwryw.

Neges olau

Mae rhai anifeiliaid y nos yn anfon neges mewn ffordd ryfedd.

Mae pryfed tân yn fflachio fel goleuadau i roi arwyddion i'w gilydd. Mae'r goeden hon yn llawn pryfed tân.

Mae pryfyn tân yn fflachio â'i fol.

Mae brogaod yn bwyta pryfed tân. O fwyta gormod, maen nhw'n pefrio.

Mae golau'n hongian o ên dreigbysgod. Mae perdys yn dod i edrych arno ac yn cael eu bwyta.

Mae cyrff magïod benyw'n pefrio.

Mae magïod gwryw'n hedfan i gwrdd â'r benywod sy'n pefrio.

Draenogod

Mae'r draenog yn hela am fwyd yn y nos pan fydd trychfilod, mwydod a gwlithod o gwmpas.

Mae draenog yn ffroeni am fwydod, cyn cloddio i'w codi.

Os daw cadno, mae'r draenog yn rholio'n belen bigog.

Mae eisiau bwyd ar y cadno, ond dydy e ddim yn hoffi pigau. Mae'n mynd i ffwrdd.

Dim ond ychydig ddiwrnodau oed yw'r draenogod bach hyn.

Dydyn nhw ddim wedi agor eu llygaid eto a dydy eu pigau ddim yn rhy finiog.

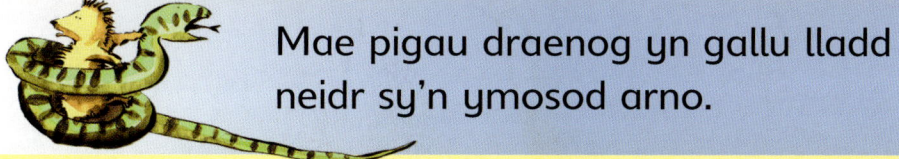
Mae pigau draenog yn gallu lladd neidr sy'n ymosod arno.

Y nos a'r dydd

Mae rhai anifeiliaid o gwmpas yn y dydd a'r nos hefyd.

Yn y nos mae teigrod a chathod mawr yn hela fel arfer. Mae cathod llai yn hoffi gwneud yr un fath.

Mae llygaid cath yn disgleirio yn y tywyllwch.

Anifail y nos yw'r cangarŵ fel arfer ond mae'n dod allan i dorheulo yn y dydd.

Bydd cwningod yn rhy boeth yn y dydd ac yn rhy oer yn y nos.

Maen nhw'n dod allan wrth iddi nosi neu ddyddio.

O'r blaen, dim ond yn y nos roedd cadnoid yn chwilio am anifeiliaid i'w bwyta.

Nawr, maen nhw'n dod allan yn y dydd hefyd, i fwyta bwyd mae pobl wedi gadael ar lawr.

Geirfa

Dyma rai o'r geiriau yn y llyfr hwn sy'n newydd i ti, efallai. Mae'r dudalen hon yn rhoi ystyr y geiriau i ti.

 nosol – yn effro ac yn brysur yn y nos. Mae anifail nosol yn gorffwyso yn y dydd

 hela – chwilio am anifeiliaid, eu dal a'u lladd, i'w bwyta fel arfer.

 ffroeni – arogli i chwilio am rywbeth.

 crafanc – y rhannau caled, miniog fel ewinedd hir ar flaen bysedd anifeiliaid.

 ffau – twll neu dwnnel y mae anifail yn ei gloddio yn y ddaear i fyw ynddo.

 gwryw – anifail sy'n gallu dod yn dad. Gwrywod yw bechgyn a dynion.

 benyw – anifail sy'n gallu dod yn fam. Benywod yw merched a menywod.

Gwefannau diddorol

Os oes gen ti gyfrifiadur, rwyt ti'n gallu dysgu rhagor am anifeiliaid y nos ar y Rhyngrwyd.

I ymweld â'r gwefannau hyn, cer i **www.usborne-quicklinks.com**.

Caiff y gwefannau hyn eu hadolygu'n gyson a chaiff y dolenni yn 'Usborne Quicklinks' eu diweddaru. Fodd bynnag, nid yw Usborne Publishing yn gyfrifol, ac nid yw chwaith yn derbyn atebolrwydd, am gynnwys neu argaeledd unrhyw wefan ac eithrio'i wefan ei hun. Rydym yn argymell i chi oruchwylio plant pan fyddant ar y Rhyngrwyd.

Bochdew yn gwrando am arwydd o beryg.

Mynegai

baedd daear, 10
bleiddiaid, 22
brogaod, 9, 19, 24
cadno, 11, 26, 29
cangarŵ, 28
cathod, 28
coala, 5,
criciedyn, 23
cwningod, 29
diogyn, 17
draenogod, 26–27
dreigbysgod du, 6–7
geco, 9
gila, 11
gwalchwyfyn yr helyglys, 18
gwlithod, 14

hipos, 14
llewpard, 4
llwynog, 11, 26, 29
llygod cangarŵ, 15
magïod, 25
moch daear, 16
mwncïod y nos, 5, 23
oposwm, 18
pathew, 16
pryfed tân, 24
racwniaid, 3
tarsier, 8
teigrod, 9, 28
troellwr llydanbig, 19
tylluanod, 12–13
ystlumod, 20–21

Cydnabyddiaeth

Clawr: Zoe Wray
Trin ffotograffau: John Russell, Emma Julings a Zoe Wray

Cydnabyddiaeth lluniau

Mae'r cyhoeddwyr yn ddiolchgar i'r canlynol am ganiatâd i atgynhyrchu deunydd:
© **Alamy Images** 13, © **Bruce Coleman** (Alain Compost) 8, (Kim Taylor) 20 a 28; © **CORBIS** (Niall Benvie) clawr, (Joe McDonald) 1, (W. Perry Conway) 3, (George McCarthy) 16, (Staffan Widstrand) 19; © **FLPA – Images of Nature** (A Christiansen) 11, (Foto Natura Stock) 17, (Christ Mattison) 18, (Albert Visage) 21, (Mark Newman) 22; © **Getty Images** (Gary Bell) 5, (JH Pete Carmichael) 9, (Jonathan Gale) 29; © **Heather Angel** (Peter David) 25; **Nature Picture Library** (David Shale) 25: © **NHPA** (Stephen Dalton) 6–7, (Christophe Ratier) 14, (Dr Ivan Polunin) 24; © **Oxford Scientific Films** (Alan Root/SAL) 10, (Doug Bertran/SAL) 15; © **Science Photo Library** (Gregory Dimijian) 23; © **Warren Photographic** (Jane Burton) 27.
Ffotograff ar dudalen 31 gan Tim Fiach.

Cyhoeddwyd gyntaf yn 2003 gan Usborne Publishing Ltd., Usborne House, 83-85 Saffron Hill, London EC1N 8RT.
Cyhoeddwyd gyntaf yng Nghymru yn 2013 gan Wasg Gomer, Llandysul, Ceredigion SA44 4JL.
www.gomer.co.uk
Cedwir pob hawl. Argraffwyd yn China.

G. REX SMITH

Medieval Muslim Horsemanship

A FOURTEENTH-CENTURY ARABIC CAVALRY MANUAL

THE BRITISH LIBRARY

BRITISH LIBRARY BOOKLETS

It is the aim of this series of booklets to introduce the British Library to the general public by drawing attention to many fascinating aspects of its collections which are of interest to the layman as well as the scholar. Many of the items mentioned and illustrated in the booklets are frequently on exhibition in the British Library's exhibition galleries in the British Museum building in Great Russell Street, London W.C.1.

ACKNOWLEDGEMENTS

The author wishes to record his indebtedness to the following, all of whom have read his draft and have made suggestions for its improvement: Professor Donald Little, Miss Elaine Paintin, Dr Michael Rogers, Mr Jack Smart and Miss Norah Titley.

The illustration on the back cover is reproduced by courtesy of the Trustees of the British Museum.

© 1979 The British Library Board
Published by the British Library,
Great Russell Street, London WC1B 3DG
BL British Library Cataloguing in Publication Data
Smith, Gerald Rex
   Muslim horsemanship.
   1. Horsemanship—Arabia—History
   I. Title II. British Library. Reference Division
   798'.2'0953   SF284.A/
   ISBN 0-904654-12-5
Designed by Peter Campbell
Set in Monotype Garamond
Printed in Great Britain
by the Oxley Press (Nottingham) Ltd

Introduction

This booklet is a study of a 14th-century Arabic manuscript (Add 18866) preserved in the Department of Oriental Manuscripts and Printed Books of the British Library. The manuscript, purchased in a London sale-room in the 19th century, is one of the treasures of the Arabic collection in the Department and can usually be seen in its general exhibition. It is a manual of horsemanship used by Mamluk cavalrymen, the men who opposed the Crusaders from Europe in the Holy Land. They were skilled soldiers and horsemen whose equestrian games, performed in stadia, were exciting spectator sports for the Mamluks who flocked to them in much the same way as did their European military counterparts to jousts and tournaments in the age of chivalry.

The manuscript contains 18 illustrations, the full range of which have not, to the knowledge of the writer, previously been published or studied in depth. Photographs of all these appear in this booklet. They include vivid scenes showing the horses and their equipment and the military costumes and weapons of the cavalrymen of medieval Egypt and Syria. At the same time the paintings are fine examples of Mamluk art in their own right.

The literal translation of the Arabic title of the work is *An End to Questioning and Desiring [Further Knowledge] concerning the Learning* (variant, *Teaching*) *of the Different Exercises of Horsemanship*. This long title has been abbreviated to *Horsemanship* throughout the booklet. The text remains unpublished and the writer knows of no translation of it into any European language. The booklet has been written with the general reader in mind. The only concessions made to the Arabist and Islamic scholar are the inclusion in the text in brackets of certain Arabic technical terms and the addition of appendices and notes to supplement the text. Suggestions have been made for further reading designed to satisfy the general reader whose interest has been stimulated by an aspect of this study.

THE MAMLUKS AND THEIR EQUESTRIAN GAMES

Saladin, the ruler known in the West for his campaigns against the Crusaders, and his family, the Ayyubids, ruled over Egypt between the years 1169 and 1250. The Ayyubids were followed by a dynasty known as the Mamluks (*mamlūk* in Arabic means 'owned', 'possessed'), since they were originally the slaves of the Ayyubids. The Mamluks held sway between 1250 and 1517 and took over the territories of Egypt, Syria and Palestine. They were of two distinct lines, the Baḥrīs (1250–1390) and the Burjīs (1382–1517). The Baḥrīs were so named after their original barracks on an island in the middle of the Nile (Baḥr al-Nīl) in Cairo and the Burjīs, also called Circassians, after their barracks in the Cairo Citadel (al-Burj). The Baḥrī Mamluks were in the main originally Qipchaqs, a Turkish tribe in southern Russia, with an admixture of Mongol and Kurdish blood. The Burjīs were mainly Circassians from the Caucasus.

The military power of the Mamluks in the territories over which they ruled stemmed the advancing tide of the vast Mongol hordes which had already destroyed Baghdad and the Abbasid caliphate in 1258 and which were now sweeping westwards from within the borders of China. Under Sultan Quṭuz (reigned 1259–60) the Mamluk army defeated the Mongols at the famous battle of 'Ayn Jālūt in Syria in 1260. By the end of the 13th century the Mamluks had also destroyed the remaining Syrian and Palestinian strongholds of the Crusaders who had first arrived in the area from Europe in the 11th century. The Circassian Mamluks were themselves, however, supplanted by the Turkish Ottomans in 1517, thus heralding Turkish rule throughout the Middle East which was to continue down to the First World War.

Although they were originally of slave status, this implied no social stigma; on the contrary many Mamluks reached high positions of state. For all of them the Mamluk military régime insisted on a strict education and special schools were set up in the Cairo Citadel.[1] Naturally enough in a military administration such as this, although subjects like Qur'ān studies, the religious sciences etc. were not neglected, great emphasis was placed on the education of a warrior

---

1 Folio 97a. 13×20·5 cm. The Arabic caption reads 'Illustration of two horsemen whose lance-heads are between each other's shoulder-blades.'
Two riders bearing lances in a jousting exercise passing at the gallop, both carrying maces. This is an exquisite painting, though unfortunately the faces have been deliberately disfigured, and it is unique in the manuscript in its inclusion of haloes round both riders' heads. Comparing this illustration with the others and particularly in view of the differing quality seen in the eighteen paintings, the suggestion is made that this is the work of the master-artist and the remainder that of his pupils. The halo does of course figure not infrequently in Islamic art and it is thought to be a survival from Sasanian times. It appears in the *Maqāmāt* illustrations and the master-artist is here working in a tradition he knows and in which he was brought up. The hare on the left is a motif particularly common in Islamic ceramics.[14]

ثم يخرج الطالب من تحت سنانه بين كتفي المطلوب ثم يخرج الطالب فيصير مطلوباً والمطلوب طالباً ثلث حركات الصف مخالفات متواليات كمثل القوس شرطوا لا جميعاً ويخرج المبتدي الخروج نحو الموكب ثلث حركات متواليات بنقلات ملاح وسنانه الى وجه الثاني وسنان الثاني بين كتفي المبتدي ثم يخرج الثاني ثلث حركات متواليات مخالفات بنقلات ملاح وسنانه في وجه المبتدي ثم يخرج المبتدي حركة اخرى ويرجع الى النا ورد يميناً ويدورا جميعاً حلقة واحدة ثم يخرج الثاني خلفه والمبتدي في طلبه ويرجعا الى النا ورد فيدورا حلقة واحدة ويقطع كل الى ارضه وهذا الوجه فهو مستشرق ومنقول من الموارنة ومختصر منه الاترى ان

élite and in particular on the training of first-class cavalrymen. For the latter a mastery of the prescribed equestrian exercises was essential. These exercises appear to have developed quickly into organised games into which an element of competition was introduced and which took place before large crowds in the specially built and elaborate stadia or hippodromes of the important towns of the sultanate, especially of Cairo. Such are the games which form the greater part of the subject-matter of *Horsemanship*.[2] Since we know that the majority of hippodromes, in Cairo at least, were built and flourished under the Baḥrī Mamluks (1250–1390), we can assume that the games were more popular during this period. The famous Sultan Baybars (1260–1277) in particular was a builder of hippodromes and patron of the equestrian games. They clearly declined during the later Burjī period (1382–1517), though their popularity must have waxed and waned at the whim of the individual sultan or even, at times perhaps, of high state officials.

Apart from those exercises described in *Horsemanship*, the following were also, amongst others, considered part of the science of horsemanship: polo, a game common with the Ayyubids, the Mamluks' predecessors, and played in the hippodromes; the *qabaq* or gourd game, entailing shooting arrows at a gourd target at the top of a high pole from a moving horse;[3] and the *birjās* game, in which a palm staff was thrown by mounted horsemen.[4]

Those with proven expertise in one or more branches of equestrian games were given the title 'master' (*muʿallim*). It is probable that the individual would specialise in one particular branch, presumably after reaching the required proficiency in all, and the author of *Horsemanship* tells us that he relied heavily on such a master for information in his book on the lance games.

ARABIC MILITARY LITERATURE

Although a large proportion of the Arabic histories and chronicles from early times includes descriptions of battles, sieges and all types of military activity, it is not until the 11th century that we begin to detect what can be broadly termed military literature. It now seems clear that the presence of the Crusaders in the Middle

---

2 Folio 99a. 23 × 20·5 cm. 'Illustration of a number of horsemen taking part in a contest, their lances on their shoulders.'
Four riders in a team game cantering round the hippodrome pool in a clockwise direction. The composition is symmetrical and even the fish in the pool are painted head to head to add to this effect. There is a lotus blossom at each corner of the pool.[15] The riders are young and beardless. They are clearly novices.

كانت رماحهم على أكافهم فشوطهم لحث شديد فاذا فعلوا ذلك وقع المخالف على اصحاب الميسره فيخرجوا مخالفات ويخرجوا الذى لهم مثلهم ثم يخرجوا المبتدا حرجه ويدوروا واحدا وردا وحدا ويقطع كل فى ارضه

وهذا الميدان فهو حربى جدّ كله وفيه يتبين الفارس الماهر لانه لا يفلت من هذا الميدان حرث كان او مبدأنى الاكل حاذق واذا فعلت هذه الاسواط واحد من ظفّه ورمحه من خلفه ورمحه على كتفه فليرد يده الى العنان ويقبض بكلتا هما على عقب الرمح وحطه من كفه ويعطل من تحته ومن مشائى هذا الوجه

East with their greater reliance on cavalry and their superiority in many types of weaponry helped to produce a spate of such compositions.[5] The reality of a permanent, highly organised standing army came only from 1169 onwards, under the Ayyubids, the rulers of Egypt and Syria prior to the Mamluk sultanate and it is not really surprising that important manuals for the improvement of military tactics, weaponry and waging war are associated with them. These were the prototypes of Mamluk military literature, of which *Horsemanship* forms a part.

Arabic military literature has conveniently been divided into three types:[6] works of horsemanship; archery; and military tactics and organisation. *Horsemanship* undoubtedly belongs to the first category, though it must be said that certain later chapters might seem to belong rather to the last. It was the second and third types, archery and military tactics, which had direct relevance to the battlefield. The flame of the composition of these genres was fuelled by the incursions and continued presence of the foreign infidel Crusaders within the borders of Islam. The books of horsemanship attempted generally to provide all the necessary information for the care and training of horses, skill with all types of weapons and sometimes even a little elementary veterinary medicine. *Horsemanship* was thus first and foremost of relevance to the games and exercises performed in the hippodromes in the Mamluk state.

ARABIC MANUSCRIPT ILLUSTRATION

Islam from the first discouraged any form of pictorial art, for it was considered that this was tantamount to setting up idols to be worshipped along with God. From the 7th century onwards the divine word in the form of the Qur'ān began to be copied, but even illumination of the resulting manuscripts was slow in developing. This deep-seated distaste for illustration, pictorial art as opposed to illumination, abstract designs and patterns, continued among the Arabs who finally gave way reluctantly only in the case of certain types of manuscript.

From the 11th century certain secular manuscripts came to be

---

3 Folio 101a. 14·5 × 20·5 cm. 'Illustration of a horseman taking part in a game with a lance, the lance-head being in his hand and its shaft to his rear.'
The lance-head here clearly means that part of the shaft near the head.

4 Folio 109a. 13·5 × 20·5 cm. No caption. A single rider carrying two lances in horizontal position. The picture is framed with stylized flowers. The horseman wears a beard and is clearly older than riders portrayed in earlier illustrations, a man of some experience.

موذج من سلاح الفارس المسلم في العصور الوسطى

adorned with illustrations, in particular the scientific manuscripts. Thus one finds manuscripts on astronomy and medicine among the first to be illustrated, followed by works on automata and veterinary and zoological texts, and of course ultimately works on horsemanship and the military arts. Probably the only non-scientific text to be illustrated was the *Kalīlah wa-Dimnah,* a collection of animal tales, which was a favourite for illustration from the 12th century onwards. Such encyclopaedias as '*Ajā'ib al-makhlūqāt* ('The Wonders of Created Things') also included some fine paintings to illustrate its diverse subject-matter.

The zenith of Arab painting, however, undoubtedly came with the superb 13th-century illustrations of the *Maqāmāt* ('Assemblies') of Ḥarīrī. These are a series of humorous stories, written in complex rhymed prose about a rather likeable vagabond named Abū Zayd. The hero is depicted against many different types of backcloth, the house, the desert tent, the bazaar and even the sea. These illustrations were produced in Iraq, mainly in Baghdad.

In 1258, however, Islam was dealt a tremendous blow. Its capital city, Baghdad, the centre of manuscript painting, was sacked by invading Mongols and the caliphate, an office instituted on the death of the Prophet Muḥammad in 632, was destroyed. Those artists employed in Iraq in the 13th century were compelled to flee westwards before the Mongol armies and they found refuge in Syria, where there was already a tradition of painting, and in Egypt. Cairo and Damascus continued after this as centres of Arab painting. Despite the Mamluks' victory over the Mongols preventing Mongol penetration into southern Syria and Egypt, the new régime, as it became the governing force in Iraq and the eastern Islamic world, absorbed a great deal of Mongol influence. This influence may be manifesting itself here in the facial appearance of the riders in the illustrations. It may also be, however, that this was how the Mamluk artists viewed the Turks in the sultanate who had originated in Central Asia.

---

5 Folio 122b. 16·5 × 20·5 cm. 'Illustration of a horseman with a sword in his hand. His sleeve is wound (?) over his hand and he rises out of his saddle as he strikes with the sword.'

ادني الفرس حتى يحصل على مصادك الايسر وانفض يدك اليمنى واقطع والرادي في
هذا الباب من المضربين لانهما ضربتان شديدتان صعبتان لا يضربهما الا ماهر
ومونعهما تحت الركاب الايسر فاذا اخفت من الوقعه عن الفرس في هاتين الضربتين
فاولا بندائك في العلم فسوة ان تقرب يدك اليسرى مع العنان وهي معطاة
بكمك الى قربوس السرج تعتمد عليه فاذا فعلت ذلك واستوى لك مائلته لك
فاخذ واخذا جيدا واضرب فانك ترجع الى مرجلك فاذا احللت ذلك واردت
سراعته لهاتين الضربتين فاضرب يدك الى المعرفة الفرس واخذر واضرب

صورة فارس قد وضع ركابه وكمك على جمع ومصادر ذلك يجب دوس خيبة السيف

وارجع الى مرجلك فهو امون عليك من الاول فاذا استمرت على الضرب باحد الضربين
فقد جسرت عليها فاخذ بعد ذلك واضرب ان شئت بغير سراج ان شاء الله تعالى

'Horsemanship' and its illustrations

The illustrations show the horses and their equipment, the apparel of the riders and their weapons. The author of *Horsemanship* prefaces the work firstly with the customary general pious phrases and utterances in rhymed prose and then with an introduction more relevant to the book itself, extolling the virtues of the Holy War. The sub-headings of the introduction can be literally translated as follows: 'Inciting (others) to take part in the Holy War'; 'The excellence of the Holy War'; 'Seeking martyrdom'; and 'Spending one's wealth for God's cause'. The introduction is profusely illustrated with quotations from the Traditions of the Prophet Muḥammad and from his Companions and other famous personages.

In the illustrations the horses depicted do not have the appearance of the pure-bred Arab. They may well be Barbs or Barb crosses. The Barb, a native of North Africa, might have served as basic stock for the Mamluk cavalry, though we can assume that Arab, as well as Turk and Turkoman blood had established itself in Syria and Egypt, for the latter breeds must have immigrated westwards with their eastern masters from as early as the 9th century.[7] At any rate, if the artists have portrayed them realistically, we have a stocky horse with quite short legs, a thick, strong body and rather long neck and head. They are painted in a wide variety of colours in the illustrations. All the horses shown in the manuscript are equipped with the same caparisons (saddle, bridle, etc.). These are painted mainly in gold, though one should not perhaps assume that even senior cavalry officers in the Mamluk army were fitted out with gold-plated equipment. Gilt spurs and stirrups are singled out in some sources,[8] however, and other articles of horse equipment might also have been such.

It is surprising to find that, in a number of illustrations, the horses wear no girth. It was first thought that this was due to carelessness on the part of the artists who had merely forgotten to include the girth. However, there are examples of girthless horses in both orien-

---

6 Folio 125a. 14 × 20·5 cm. 'Illustration of a horseman with a sword in his hand with which he strikes from the horse's ear as far back as its right croup.'
The rider carries a mace, the handle of which protrudes below his outer garment.

الباب السابع من العمل بالسيف واسمه المنجّم

وهو انك اذا فرغت من المنصف وحصل السيف في شمالك وانت دايرٌ في الـ ورد
فدر على حالك ثم اضرب بيدك اليمنى لاقدام السيف فخذه بخريده واضرب به شمالاً
من اذن الفرس اليسرى لاكَهله الايسر وانزع من كَهله الايسر الى كَهله الايمن
ثم ارسل السيف بيدك الى قدام جبهتك وانزل السيف فتله حول وجهك واقبضه

في الثانيه نفضه مليحه باسطه كوَ يمينك تفعل ذلك ثلاثًا ثم ردّ السيف من لاحِبه
يسارك من فوق واسكن حتى يضع ذنابته على فهمك الايمن ثم نقلت يدك الى المعتضد
ثم تقبض القايم باصبعك الخنصر والبنصر وعسَل السيف بشل مرفقك فاذا حصل

tal and western art.⁸ᵃ A late 16th-century Andalusian Arabic text mentions the phenomenon, though it indicates that one would only ride a girthless horse if it were absolutely necessary, say in battle when the girth had been cut. It seems most unlikely that, even as an exercise, Mamluk cavalrymen would regularly have practised riding without the girth. All the horses wear a bridle of familiar appearance and a curb bit with curved and ornamental side metals to which the reins are attached. The latter are often tied up to shorten them. Where the noseband joins the cheek piece there appears to be a small circular ornament of some kind and a larger one placed at the junction of the cheek piece, the browband and the head piece. The throat latch everywhere appears tight across the cheek and under the throat. There is a purely ornamental neck band, broad on top of the neck, narrowing to join under the neck with a circular medallion.

The saddle shows a prominent pommel and cantle. To the former is attached a breast strap⁹ which hangs loosely round the front of the chest. It is similar to the neck strap which supports the martingale, except for its apparent attachment to the pommel. A crupper runs across the saddle-cloth and under the tail presumably from the cantle or the rear of the saddle. This in turn has a strap hanging down at right angles to it. The flap of the saddle is rounded in the familiar manner. The stirrup is a single triangular-shaped metal piece. The saddle-cloth with elaborate floral and other coloured designs stretches well back towards the tail behind the saddle and comes to a sharp point over the thighs of the horse. The tail is normally tied up in a knot. The seat of the rider is generally forward on the withers. The length of the stirrup must be such that the knee is slightly bent, though this is hidden in all cases by the rider's long outer garment.

The horsemen, with only one exception, wear the same head-gear, a cap, usually yellow or brown, around which a white turban is wound. Long black hair falls down the back and, where it can be seen, in a pigtail. A number of riders are young and beardless, evidently novices, though others wear beards and moustaches. The rider wears a colourful outer garment which reaches almost down to the ankles as he sits astride his mount. The sleeves are either wrist-length or they drop to just below the elbow, revealing a usually plain coloured under garment to the wrist. In a number of pictures the rider's outer garment flaps open from the waist revealing a different coloured lining and a long under robe. The outer garment has a belt of plain material, usually painted in gold, round the waist, which collects it to the body, for the robe appears to be otherwise open

---

7 Folio 127b. 14×20·5 cm. 'Illustration of a horseman with the edge of the sword under his right armpit, the hilt in his left with the reins.'

القلام الى يسارك مواضرب بيدك اليمنى لادبانه ورده فوق ادنى لعرش حتى يرحه على قضادك ١ لاشتر واقطع ه هدا الوجه فغيه ثلث ضربات صعبات وهو وجه منقول حدث لان كل الوجه من الواجب اخترعت وهى اصلها ولا ينبغى لمن عمل بالسيف ان يزيد بعد الجولان بعدان عمل الواجب الكثر وجهين حرعا اجب من الاحدى عشر وجها فيصير العمل جولان وتلته وجوه لا بد من الواجب والامتى ازاد صجر الناس منه وملوا ولم رغب كمّنول اذا اختصّ فى العمل واذا ما فرغت من العمل بالسيف على ما زنيته لك فاعتمد

قصد ا فیما یحتاج إلیه العاملُ بالسَّیفِ ولا بُدَّلَه

down the front, though perhaps attached at the shoulder. The collar, cuffs and hem of the robe are trimmed with a golden band. A strip of gold also runs round the sleeve, high up round the biceps and under the armpit. Most horsemen wear plain white boots, though some are grey and brown and one or two simply decorated. All sport long, sharp spurs, usually painted gold, though they were not necessarily so in real life.[10]

The horsemen carry a variety of weapons. The object seen frequently at the rider's right knee is his mace, the handle of which sometime protrudes below the hem of his outer garment. This weapon obviously came in various shapes and sizes, though the favourite has a cubic head, thus presumably resembling a mallet. The mace had to be tightly secured beneath the stirrup-leather to prevent it from working loose and hampering the rider, or worse, dropping out altogether, an enormity to be likened to the guardsman who drops his rifle on parade! Mamluk maces were of iron and steel.[11] Other weapons and equipment illustrated in the manuscript are the lance (two types are shown, one shorter than the standard), the sword, invariably of the slightly curved variety, the bow and at least two types of shield. The text has two distinct words for the shield: *daraqah,* the hide and *turs* the wooden or metal shield and both are portrayed in the pictures. One helmet is shown which merely protects the head, while the neck is left exposed. The helmet does not include a nasal.

The author begins the work with a section on archery. Despite the technicalities of the subject, the section is short. Its brevity is particularly surprising because it was during the Ayyubid (1169–1250) and Mamluk periods that the bow reached its high-water mark as a cavalry weapon. Although the bow was popular and important on the battlefield, however, archery games and exercises may well not have been. One would also have expected illustrations in this section.

---

8 Folio 113a. 13·5 × 20·5 cm. Single horseman who has transfixed a bear with his lance and carries a mace at his right knee. The text mentions incidentally that this particular lance, shorter than the regular type, is useful for dealing with wild animals. The youth, obviously a novice, wears a pigtail.

Pages 18 *and* 19 *following*

9 Folio 121a. 14 × 20·5 cm. 'Illustration of a horseman performing a sword exercise.'
The saddle-cloth features a lotus leaf.

10 Folio 135a. 13 × 20·5 cm. 'Illustration of two horsemen wheeling round, with a sword in each one's hand on the horse's back.'

ونفعل مثل ذلك من جهة اليسار شوار فع بدك وهز المزراق وافضه واجلا قد حصل على عكفل فرنك تفرغ عليك من طفك فافصده من جهته من الجانب الايمن والسر نفعله لك مرارا واتت داير في الناور وشر تلوح بالمزراق خلفه على روس الخيل وان كنت ممن يحسن العمل بها فانحل وا عل الرفا بـ الخراسانيه

الخراسانيه واعلم شيي من الهادين المتقدمه شراد المزراق فوق راسك واقطع والطعن بالمزراق والحربه واحد لانهما اقصر من الرمح

الباب التاسع والعشرون فيما يجاور المسايل الوا على الزراق وما الذي ينبغي ان يكون مع الزارق **الجواب** ان نكون معه

الغرس إلى كفله واعقد في وجه الموكب عقدة ملحبة ورد السيف الى متنك الايمن
وهى حلة الثلاثة وتسير ملاصقا للموكب حتى توافى ظهره ولتظهر كل الموكب وسل السيف
سلفا وجهك وأمنه على ذكر السترى واسرح الأرض ورد الغرس إلى وجه الموكب
يسارا واعمره إلى وبسط الموكب وعنك في عين كل واحد تراعيه فاذا احصلت في
الميسره فسل السيف وانطر من نحته واد الغرس إلى الموكب على يمنك ونقضت
بالسيف في ورائك فاذا واجهت الموكب فافتح في وجه الناس فتحة باسطه كا
وصفت لك واعقد عقدة ملحبة ورد السيف على متنك الايمن وشد بدرك عليه
بلا لعب ورأسه عند ركظلك للغرس ورد الغرس شمالا حتى توافى بميسة الموكب

وقريا حتى يصل كل واحد منكما الى موضع ابتدا به شوط دارسكما يمينا وافتحا كل واحد في وجه
صاحبه ورد ا لسيفين فايمن على زند كما مع العنان وقرا حتى يصل صاحب الميمنه
الى زا يها ويصل صاحب الميسره الى زا يها شوط سبعا شمالا اغز كل واحد
منكما الى صاحبه حتى يلتقيان في وسط الميدان ثم ليغبط كل واحد منكما الى وجه
صاحبه وخرج صاحب الميمنه مخالفا الى وسط الموكب ويضرب ضربه تغيله
من اذن الفرس اليمنى بالاكفله الايمن ويرد راس فرسه شمالا الى الى الميمنه
وتولي ظهرك الموكب وسبل سيفه وينظر من تحته الى ازا الميمنه وصاحب
الميسره الى خلفه وكلا ضارب ضربه فتح هو فتحه شوط يرد صاحب الميمنه فرسه يمينا
ويرد صاحب الميسره فرسه شمالا الى الموكب مخالفا وصاحب الميمنه خلفه فخرج صا
ازا الميسره ثلث خرجات مخالفات ثم خرج صاحب الميمنه شمالا وطلب

وعارض وهو يميد البسرى وغمز على وسط خط الميدان حتى يصلوا الى وسط الموكب
ثم يتناول العنان مع الدرقة بشماله ويضرب بقائم السيف قبة الدرقة وشي عليها
بالدبابة وتزدر فرسك يميناً ويدرق بالدرقة عن كفل العزيز ويرجع على خط الداس

الكبير وزجى الى خلفه يفعل كفعل الاول ويرد فرسه شما لا على خط الدارج الكبير
وزجى الثالث يفعل كفعل صاحبه ويرد فرسه يميناً وزجى الاول فيفعل كفعل ولا يرد

The lance has pride of place in *Horsemanship* and is allotted considerable space in it. Though a weapon of less popularity with the Mamluk cavalryman and of less complexity in itself than the bow, it was evidently more employed in the exercises and games. The section on the lance includes five illustrations, and the author draws heavily on Najm al-Dīn al-Aḥdab, described as a master who was the inventor of many of the exercises described.

The author enumerates the various exercises with the sword, giving each of them its technical term and speaks of the different types of sword used. He includes in this section also exercises involving the sword together with other weapons and equipment, e.g. the sword with the hide shield, the sword with the shield and fire (see illustration 14), an exercise with two swords, with two horsemen carrying swords etc. The section on sword instruction includes no fewer than thirteen illustrations, many more than the lance book described above. The heavier wooden or metal shield is dealt with, in the main, in a question and answer style, a form of presentation which rounds off the majority of sections.

In their choice of colours the artists tread a middle path, for the colours are neither bright and gaudy nor pale and weak. They see that both horse and rider are of equal importance and they never allow one to outshine the other. The two comprise the same artistic unit which ideally they form in reality on the exercise ground while performing their exercises. The movement of the horses is fully expressed and it is not difficult to visualise their speed. Stylized flowers serve to frame the picture and are not infrequently found in pre-Mongol Arabic manuscripts, for example in some of the illustrated *Maqāmāt*. But perhaps they also represent the flowers, shrubs and trees which were sometimes planted to adorn the hippodrome.[12]

The contents of *Horsemanship* indicate clearly that the work is primarily designed for the teaching and learning of equestrian exercises and games as practised in the hippodrome. The later lessons are of direct relevance to the battlefield and all instruction in the exercises and games was clearly of indirect value to the good practical cavalryman. But it must be said that the manual itself, its style and presenta-

---

11 Folio 140a. 18·5 × 20·5 cm. 'Illustration of four horsemen, each one having a sword and a hide shield and each one carrying his shield on the horse's croup.'
The riders canter round a circular hippodrome pool in an anti-clockwise direction. All the riders have the reins looped over their right arms. As in the case of the earlier illustration this one shows absolute symmetry in the spacing of the horses and riders and the flowers round the pool, even the ripples!

tion smack of the hippodrome rather than the field of battle. The style is basically simple, straightforward and direct with second person singular verbs and pronouns. The question and answer presentation is common throughout the work. It is, however, written in extremely corrupt Arabic abounding in colloquialisms and grammatical errors. The only real difficulty in comprehension lies in the phlethora of obscure technical terms, many of Persian and Turkish origin, but presumably not obscure to the Mamluk cavalryman! Parts of the text were undoubtedly used during training in the hippodromes, though to the 20th-century observer it appears extremely complex and attempting to follow the rules of the exercises in detail without the benefit of practical demonstration is very difficult.

After the work's composition sometime before 1348, it must have been commissioned for copying as required by the masters of the hippodromes and by cavalry officers. It also seems that exquisite copies like the subject of this study and the Chester Beatty Library manuscript referred to on p. 28 below would have been destined for important libraries rather than for a practical purpose. The popularity of *Horsemanship* must have waxed and waned too with that of the games themselves.[13] The illustrations add little or no information on the exercises to what can be derived from the text. They are, therefore, to be seen as works of art and not as practical diagrams. But it is evident that the paintings in this and similar manuscripts are of paramount importance for information about the horses and caparisons used by the Mamluk cavalry, their costumes, at least those of the military, and their weapons. They are of value also to the art historian and represent a milestone in Arabic manuscript illustration, albeit a display of talent in a generally declining art.

---

12 Folio 129b. 13×20·5 cm. 'Illustration of a horseman with a small shield round his neck and a sword in his hand which he brandishes to left and right.'
It is surprising that no mention is made of the bow in the caption or in the text at this point. It seems that the sword is being rested across the right elbow while the bow is being carried with the reins in the left hand. The prominent nock and black feathers of the arrow make it clear that the arrow-head is pointing back towards the rider and perhaps the bow is unbraced and the string slung over the rider's shoulder for added support. The arrow may have been added at a later date.

الى شمالك مع العنان ثم اضرب يدك اليمنى الى دبابته ومده سرا الى الفرس حتى يكون على
فصادك الايسر ثم ادخل يدك اليمنى الى مقبض الدرقة فمكن ابهامك للثة السبابة الو[سطى]
والبنصر من المقبض ثم اخرجهما من تميز يدك وترخي توا حتى الى المسك شم اضرب يدك
اليمنى والدرقة فيها الى قايم السيف جرده واعقده من فوق راسك بغوصة مليحة يخت
السيف ثم شد يدك وغطي بالدرقة وجهك وانظر من تحتها والسيف معارض دبابته
نحو ادنك اليسرى ودراس فرسك شمالا وسر با الى الموكب حتى تنتهى الى اراى الميمنة
ثم ادر دبابة السيف حواذنك اليسرى والدرقة بين عينيك تغطي بها وجهك وراس
فرسك يمناه شم سر با الى الموكب كله حتى تنتهى الى اراى الميسرة ثم اعطهم الى الموكب وادر
دبابة السيف حواذنك اليمنى وغطي بالدرقة وجهك ودراس فرسك وسر موازنا الموكب كله

حتى ينتهي إلى الميمنة ثم ولي ظهرك وردّ راسك ورنك شمالاً إلى الموكب وادر بابه السيف
خواذنك اليسرى وعطّى باالدردوجهك وسرموا زيا الموكب كله حتى ينتهي إلى الميسرة
ثم ولي ظهرك الموكب وردّ راسك ورنك يمنا إلى الموكب وادر الباب وادخل النمي عط
بالدردوجهك ثم سرموا زيا الموكب كله حتى ينتهي إلى الميمنة ثم ولي ظهرك

الموكب وهذا الفريب يلعبه حيث وادخل الناور ود وحرد السيف والدرك هي في كفك
مع القائم ولوح به يمنا وشمالا اشراد خل بابه السيف تحت ابطك الايمن وسلّم القائم
إلى يسارك مع العنان ثم اضرب بدك النمي إلى المقدار شبر من الأبابه ومده بين دي
العرين حتى تركه على عادك الاسترامة ثما قايم بين عيدك وادخل الدرقة بين
وجهك وبين السيف وردّ السيف إلى تحت ابطك الايمن وبرق السيف في وجوه القيام

13 Folio 130a. 15 × 20·5 cm. 'Illustration of a horseman with a hide shield over his face, the sword edge under his right armpit and the hilt on his left.'
Here the rider holds the reins in his right hand, an unusual occurrence not mentioned in the Arabic caption.

اوطنب مر وصل اوما ينوم مقامه وتيف الغلام في الميمنه و ادخلات وا غمل سدا
عل السيف والدرقه حتى ينتهى الى دخل الناود فندون اورداحتى تصل الى الغلام في
الميمنه ثم ناول منه اللات لنود والصغى المدور في وسط الدرقه وآخر بين
احدها على الحديد من الفلسنوه ما بعرض والاخرى على ذبابه السيف وشرع على
حالك في با اورد ک حتى ينتهى الى غلامک بذبابه السيف كما يال للبد اليشمع
وهى اول من عبرها في هذا الوقت فان زل للبد المستقل بالمشاعله با النفط يشتعل شی
اوى بالذبابه الى اللبد الذى في وسط فلسنوتک فانه يشتعل ثم اوى بالذبابه الى
اللبد الذى على وسط الدرقه کانک تنضرب الضراب التى رسمتها في عمل السيف

والدرقه فانه يشتعل للكل فناول النار ونه السفط فالافاک ملا فاک نفطا واعل شرا نح

14 Folio 131b. 15×20.5 cm. 'Illustration of a horseman with an iron helmet on his head, with a sword. Fire glows in the helmet, the sword blade and in the middle of the shield.'
This is the only example in the manuscript illustrations of a helmet. There is no nasal and the ears are unprotected. The fire is produced by burning pieces of cloth dipped in saltpetre and placed on the shield, sword and helmet. This must have been a spectacular exercise. There has been a deliberate attempt to mutilate this painting.

من كفله الايمن الى كفله الايسر ورده من فوق كفك الايمن على صدرك مردا على
السيف الذي في يمينك وخذ بشارك العنان ثم اخرج يمينك بالسيف بنجيدا
باسطه ورد دابه سيفك الايسر تحت ابطك الايمن دابه سيفك الايمن

صورة فارس لعبه كشف ذراعه اليمنى ونزع بها كلعبه الاسبردق شهد ورد ا بموتنى اظهر اليمنى

تحت ابطك الايسر وقاعده مع يدك على متنك الايمن يع سرباز آي الموكب
كله حتى ينتهى الى الميسره ثم اعزم على الموكب وافتح السيف الذي في يمينك في
الموكب فتحةً باسطة ورده من فوق كشفك الايسر على السيف الذي في يدك
اليمنى حتى يحصل القائم على متنك الايمن فارتكخالوم من فوق ورد راس فرسك
شمالا موازيا للموكب كله حتى ينتهى الى الميمنه ثم اذا ظهر الموكب وسل يدك
اليمنى بالسيف فانظر من نحته ثم اضرب ضربةً ثقيلة من اذن الفرس اليمنى الى قفله

The Author and the manuscript

THE AUTHOR

Although his name appears nowhere in the manuscript, we know from other sources[16] that the author of *Horsemanship, Nihāyat al-suʾl,* was Muḥammad b. ʿIsā b. Ismāʿīl al-Ḥanafī al-Aqṣaraʾī who died in Damascus in 1348. With the exception of the fact that he spent most of his life there, biographical details are lacking. The master of the lance, Najm al-Dīn al-Aḥdab, was his teacher and the exercises he learnt he had corrected by a Baḥrī Mamluk in the Citadel of Damascus.

A DESCRIPTION OF THE MANUSCRIPT

The British Library MS, Add 18866, which is the subject of this study has a well-preserved brown goat-skin binding. It is decorated very simply with circular blind-tooled designs, one each on the back, front and flap. The back and front also have borders made up of both straight and wavy lines tooled close to the edge of the binding. The section of the flap protecting the leaves of the MS is divided up into three tooled rectangles with small central designs and lines forming borders round the edges. The binding is in all probability contemporary with the copying of the MS in the 8th/14th century, although there is evidence of later repair work having been carried out.

The MS, measuring 31 × 22 cm, contains 292 folios, 19 lines to the page. The title page on folio 1a gives the rhyming title of this Arabic work as *Nihāyat al-suʾl wa-'l-umniyyah/fī ʿilm al-furūsiyyah* (literally 'An end to questioning and desiring [further knowledge] concerning the science of horsemanship').[17] The more commonly used title is in fact that found in the colophon on f 292a . . . *fī taʿallum aʿmāl al-furūsiyyah* (literally ' . . . concerning the learning of the different exercises of horsemanship').[18]

As can be clearly discerned from the plates, the MS was copied in a

---

15 Folio 132b. 14 × 20·5 cm. 'Illustration of a horseman with a sword in his right hand, its blade on his left shoulder and a sword in his left hand whose blade is under his right armpit.'
This time the rider sports a beard.

legible Arabic *naskhī* hand on thick, lightly polished, cream paper, the main text being in black ink, with all the chapter headings and numerous sub-headings within the chapter in red ink in an often bold *naskhī*. The scribe is named in the colophon as Aḥmad b. 'Umar b. Aḥmad al-Miṣrī al-Adamī and he completed the copying on Thursday, 10 al-Muharram, 773 A.H., 25 July, 1371. It is of either Syrian or Egyptian provenance.

The MS contains 18 coloured paintings[19] illustrating the various exercises practised by the Mamluk cavalryman and these are dealt with in detail above. There are also diagrams of cavalry manoeuvres and ff 93b–94a and 209b–210a are taken up with plans of battle formations.

A note on the back fly-leaf reads: 'Purchased at the sale of Sir Tho Reade at Sotherby's, 28 Jany. 1852. (Lot 94.).'

Other MSS of *Nihāyat al-su'l* are preserved in the British Library (three, Or 3631, with extremely crude illustrations, and the unillustrated Add 23488 and Add 23487), Paris (2828), Cambridge (Qq 277), Chester Beatty Library, Dublin (uncatalogued in 1974), Cairo (J/N KH 391 N 'A 17739) and Istanbul (at least two copies, Süleymaniye, 4044 and Topkapi Saray, A 2651). Of those known to be extant, only the Chester Beatty MS was copied before the British Library MS, Add 18866, and this would seem to be the only one to vie with it in the artistic merit of its illustrations.[20]

16 Folio 134a. 13×20·5 cm. 'Illustration of a horseman with a sword in his [right hand the blade of which is on his left shoulder. In his left hand is a sword] the blade of which is under his right armpit.'
There is an omission of several words from the Arabic caption, for the illustration reveals that the rider in fact carries two swords by their blades in this exercise and he leaves the reins on the horse's neck. The omitted text of the caption has been supplied between square brackets from other manuscripts of the work. Although it cannot be satisfactorily read there is a deliberate attempt to portray Arabic calligraphy in gold on the rider's outer garment.

بساركْ وسَيفكْ الايسرْ عن يمينكْ الى قدام ثم يمينكْ عن يمينكْ وشمالكْ عن شمالكْ كل ثلاث من هنا وثلاث من هنا ثم امنع بيمينكْ عن يسارك وبساركْ عن يمينكْ الى الخلف ثلاث من هنا وثلاث من هنا ثم اقم السَيفَ الايسرْ على كَفكْ الايسرْ وادخل بابا به شَيفكْ الايمن تحت ابطكْ الايمن ومدها بالقائم

الى كَتفكْ الايسرْ وادخل بدْ بابه شَيفكْ الايمن تحت ابطكْ الايمن ومدها بالقائم الى كَتفكْ الايسرْ وادخل بدْ بابه شَيفكْ الايمن تحت ابطكْ الايمن ومدها الى كَتفكْ الايسرْ وطامن براسكْ وانقض باثنائكْ على نصفِ السَيفِ وانقض بكَركْ اليمنى وردها من تحت العنان وانقض على قائم السَيفِ وجرده وامنع الى قدام بيمينكْ عن يمينكْ وشمالكْ عن شمالكْ ست دفعات كما رسمتُ لكْ ثم اَشَيفكْ

وبرق بها في وجه الموكب ثم اعقد بها عقدة مليحة واعدها الى المنكب الايمن وعنك الى الموكب ودع علاجها لك حتى تنتهى الى الميسره فاضرب بيدك اليمنى على قائم السيف الذى كان يزيك بجرده من موضع الجهاد زعقده من فوق رأسك نحو صه ورد راس فرسك شمالا واعط وجهك بالدرقه وانظر من تحتها الى الموكب فيسل السيف معارضا نحو يمنك ودب به السيف الذى ستارك تحت ابطك الايمن وسر بازاى الموكب كله حتى تنتهى الى ازاى لميمنه ثم حط يدك اليمنى بين يديك وسلم بها العنان كهيئتها بالسيف والدرقه وحاصر يدك اليسرى بقبضه من فوق اذى الفرس الى كفله الاستر واعقد من رأسك عقدة مليحة وعطف

17 Folio 136a. 16 × 20·5 cm. 'Illustration of horseman with two swords and two small hide shields, one up at his face and the other in his hand with the sword.'
The rider carries a long-handled mace, protruding at his right knee and beneath his outer garment. The rein appears to be looped over his left arm.

18 Folio 138b. 13·5 × 20·5 cm. 'Illustration of a horseman with a lance in his hand which he is dragging behind him, while there is a shield in his other hand.'
Note the tassel on the neck band and behind the rider on the saddle-cloth.

CONTENTS OF THE BRITISH LIBRARY MS, ADD 18866

General introduction of pious phrases and utterances	
Introduction	1b
The bow	27b
The lance	42b
The sword	118a
The shield	151b
The mace	152b
'The art of soldiers and cavalrymen'	153a
Weapons	161b
Conscription and assembling troops	197b
Battle lines	211b
Incendiaries and smoke devices	235b
Division of spoils	240b
'What the soldier requires' – miscellany of useful hints	281a

نهاية السؤل والأمنية في تعلم أعمال الفروسية
في أمور السلطنة

كتابٌ فيه

نهاية السؤل والأمنية في علم الفروسية
وعُبُرْ ذلك

وفيه علم رماية النشاب وفيه
علم الوادن الحربية وفيه معرفة
علم البنود والسارح وفيه
مسائل وفتاوى لا يُستغنى
عنها في دار الحرب وملخّص
الـ ... القادر من الفرس
وفيه كرامهم للجراحات
وشقاقات العيوب
والسلاحات
وفيه قوله
جلّ جلاله

والحمد لله ربه وصلى الله على سيدنا محمد ... وشيخ الـ...
عليهم

في خرقة رقيقة وعُصرت في إناء فيه ما أخوه يخرج ما فيه من الموم ويبقى النقاء نزل حتى يصفو امتزج بنصيب الماعنة ويلقى عليه زيت وصبر حتى يجمع ويستعمل نافع ان شاء الله تعالى ثم كتاب السؤل والأمنية

في تعلم اعمال الفروسية ووافق الفراغ من تحريره بحمد الله تعالى وحسن توفيقه وتيسيره في يوم الخميس يوم عاشوراء من شهر الله المحرم سنة ثلاث وسبعين وسبعماية من الهجرة النبوية على صاحبها افضل الصلاة والسلام على يد العبد الفقير الى الله

احمد بن عمر بن احمد المصري الادمي عفا الله عنه وعن والديه وعن من دعا له بالتوبة والرحمة والمغفرة والتجاوز عنه هو ساير اموات المسلمين اجمعين من شاءُ ل لا رب له ا معارها بارب العالمين وحسبنا الله ونعم الوكيل وصلى الله على سيدنا محمد خير خلقه واله وصحبه وسلم تسليما كثيرا اليوم الدين

NOTES

1 *Cf.* D. Ayalon, *L'Esclavage du Mamelouke,* Jerusalem, 1951, 9 *et seq.*; also H. Rabie, 'The training of the Mamluk fāris', in V. J. Parry and M. E. Yapp, *War, Society and Technology in the Middle East,* London, 1975, 153 and *passim.*

2 I have here drawn heavily on Ayalon's article, 'Notes on the *Furūsiyya* exercises and games, etc.', *Studies in Islamic History and Civilization, Scripta Hierosolymitana,* IX, Jerusalem, 1961.

3 *Cf.* J. D. Latham and W. F. Paterson, *Saracen Archery,* London, 1970, 71, 77–8, Plates 13 and 14; Rabie, 'Training', 160 and Plate VI, describing another *qabaq* exercise also.

4 *Cf.* Latham & Paterson, *Archery,* 83–4; Rabie, 'Training', 156 and Plate I.

5 *Cf.* G. T. Scanlon, *A Muslim Manual of War,* Cairo, 1961, 4–5; also A. R. Zaki, 'Military literature of the Arabs', *Cahiers d'histoire égyptienne,* VII, 1955, 149.

6 Firstly by H. Ritter, '*La Parure des Cavaliers* und die Literatur über die ritterlichen Künste', *Der Islam,* XVIII, 1929, and also by Scanlon, *Manual.* Perhaps a fourth division should be added, viz. those works purporting to be military, but which belong in fact to the *adab* genre of literature.

7 D. Ayalon, 'Payment in Mamluk Military Society', *Journal of Economic and Social History of the Orient,* I, 1958, 263–4, provides evidence that the Mamluks imported Arabs from Arabia and other horses from Libya and North Africa.

8 *Cf.* L. A. Mayer, *Mamluk Costume,* Geneva, 1952, 35.

8a *Cf.* L. Mercier, *La Parure des Cavaliers et l'Insigne des Preux,* Paris, 1924, Plate XXXIII and C. Chenevix-Trench, *A History of Horsemanship,* London, 1970, 106, Paolo Uccello's 'The Hunt', 15th century Italian.

9 Arabic *labab*; *EI²,* 'Furūsiyya', 955.

10 *Cf.* Mayer, *Costume,* 35

11 Mayer, *Costume,* 46; Latham & Paterson, *Archery,* 72.

12 *Cf.* Ayalon, 'Notes', 43.

13 But *cf.* David James, 'Mameluke painting at the time of the Lusignan Crusade, 1365–70', *Humaniora Islamica,* II, 1974, *passim* and particularly 86.

14 *Cf.* T. W. Arnold and A. Grohmann, *The Islamic Book,* Paris, 1929, 66 and Arnold, *Painting in Islam,* New York, 1965, 95–6. For the hare motif, *cf.* A. Lane, *Early Islamic Pottery,* London, 1947, e.g. Plates 23, 28 and 34.

15 Ayalon, 'Notes', 43 (*baḥrah*) and 44 (*ḥawḍ*). Both words are used for the hippodrome pool. For the lotus flower, *cf.* W. H. Goodyear, *The Grammar of the Lotus,* London, 1891, in particular 36.

16 Brockelmann, *GAL,* S II, 167; James, 'Painting', 74.

17 This is the only word which can be used to translate *furūsiyyah,* though it is inadequate.

18 James, 'Painting', 73, completely mistranslates the title.

19 Not 12 as in James, 'Painting', 75.

20 James, 'Painting', 74–5.

FURTHER READING

Bosworth, C. E.: 'Armies of the Prophet' in Lewis, B. (ed.), *The World of Islam,* London, 1976, chapter 8

Cambridge History of Islam. Eds. Holt, P. M., Lambton, A. K. S. and Lewis, B., Cambridge, 1970, I, part 2, chapter 2

Encyclopaedia of Islam. 2nd ed. – article 'Faras'

Ettinghausen, R.: *Arab Painting,* Geneva, 1962

Faris, N. A. and Elmer, R. P.: *Arab Archery,* Princeton, 1945

Gray, B.: *Persian Painting,* Geneva, 1963. Repr. 1977

Löfgren, O. and Lamm, C. J.: *Ambrosian Fragments of an Illuminated Manuscript Containing the Zoology of al-Ǧāḥiẓ,* Uppsala, 1946

Meredith-Owens, G. M.: *Persian Illustrated Manuscripts,* London, 1973

Meredith-Owens, G. M.: *Turkish Illustrated Manuscripts,* London, 1963

Popper, W.: 'History of Egypt, 1382–1469' in *University of California Publications in Semitic Philology*' VIII–XVII, Berkeley and Los Angeles, 1954–57

Quatremère, M.: *Histoire des Sultans Mamlouks de l'Egypte,* 2 vols., Paris, 1837–42

Rice, D. T.: *Islamic Art,* London, 1975

Titley, N. M.: 'Islam' in Vervliet, H. D. L. (ed.), *The Book Through Five Thousand Years,* London and New York, 1972, 51–70

Bettina Bódi's *Videogames and Agency* is a unique and indispensable book for scholars, students, and game designers. By considering agency as an affordance of videogames that is firmly rooted in their developers' design ethos, Bódi ties together theoretical perspectives and industry practices of agency. Thoroughly researched, yet immensely readable, the book gives a much needed introduction to a central issue in the study of video games.

— **Dr Hans-Joachim Backe,** *Associate Professor, Center for Digital Play, ITU Copenhagen, Denmark*

Videogames and Agency offers an important contribution to debates around a central concept in Game Studies, providing a new framework to think through the relationship between production context, design and player agency. Using paratextual and textual analysis, Dr Bettina Bódi works adeptly across three engaging case studies to broaden our understanding of how games and their designers afford and constrain player action. This is vital reading for anyone who wants to understand more about one of the key questions in games research.

—**Dr Nick Webber,** *Associate Professor in Media, Birmingham City University, UK*

Videogames and Agency

Videogames and Agency explores the trend in videogames and their marketing to offer a player higher volumes, or even more distinct kinds, of player freedom. The book offers a new conceptual framework that helps us understand how this freedom to act is discussed by designers, and how that in turn reflects in their design principles.

What can we learn from existing theories around agency? How do paratextual materials reflect design intention with regards to what the player can and cannot do in a videogame? How does game design shape the possibility space for player action? Through these questions and selected case studies that include AAA and independent games alike, the book presents a unique approach to studying agency that combines game design, game studies, and game developer discourse. By doing so, the book examines what discourses around player action, as well as a game's design can reveal about the nature of agency and videogame aesthetics.

This book will appeal to readers specifically interested in videogames, such as game studies scholars or game designers, but also to media studies students and media and screen studies scholars less familiar with digital games.

Bettina Bódi is a lecturer in media at Leeds Beckett University, UK. Dr Bódi's research considers agency in and around videogames, as afforded by game design, and as discussed in paratexts and promotional surrounds.

Routledge Advances in Game Studies

Forms and Functions of Endings in Narrative Digital Games
Michelle Herte

Independent Videogames
Cultures, Networks, Techniques and Politics
Edited by Paolo Ruffino

Comics and Videogames
From Hybrid Medialities to Transmedia Expansions
Edited by Edited by Andreas Rauscher, Daniel Stein, and Jan-Noël Thon

Immersion, Narrative, and Gender Crisis in Survival Horror Video Games
Andrei Nae

Videogames and the Gothic
Ewan Kirkland

Longing, Ruin, and Connection in Hideo Kojima's Death Stranding
Amy M. Green

Manifestations of Queerness in Video Games
Gaspard Pelurson

Representing Conflicts in Games
Antagonism, Rivalry, and Competition
Edited by Björn Sjöblom, Jonas Linderoth, and Anders Frank

Videogames and Agency
Bettina Bódi

Videogames and Agency

Bettina Bódi

LONDON AND NEW YORK

Designed cover image: © Getty Images

First published 2023
by Routledge
4 Park Square, Milton Park, Abingdon, Oxon OX14 4RN

and by Routledge
605 Third Avenue, New York, NY 10158

Routledge is an imprint of the Taylor & Francis Group, an informa business

© 2023 Bettina Bódi

The right of Bettina Bódi to be identified as author of this work has been asserted in accordance with sections 77 and 78 of the Copyright, Designs and Patents Act 1988.

All rights reserved. No part of this book may be reprinted or reproduced or utilised in any form or by any electronic, mechanical, or other means, now known or hereafter invented, including photocopying and recording, or in any information storage or retrieval system, without permission in writing from the publishers.

Trademark notice: Product or corporate names may be trademarks or registered trademarks, and are used only for identification and explanation without intent to infringe.

British Library Cataloguing-in-Publication Data
A catalogue record for this book is available from the British Library

Library of Congress Cataloging-in-Publication Data
Names: Bódi, Bettina, author.
Title: Videogames and agency / Bettina Bódi.
Description: Abingdon, Oxon ; New York, NY : Routledge, 2023. | Series: Routledge advances in game studies | Includes bibliographical references and index.
Identifiers: LCCN 2022042697 (print) | LCCN 2022042698 (ebook) | ISBN 9781032285092 (hardback) | ISBN 9781032288475 (paperback) | ISBN 9781003298786 (ebook)
Subjects: LCSH: Agency (Philosophy) in video games. | Video games—Marketing. | Video games—Design.
Classification: LCC GV1469.34.A34 B63 2023 (print) | LCC GV1469.34.A34 (ebook) | DDC 794.8—dc23/eng/20221017
LC record available at https://lccn.loc.gov/2022042697
LC ebook record available at https://lccn.loc.gov/2022042698

ISBN: 978-1-032-28509-2 (hbk)
ISBN: 978-1-032-28847-5 (pbk)
ISBN: 978-1-003-29878-6 (ebk)

DOI: 10.4324/9781003298786

Typeset in Sabon
by Apex CoVantage, LLC

Contents

Acknowledgements ix

Introduction 1

1 Understanding Agency 13
  Agency in Game Studies 13
  Agency in Game Design 17
  Toward a Conceptualisation of Agency 22

2 A Multidimensional Heuristic Framework for Analysing Player Agency 41
  Agency Afforded in Space: The Spatial-Explorative Dimension 43
  Agency Afforded in Time: The Temporal-Ergodic Dimension 48
  Agency Over the Avatar and Its Surroundings: The Configurative-Constructive Dimension 53
  Agency and Narrativity: Narrative-Dramatic Dimension 58

3 An 'Active Cinematic Experience': Naughty Dog's *Uncharted* Series 75
  Naughty Dog and the Uncharted Franchise 76
  Developing Uncharted 4: A Thief's End 87
  Agency and a 'Cinematic Feel' 100

4 'A Compelling Story with Choices That Matter': BioWare's *Mass Effect* Series 119
  BioWare and the Mass Effect Franchise 120
  Developing Mass Effect: Andromeda 128
  Narrativity, Eventfulness, and Agency 142

5 'The World Is Your Play-Doh': System Era Softworks and
   Astroneer   161
   Independent Games: Definitions and Trends 162
   Developing Astroneer 168
   Agency and Playfulness 182

   Conclusion   206

   Index   212

Acknowledgements

This book is a continuation of my doctoral project at the University of Nottingham, which was funded by the Midlands3Cities Doctoral Training Partnership, the National Productivity Investment Fund, and the University of Nottingham Vice Chancellor's Scholarship for Research Excellence. As such, I would first like to thank the Arts and Humanities Research Council and UK Research and Innovation, as well as the University of Nottingham for enabling me to carry out this work. I could not thank enough my thesis supervisors Elizabeth Evans, Jan-Noël Thon, and Roberta Pearson for always knowing what to say to keep me going. It was a difficult journey, as PhDs often are, but it made me the scholar I am today and I would not change anything. I am eternally grateful to the PhD community at the University of Nottingham for being not only inspiring colleagues, but also great friends. In particular, Emma Humphries, Isabel Story, Judit Varga, Abi Rhodes, Dave Young, Rob Stenson, Ivan Marković, Niki Cheong, and Niall Docherty offered not only peer support but friendship throughout the years. Special thanks to Claire Burdfield and Valentina Anania for endless hours of brainstorming, proofreading, and just being all-round wonderful humans. The thesis was expertly examined by Helen Kennedy and Hans-Joachim Backe, who both went out of their way to give me a good defence experience despite the viva being impacted by the pandemic. I am thankful for their thorough examination, and for their recommendation to award the project the highest distinction.

Throughout the preparation of this book, I worked multiple part-time and permanent jobs at various universities. Developing and teaching modules on widely different subjects, such as graphic design at Nottingham Trent University, creative industries at University of Nottingham, or social media at De Montfort University gave me respite from thinking constantly about videogames, and broadened my perspective on the many ways different media engage us. As it was the case for many working from home during the pandemic, my colleagues at these institutions were also my main connection to the outside world during the last couple of years spent indoors. For this, and for those Teams and Zoom meetings that eventually turned into a virtual post-work visit to the pub, I am grateful.

Thanks to the reviewers for their insightful comments and recommendations, as well as the editorial team at Routledge for accommodating the challenges life can throw in one's way.

I want to thank my mother and sister, who have always supported me with a kind of unconditional love only family can. And finally, thank you R., for being a constant, tea-brewing, game-playing, happy-making presence throughout.

Earlier versions of some of the ideas presented in Chapters 1, 2, and 5 appear in the following articles and I am grateful for permission to draw on them here:

- Bódi, B. (2021). 'Can Playfulness Be Designed? Understanding Playful Design through Agency in *Astroneer* (2019).' *Eludamos: Journal for Computer Game Culture* 12 (1): 39–61. https://doi.org/10.7557/23.6362
- Bódi, B.; Thon, J.-N. (2020). 'Playing Stories? Narrative-Dramatic Agency in Disco Elysium (2019) and Astroneer (2019).' *Frontiers of Narrative Studies* 6 (2): 157–190. https://doi.org/10.1515/fns-2020-0012
- Bódi, B. (2020). 'Procedural Content Generation, Player Agency, and Playfulness in Survival-Crafting Game Astroneer.' *Proceedings of 2020 DIGRA International Conference: Play Everywhere.* Available from: www.digra.org/digital-library/publications/procedural-content-generation-player-agency-and-playfulness-in-survival-crafting-game-astroneer/

Introduction

Technological advancement makes it possible for videogames[1] to offer increasingly complex gameplay experiences (Dovey and Kennedy 2006: 51; Kerr 2017: 29–30). This is perhaps even more powerfully felt now that we are on the doorstep of the next console cycle, with PlayStation 5 and Xbox Series X set to launch in late 2020, and *Microsoft Flight Simulator 2020* (Asobo), a game which recreates Earth's detailed geography, live traffic, dynamic weather, and its every airport using Bing Maps and Microsoft Azure's AI, having come out to PC in August 2020. With more sophisticated hardware and software comes more complex content, and the more power the player is promised to have over said content, the more attractive and marketable the product is—as seen, for example, throughout the marketing campaign leading up to the release of *The Legend of Zelda: Breath of the Wild* (Nintendo 2017), which offers the vast open world of Hyrule, the biggest and most homogenous one in the franchise yet.[2] This tendency to aspire for games offering more agency is ever so apparent when looking at the kinds of products videogame publishers have been favouring over the past decade or so: *The Witcher* (CD Projekt Red 2007), *Assassin's Creed* (Ubisoft Montreal 2007), *Elder Scrolls* (Bethesda Softworks 1994), or *Red Dead Redemption* (Rockstar San Diego 2010), just to name a few, are all videogame franchises with numerous instalments, all designed as open worlds where the player has more freedom to do as they please compared to other, more restricted videogames. Recent installations of long-standing franchises offering linear gameplay also embraced this trend. For example, *Call of Duty: Modern Warfare*'s Spec Ops mode (Infinity Ward 2019) and *Call of Duty: Warzone* (Infinity Ward 2020) both feature more player freedom than previous instalments of the franchise, as does *Metal Gear Solid V: The Phantom Pain* (Kojima Productions 2015). This book will look into how this freedom to act is discussed by designers, and how that in turn reflects in their design principles. It will explore salient case studies to discover what these discourses around player action reveal about the nature of agency and game design.

Game studies is a vast interdisciplinary field, with clusters like education, humanities/social sciences, or computer science (Karhulahti and Koskimaa

2019; Martin 2018). That being said, as Deterding (2017) points out, a divide seems to be emerging, as human-computer interaction and communication researchers are increasingly favouring their respective disciplinary outlets. This observation is supported by the findings of two recently conducted meta-analyses into the state of digital games research, where the more technically oriented survey (Nguyen et al. 2018) and a more humanities and social sciences oriented one (Quandt et al. 2015) both pointed out that the other was notably missing from their datasets. Such a growing divide reduces the opportunities for knowledge exchange. Valuable and useful critical observations about how game design works, or could work, can be made from a perspective not necessarily informed by the observer's own design practice. Collins (2004) calls this 'interactional expertise', or 'the ability to converse expertly about a practical skill or expertise, but without being able to practice it, learned through linguistic socialisation among the practitioners' (ibid. 125). My 'interactional expertise', cultivated over the years by playing and talking about games, reading design textbooks and forums, and attending the Game Design Workshop at GDC 2016, demonstrates that there is a space for non-practical expertise in better understanding game design.[3]

The broader topic of games and gaming can be studied from multiple angles of course, such as looking at the games themselves, how they are structured, or how they convey meaning (see, e.g., Atkins 2003; Juul 2005; Ryan 2006; Wardrip-Fruin 2009); observing players to see how they make sense of games, or what playing means for them (see, e.g., Gallagher 2017; Taylor 2006, 2018); or asking questions about how games are made, and what impact circumstances of production have on gameplay experiences offered (see, e.g., Nicoll and Keogh 2019; Deuze 2007: 123–144; Dovey and Kennedy 2006; Kerr 2006, 2011, 2017). This book pursues a design-oriented approach towards studying videogames and is concerned with better understanding player agency from this perspective. As such, it follows in the footsteps of similar studies that link agency to game mechanics (see, e.g., Boonen and Mieritz 2018; Cheng 2007; Habel and Kooyman 2014; Harrell and Zhu 2009; Jørgensen 2003; King and Krzywinska 2006; Sicart 2008; Tulloch 2014), as opposed to approaches with a more narrow understanding of agency as a player's ability to change the course of a videogame's story (see, e.g., Domsch 2013; Hammond et al. 2007; Stang 2019; Tanenbaum and Tanenbaum 2009, 2010). Several of the above listed contributions at least acknowledge, if not explicitly draw on, Janet Murray's widely cited definition of agency as the 'the satisfying power to take meaningful action and see the results of our decisions and choices' (Murray 1997: 126). This definition, I will argue, and the larger discussion within which it sits, frames agency as a concept relevant to videogame narrativity, and is therefore somewhat limited. However, in Murray's argument several observations are made concerning different parts of the 'game structure' (ibid. 129–140), and this will be the starting point for the multidimensional conceptualisation of agency presented in this book.

My conceptualisation of agency draws on J. J. Gibson's affordance theory, and frames agency as an affordance of game design (Gibson 1979). The aim is to examine how agency is conceptualised in different areas surrounding digital games, focusing on game studies and game design discourse, and to synthesise the findings to create a multidimensional heuristic framework for conceptualising agency in avatar-based games. In order to demonstrate its analytical power, as well as to explore how applying the framework to specific examples can bring added value to its foundations, I will look at three case studies. They will focus on individual games, the first two being part of franchises, and the last one being a stand-alone title, created by game studios with a particular design focus that draws on 'game design lineages' (Bateman and Zagal 2018), i.e., traceable lines of inspiration and evolution in game design practice over time, as enabled by technological progress and player practices. As such, the case studies, in part, offer a historical narrative of studios keeping such game design lineages alive, reconstructed primarily using the respective studios' communications. By framing the case study games and the studios that produced them as exemplifying game design lineages, rather than describing them in terms of genre, which tends to lack connotative consistency, I can observe not only *how* the games as artifacts afford and limit agency, but also *why* that may be.

The method I chose for this research is twofold. First, a paratextual analysis is conducted to establish what I call the design ethos of each studio. The word *êthos* is of Greek origin and can broadly be translated as the character of a person, a community, or an ideology.[4] In this vein, this book posits that we can reconstruct the design ethos of a game studio by looking at how they communicate their professional and artistic identity, what the aesthetics are of the games they produce over time, and how these are reported on in trade press and in journalistic outlets. Although such texts are often generated with promotional[5] intent in mind, and therefore need to be considered with a proverbial pinch of salt, the videogame industry is notoriously secretive (see, e.g., Foxman and Nieborg 2016; O'Donnell 2014), and so turning to sources like game reviews is a productive way around the invisible wall. Journalistic coverage of videogames often features suggestions for best play practice, and also speak to socio-historical context, state of the industry, technology, and trends, as well as containing recommendations for improving design, and hypotheses about design intention which exhibit various degrees of educated guessing, as found by for example Zagal and colleagues (2009: 221).

In this book, I will use 'paratext' to refer to such materials generated around the actual videogames themselves. The term 'paratext' was coined by Gerard Genette (1997a [1982]) to refer to materials that surround a literary text, created by the author, the editor, or others partaking in the publishing of a book.[6] While this notion has certainly appeared in game studies before (see, e.g., Aarseth 1997; Consalvo 2007; Jones 2008; Newman 2008), and neighbouring media disciplines, such as film and TV studies, have long embraced the analytical value of such sources (see, e.g., Caldwell 2011; Grainge and Johnson 2015; Gray 2010; Hesford 2013), it has only been in recent years that the notion of 'paratext' begun to creep in from the periphery in game studies (see, e.g., Beil et al. 2021; Booth 2015; Consalvo 2017; Dunne 2016; Fernández-Vara 2015; Švelch 2020; Vollans et al. 2017; Vollans and Seiwald 2022; Wright 2018), with some scholars still opting for alternative terms (see, e.g., 'additions' in Chapman 2016: 269). So how does this book conceptualise paratexts?

While Genette's work did elevate previously dismissed materials to the status of worthy subject of critical inquiry, there was still a suggested hierarchical relationship between the text and what surrounds it, maintained by the insistence that the author needs to authenticate such addendums, or else they cannot be considered paratexts (Genette 1997b [1987]: 9). This hierarchy was reversed in game studies, most notably, by Consalvo (2007), who argued that paratexts shape gameplay experiences 'regardless of the actual game itself' (ibid. 8). Consalvo expanded the meaning of paratext in the context of videogames to encompass everything that surrounds games, such as magazines, strategy guides, and conventions, arguing that there is a paratexts industry that generates and manages such ancillary materials (ibid.: 22–39). This expansion was not without risk, and, as Švelch (2020: n.p.) points out, the concept of videogame paratexts got so over-inflated that some even used it to describe such things as tie-in novels and web series. In this book I understand paratextual evidence as primarily including journalistic coverage (both subject specialist and more general); conventions, conferences, and other trade events; analogue and digital marketing and advertising, such as packaging, adverts, and trailers; developer, or 'dev' blogs; and official websites, blogs, forums, and verified social media accounts of games, studios, publishers, individual developers, and other participants in the production and distribution of videogames such as hardware and software companies. This way, my understanding of paratextual materials is somewhat more expansive than Genette's original definition but is also not so broad as to include all related materials that would venture over into other realms, such as transmedia expansions.[7] By using paratextual analysis, this book takes into account the technological, economic, and socio-cultural context within which decisions about player agency are made.

Having established the design ethos of the studios discussed, in the respective case study chapters I move on to look at how the (at the time of writing) latest games from the selected studios afford and limit player action, using textual analysis. Such qualitative study of videogames is of course an established method, though often deployed under different monikers (e.g., 'action analysis' in Jørgensen 2003; 'close playing' in Bizzocchi and Tanenbaum 2011). Although 'textual' has been, on occasion, used to describe specifically components of games that are literally represented via written word (see, e.g., Newman 2008: 48), framing a videogame as 'text' in a broad sense, and therefore critical engagement with it as 'textual analysis' is not novel (see, e.g., Consalvo and Dutton 2006; Kennedy 2002; Krzywinska 2003). In this book I will use textual analysis as applied to the study of videogames by Fernández-Vara (2015). More specifically, my analysis focuses less on the meanings videogames create and how those meanings could be interpreted by different audiences, and more on how the elements that have the potential to generate meanings are arranged. In other words, I am interested in what Fernández-Vara calls the 'formal aspects' (ibid. 117–172), such as game mechanics or level design, which afford and constrain the possibility space for player action.[8]

The book is structured into five chapters, with Chapter 1 concerned with the conceptual history of agency, Chapter 2 dedicated to the proposed original theoretical approach to studying it, and the remaining chapters to a case study each. Chapter 1 begins with a survey of game design and game studies literature, focused on how agency has been used, defined, and debated over the past decades. I will highlight the common denominators within respective traditions, in order to articulate a conceptualisation of agency that speaks to the threads that emerge. Chapter 2 will present my conceptualisation of agency as the possibility space for avatar action as afforded and constrained by game design. Relying on both game studies and game design discourses, this chapter maps the four dimensions in which I argue player action can be most prominently realised in. In simple terms, I will distinguish between agency in space, in time, by allowing customisation of the avatar and its surroundings, and over narratively charged content. These two chapters will 1) identify and evaluate prominent perspectives on agency across disciplines; 2) extract common themes that appear across literature to be used pillars for a conceptualisation of agency; and 3) distinguish between multiple dimensions across which player agency as expressed via avatar action can manifest during gameplay.

The following Chapters 3, 4, and 5 are dedicated to case studies of game studios that make avatar-based videogames, to examine how dimensions of agency support and undermine each other, and also to explore how individual contexts enrich the foundations of the heuristic framework. Naughty Dog, and their Indiana-Jonesian action-adventure game *Uncharted 4: A Thief's End* (2016) in Chapter 3 is the first case study of this book because it exemplifies a very high degree of designer control over player action, and subsequently, player progression. As such, the application of the conceptualisation of agency proposed in this book, along with the multidimensional heuristic framework, onto a game that may at first seem so devoid of player agency highlights the analytical power of both. Exploring the design history of both studio and franchise allows me to consider how the player's ability to act is discussed by developers coming from a fairly standard videogame production environment and adhering to a traditional press cycle, where the studio's design ethos and the franchise's brand identity remains relatively intact over the years. It also allows for an examination of the constraints and affordances on player action in the traditional 1990s genre of platforming, and trace how this design lineage evolved over the past two decades. This case study will also introduce the notion of cinematic design, survey how this quality is conceptualised by developers, what this means for agency across dimensions, and compare these discussions to how a cinematic quality is achieved in the final product.

Chapter 4 is dedicated to the second case study of BioWare and their sci-fi action role-playing game *Mass Effect: Andromeda* (2017). It is a counterexample to the previous chapter, whereby both the design ethos of the studio and the brand identity of the franchise changed over the years. This chapter shows how changes in the composition of development and leadership teams, publishers, production pipelines, and technologies can impact player agency, and what consequences that has on the identity of the franchise. Moreover, it traces the evolution of the design lineage of role-playing games, and their subsequent merging with action-adventure design principles particularly in the AAA market, in terms of agency dimensions. By looking at an open world game whose gameplay is characterised by comparatively less salient designer control than the previous case study, this chapter demonstrates the dynamic nature of agency dimensions and how they support each other, but it also shows how they can undermine each other and therefore obstruct meaningful play.

Chapter 5 focuses on System Era's sandbox survival crafting game *Astroneer* (2019). This final case study chapter expands the scope of my inquiry by applying the heuristic framework to not just a different game design model, but also a different production context. As the studio was founded by former AAA developers who had gone independent, this case study is an opportunity to show how differently, compared to the other case studies, a game can be produced, and how differently design intention is communicated with regards to player action. In this way, this example is a good contrast to the previous two case study examples, which were both AAA games. Since System Era is a relatively young studio and, as such, there was not much in line of a design history to examine, this example instead allowed me to discuss what independence can mean in the context of videogames, and what implications that can have for player agency. At the same time, *Astroneer* exemplifies a game design lineage of survival crafting sandbox games stemming from *Minecraft*. The relatively few constraints that such a game places on player action make this an illustrative final case study.

The ways in which videogames afford agency changes with the evolution of technology and diversification of production practices. This book contributes to our understanding of agency in videogames by offering a conceptualisation informed by game design and an analytical framework that speaks to multiple dimensions in which avatar action can be realised, and as such is flexible and could adapt to this diversification. The following chapters provide a detailed examination of agency within a particular slice of the current videogame landscape, by tracing how different production contexts communicate design intention over time, and also how now-ubiquitous models of game design have evolved in terms of how they afford and constrain player action. By doing so, this book brings to light agency dynamics in and around videogames.

Notes

1 From here and throughout, I will use 'videogame' as an umbrella term to encompass the various labels used to refer to these interactive artifacts, such as computer game, digital game, electronic game, etc.
2 See for example how Reggie Fils-Aimé, Nintendo America's president, speaks about the game at E3 2016 (Nintendo 2016), or *Zelda* creator Shigeru Miyamoto's words on how important it was for them to offer players more choices in the new open world environment (Hilliard 2017: 44).
3 After all, some studios are already looking for 'Game Concept Designer' roles where technical experience is not among the essential criteria. See Jouin (n.d.) hiring for Ubisoft, for example.
4 Notably, Aristotle lists 'êthos', or 'character' in most translations, as one of three modes of persuasion in *Rhetoric* (cf. Cope 1970 [1877]).
5 For more on videogames and marketing, see, e.g., Kline et al. 2003; Kerr 2006: 43–101; Nieborg 2011: 113–118; Zackariasson and Dymek 2016; Zackariasson and Wilson 2012.
6 Genette (1997b [1987]: 5) later breaks down paratext into the subgroups of 'peritext' (all things within the immediate surrounds of a book, such as its cover, the title, or notes intertwined) and 'epitext' (materials that are more loosely connected to the text, such as interviews with the author). However, this spatial distinction is of little relevance when applied to a digital artifact such as a videogame (cf. Švelch 2020).
7 For more on transmedia, see, e.g., Jenkins 2008 on general conceptualisation; the chapters in Freeman and Rampazzo-Gambarato 2019 for a variety of approaches to the topic; Ryan 2013 or Thon 2016 on transmedia narratology; Clark 2012 or Evans 2011 on transmedia television; Freeman 2016 on early transmedia storytelling; and Kinder 1991 for an early exploration into transmedia and videogames.
8 I am not concerned with establishing what a game is, but there will be a more detailed discussion about formal aspects in Chapter 1. Many tackled the definitional challenge though, as it is an important one (cf. Arjoranta 2019), and the following is but an illustrative list. See, e.g., Avedon and Sutton-Smith 1971 or Redl et al. 1971 for early definitions; Wolf 2001 framing videogames as media; Juul's classic game model (2005: 37); the multidimensional typology of games in Aarseth et al. 2003; further classification of games in Elverdam and Aarseth 2007; Karhulahti 2020 for a phenomenological approach or, for a game design perspective, Costikyan (2005 [1999]), Crawford (1997 [1984]), or Salen and Zimmerman (2004: 80).

References

Aarseth, E. J. (1997). *Cybertext: Perspectives on Ergodic Literature*. Baltimore, MD: Johns Hopkins University Press.
Aarseth, E. J.; Smedstad, S. M.; Sunnanå, L. (2003). A Multidimensional Typology of Games. *DiGRA'03—Proceedings of the 2003 DiGRA International Conference: Level Up*. Vol. 2, pp. 48–53. Available at: www.digra.org/digital-library/publications/a-multidimensional-typology-of-games/

Arjoranta, J. (2019). How to Define Games and Why We Need to. *The Computer Games Journal* 8: 109–120.

Asobo. (2020). *Microsoft Flight Simulator 2020* [PC]. Xbox Game Studios.

Atkins, B. (2003). *More Than a Game: The Computer Game as Fictional Form*. Manchester: Manchester University Press.

Avedon, E.; Sutton-Smith, B. (eds.). (1971). *The Study of Games*. New York: John Wiley & Sons.

Bateman, C.; Zagal, J. P. (2018). Game Design Lineages. Minecraft's Inventory. *Transactions of the Digital Games Research Association* 3 (2): 13–46.

Beil, B.; Freyermuth, G. S.; Schmidt, C. (eds.). (2021) *Paratextualizing Games: Investigations on the Paraphernalia and Peripheries of Play*. Transcript Verlag.

Bethesda Softworks. (1994). *The Elder Scrolls: Arena* [PC]. Bethesda Softworks.

BioWare. (2017). *Mass Effect: Andromeda* [PlayStation 4]. Electronic Arts.

Bizzocchi, J.; Tanenbaum, T. J. (2011). Well Read: Applying Close Reading Techniques to Gameplay Experiences. In D. Davidson, ed. *Well Played 3.0: Video Games, Value, and Meaning*. Pittsburgh, PA: ETC Press, pp. 262–290.

Boonen, C. S.; Mieritz, D. (2018). Paralysing Fear: Player Agency Parameters in Horror Games. *DiGRA Nordic'18—Proceedings of 2018 International DiGRA Nordic Conference*. Available at: www.digra.org/digital-library/publications/paralysing-fear-player-agency-parameters-in-horror-games/

Booth, P. (2015). *Game Play: Paratextuality in Contemporary Board Games*. London: Bloomsbury Academic.

Caldwell, J. T. (2011). Corporate and Worker Ephemera: The Industrial Promotional Surround, Paratexts and Worker Blowback. In P. Grainge, ed. *Ephemeral Media: Transitory Screen Culture from Television to YouTube*. London: Palgrave Macmillan, pp. 175–194.

CD Projekt Red. (2007). *The Witcher* [PC]. CD Projekt.

Chapman, A. (2016). *Digital Games as History: How Videogames Represent the Past and Offer Access to Historical Practice*. London: Routledge.

Cheng, P. (2007). Waiting for Something to Happen: Narratives, Interactivity, and Agency and the Video Game Cut-Scene. *DiGRA'07—Proceedings of the 2007 DiGRA International Conference: Situated Play*. University of Tokyo. Available at: www.digra.org/digital-library/publications/waiting-for-something-to-happen-narratives-interactivity-and-agency-and-the-video-game-cut-scene/

Clark, M. J. (2012). *Transmedia Television: New Trends in Network Serial Production*. New York: Bloomsbury.

Collins, H. (2004). Interactional Expertise as a Third Kind of Knowledge. *Phenomenology and the Cognitive Sciences* 3 (2): 125–143.

Consalvo, M. (2007). *Cheating: Gaining Advantage in Videogames*. Cambridge, MA: MIT Press.

Consalvo, M. (2017). When Paratexts Become Texts: De-Centering the Game-as-Text. *Critical Studies in Media Communication* 34 (2): 177–183.

Consalvo, M.; Dutton, N. (2006). Game Analysis: Developing a Methodological Toolkit for the Qualitative Study of Games. *Game Studies* 6 (1). Available at: http://gamestudies.org/06010601/articles/consalvo_dutton#c

Cope, E. M. (1970 [1877]). *The Rhetoric of Aristotle*. Hildesheim: Olm.

Costikyan, G. (2005 [1999]). I Have No Words & I Must Design. In K. Salen and E. Zimmerman, eds. *The Game Design Reader: A Rules of Play Anthology*. Cambridge, MA: MIT Press, pp. 192–210.

Crawford, C. (1997 [1984]). *The Art of Computer Game Design*. Available at: www.digitpress.com/library/books/book_art_of_computer_game_design.pdf
Deterding, S. (2017). The Pyrrhic Victory of Game Studies: Assessing the Past, Present, and Future of Interdisciplinary Game Research. *Games and Culture* 12 (6): 521–543.
Deuze, M. (2007). *Media Work*. Cambridge: Polity Press.
Domsch, S. (2013). *Storyplaying: Agency and Narrative in Video Games*. Berlin: De Gruyter.
Dovey, J.; Kennedy, H. W. (2006). *Game Cultures. Computer Games as New Media*. New York: Open University Press.
Dunne, D. (2016). Paratext: The in-between of Structure and Play. In C. Duret and C.-M. Pons eds. *Contemporary Research on Intertextuality in Video Games*. Hershey, PA: IGI Global, pp. 274–296.
Elverdam, C.; Aarseth, E. (2007). Game Classification and Game Design: Construction Through Critical Analysis. *Games and Culture* 2 (1): 3–22.
Evans, E. (2011). *Transmedia Television: Audiences, New Media and Daily Life*. New York: Routledge.
Fernández-Vara, C. (2015). *Introduction to Game Analysis*. New York: Routledge.
Foxman, M.; Nieborg, D. B. (2016). Between a Rock and a Hard Place: Games Coverage and Its Network of Ambivalences. *Journal of Games Criticism* 1 (3). Available at: http://gamescriticism.org/articles/foxmannieborg-3-1
Freeman, M. (2016). *Historicising Transmedia Storytelling: Early Twentieth Century Storyworlds*. New York: Taylor and Francis.
Freeman, M.; Rampazzo-Gambarato, R. (eds.). (2019). *The Routledge Companion to Transmedia Studies*. New York: Routledge.
Gallagher, R. (2017). *Videogames, Identity and Digital Subjectivity*. New York: Routledge.
Genette, G. (1997a [1982]). *Palimpsests: Literature in the Second Degree*. Lincoln, NA: University of Nebraska Press.
Genette, G. (1997b [1987]). *Paratexts: Thresholds of Interpretation*. Cambridge: Cambridge University Press.
Gibson, J. J. (1979). *The Ecological Approach to Visual Perception*. Boston, MA: Houghton Mifflin.
Grainge, P.; Johnson, C. (2015). *Promotional Screen Industries*. New York: Routledge.
Gray, J. (2010). *Show Sold Separately: Promos, Spoilers, and Other Media Paratexts*. New York: New York University Press.
Habel, C.; Kooyman, B. (2014). Agency Mechanics: Gameplay Design in Survival Horror Video Games. *Digital Creativity* 25 (1): 1–14.
Hammond, S.; Pain, H.; Smith, T. J. (2007). Player Agency in Interactive Narrative: Audience, Actor & Author. *AISB'07—Artificial and Ambient Intelligence*, 2–4 April, Newcastle, UK. Available at: https://eprints.bbk.ac.uk/9955/1/9955.pdf
Harrell, D. F.; Zhu, J. (2009). Agency Play: Dimensions of Agency for Interactive Narrative Design. *Proceedings of the AAAI 2008 Spring Symposium on Interactive Narrative Technologies II*, Stanford, CA, pp. 156–162.
Hesford, D. (2013). 'Action . . . Suspense . . . Emotion!': The Trailer as Cinematic Performance. *Frames Cinema Journal* (3). Available at: http://framescinemajournal.com/article/action-suspense-emotion-the-trailer-as-cinematic-performance/
Hilliard, K. (2017). A New Take on an Old Legend: *The Legend of Zelda* Reinvents Itself for *Breath of the Wild*. *Game Informer* 287: 36–47.

Infinity Ward. (2019). *Call of Duty: Modern Warfare* [PlayStation 4] Activision.
Infinity Ward. (2020). *Call of Duty: Warzone* [PlayStation 4] Activision.
Jenkins, H. (2008). *Convergence Culture: Where Old and New Media Collide*. New York: Newyork University Press.
Jones, S. E. (2008). *The Meaning of Video Games: Gaming and Textual Strategies*. New York: Routledge.
Jørgensen, K. (2003). *Aporia & Epiphany in Context: Computer Game Agency in Baldur's Gate II & Heroes of Might & Magic IV*. Hovedfag (MA) Dissertation, Department of Media Studies, University of Bergen.
Jouin, V. (n.d.). Game Concept Designer—Green Panda Games (F/H). *Smart Recruiters*. Available at: https://jobs.smartrecruiters.com/Ubisoft2/743999713218426-game-concept-designer-green-panda-games-f-h-
Juul, J. (2005). *Half-Real: Video Games between Real Rules and Fictional Worlds*. Cambridge, MA: MIT Press.
Karhulahti, V.-M. (2020). Computer Game as a Pragmatic Concept: Ideas, Meanings, and Culture. *Media, Culture & Society* 42 (3): 471–480.
Karhulahti, V.-M.; Koskimaa, R. (2019). Canons of Games Research: An Analysis of the Most Cited Publications. *DiGRA'19—Abstract Proceedings of the 2019 DiGRA International Conference: Game, Play and the Emerging Ludo-Mix*. Available at: www.digra.org/digital-library/publications/canons-of-games-research-an-analysis-of-the-most-cited-publications/
Kennedy, H. (2002). Lara Croft: Feminist Icon or Cyberbimbo? On the Limits of Textual Analysis. *Game Studies* 2 (2). Available at: http://www.gamestudies.org/0202/kennedy/
Kerr, A. (2006). *The Business and Culture of Digital Games. Gamework/Gameplay*. London: SAGE.
Kerr, A. (2011). The Culture of Gamework. In M. Deuze, ed. *Managing Media Work*. London: SAGE, pp. 225–236.
Kerr, A. (2017). *Global Games: Production, Circulation and Policy in the Networked Era*. New York: Routledge.
Kinder, M. (1991). *Playing with Power in Movies, Television, and Video Games: From Muppet Babies to Teenage Mutant Ninja Turtles*. Berkeley, CA: University of California Press.
King, G.; Krzywinska, T. (2006). *Tomb Raiders and Space Invaders. Videogame Forms and Contexts*. London: I.B. Tauris & Co Ltd.
Kline, S.; Dyer-Witherford, N.; De Peuter, G. (2003). *Digital Play: The Interaction of Technology, Culture, and Marketing*. London: McGill-Queen's University Press.
Kojima Productions. (2015). *Metal Gear Solid V: The Phantom Pain* [PlayStation 4]. Konami.
Krzywinska, T. (2003). Playing Buffy: Remediation, Occulted Meta-Game-Physics and the Dynamics of Agency in the Videogame Version of *Buffy the Vampire Slayer*. *Slayage: The Online International Journal of Buffy Studies* 8. Available at: http://www.slayage.tv/essays/slayage8/Krzywinska.htm
Martin, P. (2018). The Intellectual Structure of Game Research. *Game Studies* 18 (1). Available at: http://gamestudies.org/1801/articles/paul_martin
Murray, J. (1997). *Hamlet on the Holodeck*. Cambridge, MA: MIT Press.
Naughty Dog. (2016). *Uncharted 4: A Thief's End*. [PlayStation 4] Sony Computer Entertainment.
Newman, J. (2008). *Playing with Videogames*. Abingdon: Routledge.

Nguyen, T.-H. D.; Melcerb, E.; Canossac, A.; Isbister, K.; Seif El-Nasr, M. (2018). Seagull: A Bird's-Eye View of the Evolution of Technical Games Research. *Entertainment Computing* 26: 88–104.

Nicoll, B.; Keogh, B. (2019). *The Unity Game Engine and the Circuits of Cultural Software*. Cham: Springer International.

Nieborg, D. B. (2011). *Triple-A: The Political Economy of the Blockbuster Video Game*. PhD Thesis, University of Amsterdam. Available at: https://dare.uva.nl/search?arno.record.id=383251

Nintendo. (2016). *Reggie Kicks Off Nintendo E3 2016 with the Legend of Zelda: Breath of the Wild*. Available at: www.youtube.com/watch?v=oalEsT7RyFI

Nintendo EPD. (2017). *The Legend of Zelda: Breath of the Wild*. [Nintendo Switch] Nintendo.

O'Donnell, C. (2014). *Developer's Dilemma. The Secret World of Video Game Creators*. Cambridge, MA: MIT Press.

Quandt, T.; Looy, J. V.; Vogelgesang, J.; Elson, M.; Ivory, J. D.; Consalvo, M.; Mäyrä, F. (2015). Digital Games Research: A Survey Study on an Emerging Field and Its Prevalent Debates. *Journal of Communication* 65 (6): 975–996.

Redl, F.; Gump, P.; Sutton-Smith, B. (1971). The Dimensions of Games. In E. Avedon and B. Sutton-Smith, eds. *The Study of Games*. New York: John Wiley & Sons, pp. 408–418.

Rockstar San Diego. (2010). *Red Dead Redemption*. [PlayStation 3] Rockstar Games.

Ryan, M.-L. (2006). *Avatars of Story*. Minneapolis, MI: University of Minnesota Press.

Ryan, M.-L. (2013). Transmedial Storytelling and Transfictionality. *Poetics Today* 34 (3): 361–388.

Salen, K.; Zimmerman, E. (2004). *Rules of Play: Game Design Fundamentals*. Cambridge, MA: MIT Press.

Sicart, M. (2008). Defining Game Mechanics. *Game Studies* 8 (2). Available at: http://gamestudies.org/0802/articles/sicart

Stang, S. (2019). "This Action Will Have Consequences": Interactivity and Player Agency. *Game Studies* 19 (1). Available at: http://gamestudies.org/1901/articles/stang

Švelch, J. (2020). Paratextuality in Game Studies: A Theoretical Review and Citation Analysis. *Game Studies* 20 (2). Available at: http://gamestudies.org/2002/articles/jan_svelch

System Era Softworks. (2019). *Astroneer* [PC]. System Era Softworks.

Tanenbaum, K.; Tanenbaum, T. J. (2009). Commitment to Meaning: A Reframing of Agency in Games. *Proceedings of the 8th Conference on Digital Arts and Culture (DAC)*, 12–15 December, Irvine, CA. Available at: https://escholarship.org/uc/item/6f49r74n

Tanenbaum, K.; Tanenbaum, T. J. (2010). Agency as Commitment to Meaning: Communicative Competence in Games. *Digital Creativity* 21 (1): 11–17.

Taylor, T. L. (2006). *Play Between Worlds: Exploring Online Game Culture*. Cambridge, MA: MIT Press.

Taylor, T. L. (2018). *Watch Me Play: Twitch and the Rise of Game Live Streaming*. Princeton, NJ: Princeton University Press.

Thon, J.-N. (2016). *Transmedial Narratology and Contemporary Media Culture*. Lincoln, NE: University of Nebraska Press.

Tulloch, R. (2014). The Construction of Play: Rules, Restrictions, and the Repressive Hypothesis. *Games and Culture* 9 (5): 335–350. https://doi.org/10.1177/1555412014542807

Ubisoft Montreal. (2007). *Assassin's Creed* [Xbox 360] Ubisoft.

Vollans, E.; Janes, S.; Therrien, C.; Arsenault, D. (2017). Introduction: 'It's [Not Just] in the Game': The Promotional Context of Video Games. *Kinephanos: Journal of Media Studies and Popular Culture* 7 (1): 1–6.

Vollans, E.; Seiwald, R. (eds.). (2022) *Not in the Game: History, Paratext and Games*. Berlin: Dr Gruyter.

Wardrip-Fruin, N. (2009). *Expressive Processing: Digital Fictions, Computer Games, and Software Studies*. Cambridge, MA: MIT Press.

Wolf, M. J. P. (2001). The Video Game As a Medium. In M. J. P. Wolf, ed. *The Medium of the Video Game*. Austin, TX: University of Texas Press, pp. 13–34.

Wright, E. (2018). On the Promotional Context of Historical Video Games. *Rethinking History: The Journal of Theory and Practice* 22 (4): 598–608.

Zackariasson, P.; Dymek, M. (2016). *Video Game Marketing: A Student Textbook*. New York: Routledge.

Zackariasson, P.; Wilson, T. L. (2012). Marketing of Video Games. In P. Zackariasson and T. L. Wilson, eds. *The Video Game Industry: Formation, Present State, and Future*. New York: Routledge, pp. 57–75.

Zagal, J. P.; Ladd, A.; Johnson, T. (2009). Characterizing and Understanding Game Reviews. *FDG'09—Proceedings of the 4th International Conference on the Foundations of Digital Games*. Orlando, FL: ACM, pp. 215–222.

1 Understanding Agency

The notion of agency is generally understood to refer to our ability to act in the world, within the societal context that prescribes our everyday life. As such, thinkers interested in the human condition, such as philosophers, sociologists, and anthropologists, have long been preoccupied with the meaning and impact of the term. Martin Heidegger (1977 [1932]) wrote that in the new technological age everything is either a representation (or picture), or a spectator of said representation, and therefore human agency is manifest in this cycle of expression and spectatorship. Michel Foucault (2013 [1982]) saw agency as eternally determined by power relations, and Anthony Giddens (1984) famously argued for something similar in his 'structuration theory', where he attempted to reconcile a tension between whether it is societal structure, or human agency which moulds our behaviour. Within the context of science and technology studies, Bruno Latour (2005) expanded the notion of agency as part of his Actor-Network Theory, arguing that not only human, but nonhuman actors, too, can be part of networks within structures of society and natural ecology. The concept of empowered ability to take action is also ubiquitous in media studies, not only concerning media reception (e.g., 'interpretive inference' in Bordwell 1989; 'participatory culture' in Jenkins 2012 [1992]) but also with regard to medial representation (e.g., Meyers 2008 on women; Downing and Husband 2005 on race; Mukherjee 2017 on postcolonialism). However, agency as understood in this book is not so much about any of the above. Instead, I propose to take a step back and think about agency in videogames in terms of what creates the possibility for it to manifest in the first place.

Agency in Game Studies

Broadly speaking, we can find three rather different approaches to studying agency in game studies. First, agency is often discussed in terms of diversity, representation, and community participation in and around videogames (e.g., Banks 2013; Gray and Leonard 2018; Joseph 2018; Ruberg and Shaw 2017; Shaw 2014; Sotamaa 2007), Second, we have narratologically oriented approaches which understand agency as a player's ability to change

DOI: 10.4324/9781003298786-2

the course of a videogame's story (e.g., Domsch 2013; Hammond et al. 2007; Stang 2019; Tanenbaum and Tanenbaum 2009, 2010). These are mostly influenced by Murray's definition of agency. Third, we have a linking of agency to game mechanics, platforms, and the material affordances of videogames (e.g., Boonen and Mieritz 2018; Brock and Fraser 2018; Cheng 2007; Habel and Kooyman 2013; Harrell and Zhu 2008; Jørgensen 2003a; Keogh 2018a; King and Krzywinska 2006; Tulloch 2014). The approach in this book is more in line with this last cluster of work. As such, these sources will be discussed in more detail in the section dedicated to establishing my conceptualisation of player agency. But before I do this, I will (1) review the prevalent narratologically oriented approach to thinking about agency and the advantages and disadvantages it has, and (2) identify some (other) early texts which paved the way for a broader conceptualisation of agency as avatar action.

The long conceptual history of agency in game studies is intertwined with the tides that have defined the field so far. First, and perhaps most fundamentally, the question of whether games are stories or not, and if so, how. In the early years, Janet Murray (1997) and Espen Aarseth (1997) spearheaded two rather different approaches to games and narrativity. Murray found computer games to be the next step in the evolution of narrative, one that offers interactivity in a way literature and film do not, while Aarseth argued that we cannot simply regard games solely as derivative of literary texts and therefore we should study them with a new disciplinary approach. For a while, this opposition was referred to as the 'ludology/narratology debate', with further entries (e.g., Atkins 2003; Eskelinen 2001b; Frasca 1999; Jenkins 2006; Murray 2005; Pearce 2004) complicating the issue even more.[1] However, most parties have since dismissed that there was ever much of a debate, and agree that it was a matter of misunderstanding and misinterpretation (Frasca 2003; Aarseth 2014, 2019). There now seems to be, as Lisbeth Klastrup puts it, 'a common agreement that most games project some form of fictional world, however limited it be' (2003a: n.p.). These widely different approaches show that we can theorise the relationship between player and game system in many ways. In the following, I will review the most prominent ones, in order to outline the gap this book addresses, as well as to identify the traditions it draws on.

I first want to discuss a buzzword a lot of scholarship revolved around: 'interactivity'. Notably, Carr et al. (2003) discuss interactivity in relation to games-as-texts, while Klastrup (2003b) establishes a 'grammar of an interactive piece of work', but it is the typology of different kinds of interactivity by Ryan (2006) that marks an important milestone in the evolution of thinking about player action and the videogame object. Ryan uses 'interactivity' to describe the many relationships that can exist between 'a user and a text' (ibid. 107), and identifies player (or rather, user) choice at the heart of the process. While Ryan does cite game designer Chris Crawford on choice being a fundamental criterion of interactivity, this observation is woven into an argument for choice being narratively relevant action expressed within 'textual architectures', which in turn can be thought of as 'structures of choice' (ibid. 99). 'Textual architectures' are both traditional and interactive architectures, which Ryan splits into story (or plots) as predetermined, and discourse as individual runs of the story/plot.[2] These comprise of nodes that represent decision moments, which then weave different patterns, such as 'vectors with side branches' for discourse or 'tree' for story (ibid. 103–104), impacting the narrative experience in digital media in various ways. These structures, Ryan argues, inform different types of interactivity (ibid. 107–108). Ryan's mappings of choice patterns are an important reference point in the development of thinking about agency because although they primarily highlight the narrative potential in interactive media, they can also be seen as strategies for how player action could be manipulated by design. Metaphors like 'network', 'sea-anemone', or 'maze' are to this day recurrent when making sense of, as well as designing, progression in videogames (see, e.g., Adams 2010 [2006]: 171–175). In this sense, Ryan's work on interactivity can be seen as an early take on capturing how design can manipulate player agency.[3]

Another way to theorise player experience as afforded by the game is known by many names: 'nontrivial effort' (Aarseth 1997: 1–2), 'player effort' (Juul 2005: 36–43), 'configurative action' (Eskelinen 2001a: n.p., 2012: 275–293), or 'player performance/playformance' (Frasca 2007: 136–179). These approaches are in some ways different, but they share a focus less on meaning-making, and more on the mechanics of interaction between player and game systems. In this vein, they could be branded as a kind of formalist approach. Notably, when dissecting the aesthetics of 'ergodic literature', that is, a combination of a text and a machine that can produce multiple manifestations of said text, Espen Aarseth argues that the readers non-trivial effort to engage with the text (which in ergodic literature is more than mere eye movement) is triggered by a text's 'traversal function', which is a text's ability to reveal or hide the components[4] of the text. Doing so conceives of the traversal function as an object-property, thereby relocating the subject of query from the reader (or, rather, player) to the object (which to Aarseth in 1997 is the text). In this vein, I propose to think of agency as afforded by the mechanisms of the videogame. This makes possible an examination of how a game's design allows for interaction in order to better understand how player agency can manifest during gameplay.

Building on Aarseth's notion of nontrivial effort, Juul speaks of 'player effort' which is exerted 'in order to influence the outcome' of a game (Juul 2005: 36–37). Since most games include rules that prescribe how player action influences both the game state and the final outcome, Juul argues that player effort is part of the game, and includes it as an official component in his classic game model. Besides 'rules' and 'variable and quantifiable outcome', Juul lists 'player effort' as a property of 'the game as a formal system', thereby making player effort the property of the game on an artefact level. From this brief discussion, already we can see that from early on, player action was considered as a possibility already prescribed into the game systems. This may go without saying, but it is important to emphasise, because it enables us to ask questions about agency not of the player, but of the videogame, which is what the heuristic framework forwarded in this book proposes to do.

Lastly, the term 'agency' was also used in early theorisations of the relationship between player and game, reader/user, and text. Most prominently, Murray's definition of agency as 'the satisfying power to take meaningful action and see the results of our decisions and choices' (Murray 1997: 126) is widely cited in game studies and game design discourse.[5] Murray states that agency is a more precise concept than interactivity because '[a]ctivity alone is not agency' (ibid. 128). She argues that agency is better understood as 'aesthetic pleasure' which takes place in the mind of the person reading/playing (ibid. 128). This approach is somewhat problematic because it conditions the experience of agency with a 'narrative satisfaction' (ibid. 140), thereby narrativising the entire gameplay experience. It also implies that agency can only be achieved as a positive experience, so emotions like frustration (as triggered by a challenging in-game situation) or fear (the primary component in playing horror games) are not part of it. While videogames can certainly be considered as narratives in many ways which I will touch upon later, they are not exclusively that.

That said, Murray's approach is not entirely unproductive to a broader conceptualisation of agency. First, the notion of meaningfulness is introduced. While these early writings attach meaningfulness to a narrative quality, that is, player action has to be relevant to the projected fiction of a game for it to be more than mere interactivity, it does open up the floor to questions about what other kinds of meaningfulness there could be.[6] Second, while Murray here is preoccupied with how best to create a 'compelling narrative structure that builds on these game structures without being diminished by them' (ibid. 129), other game components less closely tied with a game's storytelling capabilities are also discussed. These other parts of the 'game structure', such as a virtual landscape offering spatial navigation (ibid. 129–137), or the problem-solving challenges different spatial arrangements afford (ibid. 137–140) hint to what other kinds of meaningfulness games can afford, and as such they will be discussed later in this chapter.

As already stated, framing player agency as narratively meaningful action has permeated academic thought since Murray's definition. An example of this is Sebastian Domsch's (2013) approach, which follows in Murray's footsteps in that it rejects mere interaction as a true realisation of agency and regards narrative repercussions as a means to attribute meaningfulness to player action (ibid. 60–61). Domsch's work links the concept of nodal structures (not at all dissimilar to Ryan's textual architectures in interactive narrative) specifically to modern videogame agency. Drawing on Bode's notion of 'future narratives', which are potential narratives that can emerge from 'nodal situations' (Bode and Dietrich 2013: 1), Domsch argues that agency is narrative choice, insofar as a narrative is understood as what 'happens in the mind of those who experience it' (Domsch 2013: 99). While there are many points that help better understand the narrative experience videogames can afford, Domsch's approach also highlights why there is a need for a thorough exploration of agency that goes beyond narrative relevance.

The main issue with Domsch's book-length study of agency and games is that discussion is seriously hamstrung by inconsistencies and inaccuracies that could have been better examined had there been more thorough exploration of key terms key terms such as 'games', 'rule' and, perhaps most unfortunately, 'agency'.[7] A more considered critical engagement with previous scholarship on agency in game studies and game design discourse could have made the forwarded points stronger.[8] Despite these issues however, there are some productive points in the argument that outline interesting conceptual distinctions. Most saliently, while maintaining that 'choice situations' are communicated via 'narrative forms' (ibid. 31–34), the notion of 'existents'[9] is used to refer to building blocks of the gameplay experience which narrative does not account for. Domsch lists game spaces and their qualities, non-player characters populating game spaces, and 'the options available to the player in any given situation as well as the consequence of each action' as such existents (ibid. 61). These, Domsch argues, allow for different 'choice situations' which are not always narratively made sense of, such as 'reflex choices' in response to time-critical challenge (ibid: 117–120). Almost self-contradictorily, Domsch therefore underscores the importance for agency (as afforded by a 'choice situation') not only of content that can be qualified narratively, but also of other kinds of content which is somehow different.[10]

This initial review of game studies broadly sketched how player action was theorised as interactivity, player effort, and agency, and also showed that agency understood as narratively relevant choice is restrictive in many ways, which is a gap this book will tap into. The argument presented in this book will use Murray's definition of agency as a starting point, asking what other kinds of meaningfulness there can be, but it will also take into account broader conceptualisations of player action as afforded by the game. It will do so by drawing on a number of traditions within game studies, combining textual analysis of games as objects, considerations of design, and the paratextual surrounds of videogames. As such, it is an approach invested in better understanding game design, which in turn calls for a review of how game design theories have discussed the role of design in influencing player action broadly, and the concept of agency more specifically.

Agency in Game Design

As the case study chapters will discuss in more detail, the videogame industry saw an exponential growth from the late 1980s onwards. While some designers argued that the game development landscape is too fast-paced for there to be any consistent recording of design theories (see, e.g., Dille and Platten 2007), in parallel with the size of the industry grew a need for compiling knowledge of good design practices. Recognising this need, game designer Chris Crawford organised what would be known as the first Game Developers' Conference, or GDC, in his living room in 1988 (Campbell 2013). This spawned a new era in game design, where more and more effort was put towards creating a knowledge bank of design practice. In the early years, the most typical approach was to put one's own experiences into writing, usually without much reference to other designers' work, or existing theories.[11] An important first milestone in this journey is Greg Costikyan (2005 [1999]), whose essay identified the role of the designer as manipulator of player action.

Costikyan theorises the relationship between player and game in the form of a series of questions that every designer should ask themselves: 'What are the players' goals? Can the game support a variety of different goals? What facilities exist to allow players to strive toward their various goals?' (Costikyan 2005[1999]: 197). Highlighting the 'facilities' that a designer can create in order to enable players work towards their goals aligns with the approach taken by Aarseth and Juul, which shows that at a time when critical discussions around games were mostly pre-occupied by whether they are narratives or not, and by extension, whether agency is narratively validated player action or not, there were still some common truths acknowledged by both scholars and designers: namely that it is the entirety of game systems which facilitate player action in the first place.

What followed was an avalanche of game designers creating analytical models to better understand how the games they create facilitate play (e.g., the '400 Project' in Falstein 2002; 'Formal Abstract Design Tools' in Church 2005 [1999]; 'dramatic game dynamics' in LeBlanc 2006; 'neo-Aristotelian theory of interactive drama' in Mateas and Stern 2005[12]; 'game design patterns' in Björk and Holopainen 2005; the '5 dimensions of play' in Vandenberghe 2012). There are two contributions from this list that are of particular relevance to the argument presented in this book: Church, due to his foundational conceptual work which many draw upon in the following years, and Björk and Holopainen whose methodological approach I share. Others, such as Mateas and Stern (2005) and LeBlanc (2006), will be engaged with in more detail later in this chapter.

One of the 'Formal Abstract Design Tools' Church proposes is called 'intention' and he defines it as a

> process of accumulating goals, understanding the world, making a plan and then acting on it . . . intention can operate at each level, from a quick plan to cross a river to a multi-step plan to solve a huge mystery.
> (Church 2005 [1999]: 372)

Unfortunately, Church does not unpack these tools much further, leaving a lot of stones unturned. What is introduced however, is another tool called 'perceivable consequence', which is a 'clear reaction from the game world to the action of the player' (ibid. 373). This foregrounds 'intention' as realised in dialogue with feedback from the game systems—an approach that shares a lot with Murray's definition of agency discussed earlier in this chapter. However, Church makes it clear that intention is not a yes or no question, but a matter of degrees, and he also underscores the role game system feedback plays in this in ways that Murray does not. Thus, Church grounds Murray's theoretical observations in more practice-oriented writing, thereby shifting the emphasis from narrative meaningfulness to the importance of all aspects of game design.[13]

Björk and Holopainen (2005) forward a way to analyse games, identify problems in design, and find solutions for them.[14] This text is especially relevant for method and methodology-related reasons, as the multidimensional framework of agency follows closely in their footsteps when it comes to analysis and theory work. First, they propose the concept of 'game design patterns' to capture commonly recurrent formations, and a 'component framework' that these can be compiled into, which then, in turn, can be used to better understand individual iterations of game design. This is similar to how the heuristic framework for analysing agency in this book is constructed: I propose analytical dimensions, which then can be used as a lens to look at games with. Second, they argue that asking questions about gameplay can be done not just by collecting data from actual players, but also by studying the games themselves:

> As a rule-based activity, however, games have explicit requirements and more clear-cut boundaries than other activities; their explicit formality makes it possible to study gaming activity in a detailed way without having to observe the people who play games, making it easier to focus on the activity itself instead of the people.
> (Björk and Holopainen 2005: 422)

While this approach to analysis was implied in many of the texts I discussed in the review of game studies (e.g., Aarseth 1997; Juul 2005; Murray 1997), it is in game design writings that we find it articulated ever so clearly.

Somewhat overlapping with this early period of game design theorisation discussed so far was a time of game design programmes at colleges and universities being launched, predominantly in the US. For example, the Game Design and Development Program at Michigan State University launched in 2005 (msu.edu 2020), the MIT Game Lab launched in 2006 (Whitacre 2012), as did the Computer Games Design programme at UC Santa Cruz (Stephens and McGirk 2019). As a result, there was an increasing need to create a systematic curriculum for game design students, which spawned the publication of several influential game design textbooks. Most of these

20 *Understanding Agency*

offered detailed examinations of all aspects of game design (e.g., Adams 2010 [2006]; Fullerton 2014 [2004]; Rogers 2010; Rouse 2005; Salen and Zimmerman 2004; Schell 2015 [2008]), while others approached the challenge from a very specific angle, such as dissecting what the notion of 'fun' means (Koster 2004), game character development (Isbister 2006; Sheldon 2004), or the elusive experience of good 'game feel' (Swink 2008). There was also a growing number of anthologies and more traditionally structured textbooks with multiple contributing authors who were typically a mixture of designers and scholars (see, e.g., Bateman 2007, 2009; Harrigan and Wardrip-Fruin 2004, 2007, 2009). Throughout this chapter I will draw on these works in various degrees of detail, but there are two designers amongst the above listed who offer two widely different definitions of agency, which represents the broader trends in game designer discourse at the time: Boon (2007) and Adams (2010 [2006]).

In Bateman's 2007 textbook about game writing, a chapter by designer Richard Boon sketches an approach to agency similar to what is proposed here: as player action determined by designer-implemented rules. Boom writes: '[a]gency refers to the capacity for a player to effect meaningful changes in a game world, or at least the illusion that the player has this capacity' which he also thinks about in terms of player action:

> the rules of the game determine the possibilities for player agency; in totality, these rules create the game-space within which the player can act.
>
> (Boon 2007: 63)

Although what 'meaningful change' means is not specified, it is implied when Boon argues that the main way to deliver narrative content that is meaningfully crafted is 'to respond to the player's actions within the game-space' (ibid.). Again, although the notion of what constitutes a 'game-space' is not specified per se, the main point to take away is that player agency is facilitated not just by one game design feature, but in collaboration amongst the many elements as determined by the rules of the game. Boon's approach echoes what has been surfacing in game studies discourse around the time, in particular represented by Jørgensen (2003a), King and Krzywinska (2006) and Sicart (2008).

A different definition of agency is offered by Adams (2010 [2006]), and it is one entirely restricted to narratively relevant player action. The keyword to Adams' work is 'player-centric game design', which is centred on empathising with the player and an emphasis on entertainment (ibid. 518). As part of this approach, Adams defines 'agency' as '[t]he power to change the direction of the player's path through the plot, and perhaps the story's future events' (ibid. 213). Later, the idea of agency as giving the player control to influence the outcome of the plot is reiterated (ibid. 221). While Adams argues that interactive stories include three kinds of events, namely 'player events', 'in-game events' and 'narrative events', the example given to illustrate this suggests an agency condition of narrative validation:

> Consider a situation in which a player must find a way to get past a security guard to enter a building. You can give the player several ways to accomplish this: through violence, or trickery, or patience—waiting until the security guard goes off shift. No matter which approach the player chooses, he still enters the building through the same door and encounters the same things on the other side. If his decision does not actually affect the future events of the story, he has no agency. But his decision about how to get through the door contributes to the plot; his own actions are part of his experience of the game.
>
> (ibid. 160)

In a somewhat contradictory manner, however, Adams also recognises 'emergent narratives', such as the many player stories generated by the game mechanics of *The Sims* (Maxis 2000), to allow for more player agency as afforded by the 'core mechanics' of the game. it is argued that if the game has less fixed sequences of events, then players get to experience more agency, playing around and experimenting with different situations that core mechanics enable (ibid. 176). The only difference between the 'violence, trickery, or patience' tactics as afforded by the three paths to neutralise the guard in Adams' first example, and the 'core mechanics' of building different houses or choosing between career paths in *The Sims*, is the volume of options. Adams' definition of agency therefore would have benefitted from a more in-depth discussion of games' narrativity and their relationship to other game mechanics, which is what my heuristic framework will do.

Although Adams regards agency as only expressed when the player can change the course of a game's story, he does talk about various other ways in which agency can be expressed. While the distinctions are productive, they continue to be linked to storyness, which limits their scope. For example, game mechanics such as challenges, moving the avatar within game spaces, or features facilitating progression such as time pressures applied by a storytelling engine, are framed as 'mechanisms for advancing the plot' (ibid. 180–182). In other words, these are the internal clock of the game (determining both challenges and predetermined story progression), and spatial navigation of game spaces. Such a framing of game mechanics implies a primacy of narrativity in videogames, which is only one lens through which videogames can be looked at. At the same time, Adams' 'mechanisms for advancing the plot' offer a way to break down possible player action into different *dimensions*, which is what the second chapter in this book will focus on.

With the proliferation of the internet, expertly curated online resources also became widely available, such as the *GDC Vault*, which is an online library of talks given at all Game Developers' Conferences to date, or *Gamasutra*, a website offering videogame-related news, job ads, blog posts, podcasts, and many more. Both showcase a mixed bag in terms of designers conceptualising agency. We can find talks and essays where developers define agency regarding overall game design (see, e.g., Casteel 2015; Costiuc 2018; Taylor 2017; Worch 2014). But there are also many who zoom in on narrative relevance (see, e.g., Bycer 2015; Leone 2019; Marchal and Yorke 2018). These two short lists represent what is broadly the case both in game studies and in game design: that, besides the player-focused scholarship briefly mentioned in the introduction to this chapter, there are two main approaches to framing agency. One which frames it as having the power to change the development of a story; and one which argues that agency is something afforded by a broader variety of game components. In the following, I propose a conceptualisation of agency which speaks to the many ways in which player action can be deemed meaningful.

Toward a Conceptualisation of Agency

As the brief survey of agency in game studies and game design above showed, we can frame player freedom and strategies to constrain it in different ways. This book proposes a multidimensional framework that aims to capture this variety, and at the core of that framework is a conceptualisation of agency that is interested in the affordances of game design. I am deliberately avoiding the term 'definition', because a definition implies exclusivity, and by no means do I think in these terms, or want the argument to seem exclusive. What is propose here is one way of thinking about agency, rather than a golden measure. Although there is danger in a conceptualisation being too loose, there is value in this flexibility: by steering away from solid definitions, the conceptualisation of agency and its multiple dimensions proposed here maintain the possibility for adaptation to the constantly evolving medium of videogames. How, then, can we begin? Videogames being an interactive medium (in the sense Ryan understands the term), one could assume that they afford full agency, as that is the direct consequence of interactivity: I can only feel like I have a say in what happens on screen if I can, actually, do things on screen. Some scholars raised that that is not quite the case (e.g., 'reactive agency' in Arsenault and Perron 2009: 119–120; 'illusory agency' in MacCallum-Stewart and Parsler 2007: 6; 'illusion of agency' in Charles 2009). My conceptualisation of agency maintains that it could manifest to a very low degree, or indeed, be constrained altogether, but that it is equally as productive to explore how it is thus reduced or constrained as it is to point out how it is afforded.

I argue that agency can be conceived of as a matter of degrees. This approach is drawn from Ryan's (2009) conceptualisation of interactivity similarly being a spectrum. As such, I propose that, in the context of avatar-based games,

> player agency can be conceptualised as the possibility space for meaningful choice expressed via player action that translates into avatar action, afforded and constrained by a game's design.

Understanding Agency 23

Below I build my conceptualisation of agency broken down into five statements. They draw on themes and concepts which surround agency in game design and game studies discourse: meaningful player choice, player/avatar action, affordance of design, being designed, and possibility space.

Agency Is Meaningful Player Choice

As Murray points out, 'activity alone is not agency' (Murray 1997: 128). Therefore, to argue that all player action is a manifestation of agency is problematic, as doing so would raise the question of why not just use 'interactivity' instead of 'agency' to describe this elusive phenomenon. But meaningfulness of action does not only come from narratively relevant consequences of said action. As discussed earlier, Murray attaches the notion of meaningfulness to that of agency, but proceeds to qualify agency as narratively meaningful later on, thereby reducing the concept's general applicability. Murray's definition is an important starting point, however, there are other ways of thinking about meaningfulness which speak to more than a game's representational qualities.

Notably, Salen and Zimmerman advocate for meaningful play to be 'the goal of successful game design' (Salen and Zimmerman 2004: 37), and offer two definitions: one 'descriptive', and one 'evaluative'. I am including both in full below, as they form a core part of my conceptualisation of agency:

> The descriptive definition of meaningful play: Meaningful play in a game emerges from the relationship between player action and system outcome; it is the process by which a player takes action within the designed system of a game and the system responds to the action. The *meaning* of an action in a game resides in the relationship between action and outcome.
>
> The evaluative definition of meaningful play: Meaningful play is what occurs when the relationship between actions and outcomes in a game are both discernible and integrated into the larger context of the game.
>
> Discernibility means that a player can perceive the immediate outcome of an action. Integration means that the outcome of an action is woven into the game system as a whole.
> (Salen and Zimmerman 2004: 37, orig. emphasis)[15]

There are two key take-aways from this. First, that meaningfulness of play emerges from the interaction between player and system, and therefore is not an inherent quality of either alone. It does not exist in and of itself, but emerges in the feedback loop between the two, one triggering the other. Second, for meaningfulness to successfully emerge, the impact of player action on the game system needs to be palpable and relevant within the game itself. Not only must there be a feedback loop, the points of interaction within the loop must be at least perceptible, if not obvious to the player, and relevant within the context of the action. For example, in a shooter game, the avatar may have a gun, and so the player may be able to make the avatar shoot at an in-game object, such as a wooden crate. However, if the crate does not explode with a loud bang and cracks, if there are no splinters flying everywhere injuring the avatar, or if no non-player character comments on this mayhem, did they really shoot that crate? Was the action meaningful? This is what Salen and Zimmerman mean by 'discernible' and 'integrated' relationship between action and outcome, and this is how meaningfulness is understood in my conceptualisation of agency.

In a similar vein, I argue that player choice is meaningful choice about what action to take in the game. Game designer Jesse Schell draws on Salen and Zimmerman's notion of meaningfulness when he writes:

> [a] good game gives the player meaningful choices. Not just any choices, but choices that will have a real impact on what happens next, and how the game turns out.
>
> (Schell 2015 [2008]: 179)

Meaningfulness is also at the heart of Kristine Jørgensen's (2003a, 2003b) definition of agency. Jørgensen argues that agency is when the solutions players find to problems are executable and contribute towards game progression. Drawing on philosophical theories of action, she further adds that intentionality, meaningfulness, and an effect that is detectable but not necessarily expected, are all conditions necessary for an action to be considered an expression of agency (Jørgensen 2003b: 2). In a later contribution specifically theorising the many roles of interfaces in gameplay, she adds:

> As long as game-system features provide appropriate information for meaningful gameplay, they are not alienating but create a sense of engagement and attachment by giving the player agency within the gameworld.
>
> (Jørgensen 2013: 3)

Jørgensen's arguments are useful insofar as they ask questions about agency as an ability to take action, rather than meaning-making as triggered by said action. However, there are two ways in which the approached pursued in this book departs from this. First, Jørgensen's focus is on the player, and I want to focus on the design of the game, because that allows for a consideration of many more possible iterations of player action than observing the few that take place in individual game sessions. Second, especially in later work Jørgensen draws largely on Nitsche's (2008) understanding of videogames according to spatial planes, and analyses the gameplay experience in terms of the spaces it takes place in. The conceptualisation proposed in this book expands the scope of the enquiry beyond a spatial dimension.

In summary, the approach presented here is concerned with in crude terms, not only whether agency is there, but also whether it is not, and how.

Understanding Agency 25

An important condition of agency was identified, namely that interactivity alone is, indeed, not agency, but that player action needs to have a quality of meaningfulness. The above has also clarified that meaningfulness in the conceptualisation forwarded in this book is understood not just in a narrative dimension, but more broadly when looking at the interaction between player and system. In avatar-based games, this most typically happens via an avatar, and this is what the next pillar is dedicated to.

Agency Is Player/Avatar Action

In an isometric strategy game such as *Age of Empires II* (Ensemble Studios 1999) or in god games such as *The Sims* (Maxis 2000), the player gets to control multiple in-game entities, thereby exerting their capacity for meaningful action not just over one or two characters, but over entire families, or armies, while also getting to alternate which in-game entity they control at any given time. In avatar-based games, player action translates into the game via the actions of the avatar.[16] They interact with the gameworld[17] through that one entity, whether that is an actual human, like Gordon Freeman in *Half Life* (Valve 1998), animal, like Donkey Kong, or neither, like a strange sticky ball in *Katamari Damacy* (Namco 2004). The qualities of this in-game manifestation of the player, and the implications these qualities have on the overall experience, have been approached from different angles in gaming-related discourses (see, e.g., Blom 2019; Linderoth 2005; Meretzky 2001; or Willumsen 2018 for avatars in design; Isbister 2006 on a psychological approach to character design; Westecott 2009 for avatars and performativity; Bayliss 2007 on player engagement; and Klevjer 2006 or Vella 2015 on avatar as a phenomenological entity). A common thread in many, though not all, of these approaches is the differentiation between what a character is versus what an avatar is.

Generally speaking, an avatar can be described as a kind of 'visual and . . . audial representation of a player within the digital game environment' (Tymińska 2016: 102). Avatars can also be framed as a 'vicarious body' used to interact with the game system as well as its representational world (Klevjer 2006: 95–96). In a later publication, Klevjer emphasises a distinction between avatar as 'playable character or persona' and avatar as a vehicle for the player's 'embodied agency and presence' (Klevjer 2012: 17) in the game. Daniel Vella draws solid lines between the avatar and character when arguing that they are two elements of the 'playable figure' (Vella 2015: 221). He argues that besides its representational significance, the avatar, insofar as the game system is concerned, serves as the translator of player action to in-game action:

> The player acts *on* the other components of the game system *through* the avatar, making it the singular point of origin of all the lines of action the player directs towards the components of the game system.
> (ibid. 225, orig. emphasis)

This dual function of the avatar will be discussed in more detail when unpacking the dimensions of the heuristic framework. For now, it is sufficient to stress that indeed, as Vella argues, agency can be a kind of 'capacity to act upon a gameworld' (ibid. 167). Accordingly, avatar action is an important part of deconstructing agency, as it translates player choice into the game system. Looking at what the avatar can and cannot do therefore is indicative of how player action and from that, player choice, is allowed or constrained. This brings me to the next quality of agency: something afforded and constrained by game design.

Agency Is Afforded by Design

If agency can be framed as meaningful player action expressed as avatar action, then it follows that we need to consider how a videogame allows said action. Atkins and Krzywinska (2007: 6) argue that 'the parameters of what player can and can't do are scripted into a game'. Wardrip-Fruin and colleagues (2009: 7, orig. emphasis) point out that agency is a phenomenon 'that occurs when the actions players desire are among those they can take *as supported by an underlying computational model*'. Although there have been a variety of terms used to refer to the building blocks of videogames (e.g. 'unit operations' in Bogost 2006: 42; 'ludemes' in Browne et al. 2019), this support can be better understood with the help of Juul's description of rules.[18] These, he argues, do two distinct things:

> rules specify *limitations* and *affordances*. They prohibit players from performing actions such as making jewellery out of dice, but they also add meaning to the allowed actions and this *affords* players meaningful actions that were not otherwise available; rules give games *structure*.
>
> (Juul 2005: 58, orig. emphasis)

'Affordance' is a term introduced by psychologist J.J. Gibson in his seminal work *The Ecological Approach to Visual Perception* (1979), and refers to an object property which enables interaction: for instance, the 'grasp-ability' of a handle, the 'tie-ability' of rope (ibid. 125). In other words, an object can afford some kinds of interaction by means of limiting others. Designer Donald Norman reiterates this in his similarly influential book *The Design of Everyday Things* (2002 [1988]): 'the perceived and actual properties of the thing, primarily those fundamental properties that determine just how the thing could possibly be used' (ibid. 9). Talking about the relationship between game rules and meaningful player action, Juul's argument cited above underscores the importance of acknowledging that an affordance can also be considered a limitation.

Specifically with regards to agency, Mateas and Stern (2005) forward what they call a neo-Aristotelian theory for analysing game, as part of which they propose a

> prescriptive, structural model for agency. A player will experience agency when there is a balance between the material and formal constraints. When the actions motivated by the formal constraints (affordances) via dramatic probability in the plot are commensurate with the material constraints (affordances) made available from the levels of spectacle, pattern, language, and thought, then the player will experience agency. An imbalance results in a decrease of agency.
>
> (Mateas and Stern 2005: 654)

I want to draw attention to two crucial points made here. First, Mateas and Stern, like Juul, use the term 'affordance' to refer to 'formal and material constraints' of a game. Second, they link the notion of agency to these affordances. However, Mateas and Stern only limit their observations to interactive drama, and as such, they do not discuss further the many types of 'formal' and 'material constraints' which are not primarily there to serve a narrative purpose.[19] Elsewhere, Salen and Zimmerman argue that 'rules limit player action' (Salen and Zimmerman 2004: 122). Eskelinen (2012: 275) points out that 'the behaviour of every necessary element of the game, including its players, is controlled and constrained by rules'. A more positive spin on the relationship between game rules and player action is offered by Tulloch (2014), who connects rules to theories of power, and argues that seeing rules as restrictive is problematic and in many ways a result of thinking about power as something that is enforced from an external source. Tulloch stresses that rules in fact support the construction of possibilities, and as such agency should not be viewed as something that emerges *despite* rules, but *because of* rules. In other words, looking at how rules enable player action is a productive approach to better understanding agency. But rules are a rather narrow category, as videogames are made up of much more than just rules. How can this be broadened out?

It is beyond the scope of this book to address the many ways in which the question about what a videogame is can be answered. There are numerous contributions to game design theory which propose different frameworks to better understand the structural components of games. For example, Hunicke and colleagues (2004) break down games into three distinct components of 'rules', 'system', and 'fun', which they then link to the design concept of 'mechanics', 'dynamics', and 'aesthetics'. Additionally, as discussed in the literature review, Björk and Holopainen (2005) propose a component framework and design patterns which are commonly found combinations of said components. Indeed, there is no shortage of terms used to analyse and classify what videogames are comprised of.

Since the conceptualisation of agency presented here attributes meaningfulness to the interaction between player and system, I am going to follow Sicart's approach who, when defining what game mechanics are, argues that they are 'methods invoked by agents, designed for interaction with the game state' (Sicart 2008: n.p.). The notion of game mechanics is an often discussed one, with designers and scholars alike trying to pin down the relationship between rules and mechanics with various degrees of complexity (see, e.g., Järvinen 2008; Jørgensen 2013; Rouse 2005). It is important to acknowledge the variety of definitions offered, but instead of the details of terminology, such as the relationship between rules and mechanics, what helps more with understanding how avatar action is afforded is the emphasis on the relational dynamic between the player and the game—in other words, the invocation, the act of affording or constraining in a broader, more holistic sense. As Gregersen and Grodal observe, '[t]he extent to which an embodied sense of agency, ownership, and personal efficacy is fostered by games is very much a question of *overall design*' (2009: 67, my emphasis). I will therefore use the umbrella term 'game design' to refer to that which affords avatar action within the software, as created by developers.[20] As such, we can understand more about player agency by looking at how it is afforded by the design of a game, both on an algorithmic level, as well as on the level of audiovisual rendering of its governing rules.

Agency Is Designed

Framing agency as afforded by the game's design emphasises that it can be viewed as an object-property, in the veins of Aarseth and Juul's approach discussed in the brief survey of game studies literature above. Doing so slightly repositions the emphasis from asking 'what' is enabling agency to 'who'. This may seem like splitting hairs, but it has important methodological consequences when it comes to applying this conceptualisation of agency, especially in the case of a medium where creative collaboration and fan labour are very common.[21] Developers are very much aware of their role in setting into stone what players can and cannot do. For example, Lankoski and colleagues (2003: n.p.) observe that 'by setting goals, scripting pre-defined actions and choosing what kind of actions to implement, the game designer can restrict the player's freedom'. Hunicke and colleagues (2004: 1) say this, too: '[a]ll artifacts are created within some design methodology'.

Indeed, as Costikyan's (2005 [1999]) essay demonstrates, designers have acknowledged that part of their work is ushering players in certain directions from early on. Following this line of thought, and what has already been established above about agency being afforded by game design, we can frame agency as designed. However, as, Salen and Zimmerman point out, design can only ever prescribe player action indirectly, as player behaviour can never be directly designed, only the rules of the system within which the

Understanding Agency 29

behaviour occurs (Salen and Zimmerman 2004: 168). This emphasis on the fact that gaming activity will always be designed, and always indirectly, is reiterated by Björk and Holopainen as well, who argue that gaming activity can be 'treated as an objective material to be shaped by the designer' (Björk and Holopainen 2005: 422). Similarly, Jesse Schell calls design affording player action 'indirect control' (2015 [2008]: 284–298). In other words, game designers are only ever partially responsible for how the gaming experience unfolds. That being said, while acknowledging that there can never be direct control, Schell proposes a way to think about how player action *can* be designed to a degree. It is important at this point to reconstruct his approach in some detail, because Schell's terminology is widely used by game designers, as it will be seen in their recurrence throughout the case study chapters to follow in this book.

At the core of Schell's theory is a specific understanding of space: a mathematical construct characterised as discrete and continuous, with a number of dimensions, containing bound areas which may or may not be connected (ibid. 131). This space is populated by 'objects', which are the *nouns* of game space. They have 'attributes' and 'states', which are the *adjectives*, such as their position in said space (ibid. 136). Schell then ranks layers of 'knowers' according to how much of the attributes and states are revealed in the game, arguing that these dynamics are crucial to gameplay and game design:

> Game playing is decision making. Decisions are made based on information. *Deciding the different attributes, their states, and who knows about them is core to the mechanics of your game.* Small changes to who knows what information can radically change a game, sometimes for the better, sometimes for the worse.
>
> (ibid. 140, my emphasis)

Schell argues that this decision-making translates into play via *action*. Actions are the *verbs* of game mechanics, and they answer the question 'What can the player do?' (ibid. 140). The more verbs there are, the more objects they can act on, the more ways there are to combine operative actions into resultant action, the more subjects there are to implement action, and the more emergent gameplay becomes (ibid. 142). Frasca (2007: 123–125) and Järvinen (2008: 263–265) also talk about mechanics described as verbs, but what they only imply about agency being designed, Sicart makes explicit: '[a]gency is designed, too: designers think about ways for players to experience the game' (Sicart 2013: 50). Building on these approaches, I argue that agency as expressed via avatar action can be considered as the enactment, the realisation of these verbs. Therefore, agency can be thought of as designed, and we can therefore analyse a game's design in terms of agency to understand more about how it affords or limits player action as expressed via avatar action.

Agency Is Possibility Space

A notion that links all the aspects discussed so far is that of 'possibility space', which can be described in terms of the affordances and limitations of game design. Framing videogames as systems that create, or withdraw, possibility for action has a long history in game studies and game design discourses: Aarseth (1997: 3) argues that 'inaccessibility [of paths] does not imply ambiguity but, rather, an absence of possibility'; Murray (1997: 152) acknowledges that 'interactors can only act within the possibilities that have been established by the writing and programming'; Järvinen (2008: 254) frames game mechanics as a 'means to guide the player into particular behaviour by constraining the space of possible plans to attain goals'; Bogost (2008: 120) also says that the 'possibility space of play includes all of the gestures made possible by a set of rules'); or, somewhat more poetically, Jensen (2013: 76) writes '[p]ossibility spaces are sites of constant conflict between order and chaos, between constraints and open-ended play'. My conceptualisation of agency as a possibility space taps into this tradition of describing the videogame artifact as a container of possible, yet unrealised player action. More specifically, and going back to the very core of how my conceptualisation of agency draws on the notion of meaningful action, Salen and Zimmerman forward a fitting definition:

> [a possibility space] is the space of all possible actions that might take place in the game, the space of all possible meanings which can emerge from a game design. . . . The space of possibility is designed (it is a constructed space, a context), it generates meaning (it is the space of all possible meanings), it is a system (it is a space implied by the way elements of a system can relate to each other), and it is interactive (it is through the interactive functioning of a system that the space is navigated and explored).
>
> (Salen and Zimmerman 2004: 67)

Taking into account all of the above, and to conclude this section on theorising agency in avatar-based videogames, let me reiterate my conceptualisation of agency: player agency can be conceptualised as the possibility space for meaningful choice expressed via player action that translates into avatar action, afforded by a game's design.

How can we put this to action? This framing of agency yields a fairly accessible and feasible methodology: we can better understand how player agency can manifest by analysing a game's design. What follows is a heuristic framework offering analytical distinctions between main ways in which affordances and limitations of avatar action can manifest.

Notes

1 See Eskelinen 2012: 211–233 for an in-depth discussion of each contribution.
2 In simple terms, 'story' is what is told, whereas 'discourse' is how it's presented to the reader (see, e.g., Chatman 1978; Culler 1981). The difference between 'story' and 'plot' is often seen to hinge on the temporal arrangement of events, where 'story' is regarded as a chronological rendering of events, whereas 'plot' is a more complex construction. For more on the many conceptualisations of 'plot', see Dannenberg 2010.
3 For a deeper exploration into the poetics of interactive narratives, see Ryan 2009.
4 Specifically, Aarseth writes that the traversal function is 'the mechanism by which scriptons are revealed or generated by textons and presented to the user of the text', where 'scriptons' are strings of information 'as they appear to readers' and 'textons' are strings of information 'as they exist in the text' (Aarseth 1997: 62).
5 Murray's writings on agency had considerable influence in game studies and game design (e.g., Darley 2000; Grodal 2000, 2003; Montfort 2003; Tanenbaum 2008; Tanenbaum and Tanenbaum 2009, 2010; Dinehart 2009; Gazzard 2011; Mukherjee 2015; Koenitz 2018), as well as in other disciplines (e.g., in television studies see Hills 2009; Mittell 2009).
6 In more recent work, Murray moves away from a narrative-heavy approach: '[a]gency results when the interactor's expectations are aroused by the design of the environment, causing them to act in a way that results in an appropriate response by the well-designed computational system. This matching of the interactor's participatory expectations and actions to the procedural scriptings of the machine creates the pleasurable experience of agency' (Murray 2011: 12). Such an adjustment can be seen as more inclusive of different game components that may not be connected to the storytelling features of videogames. In game design, Salen and Zimmerman (2004) explored this in more depth, which will be discussed in the 'Agency is Meaningful Player Choice' part of this chapter.
7 For example, the focus of the argument seems to be on avatar-based games as implied by the underscoring of the player character as a spatial stand-in for the player (Domsch 2013: 4). Most of the examples are indeed avatar-based games such as *Bioshock* or *Deus Ex*, however, other times 'world-building games' (ibid. 23), or non-digital games like chess or Tic-Tac-Toe (ibid. 117) are mentioned. Similarly, the notion of 'rules' is used to describe a variety of things, from real world physics through simulated physics (ibid. 14–48), game design (ibid. 53–72), and social contracts and value systems (ibid. 163–167). While the term 'agency' is at the core of the argument, there are conflicting definitions: at times, Murray is cited, other times the discussion centres around human agency (see ibid. 60).
8 Perhaps the most striking omission can be found in the section discussing how nodes can create linear or nonlinear narratives (Domsch 2013: 58–95), yet neither Aarseth's writings on nonlinearity, nor Ryan's 'interactive architectures' are mentioned. Similarly, in the section talking about storyworlds in terms of affordances and limitations contains only a passing mention of Juul, and Salen and Zimmerman in a footnote (ibid. 16). In a book review, Backe singles out the lack of engagement with previous academic discourse as one of the greatest weaknesses of the book: that while it engages with core theory, 'the way the established theories are used is puzzling' (Backe 2017a: 766).
9 Things that make up a story, such as characters, spaces, or events. See Chatman 1978: 107 for the original definition; Prince 1987 who includes events, or

Herman 2002: 115–169 for a more detailed breakdown of different existents contained within a storyworld.
10 Another significant portion of Domsch's book is dedicated to dissecting how moral choices (which he calls 'valorisation choice') impact agency. My focus here is not morality, but for a detailed examination of ethics and agency see Sicart 2009, 2013.
11 Notable exceptions are Bartle 1996, 2004.
12 See also Mateas 2000, 2001; Mateas and Stern 2007.
13 Though some argue that there are differences between their approaches, with regards to their philosophical implications (see, e.g., Backe 2017b).
14 It needs stressing that they do so with thorough cross-referencing of existing game design research, as well as influential work from other disciplines, such as Christopher Alexander and colleagues' (1977) seminal work on pattern languages in architecture and urban design.
15 This understanding of meaningful action has a lot in common with that of action theorist Donald Davidson (2002: 43–63), who argued that for agency to manifest, the action must be intentional, meaningful, and have a certain affect.
16 Originating in the Sanskrit word avatāra (अवतार) (Liboriussen 2014).
17 I use gameworld to refer to the entirety of game spaces, including non-diegetic interfaces, menus, etc. Terminology will be discussed in more detail later.
18 Some challenge the primacy of rules (and mechanics) in game-related discourses. For example, Vargas-Iglesias and Navarrete-Cardero (2020) argue that a formal analysis of videogames should focus on the reality constructed by both the game systems and the player.
19 It must be added that Mateas and Stern introduce additional complexity to their understanding of agency a few years later when distinguishing between 'local' and 'global' agency, where the former is 'when the player's actions cause immediate, context-specific meaningful reactions from the system' and the latter is when 'the global shape of the experience is determined by player action' (Mateas and Stern 2005: 203–204).
20 Agency and technology are explored in more detail in science and technology studies. See, e.g., Callon and Latour 1981 or Latour 2005 for an introduction to 'actor-network theory'. For more on actors in and around gameplay, see, e.g., Taylor 2009 or De Paoli and Kerr 2010. More specifically, agency in the creation of videogames is discussed in, e.g., Banks 2013; Deuze et al. 2007; Dyer-Witheford and de Peuter 2009: 3–33; Keogh 2018b; Hadas 2020: 141–179.
21 For more on fan co-creation, see Kücklich 2005 on playbour; Pearce 2002 or Poremba 2003 on the player-author; Consalvo 2007 or Sotamaa 2010; or more recently, Joseph 2018 on modding.

References

Aarseth, E. J. (1997). *Cybertext: Perspectives on Ergodic Literature*. Baltimore, MD: Johns Hopkins University Press.

Aarseth, E. J. (2014). Ludology. In M. J. P. Wolf and B. Perron, eds. *The Routledge Companion to Video Games*. Abingdon: Routledge, pp. 185–189.

Aarseth, E. J. (2019). Game Studies: How to Play—Ten Play-Tips for the Aspiring Game-Studies Scholar. *Game Studies* 19 (2). Available at: http://gamestudies.org/1902/articles/howtoplay

Adams, E. (2010 [2006]). *Fundamentals of Game Design*. 2nd ed. San Francisco, CA: New Riders.

Alexander, C.; Silverstein, M.; Ishikawa, S. (1977). *A Pattern Language: Towns, Building, Construction*. New York: Oxford University Press.

Arsenault, D.; Perron, B. (2009). In the Frame of the Magic Cycle: The Circle(s) of Gameplay. In B. Perron and M. J. P. Wolf, eds. *The Video Game Theory Reader 2*. London: Routledge, pp. 109–131.
Atkins, B. (2003). *More Than a Game: The Computer Game as Fictional Form*. Manchester: Manchester University Press.
Atkins, B.; Krzywinska, T. (eds.). (2007). *Videogame, Player, Text*. Manchester: Manchester University Press.
Backe, H.-J. (2017a). Sebastian Domsch. *Storyplaying: Agency and Narrative in Video Games*. Narrating Futures 4. Berlin/Boston, MA: De Gruyter, 2013, 190 pp., 1 table, € 79.95/£ 59.99/$ 112.00. *Anglia* 135 (4): 763–767. https://doi.org/10.1515/ang-2017-0074
Backe, H.-J. (2017b). Two Ways through the Looking Glass. Game Design as an Expression of Philosophy of Action. *11th International Philosophy of Computer Games Conference: Action in Games*, 28 November–1 December, Kraków. Available at: https://gamephilosophy2017.files.wordpress.com/2017/11/backe_pocg2017.pdf
Banks, J. (2013). *Co-Creating Videogames*. London: Bloomsbury Academic.
Bartle, R. (1996). Hearts, Clubs, Diamonds, Spades: Players Who Suit MUDs. *MUD*, 28 August. Available at: http://mud.co.uk/richard/hcds.htm
Bartle, R. (2004). *Designing Virtual Worlds*. Indianapolis, IN: New Riders.
Bateman, C. (ed.). (2007). *Game Writing: Narrative Skills for Videogames*. Boston, MA: Charles River Media.
Bateman, C. (ed.). (2009). *Beyond Game Design: Nine Steps Toward Creating Better Videogames*. Boston, MA: Charles River Media.
Bayliss, P. (2007). Beings in the Game-world: Characters, Avatars, and Players. *IE'07: Proceedings of the 4th Australasian Conference on Interactive Entertainment*, pp. 1–6. Available at: https://dl.acm.org/doi/10.5555/1367956.1367960
Björk, S.; Holopainen, J. (2005). Games and Design Patterns. In K. Salen and E. Zimmerman, eds. *The Game Design Reader: A Rules of Play Anthology*. Cambridge, MA: MIT Press, pp. 410–437.
Blom, J. (2019). *The Dynamic Game Character: Definition, Construction, and Challenges in a Character Ecology*. PhD Dissertation, IT University of Copenhagen.
Bode, C.; Dietrich, R. (2013). *Future Narratives: Theory, Poetics, and Media-Historical Moment*. Berlin: De Gruyter.
Bogost, I. (2006). Comparative Video Game Criticism. *Games and Culture* 1 (1): 41–46. https://doi.org/10.1177/1555412005281775
Bogost, I. (2008). Persuasive Games: Texture. *Gamasutra*, 7 May. Available at: www.gamasutra.com/view/feature/132053/persuasive_games_texture.php?page=2
Boon, R. (2007). Writing for Games. In C. Bateman, ed. *Game Writing: Narrative Skills for Videogames*. Boston, MA: Charles River Media, pp. 43–69.
Boonen, C. S.; Mieritz, D. (2018). Paralysing Fear: Player Agency Parameters in Horror Games. *DiGRA Nordic'18—Proceedings of 2018 International DiGRA Nordic Conference*. Available at: www.digra.org/digital-library/publications/paralysing-fear-player-agency-parameters-in-horror-games/
Bordwell, D. (1989). *Meaning Making: Inference and Rhetoric in the Interpretation of Cinema*. Cambridge, MA: Harvard University Press.
Brock, T.; Fraser, E. (2018). Is Computer Gaming a Craft? Prehension, Practice and Puzzle-Solving in Gaming Labour. *Information, Communication and Society* 21 (9): 1219–1233. https://doi.org/10.1080/1369118X.2018.1468920
Browne, C.; Soemers, D. J. N. J.; Piette, E.; Stephenson, M.; Conrad, M.; Crist, W.; Depaulis, T.; Duggan, E.; Horn, F.; Kelk, S.; Lucas, S. M.; Neto, J. P.; Parlett, D.;

Saffidine, A.; Schädler, U.; de Voogt, A.; Winands, M. H. M. (2019). Foundations of Digital Archæoludology. Report from Dagstuhl Research Meeting 19153. *ICGA Journal* 41 (3): 1–21.

Bycer, J. (2015). Player Agency: How Game Design Affects Narrative. *Gamasutra*, 26 January. Available at: www.gamasutra.com/blogs/JoshBycer/20150126/234961/Player_Agency_How_Game_Design_Affects_Narrative.php

Callon, M.; Latour, B. (1981). Unscrewing the Big Leviathan: How Actors Macrostructure Reality and How Sociologists Help Them to Do So. In K. D. Knorr-Cetina and A. V. Cicourel, eds. *Advances in Social Theory and Methodology: Toward an Integration of Micro- and Macro-Sociologies*. Boston, MA: Routledge & Kegan Paul, pp. 277–303.

Campbell, C. (2013). GDC. The Gathering of Game Makers. *Polygon*, 25 March. Available at: www.polygon.com/features/2013/3/25/4128022/gdc-gathering-of-game-makers

Carr, D.; Schott, G.; Buckingham, D. (2003). Textuality in Video Games. *DiGRA'03—Proceedings of the 2003 DiGRA International Conference: Level Up*, pp. 144–155. Available at: www.digra.org/digital-library/publications/textuality-in-video-

Casteel, B. (2015). RTS Economics and Player Agency. *Gamasutra*, 24 November. Available at: www.gamasutra.com/blogs/BrandonCasteel/20151124/260137/RTS_Economics_and_Player_Agency.php

Charles, A. (2009). Playing with One's Self: Notions of Subjectivity and Agency in Digital Games. *Eludamos: Journal for Computer Game Culture* 3 (2): 281–294. https://doi.org/10.7557/23.6010

Chatman, S. (1978). *Story and Discourse: Narrative Structure in Fiction and Film*. Ithaca, NY: Cornell University Press.

Cheng, P. (2007). Waiting for Something to Happen: Narratives, Interactivity, and Agency and the Video Game Cut-Scene. *DiGRA'07—Proceedings of the 2007 DiGRA International Conference: Situated Play*. University of Tokyo. Available at: www.digra.org/digital-library/publications/waiting-for-something-to-happen-narratives-interactivity-and-agency-and-the-video-game-cut-scene/

Church, D. (2005 [1999]). Formal Abstract Design Tools. In K. Salen and E. Zimmerman, eds. *The Game Design Reader: A Rules of Play Anthology*. Cambridge, MA: MIT Press, pp. 366–380.

Consalvo, M. (2007). *Cheating: Gaining Advantage in Videogames*. Cambridge, MA: MIT Press.

Costikyan, G. (2005 [1999]). I Have No Words & I Must Design. In K. Salen and E. Zimmerman, eds. *The Game Design Reader: A Rules of Play Anthology*. Cambridge, MA: MIT Press, pp. 192–210.

Costiuc, S. (2018). Play, Don't Show. *Gamastura*, 19 November. Available at: www.gamasutra.com/blogs/StanislavCostiuc/20181119/330954/Play_Dont_Show.php

Culler, J. (1981). *The Pursuit of Signs: Semiotics, Literature, Deconstruction*. Ithaca, NY: Cornell University Press.

Dannenberg, H. P. (2010). Plot. In D. Herman, M. Jahn, and M.-L. Ryan, eds. *Routledge Encyclopedia of Narrative Theory*. London: Routledge.

Darley, A. (2000). *Visual Digital Culture: Surface Play and Spectacle in New Media Genres*. London: Routledge.

Davidson, D. (2002). Agency. In *Essays on Actions and Events: Philosophical Essays*. 2nd ed. Oxford: Oxford University Press, pp. 43–63.

De Paoli, S.; Kerr, A. (2010). The Assemblage of Cheating: How to Study Cheating as Imbroglio in MMORPGs. *The Fibreculture Journal* 16. Available at: http://sixteen.fibreculturejournal.org/the-assemblage-of-cheating-how-to-study-cheating-as-imbroglio-in-mmorpgs/

Deuze, M.; Martin, C.; Allen, C. (2007). The Professional Identity of Gameworkers. *Convergence* 13 (4): 335–353. https://doi.org/10.1177/1354856507081947

Dille, F.; Platten, J. Z. (2007). *The Ultimate Guide to Video Game Writing and Design*. New York: Random House.

Dinehart, S. (2009). Dramatic Play. *Gamasutra*, 3 August. Available at: www.gamasutra.com/view/feature/4061/dramatic_play.phpwww.gamasutra.com/view/feature/4061/dramatic_play.php8/3/2019

Domsch, S. (2013). *Storyplaying: Agency and Narrative in Video Games*. Berlin: De Gruyter.

Downing, J. D. H.; Husband, C. (2005). *Representing 'Race': Racism, Ethnicities, and the Media*. London: SAGE.

Dyer-Witheford, N.; de Peuter, G. (2009). *Games of Empire: Global Capitalism and Video Games*. Minneapolis, MI: University of Minnesota Press.

Ensemble Studios. (1999). *Age of Empires II: The Age of Kings* [PC]. Microsoft.

Eskelinen, M. (2001a). The Gaming Situation. *Game Studies* 1 (1). Available at: www.gamestudies.org/0101/eskelinen/

Eskelinen, M. (2001b). Towards Computer Game Studies. *Digital Creativity* 12 (3): 175–183.

Eskelinen, M. (2012). *Cybertext Poetics: The Critical Landscape of New Media Literary Theory*. London: Bloomsbury.

Falstein, N. (2002). Better by Design: The 400 Project. *Game Developer Magazine* 9 (3): 26.

Foucault, M. (2013 [1982]). Afterword: The Subject and Power. In H. Dreyfus and P. Rabinow, eds. *Michel Foucault: Beyond Structuralism and Hermeneutics*. Chicago, IL: University of Chicago Press, pp. 208–226.

Frasca, G. (1999). Ludology Meets Narratology. Similitude and differences between (video)games and narrative. *Ludology*. Available at: https://ludology.typepad.com/weblog/articles/ludology.htm

Frasca, G. (2003). Ludologists Love Stories, Too: Notes From a Debate That Never Took Place. *DiGRA'03—Proceedings of the 2003 DiGRA International Conference: Level Up*. Available at: www.digra.org/digital-library/publications/ludologists-love-stories-too-notes-from-a-debate-that-never-took-place/

Frasca, G. (2007). *Play the Message. Play, Game, and Video Game Rhetoric*. PhD Dissertation, IT University Copenhagen.

Fullerton, T. (2014 [2004]). *Game Design Workshop: A Playcentric Approach to Creating Innovative Games*. 3rd ed. Boca Raton, FL: CRC Press.

Gazzard, A. (2011). Unlocking the Gameworld: The Rewards of Space and Time in Videogames. *Game Studies* 11 (1). Available at: http://gamestudies.org/1101/articles/gazzard_alison

Gibson, J. J. (1979). *The Ecological Approach to Visual Perception*. Boston; MA: Houghton Mifflin.

Giddens, A. (1984). *The Constitution of Society*. Berkeley, CA: University of California Press.

Gray, K. L.; Leonard, D. J. (eds.). (2018). *Woke Gaming: Digital Challenges to Oppression and Social Injustice*. Seattle, WA: University of Washington Press.

Gregersen, A.; Grodal, T. (2009). Embodiment and Interface. In B. Perron and M. J. P. Wolf, eds. *The Video Game Theory Reader 2*. New York: Routledge, pp. 65–84.

Grodal, T. (2000). Video Games and the Pleasures of Control. In D. Zillmann and P. Vorderer, eds. *Media Entertainment: The Psychology of Its Appeal*. London: Routledge, pp. 197–213.

Grodal, T. (2003). Stories for Eye, Ear, and Muscles. In M. J. P. Wolf and B. Perron, eds. *The Video Game Theory Reader*. New York: Routledge, pp. 129–156.

Habel, C.; Kooyman, B. (2014). Agency Mechanics: Gameplay Design in Survival Horror Video Games. *Digital Creativity* 25 (1): 1–14. https://doi.org/10.1080/14626268.2013.776971

Hadas, L. (2020). *Authorship as Promotional Discourse in the Screen Industries: Selling Genius*. London: Routledge.

Hammond, S.; Pain, H.; Smith, T. J. (2007). Player Agency in Interactive Narrative: Audience, Actor & Author. *AISB'07—Artificial and Ambient Intelligence*, 2–4 April, Newcastle. Available at: https://eprints.bbk.ac.uk/9955/1/9955.pdf

Harrell, D. F.; Zhu, J. (2008). Agency Play: Dimensions of Agency for Interactive Narrative Design. *Proceedings of the AAAI 2008 Spring Symposium on Interactive Narrative Technologies II*, Stanford, CA, pp. 156–162.

Harrigan, P.; Wardrip-Fruin, N. (2004). *First Person: New Media as Story, Performance, and Game*. Cambridge, MA: MIT Press.

Harrigan, P.; Wardrip-Fruin, N. (2007). *Second Person: Role Playing and Story in Games and Playable Media*. Cambridge, MA: MIT Press.

Harrigan, P.; Wardrip-Fruin, N. (2009). *Third Person: Authoring and Exploring Vast Narratives*. Cambridge, MA: MIT Press.

Heidegger, M. (1977 [1932]). The Age of the World Picture. In *The Question Concerning Technology and Other Essays*. New York: Garland Publishing.

Herman, D. (2002). *Story Logic: Problems and Possibilities of Narrative*. Lincoln, NE: University of Nebraska Press.

Hills, M. (2009). Absent Epic, Implied Story Arcs, and Variation on Narrative Theme: *Doctor Who* (2005–2008) as Cult/Mainstream Television. In P. Harrigan and N. Wardrip-Fruin, eds. *Third Person: Authoring and Exploring Vast Narratives*. Cambridge, MA: MIT Press, pp. 333–343.

Hunicke, R.; LeBlanc, M.; Zubek, R. (2004). MDA: A Formal Approach to Game Design and Game Research. *Proceedings of the Challenges in Games AI Workshop, 19th National Conference of Artificial Intelligence*. San Jose, CA: AAAI Press.

Isbister, K. (2006). *Better Game Characters by Design: A Psychological Approach*. Burlington, MA: Morgan Kaufman.

Järvinen, A. (2008). *Games without Frontiers: Theories and Methods for Game Studies and Design*. PhD Thesis, Tampere University.

Jenkins, H. (2006). Game Design as Narrative Architecture. In K. Salen and E, Zimmerman, eds. *The Game Design Reader: A Rules of Play Anthology*. Cambridge, MA: MIT Press, pp. 670–689.

Jenkins, H. (2012 [1992]). *Textual Poachers: Television Fans and Participatory Culture*. New York: Routledge.

Jensen, G. H. (2013). Making Sense of Play in Video Games: Ludus, Paidia, and Possibility Spaces. *Eludamos: Journal for Computer Game Culture* 7 (1): 69–80.

Jørgensen, K. (2003a). *Aporia & Epiphany in Context: Computer Game Agency in Baldur's Gate II & Heroes of Might & Magic IV*. Hovedfag (MA) Dissertation, Department of Media Studies, University of Bergen.

Jørgensen, K. (2003b). Problem Solving: The Essence of Player Action in Computer Games. *DiGRA'03—Proceedings of the 2003 DiGRA International Conference: Level Up, 2003. Volume: 2.* Available at: www.digra.org/digital-library/publications/problem-solving-the-essence-of-player-action-in-computer-games/
Jørgensen, K. (2013). *Gameworld Interfaces.* Cambridge, MA: MIT Press.
Joseph, D. J. (2018). The Discourse of Digital Dispossession: Paid Modifications and Community Crisis on Steam. *Games and Culture* 13 (7): 690–707. https://doi.org/10.1177/1555412018756488
Juul, J. (2005). *Half-Real: Video Games between Real Rules and Fictional Worlds.* Cambridge, MA: MIT Press.
Keogh, B. (2018a). *A Play of Bodies: How We Perceive Videogames.* Boston, MA: MIT Press.
Keogh, B. (2018b). From Aggressively Formalised to Intensely In/formalized: Accounting for a Wider Range of Videogame Development Practices. *Creative Industries Journal* 12 (1): 14–33. https://doi.org/10.1080/17510694.2018.1532760
King, G.; Krzywinska, T. (2006). *Tomb Raiders and Space Invaders. Videogame Forms and Contexts.* London: I.B. Tauris & Co Ltd.
Klastrup, L. (2003a). Paradigms of Interaction: Conceptions and Misconceptions of the Field Today. *Dictung Digital* 4. Available at: www.dichtung-digital.org/2003/issue/4/klastrup/index.htm
Klastrup, L. (2003b). A Poetics of Virtual Worlds. *MelbourneDAC2008–5th International Digital Arts & Culture Conference, RMIT University, School of Applied Communication,* 19–23 May, Melbourne, pp. 100–109. Available at: http://citeseerx.ist.psu.edu/viewdoc/download?doi=10.1.1.693.3554&rep=rep1&type=pdf
Klevjer, R. (2006). *What Is the Avatar? Fiction and Embodiment in Avatar-Based Singleplayer Computer Games.* PhD Thesis, University of Bergen.
Klevjer, R. (2012). Enter the Avatar: The Phenomenology of Prosthetic Telepresence in Computer Games. In J. Sageng et al., eds. *The Philosophy of Computer Games. Philosophy of Engineering and Technology 7.* Dordrecht: Springer, pp. 17–38.
Koenitz, H. (2018). What Game Narrative Are We Talking About? An Ontological Mapping of the Foundational Canon of Interactive Narrative Forms. *Arts* 7 (4): 51.
Koster, R. (2004). *Theory of Fun for Game Design.* Phoenix: Paraglyph Press.
Kücklich, J. (2005). Precarious Playbor: Modders and the Digital Games Industry. *The Fibreculture Journal* 5. Available at: http://five.fibreculturejournal.org/fcj-025-precarious-playbour-modders-and-the-digital-games-industry/
Lankoski, P.; Heliö, S.; Ekman, I. (2003). Characters in Computer Games: Toward Understanding Interpretation and Design. *DiGRA'03—Proceedings of the 2003 DiGRA International Conference: Level Up.* Available at: www.digra.org/digital-library/publications/characters-in-computer-games-toward-understanding-interpretation-and-design/
Latour, B. (2005). *Reassembling the Social: An Introduction to Actor-Network-Theory.* Oxford: Oxford University Press.
LeBlanc, M. (2006). Tools for Creating Dramatic Game Dynamics. In K. Salen and E. Zimmerman, eds. *The Game Design Reader: A Rules of Play Anthology.* Cambridge, MA: MIT Press, pp. 438–459.
Leone, R. T. (2019). Narrative Design: Player Agency. *Leoneum,* 7 March. Available at: www.rickyleone.com/blog/22-game-dev/59-narrative-design-player-agency.html
Liboriussen, B. (2014). Avatar. In M.-L. Ryan et al., eds. *The Johns Hopkins Guide to Digital Media.* Baltimore, MD: Johns Hopkins University Press, pp. 37–40.

Linderoth, J. (2005). Animated Game Pieces. Avatars as Roles, Tools, and Props. *Online Proceedings of the Aesthetics of Play Conference*, 14–15 October, Bergen. Available at: www.aestheticsofplay.org/linderoth.php

MacCallum-Stewart, E.; Parsler, J. (2007). Illusory Agency in *Vampire: The Masquerade—Bloodlines, Dichtung Digital* 37. Available at: www.dichtung-digital.org/2007/Stewart%26Parsler/maccallumstewart_parsler.htm

Marchal, C.; Yorke, J. (2018). How to Create Great Characters: Depth, Emotion and Player Agency. *GDC Vault*. Available at: www.gdcvault.com/play/1025156/How—to—Create—Great—Characters

Mateas, M. (2000). A Neo-Aristotelian Theory of Interactive Drama. *AAAI Spring Symposium on AI and Interactive Entertainment*. Available at: https://users.soe.ucsc.edu/~michaelm/publications/mateas-aaai-symp-aiie-2000.pdf

Mateas, M. (2001). A Preliminary Poetics for Interactive Drama and Games. *Digital Creativity* 12 (3): 140–152.

Mateas, M.; Stern, A. (2005). Interaction and Narrative. In K. Salen and E. Zimmerman, eds. *The Game Design Reader: A Rules of Play Anthology*. Boston, MA: MIT Press, pp. 642–669.

Mateas, M.; Stern, A. (2007). Writing *Façade*: A Case Study in Procedural Authorship. In P. Harrigan and N. Wardrip-Fruin, eds. *Second Person: Role-Playing and Story in Games and Playable Media*. Cambridge, MA: MIT Press, pp. 203–207.

Maxis. (2000). *The Sims* [PC]. Electronic Arts.

Meretzky, S. (2001). Building Character: An Analysis of Character Creation. *Gamasutra*, 19 November. Available at: www.gamasutra.com/view/feature/131887/building_character_an_analysis_of_.php

Meyers, M. (2008). *Women in Popular Culture: Representation and Meaning*. Cresskill, NJ: Hampton Press.

Mittell, J. (2009). All in the Game: *The Wire*, Serial Storytelling, and Procedural Logic. In P. Harrigan and N. Wardrip-Fruin, eds. *Third Person: Authoring and Exploring Vast Narratives*. Cambridge, MA: MIT Press, pp. 249–438.

Montfort, N. (2003). *Twisty Little Passages: An Approach to Interactive Fiction*. Cambridge, MA: MIT Press.

Msu.edu. (2020). Game Design and Development. *Michigan State University*. Available at: https://comartsci.msu.edu/research-creative-work/thematic-research-areas/game-design-and-development

Mukherjee, S. (2015). *Video Games and Storytelling*. Basingstoke: Palgrave Macmillan.

Mukherjee, S. (2017). *Videogames and Postcolonialism: Empire Plays Back*. Basingstoke: Palgrave Macmillan.

Murray, J. (1997). *Hamlet on the Holodeck*. Cambridge, MA: MIT Press.

Murray, J. (2005). The Last Word on Ludology v Narratology. *Inventing the Medium*, 28 June. Available at: https://inventingthemedium.com/2013/06/28/the-last-word-on-ludology-v-narratology-2005/

Murray, J. H. (2011). *Inventing the Medium: Principles of Interaction Design as a Cultural Practice*. Cambridge, MA: MIT Press.

Namco. (2004). *Katamari Damacy* [PlayStation 2]. Namco.

Nitsche, M. (2008). *Video Game Spaces: Image, Play, and Structure in 3D Worlds*. Cambridge, MA: MIT Press.

Norman, D. (2002 [1988]). *The Design of Everyday Things*. New York: Basic Books.

Pearce, C. (2002). Emergent Authorship: The Next Interactive Revolution. *Computers & Graphics* 26 (1): 21–29.

Pearce, C. (2004). Towards a Game Theory of Game. In N. Wardrip-Fruin and P. Harrigan, eds. *First Person: New Media as Story, Performance, and Game*. Cambridge, MA: MIT Press, pp. 143–153.
Poremba, C. (2003). *Player as Author Digital Games and Agency*. MA Thesis, Simon Fraser University.
Prince, G. (1987). *A Dictionary of Narratology*. Lincoln, NE: University of Nebraska Press.
Rogers, S. (2010). *Level Up! the Guide to Great Video Game Design*. Chichester: John Wiley & Sons.
Rouse III, R. (2005). *Game Design: Theory & Practice*. 2nd ed. Plano, TX: Wordware.
Ruberg, B.; Shaw, A. (eds.). (2017). *Queer Game Studies*. Minneapolis, MI: University of Minnesota Press.
Ryan, M.-L. (2006). *Avatars of Story*. Minneapolis, MI: University of Minnesota Press.
Ryan, M.-L. (2009). From Narrative Games to Playable Stories: Toward a Poetics of Interactive Narrative. *Storyworlds: A Journal of Narrative Studies* 1: 43–59.
Salen, K.; Zimmerman, E. (2004). *Rules of Play: Game Design Fundamentals*. Cambridge, MA: MIT Press.
Schell, J. (2015 [2008]) *The Art of Game Design: A Book of Lenses*. Burlington, MA: Morgan Kaufmann.
Shaw, A. (2014). *Gaming at the Edge: Sexuality and Gender at the Margins of Gamer Culture*. Minneapolis, MI: University of Minnesota Press.
Sheldon, L. (2004). *Character Development and Storytelling*. Boston, MA: Thomson Course Technology.
Sicart, M. (2008). Defining Game Mechanics. *Game Studies* 8 (2). Available at: http://gamestudies.org/0802/articles/sicart
Sicart, M. (2009). *The Ethics of Computer Games*. Cambridge, MA: MIT Press.
Sicart, M. (2013). *Beyond Choices: The Design of Ethical Gameplay*. Cambridge, MA: MIT Press.
Sotamaa, O. (2007). *The Player's Game: Toward Understanding Player Production Among Computer Game Cultures*. PhD Thesis, Tampere University.
Sotamaa, O. (2010). When the Game Is Not Enough: Motivations and Practices among Computer Game Modding Culture. *Games and Culture* 5 (3): 239–255. https://doi.org/10.1177/1555412009359765
Stang, S. (2019). "This Action Will Have Consequences": Interactivity and Player Agency. *Game Studies* 19 (1). Available at: http://gamestudies.org/1901/articles/stang
Stephens, T.; McGirk, J. (2019). UC Santa Cruz Launches the Country's First Graduate Program in Serious Games. *UC Santa Cruz News Center*, 19 February. Available at: https://news.ucsc.edu/2019/02/serious-games.html
Swink, S. (2008). *Game Feel: A Game Designer's Guide to Virtual Sensation*. Burlington, MA: Morgan Kaufman.
Tanenbaum, J. (2008). *Identity Transformation and Agency in Digital Narratives and Story Based Games*. PhD Thesis, Simon Frazer University. Available at: https://core.ac.uk/download/pdf/56379399.pdf
Tanenbaum, K.; Tanenbaum, T. J. (2009). Commitment to Meaning: A Reframing of Agency in Games. *Proceedings of the 8th Conference on Digital Arts and Culture (DAC)*, 12–15 December, Irvine, CA. Available at: https://escholarship.org/uc/item/6f49r74n

Tanenbaum, K.; Tanenbaum, T. J. (2010). Agency as Commitment to Meaning: Communicative Competence in Games. *Digital Creativity* 21 (1): 11–17. https://doi.org/10.1080/14626261003654509

Taylor, J. (2017). Thoughts about Game Development: Player Agency. *Gamasutra*, 5 April. Available at: www.gamasutra.com/blogs/JeromeTaylor/20170405/295263/Thoughts_about_Game_Development_Player_Agency.ph

Taylor, T. L. (2009). The Assemblage of Play. *Games and Culture* 4 (4): 331–339. https://doi.org/10.1177/1555412009343576

Tulloch, R. (2014). The Construction of Play: Rules, Restrictions, and the Repressive Hypothesis. *Games and Culture* 9 (5): 335–350. https://doi.org/10.1177/1555412014542807

Tymińska, M. (2016). Avatars Going Mainstream: Typology of Tropes in Avatar-Based Storytelling Practices. *Replay: The Polish Journal of Game Studies* 1 (3): 101–117. https://doi.org/10.18778/2391-8551.03.06

Valve. (1998). *Half Life* [PC]. Sierra Studios.

Vandenberghe, J. (2012). The Five Domains of Play. *Darklorde*. Available at: www.darklorde.com/the-five-domains-of-play/

Vargas-Iglesias, J. J.; Navarrete-Cardero, L. (2020). Beyond Rules and Mechanics: A Different Approach for Ludology. *Games and Culture* 15 (6): 587–608. https://doi.org/10.1177/1555412018822937

Vella, D. (2015). *The Ludic Subject and the Ludic Self: Analyzing the 'I-in-the-Gameworld'*. PhD Thesis, IT University of Copenhagen. Available at: https://pure.itu.dk/portal/en/publications/the-ludic-subject-and-the-ludic-self-analyzing-the-iinthegameworld(5877eb42-85c2-4795-9ffa-6625d00b3418)/export.html

Wardrip-Fruin, N.; Mateas, M.; Dow, S.; Sali, S. (2009). Agency Reconsidered. *DiGRA'09—Proceedings of the 2009 DiGRA International Conference: Breaking New Ground: Innovation in Games, Play, Practice and Theory*. Available at: www.digra.org/digital-library/publications/agency-reconsidered/

Westecott, E. (2009). The Player Character as Performing Object. *DiGRA'09—Proceedings of the 2009 DiGRA International Conference: Breaking New Ground: Innovation in Games, Play, Practice and Theory*. Available at: www.digra.org/digital-library/publications/the-player-character-as-performing-object/

Whitacre, A. (2012). MIT Game Lab Explores the Potential of Games and Play. *MIT News*, 23 October. Available at https://news.mit.edu/2012/mit-game-lab-explores-the-potential-of-games-and-play

Willumsen, E. C. (2018). Is My Avatar MY Avatar? Character Autonomy and Automated Avatar Actions in Digital Games. *Proceedings of DiGRA'18—Proceedings of the 2018 DiGRA International Conference: The Game is the Message*. Available at: www.digra.org/digital-library/publications/is-my-avatar-my-avatar-character-autonomy-and-automated-avatar-actions-in-digital-games/

Worch, M. (2014). Level Design in a Day: Decisions That Matter—Meaningful Choice in Game and Level Design. *GDC Vault*. Available at: www.gdcvault.com/play/1020570/Level-Design-in-a-Day

2 A Multidimensional Heuristic Framework for Analysing Player Agency

There are many components to the design of a videogame, which means said design can afford and limit agency in many ways. As Carr and colleagues (2003: 150) note, 'different forms of agency operate in and around players' engagement with the games'. King and Krzywinska (2006: 119) also point out that expressions of agency take different forms, which they group broadly according to whether they are conditional to game progression (such as shooting or platforming), or whether they are less constrained and more situational (which they call 'paidia-oriented'). The following chapter takes cues from both these arguments, and combines game studies and game design theory to create a multidimensional analytical framework for examining how player agency unfolds in avatar-based videogames.

Approaches to videogame agency that acknowledge multiple layers, or dimensions, are not new (see, e.g., 'personal, proxy, and collective agency' in Schott 2006). There are two such frameworks that need closer attention here, as they both propose productive conceptual and terminological solutions. Harrell and Zhu (2008) follow a similar approach to this book when they understand agency as actions that the game system allows and the player executes (ibid. 48). They highlight that agency phenomena have multiple *dimensions*, and break down the process of agency manifestation into four levels, each influencing the next in a consecutive fashion. Harrell and Zhu argue that user input influences a system's reaction (which they term 'Agency Scope/Agency Dynamic'), which then in turn creates a codependency between user and game system ('Agency Relationship'). The introduction of agency dimensions is an important step forward, but there are two areas where Harrell and Zhu's model could be specified further. First, their model works towards facilitating narratively meaningful engagement in a gameplay session and is therefore in many ways restricting agency to only be narratively relevant. Second, it implies that there is unidirectional movement between these layers, based on cause-effect relationship between them. In a similar vein, Boonen and Mieritz (2018) introduce what they call the 'Agency Parameter Model', which also hierarchifies the relationship between the characteristics in game design which manipulate agency. I suggest that due to the constant feedback loop between player and game

DOI: 10.4324/9781003298786-3

systems, a less rigid framework that emphasises mutual influence between dimensions is better suited.

Another multidimensional model is offered by Calleja (2011), who describes the different kinds of 'player involvement' that videogames facilitate. His six dimensions are:

> control and movement (*kinesthetic involvement*), the exploration and learning of the game's spatial domain (*spatial involvement*), co-presence, collaboration, and competition with other agents (human or AI) that inhabit it (*shared involvement*), the formation of an ongoing story and interaction with the scripted narrative written into the game (*narrative involvement*), the affect generated during gameplay (*affective involvement*), and the decision making undertaken in the pursuit of both game and self-assigned goals (*ludic involvement*).
>
> (ibid. 4, orig. emphasis)

The three key things to take away from Calleja's model are that involvement occurs in multiple dimensions; dimensions are not necessarily simultaneously present to the same degree; and dimensions cooperate fluidly during gameplay (ibid. 35–45). Given that player action is, in many ways, prerequisite to involvement, it could prove productive to adapt these three observations to a conceptualisation of agency, as it would allow for a more accurate capture of how meaningful player action occurs in gameplay.

That being said, as detailed as Calleja's model is, it is not directly applicable to an analysis of videogame agency. First, Calleja's analytical focus is the experience of play itself, rather than what the game affords. In contrast, agency is framed here as a possibility space of the videogame's affordances and limitations. Such conceptualisation does not capture how players interpret said affordances, but takes into account a broader range of different gameplay iterations. Second, and more importantly, Calleja mentions 'choice' and 'agency' only in the context of specific dimensions. 'Choice' is featured as part of 'ludic involvement', but arguably, all involvement has choice expressed via action as its prerequisite. 'Agency' is specifically discussed in terms of 'kinaesthetic' and 'spatial involvement', where Calleja links the notion to movement and control (ibid. 55–71, 75, 91). At the same time, 'agency' elsewhere is used as a synonym for empowerment (ibid. 198–199), which muddles the picture somewhat. In summary, Calleja's multiple dimensions are exhaustive and apt in accounting for various iterations of gameplay, and it may well be that my model for agency feeds into his model of involvement. However, this book is not dedicated to understanding immersion and affect, it is concerned with how the possibility space for player action can be better understood.[1]

This is what my multidimensional heuristic framework for analysing player agency sets out to do. Each of the dimensions draw on themes emerging from how game studies and game design discourse discuss player action and avatar action. In the section on agency being afforded by design, the importance of the support for action provided by 'an underlying computational model' (Wardrip-Fruin et al. 2009: 7) was mentioned. What was not included then was that Wardrip-Fruin and colleagues add that a designer's task is to incentivise players towards satisfying experiences, such as 'traveling across space, managing resources, engaging in battle, or making conversational moves' (ibid.). In many ways, the four dimensions proposed below tap into this seemingly throwaway list.

Regarding methodology, the framework proposed is not a map of how agency is manifested in all avatar-based videogames, but it is designed to be used in asking interesting questions about such videogames. It is not so much a typology, or a 'grounded theory' as per the social sciences tradition, where a framework is generated solely from data collection and analysis (Creswell 1997: 55–58), although the case study analyses did help qualify certain aspects of the dimensions. It is built as a toolbox of terms and concepts that can be used to analyse agency in avatar-based videogames. In this sense, it is a heuristic approach, which

> suggests ways of looking at the problems and of categorizing them; it provides possible relations between statements, sets of statements, and the like; it facilitates seeing the consequences of proposed solutions; etc.
> (Batens 2013: 61)

This approach was chosen for several reasons. First, the terms and concepts dealt with are rather complex in and of themselves, but also in relation to each other. Therefore, the kind of extensive conceptualisation of agency proposed here is better suited to acknowledge these complexities than definitional work.[2] Second, definitions tend to imply locked-in boxes, and would not allow for the flexibility that is necessary when analysing games due to the idiosyncrasies of the medium, such as the inherent ephemerality of each play session; the sheer volume of games, game genres, and genre mixes within the avatar-based spectrum; or games simultaneously catering to different individual playstyles.

The heuristic framework is designed to ask the seemingly simple question: what can the avatar do? More specifically, on what terms does the game's design allow or constrain the player's freedom to act via the avatar? I argue that, at its conceptual core, agency can be afforded in space; in time; in terms of how much the avatar and the gameworld can be tailored to players' preference; and in the development of a story. Below, I will unpack each of these dimensions.

Agency Afforded in Space: The Spatial-Explorative Dimension

This analytical dimension zooms in on how the spaces that surround the avatar in videogames afford or constrain avatar action. Agency thus can be understood in terms of different ways of describing space in videogames. Fortunately, spatiality and its relevance to videogames has been theorised extensively and from early on, producing detailed categorisations (see, e.g., Aarseth 2000; Arsenault and Perron 2009; Juul 2005: 164–167; Klastrup 2003; Nitsche 2008; Wolf 2001). These approaches are typically concerned with how to describe various spaces within games, such as dimensionality or interface, but they rarely expand on how these spatial arrangements affect player agency.[3] The spatial-explorative dimension of agency presented here aims to do that by identifying game spaces according to functions the avatar can perform, allowing for a more fine-grained analysis of the many ways in which the spatiality of videogames affords or limits the manifestation of player agency.

A commonly used term to describe videogame spaces is 'game world' or 'gameworld'. It typically refers to a totality of game spaces (see, e.g., Bartle 2004; Klastrup 2009; Klevjer 2006: 58; Wolf 2012), including interfaces (Jørgensen 2013: 56–58). At the same time, 'gameworld' sometimes describes a game's fictional world (see, e.g., Jenkins 2006; Juul 2005: 131–162). 'Gameworld' is therefore not the best term to use as it could generate confusion. Instead I will draw on Thon (2016a) who distinguishes between different levels of representation in a way that has a spatial quality: '*locally represented situations* and the more complex *global storyworld as a whole* into which they are combined' (ibid. 47, orig. emphasis). In the case of videogames, the two can be discrepant, which is a result of the medium's interactive quality: players could be simultaneously cued into making sense of events as they happen in an individual gameplay session, which would likely differ in each instance, as well as what is supposed to happen. For example, as Thon points out, an avatar running around in circles, which the player is able to make the avatar do, does not necessarily mean that the avatar (as a fictional entity) often does that, or that this behaviour is in line with their image of being, say, a fearless soldier or mighty warrior (ibid. 115–116). While the act of running is represented, and as a result can be recognised as such by players, it is not in line with how the avatar is portrayed as part of the game's storyworld.[4] Arsenault and colleagues (2015: 93) make a similar point when emphasising the disconnect between a videogame's 'fiction' and its 'visual mediation'. Drawing on the above, we can distil two spaces of representation: a global storyworld, and local situations which may be discrepant with said storyworld. Accordingly, we can frame game spaces as affording either the former or the latter.

There is, however, a third spatial quality we can attribute to videogame spaces. Burn (2006: 73) differentiates between two kinds of avatar function: 'ludic' and 'representational'. These two functions are afforded by a videogame's spaces, therefore those, too, can be qualified as ludic or representational. A similar distinction is made by Schöter and Thon (2014: 49–50), who argue that games can be described as 'ludic experiences' (where the character is being perceived as a 'game piece') or 'narrative experiences' (where the character is being perceived as a 'fictional being').[5] We can thus add ludic as the third quality of videogame spaces. Ludic space as understood here corresponds to what Schell calls 'space as a game mechanic ... a mathematical construct' with all audiovisual layers stripped away; a merely 'functional space' (Schell 2015 [2008]: 159–163). Accordingly, we can frame videogame spaces in three ways: there are game spaces that contribute to the representation of the storyworld; then there are game spaces that represent local situations that may be discrepant with the storyworld; and last, game spaces can be described according to their abstract, ludic quality. Acknowledging that representation occurs in multiple layers is important, because it helps identifying the various game spaces within which the avatar can move.

Keeping in mind the above discussed complexity of representationality in videogames, I propose that we distinguish between space-as-ludic and space-as-representational. It would be an easy step forward then to argue that there is agency afforded by ludic space, and agency afforded by representational space: moving the avatar forwards or backwards is spatial agency, and running around in beautifully rendered valleys is representational agency. However, the situation is not quite that simple as the representation of game spaces and the gameplay that takes place in them will usually have both ludic and representational qualities at the same time. Even rather rudimentary representational game spaces have the capacity to create storyworlds. A good example of this is side-scrolling platformer *Thomas Was Alone* (Bithell 2012). While the avatar and other non-player characters are represented as rectangles and the world they inhabit is also quite conceptual in its geometrically rendered geography, the game's levels still contain recognisable shapes, such as islands in water, enriching the world created by the game.

In order to better capture the different kinds of agency afforded by the navigation of ludic and representational space, I propose to further distinguish between *spatial* and *explorative* agency. On the one hand, a spatial framing of agency allows us to ask questions concerning the possibility space comprised of movements the avatar can and cannot perform in individual videogame spaces. For example, what actual motions are afforded to the avatar by the game's design? Can they walk? Jump? Sprint? Take cover? Although these actions can be executed in both the game's ludic and representational spaces, spatial agency is more closely connected to the avatar's ludic functions. Furthermore, when thinking about navigation in videogames, increasingly it is not only the avatar's methods of locomotion that we can analyse, but also the environments that allow or constrain movement (Debus 2016). The analytical lens of spatial agency thus allows us to examine how game physics, level design and arrangement of in-game objects, and perimeters of spatial progression enable or constrain spatial agency.

On the other hand, contrasted with spatial agency's closer connection to self-contained game spaces and the avatar's ludic function, explorative agency allows us to examine how more ambitious spatial arrangements in videogames afford and constrain avatar action. Framing agency as such entails more than mere spatial navigation of the avatar. Indeed, King and Krzywinska (2003, 2006: 76–123) repeatedly emphasise the importance of exploration in action-adventure games to the overall feeling of presence and embodiment, of which agency can be seen as precursor to. An explorative framing yields questions like how the game spaces are relayed (for example, are they arranged into cities or other units, see, e.g., Vella and Bonello Rutter Giappone 2018; Vella 2019), which areas of the representational space can be explored by the avatar, through what mechanics exploration is incentivised, whether movement within representational space is continuous or interrupted (by, say, load screens), or what navigation tools and superimposed interfaces aid progress. For example, numerous games make use of warp mechanics to transport the avatar from one place to another (Gazzard 2009). Altogether, these are the kind of questions that the spatial-explorative dimension allows us to ask when trying to unpack how agency works in avatar-based games.

In terms of how these two kinds of agency relate to each other and to the two kinds of spatiality in videogames distinguished above, it can be argued that spatial agency tends to be oriented toward ludic spaces, and explorative agency tends to be oriented toward the representational spaces. That said, the two are also rather difficult to detach from each other—as we will see is the case for the other dimensions as well. For example, players *can* use the avatar to explore the game spaces as ludic space. Lara Croft running around looking for a hidden object on any given level of any given *Tomb Raider* game is a manifestation of both spatial agency in the game's ludic spaces and explorative agency in the game's representational spaces, as it is both an in-game object with a collision box being moved within a rendered matrix, and a young archaeologist searching for treasure in deserted ruins. Also, as the example of *Thomas Was Alone* illustrated, spatial agency may privilege the ludic functions of game spaces, but these functions often do also contribute to the representation of the gameworld.

Let's look at a few examples in some more detail to see how these two analytical categories help us understand how the possibility space for spatial-explorative agency is created by design. In the audiovisually realistic open world shooter *Tom Clancy's Ghost Recon Wildlands* (Ubisoft Paris 2017), the game's ludic and representational space are in near-complete alignment.[6] While launching a rocket into the skybox[7] is not quite possible, the beautifully rendered vast landscapes, mountains, and ravines are freely explorable with the avatar without any loading time breaking up levels. The whole map is an island, so the edge of the world is masked with the endless vista of the ocean. On this island, whatever the eye can see, the avatar can reach. *Ghost Recon Wildlands* is also a good example to illustrate why we cannot conflate ludic space with spatial agency, and representational space with explorative agency. While it takes just over 4 hours of playtime to walk across the entire map (TheyCallMeConor 2017), simultaneously affording spatial and explorative agency to a near-equal degree, during this epic walk, the sun rises and sets multiple times. Which means that the time frame only applies to ludic space, but not to representational space.[8]

In opposition to the complete freedom to explore both the ludic and representational space provided by *Tom Clancy's Ghost Recon Wildlands'* level design is fighting game *Mortal Kombat X* (NetherRealm Studios 2015). While it also boasts an expansive representational space comprised of numerous supernatural 'realms' like Earthrealm, Chaosrealm, or Dreamrealm, these are mostly brought to life through cut-scenes and non-interactive backdrops, and as such, cannot be explored with the avatar. In contrast, the many, smaller ludic spaces of the game where the fights take place are all rather similar in terms of what kind of spatial agency they afford, and are navigable only to a very limited degree. This is mostly due to the side-scrolling tradition of beat-em-ups, a genre the *Mortal Kombat* series belongs to. While the player does control their chosen fighter's movements, the avatar will never be able to leave this restricted space, both in a ludic and in a representational sense, to interact with things in the background. They are locked into this limited space, where everything, except for the avatar's immediate surrounds, is an inaccessible decorative backdrop. In this case, the game's design affords spatial agency vertically and horizontally (by allowing the avatar to move sideways, as well as to crouch and jump), but restricts explorative agency in almost every regard.

Numerous elements of game design impact the possibility space for avatar action in a spatially relevant way. One such element is perspective, or in other words, the player's window into the game. How much of the avatar's surroundings a player can see and how precisely a game is able to emulate the avatar's spatial perspective audiovisually can have considerable implications for agency. Sharp (2013) presents a broad survey of perspective in the context of videogames, but it is Thon (2009) who offers a classification of perspectives that aligns to the conceptualisation of space presented above. He argues that perspective can be thought of as 'spatial' and 'actional', where the former is determined by a 'spatial position from which the game space is presented audiovisually', and the latter is the 'position from which the player can interact with the game space' (ibid. 279–280).[9] Perspective in both these senses is primarily relevant for spatial agency, particularly with regards to space framed as ludic, for it is one of the ways in which game designers can manipulate the possibility space for player action, and also achieve desired effects. A good example of perspective manipulation's effect on agency is the original version of horror game *Resident Evil 2* (Capcom 1998). In the game, camera angles are mostly locked in, which creates an interesting situation whereby the avatar's spatial perspective is severely limited while its actional perspective corresponds to a typical third-person game's, which makes the successful navigation of ludic space increasingly challenging. This, in turn, reduces the player's ability to understand the ludic and representational spaces around them, impairing their ability to control their avatar successfully, which ultimately contributes to the horror effect (Perron 2018: 114–115).[10] Accordingly, the spatial-explorative analytical dimension can be used to identify perspective-related affordances that have a spatial element to them, such as numbers and configurability of vantage points, or degrees of camera control.

Similarly, level design plays a major part in how agency is afforded and limited in the spatial-explorative dimension, though even developers themselves disagree on what level design is and how it relates to other aspects of designing a videogame, such as game design (in the sense of rules and challenges) or narrative design (Bleszinski 2000; Picard 2013). First, while levels, which can be thought of both as ludic and representational spaces, indeed have a spatial quality to them, they are also a unit in time (Picard 2013: 99). Therefore, looking at level design cannot simply be restricted to the spatial-explorative dimension in the analytical framework. Second, given that a 'level' is a result of collaboration between programmers, artists, game designers, and many more, it is difficult to identify where level design stops and game design begins. Kremers (2009) suggests that it is easier to understand level design through what it is for, and how it functions. He argues that its basic function is that

> if a game designer designs the gameplay *rules*, the level designer designs *how* the player is confronted with those rules . . . a game designer *formulates* the game's rules, while the level designer *interprets* them. . . . Level design is applied game design.
> (Kremers 2009: 17–18, orig. emphases)

It follows then that we cannot quite look at level design in a game as a solely spatial-explorative agency affordance, but that, at the same time, aspects of level design that may afford or limit avatar action in the spatial-explorative dimension must be considered. By manipulating things like the overall layout of the individual game spaces (both in a ludic and representational sense), the arranging them into missions, maps, or levels, or the spatial conditions of progress that determine what is available and what is not, level design is an overarching and powerful way for game designers to influence how player action is afforded in this dimension.

Agency Afforded in Time: The Temporal-Ergodic Dimension

A definitive separation between the time(s) and space(s) of videogames risks causing more problems than it would solve, therefore the line of division drawn here is primarily for analytical purposes, while maintaining that these dimensions rarely manifest in isolation. As important as it is to understand how videogames' spatiality affords player action, '[w]e should not forget that the temporal dimension of gameplay prevails on its spatial characterization' (Arsenault and Perron 2009: 113). Indeed, temporality in videogames could be construed as something above every other dimension. For example, Calleja's (2011) multidimensional model of player involvement does not separate 'temporal involvement' the way it does 'spatial involvement', but instead places temporality above all other dimensions he distinguishes between. However, an analytical dimension dedicated to unpacking how avatar action is afforded in time is a productive step towards understanding agency as afforded by design in videogames.

The complexity of the concept of time is evident when looking at the sheer volume of studies offering ontologies, frameworks, and other such structures to understand the relevance of time and temporality to videogames and play (see, e.g. Aarseth et al. 2003; Adams 2010 [2006]: 93–95, 615–616; Alvarez Igarzábal 2019; Björk and Holopainen 2005: 421–422; Elverdam and Aarseth 2007; Eskelinen 2001b, 2012: 295–312; Hanson 2018; Juul 2005: 141–156; Lindley 2005; Tychsen and Hitchens 2009; Zagal and Mateas 2010). The different layers and levels these frameworks distinguish between allow and constrain avatar action, and consequently impact agency, to different degrees. A common distinction made is between time as played and time as happenings in the game, some form of game time versus play time, game events and player events (see, e.g., 'internal' and 'external' time in Elverdam and Aarseth 2007; 'event time' and 'user time' in Eskelinen 2001b: 178; 'event time' and 'play time' in Tychsen and Hitchens 2009: 174). While this is a productive distinction, it does not quite account for how most gameplay moments will have both a representational and a ludic quality to them.

Notably, Zagal and Mateas (2010) break down the abovementioned dichotomy further by introducing 'temporal frames' as a conceptual tool for analysing game time. The four temporal frames they list are 'real-world time', 'gameworld time', 'coordination time', and 'fictive time'. 'Real-world time' corresponds to Elverdam and Aarseth's 'external time' in that it captures time as spent playing, 'in the physical world around the player' (ibid. 848). The novelty in Zagal and Mateas' model is the breaking down of Elverdam and Aarseth's meta-category of 'internal time' into 'gameworld time', 'coordination time', and 'fictive time', and it is these three 'temporal frames' that can be linked to the threefold distinction between various game spaces proposed in the previous section. 'Gameworld time' they argue, 'is established by the set of events taking place within the represented gameworld' which

> includes both events associated with abstract gameplay actions as well as events associated with the virtual or simulated world (the literal gameworld) within which an abstract game may be embedded.
> (ibid. 849)

This quote shows the limitations of the term 'gameworld', as is seen to be used to simultaneously refer to represented 'gameplay actions' as well as 'the literal gameworld'. It is therefore better to describe this kind of temporality in terms of what I argued to be locally represented situations. Related to this is 'fictive time' which is 'established through the application of sociocultural labels to a subset of events' (ibid. 850). Zagal and Mateas argue that labelling a round 'day', or a cycle of action and inaction as the biological needs of a character 'strengthen the fictive frame' of the game (Zagal and Mateas 2010: 851). This temporal frame can be connected to what I argued to be the global storyworld representation of game spaces. Lastly, 'coordination time' is 'established by the set of events that coordinate the actions of multiple players (human or artificial intelligence [AI]) and possibly in-game agents' (ibid. 850). As such, 'coordination time' is not connected so much to videogames' representationality, and more to the abstract space which I labelled ludic space above. Once again, for clarity, it is productive to maintain the conceptual distinctions drawn by Zagal and Mateas, but I suggest different terminology for better alignment with the theorisation of game spaces discussed in the previous section of this chapter, which leaves us with: real world time (unchanged), ludic time, time of local representation, and storyworld time.

Relating Zagal and Mateas' temporal frames to the threefold distinction of game spaces enables us to capture in more depth how game design affords and constrains avatar action in time. For example, day-night cycles or countdowns may be implemented in ludic spaces but not in storyworld spaces. A common such misalignment in design is when there is a ticking clock imposed in the game's representational time that does not actually exist, or only conditionally, in ludic time. Bethesda games often implement such, arguably, deceptive measures. At the beginning of *The Elder Scrolls V: Skyrim* (2011), a non-player character prompts the player to hurry and move up to the top of the tower to get away from the dragon attack. But the avatar can be left stood at the bottom of the stairs for an indefinite amount of ludic time, and the dragon will not destroy the tower. Similarly, at the beginning of *Fallout 4* (Bethesda Game Studios 2015), the player is repeatedly prompted to leave the house immediately and run towards the nearest nuclear shelter, as bombs are inbound. The prompt happens while the avatar is inside the house, but as long as they stay in the house, the nuclear attack does not begin. In situations like this, avatar action is constrained in storyworld time, but this constraint does not extend to the time of locally represented situations and ludic time.

Conceptualising videogames' temporality this way alone, however, does not account for how agency can be afforded by temporal structures. Not only can the temporal structures in a game's design afford and constrain player action, there might also be a way to influence said temporal structures. Zagal and Mateas also make this point when they note that, 'from a design perspective, player agency over a temporal frame offers novel options for gameplay while also introducing additional temporal anomalies' (2010: 952). There is thus a need for an analytical distinction that addresses not

Multidimensional Heuristic Framework to Analyse Player Agency 51

only how temporal structures in videogames impact avatar action, but also whether it is possible for the player/avatar to manipulate these. In order to address this variable, I propose to distinguish between two kinds of agency as afforded in time: *temporal* and *ergodic agency*, which together make up the *temporal-ergodic dimension*.

Temporal agency is best described as the possibility for action as afforded and constrained within the temporal structures that constitute a game's design. Framing agency in such a way brings to light the structure of pre-designed elements that constitute ludic and representational time in the game and allows us to explore how the times of various game spaces relate to each other. We can ask, for example, how the passage of time is marked, what the victory and termination conditions are, or what 'game over'[11] is, as well as how gameplay is paced (e.g., turn-based versus real-time games in Adams 2010 [2006]: 289–290), what kind of time-critical events there are (e.g., 'ticking clocks' in LeBlanc 2006), and how they are expressed in the ludic and representational spaces. A common example for a game mechanic that can shape the possibility space for temporal agency is the day-night cycle. Most avatar-based games with resource management and crafting feature such a mechanic, such as *Don't Starve* (Klei Entertainment 2013) or the *Animal Crossing* series (Nintendo 2001—). Day-night cycles tend to regulate ludic and representational time in a way that cannot be influenced by the player, and condition things such as availability of resources, or presence of danger, accordingly. Thus, the constraint imposed by design delineates the possibility space for avatar action, thereby affording temporal agency.

This being said, temporal agency alone does not speak to scenarios where the player/avatar is granted some degree of control over temporal structures in a game's design. I propose ergodic agency as a separate analytical framing which allows us to interrogate whether such manipulation of ludic and representational time is allowed. The terminological choice is a nod to Aarseth (1997), who coined the term 'ergodic' to qualify literature where non-trivial effort is required to engage with the text. He later argued that ergodic time specifically depends on user action (Aarseth 1999). Drawing on the core idea of ergodicity encapsulating the player's ability to manipulate or intervene, 'ergodic' in the temporal-ergodic analytical dimension enables us to identify those game mechanics and design elements affording or limiting player action in time that the player does have influence over.[12] As such, framing agency as ergodic allows us to ask the seemingly simple question: can the player, through their avatar, either by a press of a button or by navigating superimposed interfaces and menus such as a power wheel,[13] influence temporal structures in the game? This can happen in multiple ways. Oftentimes, ludic time, as connected to ludic space, and therefore not necessarily moving at the same pace as storyworld time, only progresses if the player makes the avatar takes a certain action, be it as simple as taking a first step after standing still, or as specific as passing a certain bush that triggers the appearance of an enemy soldier. This would be an example of how ergodic time depends on user action, as mentioned above. At the same time, there might be mechanics in place that allow ludic and representational time to be propelled forward or backward: in other words, mechanics that allow for actions like rewind, fast-forward, slow down, or speed up of time (see, e.g., Hanson 2018: 56–85; 135–155; Knutson 2018; Schmalzer 2020). Examples for this can be found in *Prince of Persia: Sands of Time* (Ubisoft Montreal 2003); *Braid* (Number One 2008), Remedy Entertainment's action-adventure shooter games like *Max Payne* (2001) and *Quantum Break* (2016); in some games by Quantic Dream, such as *Detroit: Become Human* (2018).[14]

Now, let's take a closer look at a few examples to understand how this dimension of agency can be illuminated by examining the different ways in which time is framed, as well as the degree to which the player can influence temporal structures. Oftentimes in avatar-based games there is a closer connection between real world, ludic and locally represented time, whereas storyworld time may be constructed in a way that may seem downright illogical. For example, as noted in the *Tom Clancy* example above, it takes about 4 hours of play to walk across the entire map of the game. While the pace of walking/running in the game corresponds to the pace of a person walking/running in real world time, during the walk across the map the in-game sun rises and sets multiple times, thereby creating a temporal discrepancy.[15] A radically different way of affording temporal-ergodic agency is found in *SUPERHOT* (SUPERHOT Team 2016), a first-person shooter where compared to real world time, ludic and representational time is slowed down to such an extreme that in-game objects and non-player characters are barely moving unless the player makes the avatar move, in which case everything in the game spaces matches the movement speed of the avatar. One of the most salient visual indications of how much time is slowed down can be seen on the trails of red bullets leave behind them. This way, in most gameplay scenarios (save cut-scenes), real-world time, ludic time, the time of locally represented events, and storyworld time are more closely linked together than was the case in the *Tom Clancy* example. As such, *SUPERHOT* represents a strikingly different approach to stereotypical first-person shooter game design, because instead of relying on their trigger reflexes, the player is required to think strategically, for extended periods of time, and about every one of their avatar's movements.[16] *SUPERHOT* thus creates an interesting challenge in manipulating the possibility space for avatar action in the temporal-ergodic dimension.

Indeed, the notion of challenge is important here: the temporal-ergodic dimension can also allow us to ask questions about how temporal structures requiring time-critical action in videogames impact player agency. In simpler terms, and drawing on Pias' description of action games, players will often 'carry out actions under time pressure' (Pias 2004: 135). Game design textbooks often include lists of different challenges (e.g., 'physical coordination, factual knowledge, formal logic, pattern recognition, and so forth' in Adams 2010 [2006]: 418) and these often have a time-sensitive quality to them. Time pressure can of course take many forms. On the one hand, there are challenges that require dexterity, which have a rather obvious temporal quality to them: not only does the player need to position their avatar at the right place, but they also need to press the button at the right time in order to successfully jump from platform to platform. On the other hand, there are challenging scenarios where the pressing of a button is not necessarily as time-critical, but the challenge has a set time limit, thereby applying time pressure on the player: for example, while solving a puzzle may have a time limit on it, thereby requiring the player to think quickly, the individual actions taken by their avatar may not necessarily contribute to the outcome. Karhulahti (2013: n.p.) calls these two kinds of time criticality 'time-critical performance' and 'time-critical framework'. With the analytical dimension of temporal-ergodic agency we can therefore ask how time-critical action is designed, and how challenge design of both types shapes the possibility space for player action as expressed via the avatar.

More specifically, the temporal-ergodic analytical dimension can be used to interrogate the difficulty of time-critical challenges. Scaled difficulty has been part of videogames since the arcade era (Furze 2013: 149). If the player has the window of, say, one second to execute a series of inputs or actions, then it is the highest level of difficulty. If one extends that period to two seconds to do the same thing, the level of difficulty would decrease, as they would have more time. It is the designer's role to match player skill to the difficulty of the challenge—in other words, to balance the game (Koster 2004). Therefore, by setting variables to the avatar, such as their health, damage output or, in case of shooter games, aim assistance, as well as those of non-player character characters, the designer can manipulate the possibility space in the temporal-ergodic dimension. Higher health points mean longer battles, while higher damage points mean shorter ones. Not only can this be pre-set, technology allows for some level of adaptivity to the individual player's skill. This is referred to as 'Dynamic Difficulty Adjustment' (Hunicke and Chapman 2004). The temporal-ergodic dimension of agency therefore enables us to look at how game balancing creates challenge and scales difficulty.

Agency Over the Avatar and Its Surroundings: The Configurative-Constructive Dimension

While the spatial-explorative and temporal-ergodic dimensions already cover a fair amount of possible gameplay scenarios, there are further dimensions in which game design can afford or limit player action. For one, since at the heart of the conceptualisation of agency proposed here is avatar action, there is a need for an analytical dimension to interrogate whether (and if yes, in how far) the avatar and the surrounding game spaces are mouldable, since that will inevitably impact the possibility space for avatar action. This is what this dimension focuses on. There is, of course, a long tradition of players creating their own characters in tabletop role-playing games, and this feature was also adapted to videogames very early on, particularly to those with role-playing mechanics to them (see, e.g., Bienia 2016; Carr et al. 2006: 19–21; Hitchens and Drachen 2008). In addition, the degree to which the avatar's surroundings (both in a ludic and representational sense) can be altered also impacts the possibility space for action. Being able to change the terrain or demolish buildings, though crucial to games like strategy games that have crafting and resource management as a core mechanic, is less typical of avatar-based games.[17] Or at least it had been, until a recent-ish boom in independent games triggered by the likes of *Minecraft* (Mojang Studios 2009, to be discussed in the final case study chapter). Therefore, this analytical dimension will address the changeability of the attributes of both the avatar and the world which surrounds it.

As discussed in the 'Agency Is Player/Avatar Action' section of the previous chapter, when wanting to better understand the relationship between agency and game design, we can frame the avatar (as understood in this book) in at least two ways: according to whether it is considered a game piece, or a representational object. In acknowledging this distinction, and to fit into the language used to describe analytical distinctions in this heuristic framework thus far, I framed the avatar according to their function as ludic and as representational (Burn 2006). In order to discuss how avatar characteristics can be modified I propose the term 'configuration'. In game studies 'configuration' is typically used as a metaphor for the gaming process (Eskelinen 2001a; Sicart 2008, 2011; Simons 2007), but for the purposes of this heuristic framework, I use it very specifically to refer to avatar modification. This game design affordance is one of the key components of role-playing games (see, e.g., 'characterization of player characters' in Björk and Zagal 2018: 327–329) and is becoming increasingly prevalent in other videogame genres as well (Dahlskog et al. 2015; MacCallum-Stewart et al. 2018: 173–177).

Framing agency as configurative allows us to ask questions about the degrees to which the avatar, both as a ludic and representational object, can be configured, as well as to track the impact and consequences of said configuration. What characteristics and variables does the avatar have? Can the avatar's 'figurative attributes' (Willumsen 2018), such as name, appearance, costume, weapons, or inventory be changed? If so, to what end? Does the avatar change throughout the duration of the game, and if so, how? What are the means of progress measurement and tracking (e.g., 'stratified character progression' in Peterson 2012: 341–359 v. 'non-stratified character progression' in Zagal and Altizer 2014: 2)? A common example of design affording configurative agency is the character creation process in role-playing games. Selecting visual features like hair colour, or building a character according to any one profile in the 'holy trinity' of role-playing game design, namely 'tank, healer, damager' (Björk and Zagal 2018: 326), can have implications for the avatar both in a ludic and a representational sense (Krzywinska 2007: 106).[18]

As to what kinds of attributes designers usually plan with in videogames, a non-exhaustive, but nonetheless thorough list is offered by game designer and writer Evan Skolnick:

> name, sex, race/species, age, intelligence, education type and level, profession, vocabulary, backstory, character arc/change, desire, likes, dislikes, values, key flaws, vices, physical attributes, clothing, weapons/paraphernalia.
>
> (Skolnick 2015: 134–135)

While some of the above listed attributes, such as hair colour or intelligence, may be more obvious than others when it comes to thinking about avatar configuration, it is not uncommon that characteristics like vices or values would have an impact on the avatar both in its ludic and representational function. For example, in role-playing detective game *Disco Elysium* (ZA/UM 2019), the avatar is addicted to smoking, alcohol, and drugs. Depending on which vice the player subjects the avatar to, their skills and attributes may become stronger or weaker, impacting both their ludic and representational functions. For example, smoking raises intellectual skill points, but damages health; or, non-player characters may comment on being interrogated by a detective high on speed, which could reduce their authority points, and therefore impact the success of the interrogation.

Much like with our previous two dimensions, while it is generally more likely that ludic configuration would have a greater impact on ludic space and time, and representational configuration on representational space and time, quite often there is a discrepancy between, say, how powerful a chosen weapon or piece of armour is, and how it actually looks on the avatar. The analytical framing of configurative agency is useful in picking up on such discrepancies. Games like action-role-playing game *Diablo III* (Blizzard Entertainment 2012) serve as good examples to pinpoint the potential for disconnect, particularly in the case of female avatars. In choosing armour, a player would most likely go for a set which raises the avatar's overall strength or resistance, but the visual design of the pieces may not necessarily reflect just how resilient or protective that particular piece of armour is.[19] The discrepancy between avatar configuration with regards to the avatar's ludic and representational function becomes even more apparent on one of *Diablo III*'s secret levels called Whimsyshire, which is designed to be brightly coloured and full of unicorns, quite unlike the usual theme of demonic hellscapes in the game.

Besides the configuration of the avatar, the degree to which the surrounding game spaces can be altered also shapes the possibility space for avatar action. Consequently, whether a game's design allows for this, and if yes, how, has relevance for agency. Murray described this as 'constructivist agency' (1997: 147), but I want to slightly update the concept behind it, and in order to reflect these changes will use the term constructive agency instead. For example, by chopping wood in survival game *The Forest* (Endnight Games 2014) the avatar is able to gather logs which then they can use for building shelter, but the act also angers the cannibals local to the peninsula the game takes place on. Inquiries into constructive agency are thus concerned with whether, and if so, to what degree the player is allowed to change the spaces within which the avatar exists, and more importantly, acts. Can they determine the perimeter of the world they are in? Can they physically alter it by, for example, raising or lowering terrain? Can they mine, harvest, or in other ways gather materials? And if they can, do these acts actually change the game's spaces? Can they add anything to the game space, either ludic or representational, for instance grow something or build things? These are the kinds of questions we can ask with the help of the analytical framing of agency as constructive.

Such game mechanics are typically found in non-avatar-based games, such as the dollhouse simulator *The Sims* franchise (Maxis 2000—), strategy games like the *Age of Empires* series (Ensemble Studios 1997—), or simulation games focused on the building and management of service providers and attractions, such as *Theme Hospital* (Bullfrog Productions 1997) or *Roller Coaster Tycoon* (Chris Sawyer Production 1999). However, the past decade or so saw a rise of avatar-based genres which afford the alteration of the avatar's surrounds to a similar scale. Apart from the already mentioned survival genre, or *Minecraft* (Mojang Studios 2009), which will be discussed in more detail in the last case study chapter, another typical example would be games about farming, where the player can arrange plantations and buildings in any desirable formation so long as they correspond with the rules of the storyworld, such as *Harvest Moon* (Amccus 1996) or *Stardew Valley* (ConcernedApe 2016).

Keeping in mind the threefold framing of space discussed earlier (ludic space, space of local representation, and storyworld space), we can identify interesting tensions in how constructive agency can manifest. In post-apocalyptic action-role-playing game *Fallout 4* (Bethesda Game Studios 2015) the avatar can unlock 'Settlement' sites at 30 pre-set locations within the map. Certain structures, like 'Water Purifiers' or 'Guard Posts', are pre-designed, but it is also possible to build new structures from a big selection of customisable building blocks, consisting of types of 'Walls', 'Floors', 'Roofs', 'Doors', and 'Windows', as well as a similarly huge selection of 'Furniture' and 'Decorations'. These are made from components scrapped from found structures, such as 'Steel' or 'Wood'. There is, however, an opposing logic to the surrounding world and the buildings of the 'Settlement'. While exploring the wastelands left behind by a nuclear apocalypse, the avatar is surrounded by buildings that are visibly made of, say, concrete supported by iron beams, thereby creating the physics of the storyworld with regards to how buildings are made structurally sound. Somewhat contradictorily, in the 'Settlements' it is possible to, say, place one metal sheet on the floor and erect a tower on it exclusively comprised of metal sheets, without any further structural support, and it does not fall over. Thus, in *Fallout 4* there is a tension between the laws determining structural integrity within the level of locally represented space and the broader storyworld representation, which the analytical lens of constructive agency helped us identify.

This becomes even more interesting when looking at what Fordyce (2018) calls the 'homesteading' mechanic, found for example in *Assassin's Creed II* (Ubisoft Montreal 2009). At some point in the game the player character Ezio and his family need to flee Firenze and take up residence in a nearby village called Monteriggioni. Here, they may choose to 'Renovate' their family mansion. Buildings like a 'Bank', 'Doctor', or 'Blacksmith' can be renovated, while others like a 'Well' can be placed by paying in-game currency to an architect to do it. Once paid, the building storefronts transform, and each building increases the revenue Ezio gains at regular intervals, as well as provide discount for certain gear and services. The buildings therefore have a ludic function, and they also form part of the global storyworld. But unlike in *Fallout 4*, the buildings can only be placed at their pre-set location, and there are no options for customising them either. In providing their ludic function, they are locked to the laws of the global storyworld. Therefore, while renovating these buildings comes with gameplay benefits, such as cheaper gear or increased revenue, the avatar does not actually accumulate lumber or spend time laying bricks for these buildings to come into existence. Their 'construction' also does not require the management of building staff or supplies, only the single in-game currency. This mechanic affords a much lower degree of constructive agency than *Fallout 4* does, as, although the buildings form part of the global storyworld of the game, and they are connected to an avatar's ludic function and can therefore be seen as an extension of the avatar configuration system, the buildings themselves are not built by the avatar, nor do they require actual grafting, such as resource gathering and management, from the avatar.

As already argued in this last example, a prime area of scrutiny relevant for the analytical dimension of configurative-constructive agency is that of in-game economies. Indeed, as Knowles and Castronova (2018: 310) point out, 'an economy is a game system that facilitates choice in play', and as such, in-game economies play a vital role in facilitating player agency. Costikyan offers an illustrative list of the many resources that can make up a game's economy:

> 'Resources' can be anything: Panzer divisions. Supply points. Cards. Experience points. Knowledge of spells. Ownership of fiefs. The love of a good woman. Favors from the boss. The good will of an NPC. Money. Food. Sex. Fame. Information.
> (Costikyan 2005 [1999]: n.p.)

By establishing in-game economies, setting values for goods, creating storage units different in size, or lay down rules of trade, designers can manipulate the possibility space for avatar action, and subsequently, agency, in the configurative-constructive dimension. A common way to do this is by creating systems of utility and scarcity (Fullerton 2014 [2004]: 78). Prominent ways for creating scarcity in virtual economies could be scarcity in creating the avatar, their appearance and skills; and scarcity in how goods and services are arranged (see, e.g., Baumgartner 2015; Castronova 2006).[20] Therefore, the design of research management systems, attribution of value to in-game objects, or the introduction of currencies and markets, are means in which the possibility space for avatar action in the configurative-constructive dimension can be shaped.

Agency and Narrativity: Narrative-Dramatic Dimension

As repeatedly emphasised throughout the above discussion of the spatial-explorative, temporal-ergodic, and configurative-constructive dimensions of player agency, the affordances and limitations of game design can be framed in terms of ludic and representational functions. However, so far I have only briefly commented on how videogames can represent events with varying degrees of narrative quality to them, and how this representation shapes the possibility space for avatar action. This is what the fourth and final dimension will address.

Videogame scholarship has long been occupied with examining exactly how games can be considered a storytelling medium. As mentioned at the beginning of this chapter, this topic has been hotly debated since the nascent years of the field (see, e.g., Frasca 2003a; Pearce 2005), but it is now mostly agreed upon that videogames can be perceived to exhibit various degrees of narrativity (see, e.g., Ryan 2005: 4). It comes as no surprise, then, that many have offered solutions for how to make critical observations about narrative in the context of videogames (see, e.g., Aarseth 2012; Ang 2006; Atkins 2003; Backe 2012; Jannidis 2003; Neitzel 2014; Pearce 2004; Ryan 2006: 181–203; Thon 2016a). Accordingly, at the heart of the narrative-dramatic dimension of agency is the understanding that narrativity is not a yes or no question, but a matter of degrees. Notably, Ryan (2004: 9) argued that text 'being narrative' and 'possessing narrativity' are two different things. In making this distinction, Ryan shifted the emphasis from whether a text *is* a narrative, to whether it *has* a perceivable narrative quality to it. Juul (2005: 130–133) later made a similar point, as did Jenkins (2006) when he pointed out that videogames can be considered as 'evocative spaces' capable of relaying 'spatial stories' via what he termed 'environmental storytelling'. 'Spatial stories', Jenkins argues,

> can evoke pre-existing narrative associations; they can provide a staging ground where narrative events are enacted; they may embed narrative information within their mise-en-scene; or they provide resources for emergent narratives.
>
> (Jenkins 2006: 676–677)

Although Jenkins foreground narrativity as a spatial affordance of game design, the point he makes about something other than predeterminedly narrative elements contributing to games' narrativity is important nonetheless. In this vein, the narrative-dramatic dimension in the heuristic framework is useful to examine videogames' potential to generate narratively charged events in all four ways listed by Jenkins, or as Ryan (2006: 7) puts it, videogames' 'storiness'. When thinking about this dimension, we can ask questions about what narrative elements there are in game design and whether the player has any influence over them; as well as how other, less straight-forwardly narrative elements of game design facilitate avatar action with a narrative quality to it.

The analytical framing of agency as narrative enables us to ask broader questions regarding representationality and avatar action. In other words, about what prototypically narrative elements there are, and to what degree they afford or limit avatar action. For example, is there a back story (Myers 2003)? What are the main 'story beats' (Mochocki 2020)? Are there sequences of highly limited player action that remediate other forms of media (such as photography, cinema, or comics), also known as cut-scenes (Glassner 2004: 285–288; Klevjer 2002, 2013)? Are there predetermined events that take place in the game spaces while affording some degree of avatar control, or in other words, are there scripted events (Thon 2016b)? Some have argued in the past that cut-scenes constrain player agency (Falstein 2005: 92–65; Grodal 2003; Juul 2005: 135), but that is not quite the case. For example, shooter games typically make use of cut-scenes to deliver narrative content, which may constrain agency in other dimensions as cut-scenes suspend the core gameplay loop of time-critical shootery, but they contribute to the avatar's representational function by giving them, say, motivation, or adding layers to their personality. This is what Cheng calls 'representational agency', or 'the feeling of being a star of the action movie' (2007: 17).[21] In addition, besides cut-scenes and such, framing agency as narrative also allows us to ask whether there are dialogue mechanics, where the avatar interacts with non-player characters via superimposed menus, as well as whether there are any elements of level design or art that can add to the represented storyworld, such as writings on a wall ('environmental storytelling' in Jenkins 2006). Last but not least, what kind of dialogue and scripted behaviour do non-player characters have? Through what means is game lore established? As such, narrative agency is primarily connected to the avatar's representational function, and for analytical purposes is more productive when approaching the subject of analysis as narrative representation, rather than as interactive simulation (Frasca 2003b; Thon 2016a: 107; Klevjer 2019).

Furthermore, the analytical lens of narrative agency allows us to catalogue not only what prototypically narrative elements there are in a videogame, but also how they are structured, and to what degree the player is allowed to meaningfully intervene in the designed structures. As the brief overview of game studies and game design literature earlier showed, this is a predominantly how the term 'agency' is understood. Scholars and designers alike have proposed different strategies for arranging narratively relevant content in videogames,[22] and a general theme such structurations revolve around is whether the player is guided through a singular path in their experience of the predetermined narrative, akin to the kind of experience film or literature typically offers, or whether the narrative experience is planned to be less linearly designed. This problem has been thoroughly discussed under the moniker of 'nonlinearity' and variations thereof.[23] While the concept of nonlinearity is at the heart of the analytical framing of narrative agency, we need to distinguish between the kind of nonlinearity that stems from the interactivity inherent to the medium of videogames, and a nonlinearity that is designed into the narrative affordances of the game (Thon 2016b). Focusing on the latter, by framing agency as narrative, we can ask questions such as: are there forking paths in the story (Aarseth 1994)? What metaphors can be used to describe their structure, for instance: a vector with side branches, a tree, or a maze (Ryan 2015: 165–175)?

A straightforward example of design affording narrative agency can be found in games by Telltale Games and Quantic Dream. These studios are well-known for making games where the core gameplay loop is centred on players making decisions in dialogue trees or Heads-Up Displays (or HUD) about how the narrative should progress. In *Detroit: Become Human* (Quantic Dream 2018), the player controls three avatars whose individual plotlines collide several times during the overarching narrative thematising the complications of self-aware artificial intelligence. Gameplay mainly consists of narratively meaningful decision-making challenges embedded in scripted events that restrict avatar action to various degrees in the other dimensions. As the player/avatar is repeatedly prompted to choose between options for how the plot should continue, they realise any one of many complex sequences of events as afforded by the vast network of choice trees in the game.

That said, game design can also afford another kind of narrativity-related agency, which emerges from interaction with the game as a ludic system. Indeed, game mechanics that govern the rules, goals, challenges, and other structures in games' design are not necessarily meant to be narrative in the same way as cut-scenes or scripted sequences are, but they still have the possibility to generate events with a narrative quality to them. As Salen and Zimmerman (2004: 384) point out, the events generated by the game as a ludic system are linked by a cause-and-effect relationship, and are therefore exhibiting a logical, context-dependent and therefore dynamic and non-repeatable sequence, which can be interpreted by the player as narrative. For example, spotting a rare and tough enemy when the avatar is low on health and supplies presents a unique prospect: does the player/avatar take the risk of facing the difficult enemy in pursuit of glory, and hopefully valuable loot, or do they retreat to attend to their health and restore their dwindling supplies? The analytical lens of dramatic agency aims to address whether, and if so, how, this narrativity is facilitated by design.[24]

Dramatic agency can be facilitated by what Chandler (2007) calls 'mythocentric narrative design', which, juxtaposed to 'logocentric narrative design' which is controlled and highly predetermined by the designer, is

> [w]ide-open and free-ranging and consists of arenas for player action that have been created by the developers. The player, as author of the core experience, gets to choose the goals and means of the game experience. Unlike logocentric design, the developers are *facilitators, not creators*, of the events that transpire.
>
> (Chandler 2007: 108, my emphasis)

Framing agency as dramatic therefore targets narrative quality that is emergent, 'facilitated' and not 'created' by design, thereby exhibiting a different degree of predetermination in the delivery of narratively relevant content when compared to the affordances discussed in the section above on narrative agency. Because they are so closely connected to the mechanics that govern ludic functions in the game, dramatic agency affordances create a possibility space for stories that are context-dependent, and therefore will not recur in the same way across different playthroughs, unless we are to re-enact each step taken by the player/avatar that generated the first iteration, and even then, depending on how sophisticated the audiovisual representation is in the game, we might end up with a different series of events. As such, the manifestation of dramatic agency is more connected to the avatar's ludic function than narrative agency is, but not exclusively so: ludic events, regardless of whether they align with the storyworld, can also be represented locally. For example, the ludic function of the avatar to traverse the level as designed can be represented as running, riding a horse, or driving a car.

Choosing 'dramatic' to capture this kind of agency is a nod to an existing tradition in game design to refer to the kind of agency facilitated by a game's rules and goals as 'dramatic'. Building on Aristotelian categories for the dramatic form, Mateas (2000, 2001) proposes to think of agency in interactive drama as an inherently dramatic experience afforded by a good balance in design. Similarly, Murray describes dramatic agency as 'the cueing of the interactor's intentions, expectations, and actions so that they mesh with the story events generated by the system' (Murray 2005: 85). Specifically, dramatic agency as conceptualised in this framework is concerned with better understanding how game design supports the iteration of 'the plans and gambits, the bluffs, the stratagems, the reversals of fortune . . . a climactic struggle that builds to a satisfying conclusion' (LeBlanc 2006: 439). As such, it can be used to interrogate how what Fullerton calls 'dramatic elements' 'engage the players emotionally by creating a dramatic context for the formal elements' (Fullerton 2014 [2004]: 41). For the purposes of analysing avatar-based videogames, dramatic agency can be used to ask how game design allows or constrains the emergence of a 'player story' (Rouse 2005) in moment-to-moment gameplay. What features of the ludic system facilitate the emergence of these stories? Are they coherent with the storyworld as represented via more predeterminedly narrative game design affordances, and/or the story 'written' by the player/avatar so far (i.e., not a result of cheating, modding, or glitches)?[25]

Given its close connection to the game as a ludic system, it is likely that we can observe at least some degree of dramatic agency being afforded in most gameplay scenarios in avatar-based games. There are, however, certain design features that increase the possibility space for dramatic agency to be realised. For example, the basic design formula of roguelike games is: randomly (or semi-randomly) generated levels, inventory and experience point management, and permadeath (meaning there is no saving the game, defeat results in having to restart from the beginning of the game). Any given gameplay sequence in *Spelunky* (Mossmouth, LLC 2008), *The Binding of Isaac* (McMillen 2011), or *Enter the Gungeon* (Dodge Roll 2017) is therefore likely to be unique: the player/avatar will traverse an environment that is arranged differently in every playthrough, facing challenges that appear at different times and varied locations, earning ever-changing rewards from successfully overcoming said challenges. Since avatar death is penalised with the loss of all progress, the player will likely have to replay the same levels multiple times before succeeding. In this way, roguelike games' narrative quality can be best described as, drawing on Chandler's (2007) terminology once more, less as 'authored', and as such, delivered via standard narrative elements like cut-scenes or scripted events, and more as 'facilitated' by other, less standardly narrative, game mechanics. As such, roguelike games generally afford a high degree of dramatic agency.

To sum up, the analytical dimension of narrative-dramatic agency in the heuristic framework is useful for asking questions about how game design's narrative quality enables or constrains avatar action. Narrative agency, on the one hand, is aimed at identifying what narratively charged elements there are in game design, how they afford and constrain avatar action, what formation their structural arrangement takes, and whether the player/avatar can meaningfully intervene in their structuration. How does the game use cut-scenes, scripted events, or non-player characters in order to deliver predeterminedly narrative gameplay moments? Are there forking paths in the story? Dramatic agency, on the other hand, can be used to better understand how elements of game design that are not typically (or at least not directly) supposed to be vehicles of narrative content still contribute to the emergence of 'player stories' (Rouse 2005). How do game mechanics, such as traversal of game spaces or resource management, facilitate the manifestation of events that can be linked together in a way that they can be interpreted by the player as stories? How do these chains of events relate to the globally represented storyworld?

At this point it needs pointing out that although dramatic agency does rely on agency affordances of the other dimensions described above, this does not mean that the possibility space for avatar action in those dimensions is fundamentally foregrounded by narrativity, or that there is a hierarchy of agency across dimensions. Although the heuristic framework separated different ways in which game design can shape the possibility space for player action, these distinctions were made for analytical purposes. In no way do I want to suggest that these dimensions are, in fact, working in isolation. On the contrary, this chapter has demonstrated that agency can be better understood as more than a one-dimensional phenomenon, and although it is important to acknowledge how dimensions support each other, it is equally as interesting to ask how they do not. These questions are what the following case studies will explore in more detail. The following chapters will turn to three examples to first, test the applicability of the heuristic framework, and second, to examine the relationship between game design and player agency in more detail. The remainder of this book will explore how agency manifest in these case studies through not only the games themselves, but also through the framings and paratexts that surround the games.

Notes

1 This is not to say there isn't plenty of research on these topics. See, e.g., Csikszentmihalyi 1975 on flow, Mäyrä and Ermi 2005 or Ryan 2015: 85–114 on typologies of immersion; Järvinen 2009 or Perron 2005 on classifying emotions elicited by game design; Perron 2018: 66–127 on fear specifically; Swink 2008 or Isbister 2016: 1–42 for designer perspectives on emotion and games; Grodal 2009: 158–181 on agency and emotions during gameplay; Gregersen and Grodal 2009: 66–69 or Keogh 2018 on agency and embodiment; or the essays on cognition, affect, and emotion and videogames in Perron and Schröter 2016.
2 Though we could argue that extensive conceptualisation is a kind of definition, albeit longer. In this vein, the conceptualisation of agency and the multidimensional heuristic framework proposed in this book is best described according to the philosophical tradition of 'explication', which fundamentally is inexact and therefore cannot be proven right or wrong (Carnap 1950: 3–4), deployed when 'one wants both to rely on an *old*, existing meaning and to attach a *new*, proposed meaning' (Belnap 1993: 116, orig. emphasis).
3 This being said, the notion of agency and videogames' spatiality have been linked before, albeit through rather narrow lenses. See, e.g., Taylor 2003 for a psychoanalytical approach; Morris 2002: 89 who argues that first person shooter games have more agency because of a sense of presence and involvement granted by the immediacy of the action genre and the unique FPS perspective; or, as already mentioned, Calleja 2011: 75 for an approach from the perspective of immersion and 'habitation'.
4 For more on how videogames cue players into making sense of multiple layers of representation, see Thon 2016b, 2017.
5 A third category they introduce is the game as a 'social experience', through which lens the character is a 'representation of the player', but this is not relevant here since my investigation is limited to singleplayer design.
6 Except for the map's edges of course, where the world beyond is indirectly represented as part of the skybox.

7 Videogames' tool to create the illusion that a virtual world is bigger than it actually is.
8 Aarseth (2008) talks about a similar disconnect between how big *World of Warcraft*'s space is supposed to feel like compared to how big it is. This will be revisited in the following section on temporal-ergodic agency.
9 Thon also talks about a third kind of perspective, which he calls 'ideological perspective', but this captures how game events are evaluated by the player, it is not relevant for the conceptualisation of agency presented here.
10 Interestingly, this no longer applies to the recent remake of the game (Capcom 2019), where a combination of chase cams and moveable cameras are used. The feature has been sorely missed by original fans of the game, and there is now a Fixed Camera Angle Mod for the game for those with a nostalgic flair.
11 See Copcic et al. (2013) on permadeath, Fassone (2017) on endings in videogames, and Herte (2020) for how various ways of ending narrative videogames correspond to broader, more conventional expectations of conclusion and closure.
12 Newman (2002) further developed the concept of ergodicity and argued that an entire videogame cannot be described as ergodic, but instead, there are 'ergodic elements' in a long sequence of segmented instances of gameplay. My analytical category of ergodic agency sheds light on this potential for variability.
13 Power wheel, command wheel, or weapon wheel are all terms used to refer to a wheel-like design in action and role-playing games, which facilitate quick access to the avatar's powers or weapon inventory. It not taking up a whole screen is particularly useful in combat and other time-critical scenarios.
14 See, e.g., Alvarez Igarzábal 2019: 147–148, Atkins 2007; Davidson 2008 on *Prince of Persia: Sands of Time*; Stamenković and Jaćević 2015 on *Braid*, Hanson 2018: 167–179 on *Quantum Break*.
15 For more on the paradox of simultaneous immediacy and atemporality in audiovisual media, see Doane 2002.
16 See Backe 2016 for a more detailed analysis of how *SUPERHOT* challenges the player in time.
17 For more on how strategy games emulate historic methods of research gathering and construction, see Grufstedt (2022).
18 While my focus is single-player games, the social and self-expressive function of avatars in massively multiplayer online games is a widely researched topic. See, e.g., Banks 2017; Bartle 1996; Burn and Schott 2004; Jenson et al. 2015; Taylor 2006: 93–124; Van Looy et al. 2014.
19 A similar observation is made by Thon (2016a: 112), pointing out the discrepancy between how many items an avatar carries versus how big their apparent carrying item (e.g., backpack) is.
20 Castronova also talks of scarcity of social roles, though this aspect is not relevant for my conceptualisation, as it relates more to how the player makes sense of their experience.
21 It is also important to keep in mind that cut-scenes might be favoured by developers as a means of cost-cutting. See Sheldon 2004: 183.
22 See, e.g., 'interactive structures' in Ryan 2015: 165–175; 'logocentric v. mythocentric narrative design' in Chandler 2007: 102–108; 'three act structure' in Skolnick 2015: 12–26, 'The Hero's Journey' adapted to videogames in Rollings and Adams 2003: 93–109, or Ip 2011b.
23 See, e.g., Aarseth 1994; Backe 2012; DeMarle 2006; Ip 2011a; Miller 2004: 124–125; Rouse 2005: 223–224; also 'multilinearity' in Nelson 1993; 'non-unilinearity' in Domsch 2013: 75–95.
24 The two kinds of narrative quality we can attribute to videogames is a well-established distinction amongst scholars and game designers alike. See, e.g.,

'embedded narrative' and 'emergent narrative' (Salen and Zimmerman 2004: 382–385), 'designer story' and 'player story' (Rouse 2005: 203–206), 'push and pull narrative' (Levine 2008: n.p.), or 'scripted narrative' and 'alterbiography' (Calleja 2011: 113–134). These distinctions can all be related to another, widely discussed binary framing of videogames as systems of progression v emergence. See, e.g., Adams and Dormans 2012: 43–59; Juul 2005; Baljko and Tenhaaf 2008; Soler-Adillon 2019.

25 See, e.g., Laukkanen 2005; Sotamaa 2003, 2010 on modding; Consalvo 2007 or de Paoli and Kerr 2010 on cheating; and the chapters in Mortensen et al. 2015 on transgressive and subversive play.

References

Aarseth, E. J. (1994). Nonlinearity and Literary Theory. In G. Landow, ed. *Hyper/Text/Theory*. Baltimore, MD: Johns Hopkins University Press, pp. 51–86.

Aarseth, E. J. (1997). *Cybertext: Perspectives on Ergodic Literature*. Baltimore, MD: Johns Hopkins University Press.

Aarseth, E. J. (1999). Aporia and Epiphany in *Doom* and *The Speaking Clock*. In M.-L. Ryan, ed. *Cyberspace Textuality: Computer Technology and Literary Theory*. Bloomington, IN: Indiana University Press, pp. 31–41.

Aarseth, E. J. (2000). Allegories of Space: The Question of Spatiality in Computer Games. In M. Eskelinen and R. Koskimaa, eds. *Cybertext Yearbook 2000*. Jyväskylä: University of Jyväskylä, pp. 152–171.

Aarseth, E. J. (2008). A Hollow World: *World of Warcraft* as Spatial Practice. In H. G. Corneliussen and J. W. Rettberg, eds. *Digital Culture, Play, and Identity: A World of Warcraft Reader*. Cambridge, MA: MIT Press, pp. 111–122.

Aarseth, E. J. (2012). A Narrative Theory of Games. *FDG'12: Proceedings of the International Conference on the Foundations of Digital Games*. New York: Association for Computing Machinery, pp. 129–133.

Aarseth, E. J.; Smedstad, S. M.; Sunnanå, L. (2003). A Multidimensional Typology of Games. *DiGRA'03—Proceedings of the 2003 DiGRA International Conference: Level Up*. Vol. 2, pp. 48–53. Available at: www.digra.org/digital-library/publications/a-multidimensional-typology-of-games/

Adams, E. (2010 [2006]). *Fundamentals of Game Design*. 2nd ed. San Francisco, CA: New Riders.

Adams, E. W.; Dormans, J. (2012). *Game Mechanics: Advanced Game Design*. Berkeley, CA: New Riders Games.

Alvarez Igarzábal, F. (2019). *Time and Space in Video Games: A Cognitive-Formalist Approach*. Bielefeld: Transcript verlag.

Amccus. (1996). *Harvest Moon* [SNES]. Nintendo.

Ang, C. S. (2006). Rules, Gameplay, and Narratives in Video Games. *Simulation & Gaming* 37 (3): 306–325. https://doi.org/10.1177/1046878105285604

Arsenault, D.; Côté, P.-M.; Larochelle, A. (2015). The Game FAVR: A Framework for the Analysis of Visual Representation in Video Games. *Loading . . . The Journal of the Canadian Game Studies Association* 9 (14): 88–123.

Arsenault, D.; Perron, B. (2009). In the Frame of the Magic Cycle: The Circle(s) of Gameplay. In B. Perron and M. J. P. Wolf, eds. *The Video Game Theory Reader 2*. London: Routledge, pp. 109–131.

Atkins, B. (2003). *More Than a Game: The Computer Game as Fictional Form*. Manchester: Manchester University Press.

Atkins, B. (2007). Killing Time: Time Past, Time Present and Time Future in *Prince of Persia: The Sands of Time*. In T. Krzywinska and B. Atkins, eds. *Videogame, Player, Text*. Manchester: Manchester University Press, pp. 237–253.

Backe, H.-J. (2012). Narrative Rules? Story Logic and the Structures of Games. *Literary and Linguistic Computing* 27 (3): 243–260. https://doi.org/10.1093/llc/fqs035

Backe, H.-J. (2016). Past Time. Questionable Epistemologies of Time and Identity in *SUPERHOT* and *Metal Gear Acid 2*. *The Philosophy of Computer Games Conference*, University of Malta, 1–4 November. Available at: https://pure.itu.dk/portal/files/83324836/backe_past_time.pdf

Baljko, M.; Tenhaaf, N. (2008). The Aesthetics of Emergence. *ACM Transactions on Computer-Human Interaction* 15 (3): 1–27.

Banks, J. (2017). Multimodal, Multiplex, Multispatial: A Network Model of the Self. *New Media & Society* 19 (3): 419–438. https://doi.org/10.1177/1461444815606616

Bartle, R. (1996). Hearts, Clubs, Diamonds, Spades: Players Who suit MUDs. *MUD*, 28 August. Available at: http://mud.co.uk/richard/hcds.htm

Bartle, R. (2004). *Designing Virtual Worlds*. Indianapolis, IN: New Riders.

Batens, D. (2013). The Role of Logic in Philosophy of Science. In M. Curd and S. Psillos, eds. *The Routledge Companion to Philosophy of Science*. New York: Routledge.

Baumgartner, R. (2015). "Main Objective: Don't Starve": Representations of Scarcity in Virtual Worlds. In F. Felcht and K. Ritson, eds. The Imagination of Limits: Exploring Scarcity and Abundance. *RCC Perspectives* 2: 45–52. doi.org/10.5282/rcc/7141

Belnap, N. (1993). On Rigorous Definitions. *Philosophical Studies: An International Journal for Philosophy in the Analytic Tradition* 72 (2/3): 115–146.

Bethesda Game Studios. (2011). *The Elder Scrolls V: Skyrim* [PC]. Bethesda Softworks.

Bethesda Game Studios. (2015). *Fallout 4* [PC]. Bethesda Softworks.

Bienia, R. P. (2016). *Role Playing Materials*. Braunschweig: Zauberfeder.

Bithell, M. (2012). *Thomas Was Alone* [PC]. Mike Bithell.

Björk, S.; Holopainen, J. (2005). Games and Design Patterns. In K. Salen and E. Zimmerman, eds. *The Game Design Reader: A Rules of Play Anthology*. Cambridge, MA: MIT Press, pp. 410–437.

Björk, S.; Zagal, J. P. (2018). Game Design and Role-Playing Games. In S. Deterding and J. Zagal, eds. *Role-Playing Game Studies: Transmedia Foundations*. New York: Routledge, pp. 323–336.

Bleszinski, C. (2000). The Art and Science of Level Design. *Game Developers Conference 2000 Proceedings*. Available at: www.gamedevs.org/uploads/the-art-science-of-level-design.doc

Blizzard Entertainment. (2012). *Diablo III* [PC]. Blizzard Entertainment.

Boonen, C. S.; Mieritz, D. (2018). Paralysing Fear: Player Agency Parameters in Horror Games. *DiGRA Nordic'18—Proceedings of 2018 International DiGRA Nordic Conference*. Available at: www.digra.org/digital-library/publications/paralysing-fear-player-agency-parameters-in-horror-games/

Bullfrog Productions. (1997). *Theme Hospital* [PC]. Electronic Arts.

Burn, A. (2006). Playing Roles. In D. Carr, D. Buckingham, A. Burn, and G. Schott, eds. *Computer Games: Text, Narrative and Play*. Cambridge: Polity Press, pp. 72–87.

Burn, A.; Schott, G. (2004). Heavy Hero or Digital Dummy? Multimodal Player-Avatar Relations in *Final Fantasy 7*. *Visual Communication* 3 (2): 213–233. https://doi.org/10.1177/1470357043041

Calleja, G. (2011). *In-Game: From Immersion to Incorporation*. Cambridge, MA: MIT Press.

Capcom. (1998). *Resident Evil 2* [PC]. Capcom.

Capcom. (2019). *Resident Evil 2* [PlayStation 4] Capcom.

Carnap, R. (1950). *Logical Foundations of Probability*. Chicago, IL: University of Chicago Press.

Carr, D.; Buckingham, D.; Burn, A.; Schott, G. (eds.). (2006). *Computer Games: Text, Narrative, Play*. Cambridge: Polity Press.

Carr, D.; Schott, G.; Buckingham, D. (2003). Textuality in Video Games. *DiGRA'03—Proceedings of the 2003 DiGRA International Conference: Level Up*, pp. 144–155. Available at: www.digra.org/digital-library/publications/textuality-in-video-games/

Castronova, E. (2006). Virtual Worlds: A First-Hand Account of Market and Society on the Cyberian Frontier. In K. Salen and E. Zimmerman, E., eds. *The Game Design Reader: A Rules of Play Anthology*. Cambridge, MA: MIT Press, pp. 814–863.

Chandler, R. (2007). *Game Writing Dandbook*. Boston, MA: Charles River Media.

Cheng, P. (2007). Waiting for Something to Happen: Narratives, Interactivity, and Agency and the Video Game Cut-Scene. *DiGRA'07—Proceedings of the 2007 DiGRA International Conference: Situated Play*. University of Tokyo. Available at: www.digra.org/digital-library/publications/waiting-for-something-to-happen-narratives-interactivity-and-agency-and-the-video-game-cut-scene/

Chris Sawyer Productions. (1999). *Roller Coaster Tycoon* [PC]. Hasbro Interactive.

ConcernedApe. (2016). *Stardew Valley* [PC]. ConcernedApe.

Consalvo, M. (2007). *Cheating: Gaining Advantage in Videogames*. Cambridge, MA: MIT Press.

Copcic, A.; McKenzie, S.; Hobbs, M. (2013). Permadeath: A Review of Literature. *'13 IEEE—International Games Innovation Conference (IGIC)*, Vancouver, BC, pp. 40–47.

Costikyan, G. (2005 [1999]). I Have No Words & I Must Design. In K. Salen and E. Zimmerman, eds. *The Game Design Reader: A Rules of Play Anthology*. Cambridge, MA: MIT Press, pp. 192–210.

Creswell, J. W. (1997). *Qualitative Inquiry and Research Design: Choosing among Five Approaches*. Thousand Oaks, CA: SAGE.

Csikszentmihalyi, M. (1975). *Beyond Boredom and Anxiety: The Experience of Play in Work and Games*. Washington, DC: Jossey-Bass Publishers.

Dahlskog, S.; Björk, S.; Togelius, J. (2015). Patterns, Dungeons and Generators. *FDG'15—Proceedings of the 10th International Conference on the Foundations of Digital Games*, 22–25 June. Available at: www.fdg2015.org/papers/fdg2015_paper_30.pdf

Davidson, D. (2008). Well Played: Interpreting *Prince of Persia: The Sands of Time*. *Games and Culture* 3 (3–4): 356–386. https://doi.org/10.1177/1555412008317307

Debus, M. S. (2016). Video Game Navigation: A Classification System for Navigational Acts. *Replay: The Polish Journal of Game Studies* 3 (1): 29–46. https://doi.org/10.18778/2391-8551.03.02

DeMarle, M. (2006). Nonlinear Game Narrative. In C. Bateman, ed. *Game Writing: Narrative Skills for Videogames*. Boston, MA: Charles River Media, pp. 71–84.

De Paoli, S.; Kerr, A. (2010). The Assemblage of Cheating: How to Study Cheating as Imbroglio in MMORPGs. *The Fibreculture Journal* 16. Available at: http://sixteen.fibreculturejournal.org/the-assemblage-of-cheating-how-to-study-cheating-as-imbroglio-in-mmorpgs/

Doane, M. A. (2002). *The Emergence of Cinematic Time: Modernity, Contingency, the Archive*. Cambridge, MA: Harvard University Press.

Dodge Roll. (2017). *Enter the Gungeon* [PC]. Devolver Digital.

Domsch, S. (2013). *Storyplaying: Agency and Narrative in Video Games*. Berlin: De Gruyter.

Elverdam, C.; Aarseth, E. (2007). Game Classification and Game Design: Construction Through Critical Analysis. *Games and Culture* 2 (1): 3–22. https://doi.org/10.1177/1555412006286892

Endnight Games. (2014). *The Forest* [PC]. Endnight Games.

Ensemble Studios. (1997). *Age of Empires* [PC]. Microsoft.

Eskelinen, M. (2001a). The Gaming Situation. *Game Studies* 1 (1). Available at: www.gamestudies.org/0101/eskelinen/

Eskelinen, M. (2001b). Towards Computer Game Studies. *Digital Creativity* 12 (3): 175–183. https://doi.org/10.1076/digc.12.3.175.3232

Eskelinen, M. (2012). *Cybertext Poetics: The Critical Landscape of New Media Literary Theory*. London: Bloomsbury.

Falstein, N. (2005). Understanding Fun: The theory of Natural Funativity. In S. Rabin, ed. *Introduction to Game Development*. Boston, MA: Charles River Media.

Fassone, R. (2017). *Every Game Is an Island: Endings and Extremities in Video Games*. New York: Bloomsbury Academic.

Fordyce R. (2018). Dwarf Fortress: Laboratory and Homestead. *Games and Culture* 13 (1): 3–19. https://doi.org/10.1177/1555412015603192

Frasca, G. (2003a). Ludologists Love Stories, Too: Notes From a Debate That Never Took Place. *DiGRA'03—Proceedings of the 2003 DiGRA International Conference: Level Up*. Available at: www.digra.org/digital-library/publications/ludologists-love-stories-too-notes-from-a-debate-that-never-took-place/

Frasca, G. (2003b). Simulation versus Narrative: Introduction to Ludology. In M. J. P. Wolf and B. Perron, eds. *The Video Game Theory Reader*. New York and London: Routledge, pp. 221–235.

Fullerton, T. (2014 [2004]). *Game Design Workshop: A Playcentric Approach to Creating Innovative Games*. 3rd ed. Boca Raton, FL: CRC Press.

Furze, R. (2013). Challenge. In M. J. P. Wolf and B. Perron, eds. *The Routledge Companion to Video Games*. Abingdon: Routledge, pp. 143–151.

Gazzard, A. (2009). Teleporters, Tunnels & Time: Understanding Warp Devices in Videogames. *DiGRA'09—Proceedings of DiGRA 2009 International Conference: Breaking New Ground: Innovation in Games, Play, Practice and Theory*. Available at: www.digra.org/digital-library/publications/teleporters-tunnels-time-understanding-warp-devices-in-videogames/

Glassner, A. (2004). *Interactive Storytelling: Techniques for 21st Century Fiction*. Natick, MA: A.K. Peters.

Gregersen, A.; Grodal, T. (2009). Embodiment and Interface. In B. Perron and M. J. P. Wolf, eds. *The Video Game Theory Reader 2*. New York: Routledge, pp. 65–84.

Grodal, T. (2003). Stories for Eye, Ear, and Muscles. In M. J. P. Wolf and B. Perron, eds. *The Video Game Theory Reader*. New York: Routledge, pp. 129–156.

Grodal, T. (2009). *Embodied Visions: Evolution, Emotion, Culture, and Film.* New York: Oxford University Press.
Grufstedt, Y. (2022). *Shaping the Past: Counterfactual History and Game Design Practice in Digital Strategy Games.* Berlin: De Gruyter.
Hanson, C. (2018). *Game Time: Understanding Temporality in Video Games.* Bloomington, IN: Indiana University Press.
Harrell, D. F.; Zhu, J. (2008). Agency Play: Dimensions of Agency for Interactive Narrative Design. *Proceedings of the AAAI 2008 Spring Symposium on Interactive Narrative Technologies II,* Stanford, CA, pp. 156–162.
Herte, M. (2020). *Forms and Functions of Endings in Narrative Digital Games.* New York: Routledge.
Hitchens, M.; Drachen, A. (2008). The Many Faces of Role-Playing Games. *International Journal of Role-Playing* 1 (1): 3–21.
Hunicke, R.; Chapman, V. (2004). AI for Dynamic Difficulty Adjustment in Games. *Challenges in Game Artificial Intelligence AAAI Workshop.* Available at: http://users.cs.northwestern.edu/~hunicke/pubs/Hamlet.pdf
Ip, B. (2011a). Narrative Structures in Computer and Video Games: Part 1: Context, Definitions, and Initial Findings. *Games and Culture* 6 (2): 103–134. https://doi.org/10.1177/1555412010364982
Ip, B. (2011b). Narrative Structures in Computer and Video Games: Part 2: Emotions, Structures, and Archetypes. *Games and Culture* 6 (3): 203–244. https://doi.org/10.1177/1555412010364984
Isbister, K. (2016). *How Games Move Us. Emotion by Design.* Cambridge, MA: MIT Press.
Jannidis, F. (2003). Narratology and Narrative. In T. Kindt and H.-H. Müller, eds. *What is Narratology? Questions and Answers Regarding the Status of Theory.* Berlin: De Gruyter, pp. 35–54.
Järvinen, A. (2009). Understanding Video Games as Emotional Experiences. In B. Perron and M. J. P. Wolf, eds. *The Video Game Theory Reader 2.* New York: Routledge, pp. 85–108.
Jenkins, H. (2006). Game Design as Narrative Architecture. In K. Salen and E. Zimmerman, eds. *The Game Design Reader: A Rules of Play Anthology.* Cambridge, MA: MIT Press, pp. 670–689.
Jenson, J.; Taylor, N.; de Castell, S.; Dilouya, B. (2015). Playing with Our Selves: Multiplicity and Identity in Online Gaming. *Feminist Media Studies* 15 (5): 860–879. https://doi.org/10.1080/14680777.2015.1006652
Jørgensen, K. (2013). *Gameworld Interfaces.* Cambridge, MA: MIT Press.
Juul, J. (2005). *Half-Real: Video Games between Real Rules and Fictional Worlds.* Cambridge, MA: MIT Press.
Karhulahti, V.-M. (2013). A Kinesthetic Theory of Videogames: Time-Critical Challenge and Aporetic Rhematic. *Game Studies* 13 (1). Available at: http://gamestudies.org/1301/articles/karhulahti_kinesthetic_theory_of_the_videogame
Keogh, B. (2018). *A Play of Bodies: How We Perceive Videogames.* Boston, MA: MIT Press.
King, G.; Krzywinska, T. (2003). Gamescapes: Exploration and Virtual Presence in Game-worlds. *DiGRA'03—Proceedings of the 2003 DiGRA International Conference: Level Up.* Available at: www.digra.org/digital-library/publications/gamescapes-exploration-and-virtual-presence-in-game-worlds/
King, G.; Krzywinska, T. (2006). *Tomb Raiders and Space Invaders. Videogame Forms and Contexts.* London: I.B. Tauris & Co Ltd.

Klastrup, L. (2003). A Poetics of Virtual Worlds. *Melbourne DAC 2008–5th International Digital Arts & Culture Conference, RMIT University, School of Applied Communication*, 19–23 May, Melbourne, pp. 100–109. Available at: http://citeseerx.ist.psu.edu/viewdoc/download?doi=10.1.1.693.3554&rep=rep1&type=pdf

Klastrup, L. (2009). The Worldness of *EverQuest*: Exploring a 21st Century Fiction. *Game Studies* 9 (1). Available at: http://gamestudies.org/0901/articles/klastrup

Klei Entertainment. (2013). *Don't Starve* [PC]. 505 Games.

Klevjer, R. (2002). In Defence of Cut-Scenes. In *Proceedings of Computer Games and Digital Cultures Conference*. Tampere: Tampere University Press. Available at: http://citeseerx.ist.psu.edu/viewdoc/download?doi=10.1.1.190.1300&rep=rep1&type=pdf

Klevjer, R. (2006). *What Is the Avatar? Fiction and Embodiment in Avatar-Based Singleplayer Computer Games*. PhD Thesis, University of Bergen.

Klevjer, R. (2013). Cut-Scenes. In M. J. P. Wolf and B Perron, eds. *The Routledge Companion to Video Game Studies*. New York: Routledge, pp. 301–309.

Klevjer, R. (2019). Virtuality and Depiction in Video Game Representation. *Games and Culture* 14 (7–8): 724–741. https://doi.org/10.1177/1555412017727688

Knowles, I.; Castronova, E. (2018). Economics and Role-Playing Games. In S. Deterding and J. Zagal, eds. *Role-Playing Game Studies: Transmedia Foundations*. New York: Routledge, pp. 300–313.

Knutson, M. (2018). Backtrack, Pause, Rewind, Reset: Queering Chrononormativity in Gaming. *Game Studies* 18 (3). Available at: http://gamestudies.org/1803/articles/knutson

Koster, R. (2004). *Theory of Fun for Game Design*. Phoenix: Paraglyph Press.

Kremers, R. (2009). *Level Design: Concept, Theory, & Practice*. Natick, MA: AK Peters, Ltd.

Krzywinska, T. (2007). Being a Determined Agent in *World of Warcraft*. In T. Krzywinska and B. Atkins, eds. *Videogame, Player, Text*. Manchester: Manchester University Press, pp 101–119.

Laukkanen, T. (2005). *Modding Scenes. Introduction to User-Created Content in Computer Gaming*. University of Tampere Hypermedia Laboratory Net Series 9. Available at: https://trepo.tuni.fi/bitstream/handle/10024/65431/951-44-6448-6.pdf?sequence=1&isAllowed=y

LeBlanc, M. (2006). Tools for Creating Dramatic Game Dynamics. In K. Salen and E. Zimmerman, eds. *The Game Design Reader: A Rules of Play Anthology*. Cambridge, MA: MIT Press, pp. 438–459.

Levine, K. (2008). Storytelling in BIOSHOCK: Empowering Players to Care about Your Stupid Story. *GDC Vault*. Available at: www.gdcvault.com/play/301/Storytelling-in-BIOSHOCK-Empowering-Players

Lindley, C. A. (2005). The Semiotics of Time Structure in Ludic Space As a Foundation for Analysis and Design. *Game Studies* 5 (1). Available at: www.gamestudies.org/0501/lindley/

MacCallum-Stewart, E.; Stenros, J.; Björk, S. (2018). The Impact of Role-Playing Games on Culture. In S. Deterding and J. Zagal, eds. *Role-Playing Game Studies: Transmedia Foundations*. New York: Routledge, pp. 172–187.

Mateas, M. (2000). A Neo-Aristotelian Theory of Interactive Drama. *AAAI Spring Symposium on AI and Interactive Entertainment*. Available at: https://users.soe.ucsc.edu/~michaelm/publications/mateas-aaai-symp-aiie-2000.pdf

Mateas, M. (2001). A Preliminary Poetics for Interactive Drama and Games. *Digital Creativity* 12 (3): 140–152.

Maxis. (2000). *The Sims* [PC]. Electronic Arts.

Mäyrä, F.; Ermi, L. (2005). Fundamental Components of Gameplay Experience: Analysing Immersion. *DiGRA'05—Proceedings of the 2005 DiGRA International Conference: Changing Views: World in Play*. Available at: www.digra.org/digital-library/publications/fundamental-components-of-the-gameplay-experience-analysing-immersion/

McMillen, E. (2011). *The Binding of Isaac* [PC]. Edmund McMillan.

Miller, C. (2004). *Digital Storytelling: A Creator's Guide to Interactive Entertainment*. Burlington, MA: Focal Press.

Mochocki, M. (2020). Story Beats as Micronarrative Units for Ludonarrative Analysis. *Centre of Excellence in Game Culture Studies Blog*, 27 April. Available at: https://coe-gamecult.org/2020/04/27/story-beats-as-micronarrative-units-for-ludonarrative-analysis/

Mojang Studios. (2009). *Minecraft* [PC]. Mojang Studios.

Morris, S. (2002). First-Person Shooters: A Game Apparatus. In G. King and T. Krzywinska, eds. *Screenplay: Cinema/Videogames/Interfaces*. London: Wallflower Press, pp. 81–97.

Mortensen, T. E.; Linderoth, J.; Brown, A. M. L. (2015). *The Dark Side of Game Play: Controversial Issues in Playful Environments*. New York: Routledge.

Mossmouth, LLC. (2008). *Spelunky* [PC]. Mossmouth, LLC.

Murray, J. (1997). *Hamlet on the Holodeck*. Cambridge, MA: MIT Press.

Murray, J. H. (2005). Did It Make You Cry? Creating Dramatic Agency in Immersive Environments. *ICVS 2005: Virtual Storytelling: Using Virtual Reality Technologies for Storytelling*. Berlin: Springer, pp. 83–94.

Myers, D. (2003). The Attack of Backstories (and Why They Won't Win). *DiGRA'03—Proceedings of the 2003 DiGRA International Conference: Level Up*. Vol. 2. Available at: www.digra.org/digital-library/publications/the-attack-of-the-backstories-and-why-they-wont-win/

Neitzel, B. (2014). Narrativity of Computer Games. In P. Hühn et al., eds. *The Living Handbook of Narratology*. Hamburg: Hamburg University Press. Available at: www.lhn.uni-hamburg.de/node/127.html

Nelson, T. H. (1993). *Literary Machines*. Sausolito, CA: Mindful Press.

NetherRealm Studios. (2015). *Mortal Kombat X* [PlayStation 4]. Warner Bros. Interactive Entertainment.

Newman, J. (2002). The Myth of the Ergodic Videogame: Some Thoughts on Player-Character Relationships in Videogames. *Game Studies* 1 (2). Available at: www.gamestudies.org/0102/newman/

Nintendo EAD. (2001). *Animal Crossing* [Nintendo 64]. Nintendo.

Nitsche, M. (2008). *Video Game Spaces: Image, Play, and Structure in 3D Worlds*. Cambridge, MA: MIT Press.

Number One. (2008). *Braid* [PC]. Number One.

Pearce, C. (2004). Towards a Game Theory of Game. In N. Wardrip-Fruin and P. Harrigan, eds. *First Person: New Media as Story, Performance, and Game*. Cambridge, MA: MIT Press. pp. 143–153.

Pearce, C. (2005). Theory Wars: An Argument Against the So-Called Ludology/Narratology Debate. *DiGRA'05—Proceedings of the 2005 DiGRA International*

Conference: Changing Views: Worlds in Play. Available at: www.digra.org/digital-library/publications/theory-wars-an-argument-against-arguments-in-the-so-called-ludologynarratology-debate/

Perron, B. (2005). A Cognitive Psychological Approach to Gameplay Emotions. *DiGRA'05—Proceedings of the 2005 DiGRA International Conference: Changing Views: Worlds in Play*. Available at: www.digra.org/digital-library/publications/a-cognitive-psychological-approach-to-gameplay-emotions/

Perron, B. (2018). *The World of Scary Video Games: A Study in Videoludic Horror*. New York: Bloomsbury.

Perron, B.; Schröter, F. (eds.). (2016). *Video Games and the Mind: Essays on Cognition, Affect and Emotion*. Jefferson, NC: MacFarland & Co.

Peterson, J. (2012). *Playing at the World: A History of Simulating Wars, People and Fantastic Adventures, from Chess to Role-Playing Games*. San Diego, CA: Unreason Press.

Pias, C. (2004). Action, Adventure, Desire. In H. Hagebölling, ed. *Interactive Dramaturgies: New Approaches in Multimedia Content and Design*. Berlin: Springer, pp. 133–147.

Picard, M. (2013). Levels. In M. J. P. Wolf and B. Perron, eds. *The Routledge Companion to Video Games*. Abingdon: Routledge, pp. 99–106.

Quantic Dream. (2018). *Detroit: Become Human* [PlayStation 4]. Sony Interactive Entertainment.

Remedy Entertainment. (2001). *Max Payne* [PC]. Gathering of Developers.

Remedy Entertainment. (2016). *Quantum Break* [PC]. Microsoft Studios.

Rollings, A.; Adams, E. (2003). *Andrew Rollings and Ernest Adams on Game Design*. Indianapolis, IN: New Riders

Rouse III, R. (2005). *Game Design: Theory & Practice*. 2nd ed. Plano, TX: Wordware.

Ryan, M.-L. (2004). *Narrative Across Media*. Lincoln, NE: University of Nebraska Press.

Ryan, M.-L. (2005). On the Theoretical Foundations of Transmedial Narratology. In J. C. Meister, T. Kindt, and W. Schernus, eds. *Narratology Beyond Literary Criticism. Mediality, Disciplinarity*. Berlin: de Gruyter, pp. 1–23.

Ryan, M.-L. (2006). *Avatars of Story*. Minneapolis, MI: University of Minnesota Press.

Ryan, M.-L. (2015). *Narrative as Virtual Reality 2*. Baltimore, MD: Johns Hopkins University Press.

Salen, K.; Zimmerman, E. (2004). *Rules of Play: Game Design Fundamentals*. Cambridge, MA: MIT Press.

Schell, J. (2015 [2008]). *The Art of Game Design: A Book of Lenses*. Burlington, MA: Morgan Kaufmann.

Schmalzer, M. (2020). Play While Paused: Time and Space in Videogame Pause Menus. *Journal of Games Criticism* 4 (1). Available at: http://gamescriticism.org/articles/schmalzer-4-1

Schöter, F.; Thon, J.-N. (2014). Video Game Characters: Theory and Analysis. *Diegesis* 3 (1): 40–77.

Schott, G. (2006). Agency in and Around Play. In D. Carr et al., eds. *Computer Games: Text, Narrative and Play*. Cambridge: Polity Press, pp. 133–148.

Sharp, J. (2013). Perspective. In M. J. P. Wolf and B. Perron, eds. *The Routledge Companion to Video Games*. Abingdon: Routledge, pp. 99–106.

Sheldon, L. (2004). *Character Development and Storytelling*. Boston, MA: Thomson Course Technology.
Sicart, M. (2008). Defining Game Mechanics. *Game Studies* 8 (2). Available at: http://gamestudies.org/0802/articles/sicart
Sicart, M. (2011). Against Procedurality. *Game Studies* 11 (3). Available at: http://gamestudies.org/1103/articles/sicart_ap/
Simons, J. (2007). Narrative, Games, and Theory. *Game Studies* 7 (1). http://gamestudies.org/07010701/articles/simons
Skolnick, E. (2015). *Video Game Storytelling: What Every Developer Needs to Know about Narrative Techniques*. New York: Watson-Guptill.
Soler-Adillon, J. (2019). The Open, the Closed and the Emergent: Theorizing Emergence for Videogame Studies. *Game Studies* 19 (2). Available at: http://gamestudies.org/1902/articles/soleradillon
Sotamaa, O. (2003). *Computer Game Modding, Intermediality and Participatory Culture*. Unpublished manuscript.
Sotamaa, O. (2010). When the Game Is Not Enough: Motivations and Practices among Computer Game Modding Culture. *Games and Culture* 5 (3): 239–255. https://doi.org/10.1177/1555412009359765
Stamenković, D.; Jaćević, M. (2015). Time, Space, and Motion in *Braid*: A Cognitive Semantic Approach to a Video Game. *Games and Culture* 10 (2): 178–203. https://doi.org/10.1177/1555412014557640
SUPERHOT Team. (2016). *SUPERHOT* [PC]. Superhot Team.
Swink, S. (2008). *Game Feel: A Game Designer's Guide to Virtual Sensation*. Burlington, MA: Morgan Kaufman.
Taylor, L. N. (2003). When Seams Fall Apart. Video Game Space and the Player. *Game Studies* 3 (2). Available at: www.gamestudies.org/0302/taylor/
Taylor, T. L. (2006). *Play between Worlds: Exploring Online Game Culture*. Cambridge, MA: MIT Press.
TheyCallMeConor. (2017). *Across the Map #71 Tom Clancy's Ghost Recon Wildlands Walk Across the Map TimeLapse Video*. Available at: www.youtube.com/watch?v=BLrpwl2_Ukw
Thon, J.-N. (2009). Perspective in Contemporary Computer Games. In P. Hühn et al., eds. *Point of View, Perspective, and Focalization: Modeling Mediation in Narrative*. Berlin: De Gruyter, pp. 279–300.
Thon, J.-N. (2016a). *Transmedial Narratology and Contemporary Media Culture*. Lincoln, NE: University of Nebraska Press.
Thon, J.-N. (2016b). Narrative Comprehension and Video Game Storyworlds. In B. Perron and F. Schröter, eds. *Video Games and the Mind: Essays on Cognition, Affect and Emotion*. Jefferson: McFarland, pp. 15–31.
Thon, J.-N. (2017). Transmedial Narratology Revisited: On the Intersubjective Construction of Storyworlds and the Problem of Representational Correspondence in Films, Comics, and Video Games. *Narrative* 25 (3): 286–320.
Tychsen, A.; Hitchens, M. (2009). Game Time: Modeling and Analyzing Time in Multiplayer and Massively Multiplayer Games. *Games and Culture* 4 (2): 170–201. https://doi.org/10.1177/1555412008325479
Ubisoft Montreal. (2003). *Prince of Persia: The Sands of Time*. [PlayStation 2] Ubisoft.
Ubisoft Montreal. (2009). *Assassin's Creed II* [Xbox 360]. Ubisoft.
Ubisoft Paris. (2017). *Tom Clancy's Ghost Recon Wildlands* [PlayStation 4]. Ubisoft.

Van Looy, J.; Courtois, C.; De Vocht, M. (2014). Self-Discrepancy and MMORPGs: Testing the Moderating Effects of Avatar Identification and Pathological Gaming. In T. Quandt and S. Kröger, eds. *Multiplayer: The Social Aspects of Digital Gaming*. New York: Routledge, pp. 234–242.

Vella, D. (2019). Dwelling in Digital Game Worlds. *DiGRA'19—Abstract Proceedings of the 2019 DiGRA International Conference: Game, Play and the Emerging Ludo-Mix*. Available at: www.digra.org/digital-library/publications/dwelling-in-digital-game-worlds/

Vella, D.; Bonello Rutter Giappone, K. (2018). The City in Singleplayer Fantasy Roleplaying Games. *DiGRA'18—Proceedings of the 2018 DiGRA International Conference: The Game is the Message*. Available at: www.digra.org/digital-library/publications/the-city-in-singleplayer-fantasy-role-playing-games/

Wardrip-Fruin, N.; Mateas, M.; Dow, S.; Sali, S. (2009). Agency Reconsidered. *DiGRA'09—Proceedings of the 2009 DiGRA International Conference: Breaking New Ground: Innovation in Games, Play, Practice and Theory*. Available at: www.digra.org/digital-library/publications/agency-reconsidered/

Willumsen, E. C. (2018). Is My Avatar MY Avatar? Character Autonomy and Automated Avatar Actions in Digital Games. *Proceedings of DiGRA'18—Proceedings of the 2018 DiGRA International Conference: The Game Is the Message*. Available at: www.digra.org/digital-library/publications/is-my-avatar-my-avatar-character-autonomy-and-automated-avatar-actions-in-digital-games/

Wolf, M. J. P. (2001). Space in the Video Game. In M. J. P. Wolf, ed. *The Medium of the Video Game*. Austin, TX: University of Texas Press, pp. 51–77.

Wolf, M. J. P. (2012). *Building Imaginary Worlds: The Theory and History of Subcreation*. New York: Routledge.

ZA/UM. (2019). *Disco Elysium* [PC]. ZA/UM.

Zagal, J. P.; Altizer, R. (2014). Examining 'RPG elements': Systems of Character Progression. *FDG'14—Proceedings of the 9th International Conference on the Foundations of Digital Games*. Available at: https://my.eng.utah.edu/~zagal/Papers/Zagal_Altizer_RPG_Elements_Progression.pdf

Zagal, J. P.; Mateas, M. (2010). Time in Video Games: A Survey and Analysis. *Simulation & Gaming* 41 (6): 844–868. https://doi.org/10.1177/1046878110375594

3 An 'Active Cinematic Experience'
Naughty Dog's *Uncharted* Series

Uncharted is Sony Interactive Entertainment's PlayStation-exclusive tent pole franchise, with sales over 41 million units (Batchelor 2017), and it follows a tradition of highly linear games that restrict player action in multiple dimensions by streamlining progress. The series centres around treasure-hunting protagonist Nathan Drake and his gallery of friends and foes, has realistic audiovisual style and adheres to pulp action-adventure genre conventions with an Indiana Jonesian flare of humour. Its core mechanics are shooting and platforming. While Naughty Dog has gone through several iterations as a studio throughout its decades-long history, it retained a relatively consistent style of design. Even *Uncharted*, their longest-standing franchise, managed to keep its core brand identity of offering an 'active cinematic experience' (BluRay Trailers 2009: n.p.), despite drastic changes in leadership, which impacted design. When talking about videogames, 'cinematic' typically has two connotations. First, videogames tend to make use of 'cinematic devices, tropes and associations' King and Krzywinska (2002: 2). Indeed, a cinematic, or filmic, quality has connotations regarding audiovisual representation both in terms of form and content. Devices in game design such as 'dynamic lighting' (El-Nasr et al. 2007), weather simulation (Barton 2008), 'scripted staging' (Girina 2013), framing and composition (Chang and Hsieh 2018), as well as the borrowing of genre tropes such as horror, action, or adventure, are just some of the many ways game design re-appropriates other audiovisual media in general, and film in particular. Bolter and Grusin (2000: 19) call this 'remediation', which is the idea that a medium 'refashions its predecessors and other contemporary media'.[1] Following this concept, Rehak (2003: 103–104) and King and Krzywinska (2002: 4) both suggest that videogames can be considered as remediating cinema. The latter two in particular argue that the cinematic quality is an essential component of the gameplay experience, and not just something that was adopted in an attempt to legitimise videogames as quality entertainment (ibid.).

Second, and somewhat connected to this, is that 'cinematics' is another name for cut-scenes. As discussed in Chapter 2, while this stance is increasingly less prevalent, cut-scenes have been seen as breakers of interactivity,

DOI: 10.4324/9781003298786-4

and subsequently, immersion, especially in the late 1990s/early 2000s. Nonetheless, there is value in examining this restrictive quality further. Cutscenes do restrict the avatar in many ways, but they simultaneously work towards facilitating an emotional reaction akin to that triggered by films. 'Cinematic'-ness in games therefore also suggests that gameplay experience might trigger an emotional reaction akin to those triggered by film viewing. With this in mind, this chapter will show that Naughty Dog's aspiration for an 'interactive cinematic experience' goes beyond the photorealism of audiovisual representation and the re-appropriation of genre tropes, and explore how this design intention impacts agency across dimensions.[2]

This chapter comprises of three sections. First, the focus is on Naughty Dog's early years to identify main themes in their games' design. This section will trace the development of the studio's design ethos along two popular game series, *Crash Bandicoot* (1996–1999), and *Jak and Daxter* (2001–2013), which laid the foundations for linear 3D character-based action gameplay with platforming and shooting elements, and memorable characters. Then, the focus will be on how Naughty Dog left behind the world of cartoonish animation in favour of a more realistic audiovisual style in the instalments of the *Uncharted* franchise, while transporting game mechanics from their past titles. The second section will turn towards *Uncharted 4: A Thief's End* to examine how designers discuss their design priorities in terms of player agency. The final section will be an analysis of how agency is afforded and limited by the game's design across dimensions to achieve this cinematic quality in the game. The chapter argues that Naughty Dog maintained a consistency in style of design despite changes to leadership; and that the cinematic quality of the *Uncharted* series is achieved by affording and restricting agency across a variety of dimensions. I will argue that player agency can be realised in a number of dimensions but remains restricted in others. Thus, this chapter will examine the interplay between those dimensions and how agency is understood, sacrificed, and afforded in the development of cinematic gameplay.

Naughty Dog and the *Uncharted* Franchise

The Early Years of Naughty Dog: Crash Bandicoot *and* Jak and Daxter

Naughty Dog was founded in 1984 by old school friends Jason Rubin, an artist and visual effects designer, and Andrew 'Andy' Gavin, a programmer. This duality in leadership continues to be a defining trait of the studio's production culture to this day, with joint leads, each with their specialty, assigned to projects. Building a reputation for unique, recognisable design has been an aspiration since the studio's formation. As Rubin reminisces:

> We had this vision, even back in 1987 when we changed the name to Naughty Dog, that we wanted a game that stands out. That, someday,

people would pick up a box and say 'Oh, Naughty Dog! I know that company! That's a good company!'

(TheDarkStation88 2011: n.p.)

Arguably, the most recognisable characteristic of their games is a cinematic quality. This was, however, not at all uncommon in games around the time. The 1990s saw a boom of 3D games for mostly PC: shooters in the footsteps of *Wolfenstein 3D* (id Software 1992) and *Doom* (id Software 1993) gained popularity, while *Tomb Raider* (Core Design 1996) merged action and adventure genre conventions in 3D space, thus creating the template for many blockbuster titles to come. These games invited players to 'move through a sensationally realistic 3-D world of amazing detail' (Mobygames 2002a), or raid tombs in the 'most breath-taking 3D worlds yet seen' (Mobygames 2002b). At the same time, 2D platformers like *Sonic the Hedgehog* (Sonic Team 1991—ongoing) on Sega Megadrive, and *Super Mario Bros* (Nintendo 1985—ongoing) on the Nintendo Entertainment System, and its successor, the Super Nintendo Entertainment System, dominated the console market. The only games with 3D worlds on consoles at the time were those that were designed to run with Nintendo's graphics enhancement hardware, the Super FX chip for SNES, such as *Star Fox* (Nintendo 1994).[3] In 1994, after years of small-scale projects (mostly action and fighter games), Naughty Dog, at this point no more than 3–4 people, moved to Universal Interactive Studios' lot, who funded their work (Naughty Dog 2019). Universal and Sony greenlighted their first pitch for a project as an exclusive title for the newly released PlayStation game console.[4] With *Crash Bandicoot* (Naughty Dog 1996), the studio aspired to create a side-scrolling action game that introduced a mascot for the new PlayStation to compete with Nintendo's Mario and Sega's Sonic. However, when it came to the looks of the game, *Crash Bandicoot* offered something its competitors did not. Most importantly, it innovated in terms of texture design.[5] Co-founder Andy Gavin said about those times:

> No one else used the shading. Everyone else used the full textured mode [because] it reduced your poly count, like, dramatically. We used the textured polygons in the backgrounds for the most part—almost exclusively—and the shaded polygons in the characters. They worked well with our cartoon style.
>
> (qtd. in Nishita 2017: n.p.)

In other words, with this game, Naughty Dog aimed to recreate the depth and complexity of cartoon animation, which made them stand out in a market populated by rudimentary pixel figures. Although not yet explicitly alluding to cinematic conventions, Gavin's words above suggest they were thinking of their design in terms of another medium's visual codes.

Crash Bandicoot stood apart not just for its visual aesthetics, but for its complete overhaul of avatar-based game design. The typical approach to platformer design around the time was to follow side-scroller conventions, where the avatar moved from left to right in a 2D space, sprinting, crouching, and jumping to overcome challenges created by level design. Naughty Dog had a slightly different approach however, as co-founder Jason Rubin recalls:

> We realised that the simplest conceptual way to [innovate] was to take a 2D world that was flat, and simply rotate it. So the gameplay happened without moving it to left and right, and rather in and out. This concept we called 'Sonic's ass'. . . . The advantage to our method was, by turning the camera 90 degrees and keeping the character restricted, we could draw a lot more polygons. And the look, the density of the foliage, the amount of detail in it gave it a competitive edge.
> (TheDarkStation88 2011: n.p.)

That said, compared to its 2D platformer competitors, like *Sonic* (Sonic Team 1991) and *Super Mario Bros* (Nintendo 1985), *Crash Bandicoot* shared a lot when it came to gameplay and agency affordances, in that the player had to navigate an avatar through levels designed to set traversal challenges. However, cinematic aspirations were clear at the time, as seen in this interview segment where Gavin underscored the inspiration they drew on from film production:

> We sort of tried to take a Warner Bros style cartoon and put it in 3D. We came up with the idea of putting a camera on a kind of dolly, like they do in a movie scene. Therefore, you knew where the camera was going to be, and have a decent vantage point on the action.
> (TheDarkStation88 2011: n.p.)

By 'keeping the character restricted', the possibility space for player agency in the spatial-explorative dimensions was limited, but *Crash Bandicoot* being a platformer, time-critical action was crucial to gameplay. The game had a linear narrative and progression, with cut-scenes arranged to happen at the same place and time, thereby restraining narrative agency, which was quite common for games in the same genre of course. At the same time, the game's design afforded a low level of dramatic agency, as the platforming challenges would often generate infinitely variable player stories of trial and error. A low degree of configurative-constructive agency was also afforded by collectible items with extra lives and other benefits, and the ability to activate mechanisms that make box-bridges materialise over previously uncrossable drops, pits, and ravines. *Crash Bandicoot* was an international hit, and its avatar was marketed as the PlayStation's mascot. The franchise now includes several sequels, and a recent remake of the original trilogy for the PlayStation 4, *Crash Bandicoot N.Sane Trilogy* (Vicarious Visions 2017). By 2000, Universal sold its publishing rights to Sony, and with that, Naughty Dog became a wholly owned subsidiary of Sony Interactive Entertainment, a relationship that exists to this date. While the PlayStation allowed for low budget production, things changed with Sony's next generation hardware.

From a technological point of view, the PlayStation 2 supported the 'digital versatile disc' format, or DVD, which was heralded as the 'most successful consumer electronic device since the black and white television' (Brookey 2007: 199). Compared to their predecessor, the CD-ROM, DVDs had more storage space, while the PlayStation 2 itself had increased processing power and memory, allowing for more polygons to be displayed at any time, which meant more sophisticated visuals and more complex aesthetic and gameplay design. The console premiered titles such as *Metal Gear Solid 2* (Konami Computer Entertainment Japan 2001) and *Grand Theft Auto III* (DMA Design 2001), which would raise the bar for 3D gameplay and cinematics (Klevjer 2013: 302–303). Naughty Dog released their next commercially successful original IP for the PlayStation 2 called *Jak and Daxter* (2001), which was another platformer game but on a new game engine.

This time, the studio offered not only the illusion of 3D virtual space like in *Crash*, but proper 3D, thereby expanding the possibility space for spatial-explorative agency to be realised. Founder Jason Rubin attributed this decision to the advantageous financial position of publishers, who were to become the goliaths of today's videogame market:

> On the PS2 at the beginning, publishers were saying eesh, these games are really expensive. That ended up killing them. But other publishers, like EA, Activision, Sony, Microsoft, said 'make the biggest splash you can'. And Naughty Dog went from a team that was always trying to save money, to work as tightly as we could, to 'Hire Big, Think Big', let's put everything we have into making these games
> (PlayStation Europe 2014: n.p.)

Jak and Daxter featured Jak, the silent protagonist and player character, and his voiced side kick Daxter, who provided comic relief and banter. While in essence *Crash Bandicoot* was a rotated side-scroller, *Jak and Daxter* was an open world[6] platformer game with a fairly simple designer story. It fit into the same basket as other cartoonishly animated platformers around that time, like Sony's own *Spyro the Dragon* (Insomniac Games 1998) or Nintendo's *Banjo-Tooie* (Rare 2001). It also shared the general directions in gameplay: the player navigates the avatar through open world levels with traversal challenges to collect items, framed by a fairly simple narrative centred on defeating a series of mini-bosses, and eventually, once enough items are collected, a main boss. The dominant agency affordances in *Jak and Daxter* were in two dimensions. On the one hand, with the avatar's movements ranging from double jump, rolling into a long jump, slide-punch, slam, and spin-kick, the game's design afforded agency in the spatial-explorative dimension. On the other hand, as these actions were time-critical in that they required the player to push the right button at the right time, there was a considerable possibility space for avatar action in the temporal-ergodic dimension. The game also featured vehicle navigation on certain levels. Combat was mostly restricted to melee, and although the game did not have shooting elements per se, the player could use special powers that would enable certain ranged projectile attacks, such as fireballs. Traversal between locations was seamless, without any loading screens, which contributed to the whole experience being more fluent, less segmented by idle time spent waiting for the game to load. As I will show below, this feature was often emphasised in marketing, but *Jak and Daxter* was not yet marketed as film-like per se.

The game was heralded by critics and gamers alike as the best 3D platformer game on the console market (Satterfield 2001; Zdyrko 2001), and similar Sony titles capitalised on the winning formula with other similar games, such as *Ratchet and Clank* (Insomniac Games 2002).[7] Its sequel, *Jak II* (2003) introduced several novel mechanics, and a much bigger, darker storyworld. Jak got a voice, and the game itself was bigger, thanks to Naughty Dog revising their engine to fine-tune the overall gameplay experience. On this, Rubin said

> [a]fter *Jak and Daxter* . . . we had an engine, we got polygons on the screen, so the beauty of that is that in this game, we got to spend all of our time, the entire two years, getting better gameplay, getting more intelligent creatures, getting more stuff out there, adding to the gaming experience, as opposed to just fighting to get the stuff on screen.
>
> (Otana 2009: n.p.)

This included the introduction of a shooting mechanic, and the improvement of non—player character behaviour through more sophisticated AI: allies were joining fights, and enemies had better environmental awareness. This meant that agency was increasingly afforded in the temporal-ergodic and spatial-explorative dimensions. At the same time, with set characters, and a heavily predetermined narrative, there was not much narrative agency afforded, but due to the open-world design, plenty of dramatic agency through the exploration incentivised by the large virtual space. In terms of 'cinematic'-ness, Evan Wells, the studio's Co-President at the time of writing, said this of the *Jak and Daxter* series in retrospect:

> We were looking at the PS2 hardware and said okay, this world has to be seamless. We don't want any loads, it's got to feel immersive, we don't want there to ever be a break from the action, or for you to say 'oh, now's the time to put down the controller, I finished the level'.
>
> (PlayStation 2012: n.p.)

An 'Active Cinematic Experience' 81

In a medium where play was thus far typically structured by systematically inserted loading screens between levels, this was something of a novelty, arguably inspired by the seamlessness of other audiovisual media, such as film or cartoons. Though 'cinematic'-ness per se was not mentioned yet, it would very clearly become a priority when the studio moved away from cartoonish animation, towards the realm of photorealistic representation.

After the release of *Jak II*, the studio saw a major overhaul of staff. Studio leads Rubin and Gavin left, transitioning leadership to Evan Wells and Christophe Balestra, who were also a designer-artist duo much like their predecessors. Wells identified the safeguarding of Naughty Dog's unique company culture as a priority during the transition:

> We were dealing with making sure that we kept intact all of the flexibility that we were accustomed to working with and that we weren't changing our company culture.
> (PlayStation Europe 2014: n.p.)

Although Naughty Dog had become Sony's subsidiary, they continued to work as an independent studio, with almost no producers influencing design decisions, which is how they worked at the time of *Uncharted 4*'s development. There were no dedicated producers or managers, the 'lead' position entailed less of taking charge and more a channelling of information to the department (Reilly 2011). For an average of three hundred people, they reportedly employed two production coordinators, which, in an industry where the average is one producer for ten members of staff, is remarkably low (Digital Dragons 2018). Despite major changes like these, the studio maintained its design ethos.[8]

The Uncharted Franchise: Creating an 'Active Cinematic Experience'

Besides the surge of cartoonish platformers on consoles in the early 2000s, another genre rose to prominence in the late 1990s and early 2000s: the third person action-adventure. Games like *Prince of Persia: The Sands of Time* (Ubisoft Montreal 2003) aspired for the success *Tomb Raider* harnessed in the late 1990s. There was also a rise in popularity of shooters with deeper, darker themes and more complex forms of narrative, such as the original *Halo* trilogy (Bungie 2001, 2004, 2007) and *Tom Clancy's Splinter Cell* (Ubisoft Montreal 2002). These were both exclusive titles and are tent pole franchises to this date on Microsoft's game console, the Xbox. Sony was yet to enter this market. With the enhanced technological capacities of the PlayStation 3 released in 2006, Naughty Dog was looking to develop an original IP to flagship Sony's hardware, which ended up being *Uncharted: Drake's Fortune* (2007). According to Don Poole, former environmental modeller at Naughty Dog, *Uncharted: Drake's Fortune* was at first going to be yet another game with fantastical elements, much like *Crash Bandicoot* and *Jak*, but due to pressure from Sony to conform to changing market trends, it moved away from this original intention:

> The market had changed a lot by then. The demographic was older and gritty shooters were really dominating. Sony wanted very much to get into that market share; it pushed all of its developers in this direction. So the big push from Sony, not just at Naughty Dog but at all of Sony's development companies at the time, was to craft games for PlayStation 3 that were much more realistic. The pressure from Xbox's success with gritty shooters was a very real force on our direction at that time.
>
> (qtd. in Reeves 2011: n.p.)

And so, with *Uncharted: Drake's Fortune*, Naughty Dog took the avatar-based 3D action-platformer formula and revamped it in realistic-looking style, as a deliberate step away from the cartoony aesthetics of its preceding releases (Caron 2007). The core mechanics of the series were traversal/platforming, shooting and brawling, and puzzle challenges. It was from this point onwards that the studio began to display a consistent style of game design, in terms of both audiovisual aesthetics and gameplay. The franchise currently consists of five main titles for the PlayStation 3 and 4, and some smaller handheld and mobile games, which were developed by different studios. The first four main games, namely *Uncharted: Drake's Fortune* (2007), *Uncharted 2: Among Thieves* (2009), *Uncharted 3: Drake's Deception* (2011), and *Uncharted 4: A Thief's End* (2016) feature Nathan Drake as protagonist, and a recurring cast of friends and foes. The latest title, *Uncharted: Lost Legacy* (2017) is a smaller, shorter game led by two side characters featured in earlier games. This chapter will zoom in on the fourth title of the franchise, the one that concludes Nathan Drake's story. But before we can explore that, we need to look at the franchise's development until then, to examine the role it played in the formation of Naughty Dog's design ethos.

All *Uncharted* games focus on the protagonist embarking on an action-packed adventure across exotic locations, hunting for treasure, racing time and rivals. They take place in a world highly resembling our own, meaning they share things like geography, physics, and languages, with occasional fantastical elements in all but the fourth instalment. The overall tone, narrative, pacing, style, and characterisation in the franchise draws heavily on pulp and action-adventure films and television shows. As long-time *Uncharted* developer Richard Lemarchand said about the inspirations for the IP:

> So we looked at loads of those matinee serials: lots of chases, running around looking for treasure, unlikely allegiances with a whole crazy cast of characters, lots of narrow escapes and risky situations.
>
> (XoZen 2007: n.p.)

The first game was well-received, with many praising how it was much like playing a pulp action or adventure film of old times, and it was nominated for numerous awards from press outlets. 'Blockbuster vibes', Indiana Jones, and the film *National Treasure* are mentioned repeatedly on the game's Metacritic page.

While *Uncharted: Drake's Fortune* paved the way in a new direction for the studio, it was with the second instalment of the series, *Uncharted 2: Among Thieves* (2009) that Naughty Dog crystallised their design ethos. This time, as Lemarchand said in a conference talk, they 'wanted to create a fully playable version of a big summer blockbuster action-adventure movie' (GDC 2017a: n.p.). With *Uncharted 2*, Naughty Dog's signature gameplay crystallised into a linear narrative-driven experience with complex characters and playable high-octane chase sequences in epic set pieces with a monumental score, with actors' movements and voices captured live simultaneously as if it was a theatre production (PlayStation 2009b, 2009c). The guiding thought behind the production of each game, as Creative Director and Lead Writer Amy Hennig summarised it, was: 'how do we best replicate that action-adventure movie experience?' (Nguyen 2011: n.p.).

Indeed, it was with the second instalment that a cinematic quality became an explicitly worded priority for the studio. They pledged to create an 'active cinematic experience' with their games: not only was this phrase used as a promotional hook (BluRay Trailers 2009: n.p.), it was also presented at the Game Developers Conference as the essence of everything they do with their game design (GDC 2016a: n.p.). As Game Director Bruce Straley and Co-Lead Designer Neil Druckmann summed up at the conference, cinematic stands for 'anything of filmic quality. The cameras, pacing, performance of the actors, music, everything that makes your favourite movies great' (ibid.). This presentation also revealed that production consisted of the simultaneous development of story in tandem with gameplay, with staff members being both story and gameplay designers at any time, constantly communicating; and that the *Uncharted* brand had been based on a compiled document of action-adventure genre 'conventions and tropes' from Hollywood blockbusters like *Indiana Jones and the Raiders of the Lost Ark* (1981) and *National Treasure* (2004), such as walking into the enemy trap, or being left behind on a plane without a pilot (ibid.). These then became inspiration for 'game mechanics, set-ups, or just the tone and the vibe of the story' (ibid.). The topics discussed and language used in this GDC talk indicate that design intention was to aspire for a cinematic quality, and that the brand identity of the *Uncharted* franchise was firmly anchored in the cinematic genre of pulp action-adventure. How did Naughty Dog create the 'active cinematic experience', and what did that mean in terms of the player's agency?

The bulk of the narrative in all three games is often delivered via cutscenes, though the proportion of these versus gameplay sections shifts with each instalment, in line with the enhancement of the hardware. These cutscenes allowed designers to, as *Uncharted 2*'s Game Director Bruce Straley said in the GDC presentation mentioned above, 'leverage the language of cinema by using things like composition, close-ups, wide angle shots, basically any shot that's not over the shoulder player camera, dramatic editing' (ibid.). Aspiring for a cinematic quality in representation meant that designers placed a heavy emphasis on storytelling by creating plenty of design affordances which would deliver predeterminedly narrative moments in order to relay a linear story, thereby limiting narrative agency. As was to become a typical feature of the games, cut-scenes were embedded seamlessly, without any loading screens, which created a more organic flow, and a more filmlike experience. They typically focused on adding layers of motivation and personal history to characters, as well as exposition and context to the key moments in the plot, which left the action set-pieces to be experienced via gameplay. The *Uncharted* games also incorporated genre tropes of action-adventure, such as the overall focus on treasure hunting, the main characters' personalities, and their relationship management, drawing on melodrama.[9] All these being said, 'cinematic'-ness was not solely achieved via cut-scenes and genre inspirations, but also via game design.

From early on in the franchise, Naughty Dog developers have been vocal about the need to restrict avatar action in order to deliver the kind of experience they had in mind for *Uncharted* games. They called this design priority 'focused'. Speaking of the first game, Lemarchand and Druckmann said:

> Except for a few vehicle-based sections, *Uncharted*'s gameplay is tightly focused on a few core mechanics. This was quite a difference from the design approach of the *Jak and Daxter* series, where much of the fun was derived from the sheer variety of gameplay in the missions. This focused approach, along with the realistic world we created for Uncharted, made game design on the project quite challenging. . . . This resulted in what we feel is a much more elegant design overall.
> (Lemarchand and Druckmann 2008: n.p.)

This 'focused approach' can be further broken down with the help of the multidimensional heuristic framework. In order to enable the fast-paced gameplay at the heart of Naughty Dog's evolving design ethos within the technological restrictions of each hardware's processing power, the games' design considerably restricts the possibility space for avatar action in all four dimensions. Time-critical action is at the centre of the gameplay experience, thereby enabling ergodic agency to manifest, albeit not to a degree that is considerably more prevalent than it would be in any other action game. As the games' narrative structures are linear, in order to maintain the predetermined direction and pace of storytelling, besides genre-typical movement verbs often found in action-adventure games (such as run, jump, or take cover), agency in the spatial-explorative dimension is severely restricted throughout the first three games, though the levels gradually became larger as technology allowed, and the designers became more proficient in making use of it.[10] For the sake of maintaining designer control over player progress, temporal agency is also restricted, along with both the configuration of the avatar and the construction of objects in the game's space (bar a very low degree of agency expressed by customising the avatar's weaponry). Such a high degree of designer control over avatar action results in agency also being impaired in the narrative-dramatic dimension, though due to increasingly sophisticated technologies in animation and graphics processing, this constrained game feel began to gradually be counterbalanced with rich and lifelike representation of the game spaces and those inhabiting them.

Let's take a moment and look at how developers talked about creating an 'active cinematic experience', through the specific example of *Uncharted 2*'s train levels. I chose this example as developers said these levels were particularly challenging to design, requiring a complete overhaul of Naughty Dog's game engine in order to obtain the desired results (Gregory 2010), which shows the level of effort put towards creating a filmlike gameplay experience. The train levels were widely praised by fans and the press (Yin-Poole 2018), and fellow developers still look at Naughty Dog's feat with 'an almost religious fervour' (Bramwell 2013: n.p.). 'Chapter 13: Locomotion' and 'Chapter 14: Tunnel Vision' make up a roughly 20-minute-long playable set piece in *Uncharted 2*. They take place entirely on a moving train, which Drake, the player/avatar, has to fight his way through. Unlike similar levels in other games, this train, and everything in it, is designed to move constantly, thanks to what Naughty Dog call 'Dynamic Object Traversal System'.[11] As Lemarchand explains in the game's post-mortem:

> This system provided us with the ability to have player character Nathan Drake and all of his allies and enemies in the game able to use all of their traversal and combat abilities on any moving object. This might not seem like a big deal, but for those of us who had been working on 3D character action games for a while, [it] was pretty much the Holy Grail.
> (GDC 2017a: n.p.)

On these levels, Naughty Dog developers discussed three main strategies deployed to create an 'active cinematic experience': through audiovisual means, through difficulty, and through level design.

First, the audiovisual features in gameplay granted characters and environments a more cinematic appeal. Amongst these were the use of filmic colour palettes[12] (GDC 2017a), varied camera angles, contextual move-sets in animation, such as Drake stumbling on ice, covering his face as he runs by explosions, or furniture dynamically reacting to events. As Mike Hatfield, Lead Technical Artist on *Uncharted 2* said,

> All we want to do is blur the line between pre-computed physics stuff that we pre-process in our 3D software, and the stuff that's happening live in the game, dynamically reacting to explosions and gunfire.
> (PlayStation 2009a: n.p.)

Environments reacting dynamically to play allow for a degree of dramatic agency to be realised. Explosions are a good example of this, as they are not predetermined in occurrence, but happen only when the avatar or an enemy unit throws a grenade in the proximity of objects with explosive attributes, such as a crate. With features such as this, *Uncharted* games afford a degree of dramatic agency: the game's ludic systems, when interacted with, create player stories unique to the individual playthrough, as triggered by the interactions then and there—albeit to a lower degree when compared to the other two case study chapters.

Second, while the player's agency is severely restricted as the player cannot get off the train, the game's design, particularly in terms of traversal and combat challenges, can be rather forgiving when it comes to difficulty. Besides the lack of loading screens and minimal, if any, superimposed interfaces, this organic quality is also no doubt in service of the fluency of an 'active cinematic experience'. This is negotiated with the help of 'Dynamic Difficulty Adjustment', a technology that Naughty Dog has been using profusely since *Crash Bandicoot* (Gavin 2011). As I discussed in the previous chapter, 'Dynamic Difficulty Adjustment', or DDA, is a systemic way the game's difficulty is adjusted depending on how much the player struggles.[13] Therefore the challenge posed in combat situations affords agency in a temporal-ergodic dimension, which is further supported by this safety measure, in case the challenge proves to be too difficult for the player to ease through that section. Manipulating temporal-ergodic agency in such a way enables a more organically flowing gameplay experience.

Last but not least, another way in which Naughty Dog enhances the cinematic quality of the train level in *Uncharted 2* is by manipulating the game spaces, thereby impacting agency in the spatial-explorative dimension. Since the game could not be made as a truly open world game, as it would not have allowed for the high degree of designer control on avatar action, an alternative method was devised to create a realistic experience of progressing through a moving train. This was necessary as it would not have been possible to store and run such a resource-heavy level at the time, and similar train levels, such as the one in *Final Fantasy VIII* (Square 1999), appear to have a static train with moving background to create a similar feeling of movement. The way Naughty Dog created the illusion of the train progressing forward was to have the train not be static, but move in circles on a loop, while the background occasionally changes when the avatar is in a high-walled train carriage, or while a cut-scene is played (Gregory 2010). Thus, there is a considerable discrepancy between the ludic, locally represented, and storyworld spaces: although the player/avatar's agency affordances are restricted in the ludic and locally represented space, it appears as though the train is moving along a long, continuous path in the storyworld space. Thus, the player's spatial agency could remain quite restricted, but an illusion of movement is created in the game's representational space thereby affording explorative agency, which builds up into an action set piece. Therefore, the train levels contribute towards the franchise's brand identity as an 'active cinematic experience', thanks to the design solutions observed.

After the success of *Uncharted 2*, Naughty Dog split into two teams: one working on *Uncharted 3*, the other, led by the key developers associated with the franchise, Neil Druckmann and Bruce Straley, moved on to create a new IP for the PlayStation 3. This new game would become *The Last of Us* (2013), a multiple BAFTA-winning action-adventure-stealth survival-horror game. Unlike any of their previous games, *The Last of Us* was much darker in its narrative themes. It also introduced a more diverse stealth system and placed larger emphasis on crafting, which afforded a slower pace, especially compared to the *Uncharted* franchise. In the meantime, a small team led by Amy Hennig continued to work on the next, and planned to be final, instalment of *Uncharted*, as led by Nathan Drake.

Developing Uncharted 4: *A Thief's End*

The notion of an 'active cinematic experience' was discussed in a slightly more deconstructed way by *Uncharted 4*'s developers compared to previous instalments. As shown in the historical overview above, 'cinematic'-ness in general for Naughty Dog encapsulated an aspiration for the recreation of a summer cinema blockbuster, inspired by a mood board of Hollywood action-adventure classics and pulp television series. Not counting the inherent cinematic quality of the games' cut-scenes, we saw how developers repeatedly emphasised three tools at their disposal in order to achieve this goal: pacing, restricting player action to core mechanics, and a high audiovisual quality. *Uncharted 4*'s designers, however, no longer promoted the 'active cinematic experience' motto, and were generally less clear on what a filmic quality meant for them, though their words continued to revolve around the themes of cultural references to pulp films, creating interesting stories with believable and complex characters, and very high-quality art and animation. This may have been due to the change of Naughty Dog's public perception, particularly post-*The Last of Us*.

Up to this point, the studio was still in the process of revamping their design ethos from making cartoony platformers to producing realistically animated action-adventure games, and the voices across the paratextual surrounds promoted explicit cinematic aspirations accordingly. Developers repeatedly expressed a desire to create filmic games, as if 'filmic' was a quality marker. Indeed, when videogames still struggled to be recognised as a medium capable of offering worthwhile entertainment value, 'cinematic' in the context of games was often used as a praise, a way to elevate the cultural status of the product, especially in a promotional context (King and Krzywinska 2002: 7). However, especially after the explosive success of *The Last of Us*, Naughty Dog no longer needed to rely on such means to market their work, because by then their design style was a recognisable brand in and of itself, one with connotations for high production values and stories told akin to those of blockbusters. Therefore, throughout the years leading up to *Uncharted 4*'s release, developers were increasingly less consistent in their usage of descriptors like 'cinematic' or 'filmic', and discussed more the design priorities they established as a studio over the years, in a self-referential manner. Design intention also increasingly became about story construction and character moments both via performance captured cut-scenes and what developers described above as 'live' gameplay that elicit an emotional reaction in their players, feats that the studio championed in *The Last of Us* as well. But what did this mean for the studio's brand and image in general?

Naughty Dog is a Sony subsidiary, turning over large revenues. As such, it would not be too radical to suggest that growing pressure from market demand would steer their style of design towards crowd-pleasing mainstream—in this particular case, towards the open world action-adventure games that dominated sales across the globe, such as Ubisoft's *Assassin's Creed* and *Far Cry* series. However, Naughty Dog's developers did not acknowledge these trends as relevant, and instead stressed the importance of staying true to the *Uncharted* brand, and to the studio's design ethos. Co-Game Director Bruce Straley said that measuring against industry trends was not a concern:

> I don't care what the industry is doing. I wanna make a game that I wanna play. . . . We're not comparing what we're doing here with what other people are doing. We're comparing what's the evolution of Uncharted, what can we do with this franchise.
>
> (qtd. in Hanson 2015a: n.p.)

Similarly, Co-Game Director Druckmann reminisced:

> Sometimes we'd have a brainstorm meeting looking at different mechanics . . . and people would go 'oh that's really hard' and someone in the room will eventually say 'We're Naughty Dog'. And that statement has so much weight, and the pressure is to make sure that statement always has weight going forward. 'We're Naughty Dog. We're gonna make one of the best games out there'.
>
> (qtd. in Hanson 2015a: n.p.)

Audio Lead Phil Kovats felt like they had 'a lot of responsibility' to stay true (PlayStation 2016a: n.p.) to the brand's legacy. Although market trends, apparently, did not play that much of a part in the decisions made during *Uncharted 4*'s development, there are two major moments of change in the circumstances of production that need to be considered. First, there was technological innovation with the introduction of the next-generation gaming consoles by Sony and Microsoft. Second, there was the change in almost all leading personnel and cast members about halfway through production. The following will examine how these factors set the groundworks for how player agency was to be thought about by developers.

Changes in Hardware and Personnel

In the early 2010s, there was much anticipation around the game that was said to conclude Nathan Drake's storyline. Fans and journalists alike pitched several ideas to Naughty Dog about where they wanted the last game to go (IGN Staff 2011; Miller and Altano 2012). By this time, the *Uncharted* franchise was Sony's flagship IP on the PlayStation. Thus, it was not surprising when the company announced at the next-generation console PlayStation 4's launch that a new *Uncharted* game was also in the making. The announcement took the form of a highly suggestive trailer, with a camera pacing over a map while a man, presumably the new villain, spoke about having been abandoned by Drake and how this gave him a new purpose of revenge (PlayStation 2013). Shortly after the release of this trailer, mo-cap actors shared behind-the-scenes photos on their social media (Monaghan 2013; Stashwick 2013), but apart from these leaks, there was little coming from the studio until early 2014. After the release of *The Last of Us* (2013), its team freed up, and thus the studio was able to turn their full attention to the slowly brewing new *Uncharted* game, only to find it markedly behind schedule, and without a feasible plan for production (Schreier 2017: 36–38). Soon after, long-time *Uncharted* Creative Director Amy Hennig, *Uncharted 4* Game Director Justin Richmond, lead character artist Michael Knowland, and Art Director Nate Wells left Naughty Dog, along with actors Alan Tudyk and Todd Stashwick.

Although it is not uncommon for creators or key talent to leave production due to delays and a general state of disorganisation, the specific reason for their departure is yet to be officially explained. Many fans and journalists seem to believe they were pushed out by the rockstar-like developer duo leading the development of some *Uncharted* games and *The Last of Us*, Bruce Straley and Neil Druckmann (Orland 2015). Naughty Dog's co-presidents attempted to disperse these rumours on their developer blog but did not clarify further (Wells 2014). Wherever the truth may lie, Druckmann and Straley (Labbe 2015: n.p.) did admit to a complete overhaul of the project as it stood, beginning with the story, which, as the historical overview above showed, is what determines game mechanics in *Uncharted* games. While the transition was abrupt, it was well-organised. As Lead Environment Artist Tate Mosesian recalls, 'they had a plan, a clear plan, and they expressed it to the team. It instilled confidence' (Schreier 2017: 41). The new directorial duo continued to press the original priorities set out by Naughty Dog's then co-president Christophe Balestra, who said at the PlayStation launch event:

> We're gonna be pushing storytelling and performance capture, like always. But graphically, we're gonna see a big jump with what the team is working on right now.
>
> (PlayStation 2013: n.p.)

90   An 'Active Cinematic Experience'

This early statement set the direction in design intention as one focusing on storytelling and sophisticated audiovisuals, as consistent with the *Uncharted* brand. The big jump in graphics was made possible with the power of the PlayStation 4 console, and as we will see, developers regularly referred back to the technological affordances of the new hardware as a decisive factor in why certain decisions were made during the development of *Uncharted 4: A Thief's End*.[14]

As Sony's then-President and CEO Jack Tretton summed up, the new console delivered 'powerful graphics and speed, intelligent personalization, deeply integrated social capabilities, and innovative second-screen features' (Tretton 2013: n.p.). Most notably, with the revamped PlayStation Network, Sony expanded the kinds of services provided by the console, including new communication and social features, film, television, and music streaming, and a cloud gaming library containing previous PlayStation titles. Furthermore, the console brought about three novel technological changes which are relevant for *Uncharted 4*'s design intention. Firstly, compared to the PlayStation 3 single-core central processing unit (CPU), or the brains of the machine, as it were, the new hardware sported an eight-core CPU, with expanded memory. This meant that it could process an increased amount of data that is more complex, and at a faster speed. It also featured a more powerful graphics processing unit (GPU), which could render higher resolution 3D and a higher framerate, resulting in more pixels being displayed simultaneously, which were refreshing at a higher rate per second. In very simple terms, this meant that game systems could be more complex; the games themselves would have more audiovisual detail; and they could run more smoothly on the PlayStation 4 compared to its predecessors, or even its competition. Indeed, when it came to the competition, at its launch the PlayStation 4 outperformed its rival, Microsoft's Xbox One. Flagship franchise games such as *Call of Duty: Ghosts* (Infinity Ward 2013) or *Assassin's Creed IV: Black Flag* (Ubisoft Montreal 2013) ran at higher resolution on the PlayStation 4 (Hamilton 2013).

Moreover, it was with the PlayStation 4 that Sony revised their previous infamously problematic shading language for the PlayStation 3 (Sinclair 2017). Shading, in the context of 3D animation, refers to the process of creating ways to imitate material qualities and textures of a real-world object (Paquette 2013: 185–218). By determining valuables assigned to pixels that make up 3D objects in virtual space, such as glossiness or specularity, it is possible to imitate surface characteristics. With the new hardware, the PlayStation Graphics Library (PSGL) was replaced by PlayStation Shader Language (PSSL), which optimised the efficiency of the new console's GPU (Stenson and Ho 2013). It streamlined production pipelines because it gave programmers a new set of tools to write shaders in exactly the way the artists wanted them (Leadbetter 2013) and the PS4 had the power to execute them. Therefore, Naughty Dog, as a Sony subsidiary with access to this technology, had certainty and consistency in using development tools. This in turn made production more efficient. Such combination of technological feats meant that developers would be able to make the best of the hardware's affordances regarding game systems and graphics. These changes in hardware and personnel already hint towards how agency was shaped by design intent in *Uncharted 4*. Looking deeper into interviews with developers will reveal the ramifications of these in more detail.

A 'Cinematic Feel'

Uncharted 4's developers relied increasingly less on filmic terminology when expressing an aspiration for cinematic quality in their design. Instead, they spoke to aspects that crystallised as the studio's design ethos, loosely associated with this historic priority; and a refined commitment to story construction and consequently, conveying characters' emotional complexity. Straley said they would have loved to have mechanically interesting and new game components as a design challenge. However, although such features would have granted spectacle without doubt, he admitted that it would not be consistent with the franchise's brand identity rooted in a 'cinematic feel':

> We wanna make jetpacks, laser beams, those ideas are simple. But [the challenge is] to actually go [and focus on] what's going to create the most rich experience, and keep the pacing, so it keeps that action cinematic feel that *Uncharted*'s known for.
>
> (Gamespot 2015: n.p.)

Indeed, it is a cinematic, or filmic 'feel' that design intention as per *Uncharted 4*'s promotional paratext seems to revolve around the most. Elsewhere, Straley expanded on this concept in more detail:

> We're thinking in filmic terms, but what's important for us is how much of that we can put on the [analogue] stick. That's what we start with in the story discussions. Then, when we talk to the designers, it's like, 'This is where the characters are at, this is what we're trying to do, and these are the mechanics we're trying to exploit at this point. Let's pull those things together and make the player feel what the characters are feeling'.
>
> (qtd. in Staff 2015: n.p.)

While he acknowledged that their frame of thinking is centred on creating a film-like experience, their secondmost priority seems to have been to translate this filmic framing into interactive terms. While the desire to 'put things on the stick', that is, give as much control to the player as possible, was being acknowledged, the general approach to development was still that mechanics stem from 'story discussions'. The historical overview of the *Uncharted* franchise above explored how the design intention in previous instalments centred on the idea of creating an 'active cinematic experience'. At that time, developers discussed extensively how when it came to creating the game, and planning large scale structural matters like pacing, they thought in terms of the conventions of film and television. *Uncharted 4* was no different in this regard, and a focus on story-ness was reiterated by Druckmann:

> We have become more conscious of, more proficient at, storytelling. Whatever meeting we're having—even if it's background or character artists—we're speaking the same language. We're speaking as storytellers.
>
> (ibid. n.p.)

Designers of all disciplines set out to approach all parts of the game as a 'scene', a part of a whole, where each part is building up to an overarching narrative:

> What we're trying to do is look at everything, even the moments between cut-scenes, as a scene. There's always something that's happening with the character arc that's important.
>
> (qtd. in Staff 2015: n.p.)

Interestingly, this approach is not uncommon in film. Bordwell and Thompson (2004) propose to frame a neo-structuralist engagement with film texts through the lens of 'narrative as formal system'. They argue that a film's formal structure can be mapped according to how it deploys 'cause-effect, story-plot differences, motivations, parallelism, progression from opening to closing, and narrational range and depth' (ibid. 103). By discussing the building blocks of the designed gameplay experience in terms of 'scenes', we can argue that Naughty Dog takes an approach to structuring the game according to formal qualities also found in films.

This aspiration for filmic quality was mostly consistent with the *Uncharted* brand, as well as Naughty Dog's design ethos. That being said, in terms of the language used by developers across the paratextual corpus, there was less consistency with regards to what this 'cinematic'-ness meant, and increasingly more focus on evoking emotions in players. As to how Naughty Dog's developers intended to achieve this via design, there were two main themes salient in interviews and other paraphernalia: restricting player action to core mechanics and aspiring for never-before-seen levels of audiovisual detail. A recurrent influential factor in developer discourse around these two topics, as the following will show, was how the new technology of the PlayStation 4 facilitated innovation, and how the studio was predominantly motivated less by having to adhere to industry pressure, more by delivering design that fits the high standards laid down by their previous games.

Soon after Straley and Druckmann took over the project, they changed not just the story, but also the majority of game mechanics planned during pre-production. Previously, Hennig and her team were prototyping a variety of new ideas, which Straley recalls were mostly 'theorycraft'; a sort of 'wouldn't it be cool if . . . ?' stage in game design where there is no implementation per se, just planning, and more often than not, over-planning.[15] When Straley and Druckmann got on board, they immediately identified a new priority. As Straley recalls:

> [T]he thing that I needed to do more than anything was to pin down what the core mechanics were going to be. Sifting through the prototypes and seeing what was going to work and what wasn't. What scales. What works with something else.
> (qtd. in Schreier 2017: 45)

This proved to be quite a challenge, especially given how much more content they could now create on the new platform. As Druckmann said, a recurrent issue they were having as developers was how to create a game that offers more player choice while simultaneously maintaining the linear, filmic pacing of previous games:

> The challenge for us, the thing that has been super hard, is how do we give you more choices, and make the pacing feel just as intense as when things have been more linear.
> (PlayStation 2016b: n.p.)

They set out to overcome this challenge in a way that, at first glance, may seem somewhat contradictory: by limiting player action to what they called 'core mechanics', a very basic set of simple game mechanics that the player can familiarise themselves with relatively quickly.[16] It could be argued that if player action is limited by design, then player agency is restricted accordingly. However, as Calleja points out, 'even the most free-form activity in a virtual environment is constrained by the code which enables it' (Calleja 2011: 148). Indeed, as argued in Chapter 1, agency could be thought of not as a yes or no question, but a matter of degrees. As such, constraining player action does not automatically mean that the player has no agency. In Straley's words, it is precisely because the design puts forward simplified game mechanics that the player can 'feel empowered':

> [T]he challenges that we put in front of you in layout, and designs, and enemy designs, and classes of enemies, and the turret truck, etcetera, you have to be so familiarised with your core mechanics and dexterous on the stick, so familiarised with that language of interaction with that world that we're creating, that you need to feel empowered as a player.
> (Gamespot 2015: n.p.)

Core mechanics were already a design priority in previous games, particularly in *Uncharted 2: Among Thieves*, whose development was also led by Straley and Druckmann (PlayStation 2014b; PlayStation 2016b), and continued to be for *Uncharted 4*. The studio's idea for what the core gameplay would look like was publicised with two gameplay trailers: one shown at PlayStation Experience (PSX) in 2014, the other at E3 in 2015 (IGN 2014; PlayStation 2015a). *Uncharted* being the product of a studio with a long history in platforming games, the first gameplay trailer showed what implications this carried for the avatar's move set. It is a roughly 15-minute-long gameplay section, and it features a traversal and combat-stealth section in an open environment much bigger in size compared to previous *Uncharted* games. This trailer revealed the traversal mechanics already present in previous games, such as running, jumping, or climbing. It also introduced the new core mechanics of the climbing spike and the rope. As Lead Game Designer Kurt Margenau said, 'the biggest design thing that came out of the new hardware was literally just the bigger spaces' (PlayStation 2016b: n.p.). These were conceptualised by Naughty Dog's level designers as 'wide linear' levels, a phrasing with which they aimed to reconcile the tension between the freedom of open world level design and the constraints that go hand in hand with linear progression design (Sinclair 2016). Nevertheless, Margenau stressed elsewhere that they still intended to maintain some degree of direction:

> Everything you see, you can go to. We're not going to arbitrarily block you. It's still a directed experience. We have our beats, our big moments that we want to pitch you to, but we want to make the player come to them on their own. We're not shoving them down their throats.
> (qtd. in Farokhmanesh 2015: n.p.)

Specifically talking about spaces, co-lead game designer Anthony Newman said that thanks to the technological affordances of the new console, they could now increase the possibility space for avatar action in a spatial-explorative dimension:

> We really wanted to give more player choice, a greater sense of freedom, and exploration on these levels. . . . So one thing we're definitely doing is we're opening it up a lot more, and the memory of the PS4 is definitely allowing us to do that.
> (PlayStation 2015b: n.p.)

This approach came to be marketed as 'wide-linear' level design (Crossley 2015). these quotes show that developers expressed concerns about the challenges of mitigating increased player freedom with the simultaneous adherence to the necessary constraints that the linear narrative required, all the while wanting to expand the possibility space for the spatial-explorative dimension of agency. This design intention can be deduced from the expansion of level sizes as well as the core move set of the avatar to make traversal options more diverse, as shown in the trailers.

The trailers also reveal what core mechanics utilised in combat afforded by such 'wide-linear' design looked like at this stage in development. Technology did not just allow for there to be bigger spaces, it also allowed for non-player characters in said spaces to be more proficient in traversing them, thereby increasing the challenge in these scenarios. Designers set out to revise enemy and ally behaviours. Previously, they were scripted to a high degree, but with *Uncharted 4* the studio worked on more sophisticated AI systems that actively make decisions based on their understanding of space and their knowledge of where the player's avatar could be. Lead Animator Jeremy Yates said on this:

> We didn't want a game where you just sit behind cover, you know, the stop-and-pop, we really wanted you to move through the environment, to outsmart them, flank them, for them to be able to chase you around, just have that constant motion.
>
> (PlayStation 2016c: n.p.)

By designing more reactive, less predetermined non-player character behaviour, *Uncharted 4*'s designers endeavoured to create more challenging combat scenarios. This suggests that another key area for design intention in terms of designing agency was in the temporal-ergodic dimension. However, applying restrictions to the player character's core mechanics while diversifying non-player character actions became slightly more difficult to balance when it came to *Uncharted*'s trademark action set pieces, and example of which was revealed in the gameplay trailer showed at E3 2015 (PlayStation 2015a).

In high-octane vehicle chase sequence shown in this trailer, Drake has to advance to the front of a convoy to catch up with his brother. In doing so, he has to climb on board a truck, then move gradually towards the front all the while travelling at high speed, and shoot enemies both in his way, and on other vehicles in the convoy. During this sequence, the player is shown to have complete control of the avatar, bar a few scripted moments. Indeed, it is with such fast-moving set pieces that a very good command of the core mechanics becomes fundamental and facilitating this was a priority for the studio. As Straley said,

> So much of what we're trying to make with our games is, we wanna make them accessible. We as a studio we try to make them accessible. Accessible doesn't mean, like, dumbed down, or 'press one button and the whole sequence plays on'. We just wanna make it so that you understand that you have a relationship with the mechanics, that you chunk them easily, and you can engage them. And now you want to exploit them, and it's up to you to have that choice.
>
> (qtd. in Hanson 2015a: n.p.)

What he emphasised was the importance placed on facilitating players' 'relationship with the mechanics' as a prerequisite of enabling the player to successfully navigate these fast-paced gameplay sequences easily. This ease of access would then enable players to 'chunk them easily', and to 'exploit them' which would in turn, rather contradictorily, enable players to still tailor their playstyle to their preference to a certain degree. This emphasis on accessibility, combined with larger level sizes and the adaptive behavioural diversity of non-player characters suggests another tangent to design intention. Besides telling the linear story via predetermined, largely non-interactive cut-scenes and scripted events that do not afford much narrative agency, designers' focus seemed also to be on enabling emergent, narratively charged sequences of events, thereby affording a degree of dramatic agency to players. This focus on dramatic agency becomes even more evident when examining the other theme emerging from a survey of paratextual sources: an emphasis on highly detailed and filmic audiovisual quality.

From the first trailer since Straley and Druckmann's takeover, a photorealistic aspiration in design intention was evident. The beginning of the trailer reads 'The following trailer was captured directly from a PlayStation 4 system', which underscores the importance of the new hardware in achieving this. Although it is cinematic pre-animated footage, and not gameplay footage, the trailer still showed that the hardware is capable of successfully running highly detailed animation (PlayStation 2014a). The photorealistic details, such as Nathan Drake's stubble, wrinkles, strands of hair, as well as the wet patches of his shirt, or his torso reflecting the light showcased the power of the new technology.

Talking about how much more visual detail the new hardware allows them to convey, Druckmann said of the trailer:

> From a character standpoint, the tech really allows us to get more subtlety. We're seeing hints of that in the trailer, you know, how much we can show pain or grimaces . . . it's a subtle touch, but as he raises his eyebrows, the colour of his skin changes, the blood flows away from that compression. All those things let a realistic character become much more grounded, much more believable.
>
> (PlayStation 2014c: n.p.)

The key words to take away here are 'grounded' and 'believable', which hint towards an aspiration for a photorealistic quality. This priority in design intention is underscored by Naughty Dog's animators as well (GDC 2018). Throughout production, not only would Naughty Dog hire animators with a strong background in film, they would also host visiting seminars by animators from studios like Pixar. They also often used filmic reference points such as Roger Deakins' work for the Coen brothers (PlayStation 2015b). This suggests that on their quests to 'grounded' and 'believable' representation, they were greatly inspired by cinematic conventions.

An 'Active Cinematic Experience' 97

Naughty Dog as a studio has long had a reputation for outstanding animation and art. However, as the train level from *Uncharted 2* discussed earlier demonstrates, it is not only in cut-scenes, but also in gameplay sequences that the studio works towards highly detailed audiovisual representation. It was with the subject of art and animation that the studio's developers toured high profile game design workshops and industry events across the globe, such as the Game Developers Conference and the Special Interest Group on Computer Graphics and Interactive Techniques (SIGGRAPH), where they share their knowledge and educate other developers on their work. Just in the past few years, several such talks and seminars were given by animation and art team members on the development of *Uncharted 4*, dissecting the technical aspect of their work in great detail.[17] Talks on performance capture of not just cut-scene, but gameplay sections, such as climbing movements, as well as panels and interviews with performance capture staff and actors, were also common (PlayStation 2015c; Spottingames 2017), which demonstrate the studio's dedication not only to creating, but also promoting the importance of visual detail. Naughty Dog Artist Adam Littledale revealed a key objective for their department:

> We create the plants by hand. We go for more of an illustrative look, and more idealized to how we want to see it. We want realism but pushed a little in the ways that we want them to be pushed.
> (Reiner 2015a: n.p.)

Such attention to detail was made possible by the technological prowess of the PlayStation 4. As Druckmann said

> [t]he resolution involved in that requires a lot more work, and a lot more thought, and a lot more time. It's not just 'eh, any old dirt will do'. It's a very specific dirt, how wet is that dirt, how many pebbles are pushing up in that dirt, and you take that consideration and you apply that to everything. . . . The new hardware allows us to achieve what we've been trying to achieve the whole time, and that's just believability and complexity.
> (PlayStation 2016b: n.p.)

Druckmann here underlined the importance of consideration of minute detail and ties it back to the studio's design ethos by saying they have been working towards 'believability and complexity'. While a lot of effort was put towards designing environments with highly detailed visuals, the character model of Nathan Drake also benefited from similar attention. Reportedly, there are approximately 1200 bone-like parts in his face alone, compared to *Uncharted 3*'s 250 (Reiner 2015b). In addition to environment art and character facial animations, ragdoll animations (that is, the way bodies are animated) also benefited from the PlayStation 4's technological affordances.

The console allowed for the creation and implementation of more complex movements through the game's systems. Lead Animator Jeremy Yates said

> We also want more contextual animations. If Drake has a pistol in his hand, his animations will be different. If he has an assault rifle, those animations will be different. These differences are subtle, but you can see they are there. . . . The hit reactions have nothing to do with the animation from the attacker. It's all based on the angle from which Drake punches, and where he hits them on the body. We have a huge library of hit reactions. It's very dynamic, and you can come at it from any angle.
> (Reiner 2015b: n.p.)

Such emphasis on the enrichment of the representational world not only in cut-scenes, but also during gameplay, indicates that Naughty Dog placed demonstrable emphasis on affording dramatic agency as not only do these in-game objects and animations enrich the predetermined designer story told largely via cut-scenes, they also contribute towards a photorealistic quality in the emergent player story. Furthermore, each gameplay session, style, and angle of approach would generate a unique sequence of emergent player stories.

The same is true for the audio design team. Senior Sound Designer Robert Krekel's words reveal a salient cinematic inspiration:

> What's unique about *Uncharted* is its pulp adventure roots. As a sound guy, we all kinda feel like we always just go back to Indiana Jones.
> (Krohgie 2016: n.p.)

The pulp adventure inspiration did not just mean sound designers thought in terms of filmic reference points like Indiana Jones—they recreated actual sounds from the films using similar methods as foley artists would for film. For instance, Senior Sound Designer Jeremy Rogers went and bought the same brand bullwhip as used by Indiana Jones.

> I think one of the big sounds that's gonna show up that's iconic is the grappling hook. . . . I actually went and bought a David Morgan bullwhip, which is the same bullwhip maker that did the Indiana Jones whip that Ben Burtt, big sound designer, used for all the whip cracks and whooshes and everything. . . . We did a whole series of recordings with that. And because of that, I think it's an homage to Indiana Jones, and I think it becomes one of the iconic sounds of this *Uncharted* game.
> (Krohgie 2016: n.p.)

Actions like this show that a cinematic quality was very much of import to sound design. More specifically, developers endeavoured to capture the richness and complexity of real-world aural environments. Besides the filmic inspirations, as Audio Lead Phil Kovats summed it up, they 'really tried to make sure that as the player progresses through the story, they really felt that they were being held into different locations across the world' (Krohgie 2016: n.p.). The new hardware made it possible to design very high level of detail and variation to sounds. It allowed for things such as the implementation of what Naughty Dog's designers called a Dynamic Foliage System, which meant that depending on speed of traversal and the kind of environment, for instance running or walking through a bush, or driving on different surfaces, everything was made to sound different:

> On the jeep, each tyre is individually synthed on what it's driving on, how it's driving, is it skidding, is it losing any pressure, those kinds of things. And it really brings the jeep to life.
> (Krohgie 2016: n.p.)

Not only were the sounds complex and realistic, developers also emphasised their efforts towards creating emergent, situation-specific sound. A degree of dynamicity is not uncommon in videogames, considering that they are an interactive medium: the player could have their avatar shoot a weapon, and the sound of gunfire would be triggered then and there, as a result of the player's action, not scripted to happen in that particular moment in time.[18] However, as Senior Sound Designer Jeremy Rogers emphasised, due to the advanced sound engine, they were able to create a seamlessness in the game's audio that tied together cut-scenes and gameplay sequences into one:

> I believe the world we have created is more film-like and expansive than ever. The sound engine itself is incredibly advanced. Because of that, the audio experience is more realistic. Usually, in a game, you can tell when there is a cutscene with baked-audio in 5.1—in this game, it is seamless. There are times where we bake the audio into the scene, and there are times when the audio is happening in the actual environment on the fly.
> (Andersen 2016: n.p.)

Such a high level of detail inspired by aural cinematic tradition, but translated to the language of videogames, not always predetermined in occurrence but deliberately crafted so that they are reactionary and relative in occurrence, suggests that sound designers were placing emphasis on enabling a degree of dramatic agency not just via visual, but also audio design.

Before moving on to the textual analysis, let's review the main takeaways regarding design ethos and intention. The paratextual analysis revealed that intention was shaped less by market pressure, but by internally set high standards primarily regarding detailed audiovisual quality. The two main contextual factors with influence were the technological innovation of the PlayStation 4, and the changes in personnel, which in turn led to an overhaul of the project. The new directive was to create a game that balances a cinematic feel with as much available to the player 'on the stick' as possible. This primarily translated into working towards allowing player freedom on bigger than before levels, and giving players agency to traverse the space and tackle enemies in ways they see best fit, therefore creating a game that would afford agency in the spatial-explorative and temporal-ergodic dimension. Developers identified the challenge of balancing the freedom provided by 'wide-linear' levels with largely linear progression required to tell a story, and endeavoured to tackle this by implementing measures that still maintain some degree of control by restricting player action to core mechanics. While the heavily predetermined linear narrative structure would not leave much space for narrative agency to manifest and therefore developers did not discuss it, the emphasis placed on delivering photorealistic audiovisual detail suggested that dramatic agency would be of import to designers. The next, and final, section of this chapter will explore how agency is afforded and limited by the design of *Uncharted 4: A Thief's End*, and will question whether it matches the designers' stated intentions. This section will look at how the discourse of 'cinematic'-ness interweaving the paratextual surrounds privileges certain types of agency in the game itself.

Agency and a 'Cinematic Feel'

In terms of the general make-up of *Uncharted 4*, the main game mechanics are traversal, puzzle-solving, and combat. The main types of gameplay sequences are 'wide-linear' levels, set pieces, and cut-scenes. In order to deliver a tightly authored story, these are arranged in a linear fashion, with no branching options in the main plot. Since the game is story-driven, there are more cut-scenes at the beginning, when the main conflict is set up, while the second half of the game shifts focus toward 'wide linear' levels, with a few cut-scenes scattered for major story beats. Within wide-linear levels and set pieces (brought to life by scripted events of varying complexity), there is some degree of sideways gameplay, as opposed to the forward movement dictated by the predetermined story. For example, *Uncharted 4*'s set pieces are fully playable sequences of car chases, escapes from collapsing buildings, or a climb out of a car hanging off a cliff. Such scenes are typically represented by cut-scenes in most games as it would be rather challenging and resource-intensive to implement them in live gameplay. Set pieces in *Uncharted 4* sacrifice player freedom for spectacle and controlled pace, but there is still some degree of optionality within them: for instance, different paths are afforded down the hill in the Madagascar car chasing sequence, although they all lead to the same road. These gameplay sections afford agency across all dimensions and will be discussed accordingly. The following analysis will focus on agency in the spatial-explorative, temporal-ergodic, and narrative-dramatic dimension, since these are the most prominent ones in this game. Configurative-constructive agency will not be discussed in much detail, because in order to maintain consistency of storyworld across playthroughs, only a very low degree of agency is afforded in this dimension, bar the ability to change Nathan Drake's weapons, and the occasional movable platform.

Spatial-Explorative Agency in Uncharted 4

Generally speaking, in terms of how ludic, locally represented, and storyworld spaces relate to each other, there is no notable discrepancy besides those typical of videogames: objects populating the 3D spaces are surrounded by non-visually represented collision boxes, there is a skybox which creates the illusion of the storyworld being bigger than the locally represented space, and there is a minimally intrusive HUD disrupting the storyworld space with ludic information. This is not to say there is nothing noteworthy of spatial-explorative agency affordances in the game's design. What developers referred to as 'wide linear' levels afford the largest possibility space for avatar action across dimension in *Uncharted 4*. In these, the avatar's essential move set is comprised of running, jumping, climbing, rolling, and the context-dependent crouch and taking cover. There are also the objects of swinging rope and a climbing spike, which add some variation. While these spatial agency affordances are fairly standard for action-adventure games, assessing them within the tradition of the platformer genre, the like of which Naughty Dog produced historically with *Crash Bandicoot* or *Jak and Daxter*, reveals that they are rather reduced and simplified. The main challenge in platformer games is time-critical traversal of levels populated with obstacles. In platformer games of old, spatial agency affordances such as a 'double jump' or 'slide and jump' also enable agency to manifest in the temporal-ergodic dimension, whereby the player is required to, for instance, press X twice on the PlayStation controller within a short window of time in order to have their avatar successfully execute a double jump. In *Uncharted 4*, the platforming challenges are somewhat more forgiving in two rather salient ways. First, the area on a platform from which a jump is to be launched for it to be successful, as well as the landing zone, are quite generous and do not require the kind of precision platformer games tend to. This could be seen as a way to sacrifice challenge for organicness of flow, moving the imaginary toggle of player experience from 'game' towards 'film'. Second, there are visual markers that indicate what areas in the avatar's immediate vicinity are available for jumping on, climbing, rope-hooking, or to be climbed with the spike. Discoloured or highlighted edges, specifically textured rock surfaces, or pop-up icons indicate whether a certain move is executable or not. This, again, is arguably a means to smooth player progression, for constantly falling off edges or unsuccessfully attempting to rope every tree branch breaks the fluidity of traversal, thereby staggering the fast-paced action feel that was said to be design intention. In this way, *Uncharted 4*'s design restricts spatial agency from manifesting, and this restriction fits within design intention to keep mechanics core.

Looking at explorative agency, the PlayStation 4 is able to run larger levels efficiently, and these require the player to be able to read more complex terrains and object relations (see 'spatial literacy' in Pearce 2008). In comparison to the game's other, more constricted sections, the navigation of these wide-linear levels allow for a larger degree of freedom in planning the avatar's progression. While compared to previous instalments of the franchise, such design expands the possibility space for explorative agency, however, there is still a degree of designer control in guiding the player/avatar towards the correct route. The main routes are still labelled with *Uncharted*'s trademark yellow/white lines along edges, and developers also often use light and in-game objects as obstacles to point the player in the right direction.

These denote primarily routes across the levels, so they curb the incentive to explore available space. Girina calls these devices 'expressive lighting' and 'scripted staging', where the former serves the purpose of decorum as well as functionality (Girina 2013: 52), and the latter

> allows for a compromise between the freedom granted to the player and the control guaranteed to the narrative instance. The ultimate goal of staging is to believably convey the illusion of free will while channelling the player's activity on a predetermined route.
>
> (Girina 2013: 49)

Elsewhere, he adds '[s]cripted staging creates constraints on the freedom allowed to the player in order to make him/her experience the designed cinematic situation' (Girina 2015: 78). If we were to use Girina's terminology, we would say that these techniques thus deployed in 'wide-linear' levels ultimately convey an 'illusion of free will'. However, if we think of agency in terms of degrees, it could then be argued that there is explorative agency being afforded, only to a certain degree, with some designer authority still curbing the possibility space for avatar action, as a means of achieving the effect desired by the 'designed cinematic situation'.

In *Uncharted 4*'s set pieces, the situation is rather different, whereby avatar action in the spatial-explorative dimension is somewhat more restricted, as and when the set piece requires it to be. In general, and quite logically, the player's explorative agency is severely constrained, meaning they cannot deviate from the area in general, as well as the direction of progress. The Madagascar set piece is a good example of this. It is *Uncharted 4*'s longest interlinked sequence of action set pieces, ushering the player/avatar through a market area, an entire multi-story house, including rooftop chase, a car chase through the city, being dragged behind an enemy vehicle, fighting enemies and jumping from truck to truck, then driving again, and eventually riding the back of Sam's motorbike.

The individual sequences within this chain of events afford and limit avatar action in the spatial-explorative dimension to different degrees. At some points, for instance in the market section, all spatial-explorative agency affordances are enabled, as it is a freely navigable, albeit small, wide-linear arena. At other times, such as when riding a motorbike that Drake's brother Sam is driving, there is no agency afforded in this dimension: Drake is stuck behind his brother, and the only thing he can do is shoot at the truck in pursuit. While this section is heavily scripted, all three spaces the avatar traverses align as much as they tend to during regular gameplay (not in cut-scene), as the avatar still has control over the camera. If they were to traverse a projected video, the camera's movements would result in a distorted perspective. It can thus be seen that during such set pieces, while the game spaces appear as only slightly altered from how they tend to align in regular gameplay, the game mechanics are not only limited to core in and of themselves, they can also be further reduced if need be. This supports the delivery of a 'cinematic feel', which in this case means adhering to genre conventions of action-adventure cinema.

Last but not least, agency in the spatial-explorative dimension is most rigorously restricted in certain scripted events where the avatar is required to remain in close proximity to the non-player character who is delivering pre-determined narrative content. An example of one such sequence where only spatial agency is being afforded is in 'Chapter 2: Infernal Place'. The chapter begins in a prison with an extended walking sequence where the warden escorts the avatar to the prison grounds. In the sequence, the avatar's hands are tied back, thereby visually signalling the restriction on agency, and the level layout consists of one-way corridors and strategically placed guards obstructing the player should they try to diverge from the laid-out path.

Sections like these slow down avatar progression in order to deliver narrative content. In this case, the interactions the avatar has during his walk introduce his character for those who might be unfamiliar with its previous iterations. In summary, agency affordances in the spatial-explorative dimension vary depending on what type of gameplay segment we are looking at, but in general they are rather restricted, and are designed to enable ease of progress through the game to deliver the pace and intensity of the game's story.

Temporal-Ergodic Agency in Uncharted 4

Uncharted 4, being a story-driven game, does not allow for much tinkering when it comes to the temporal structures of the game that determine order of events and pace, since, though we can easily think of action-adventure films where time manipulation is a central theme, doing so would disrupt the specific 'playable cinema blockbuster' game feel that Naughty Dog is going for. That said, we can still review how the game's design shapes the possibility space for avatar action in this dimension. Most prominently, Quick Time Events, or 'prompt[s] that forc[e] players to make a split-second action or suffer usually painful or fatal consequences' (Rogers 2014: 196), are used in

Uncharted 4 to two ends, both having to do with enhancing the cinematic quality of gameplay by restricting avatar action even beyond core mechanics. First, these 'ergodic punctuations' are deployed to 'lend the whole scenario a sense of enhanced participatory involvement' and prompt the player to maintain more attention even to cut-scenes (Newman 2002: n.p.). During a QTE, a flashing icon pops up showing what button of the controller needs to be pressed repeatedly at a fast pace, which is often accompanied by haptic feedback from the controller itself, and a slowly growing ring-shaped progression metre indicating how long this repeated action needs to be maintained for. Second, there are QTEs in *Uncharted 4* which are unavoidable due to the game's linear progression, such as a door being locked that requires the forceful removal of an obstacle, or freeing the avatar from a headlock in close quarters combat. These embellish the avatar's core move set in certain situations (for example, there is no 'keep pounding on the gate' verb). By doing so, such QTEs allow the player/avatar to realise a slightly more complex action, thereby enhancing the realistic and natural quality in the avatar's actions.

Besides this simple prompt to time-critical action, there is more to discuss when it comes to temporal-ergodic agency affordances in *Uncharted 4*. As mentioned in the paratextual analysis, the new, more capable hardware meant that there was more space to be filled with content. As a result, there are several wide-linear combat arenas, especially towards the game's end, which afford gameplay more reminiscent of open-world games than any of the previous *Uncharted* games did. The most salient consequence of this is that *Uncharted 4*, no doubt inspired by *The Last of Us* in this, significantly expands game design affordances that enable stealth gameplay. For a franchise that was primarily geared towards run-and-gun combat, this expands temporal-ergodic agency in a novel way: by allowing the option to significantly slow down the pace of gameplay. What does this mean in practice? Players may choose to storm into a given combat arena; or they can sneak closer to enemies to tag them, much like in the genre-defining stealth series *Metal Gear Solid*. Combat arenas of levels are designed in such a way that they allow for plenty of opportunities to lurk up on enemies by providing cover such as tall grass or rock walls.

These arenas also sprawl upwards as much as sideways, which means the players can take verticality into account when planning. This is a textbook example of when an aspect of game design simultaneously affords agency in the spatial-explorative and temporal-ergodic dimension. Once enemies are tagged, the player/avatar is free to squat behind cover and strategise how best to approach the situation without any penalties in place. Thus, level design affords variation in playstyles, creating more opportunities for the player to plan and execute stealthy takedowns, such as breaking the enemy's neck, which the avatar enacts in hasty fashion at the press of a button once in correct position. By allowing such variation, *Uncharted 4* expands the possibility space for avatar action in the temporal-ergodic dimension by giving the player more power to regulate the pace of their gameplay experience.

In addition to level design, non-play character behaviour, particularly that of enemies, also contributes to the expansion of agency in the temporal-ergodic dimension. In *Uncharted 4*, enemy actions are less authored, more reactive, and in a way, dynamic. This means that compared to previously hand-crafted behaviours, such as the enemy always hiding behind that one corner, waiting to flank the player/avatar but only beginning to do so once they pass that one bookshelf or tree, enemy AI in *Uncharted 4* exhibits more systemic behaviour. That said, Naughty Dog's level designers still programmed some degree of authorial control into these behaviours by tagging combat arenas with an entrance and exit, as well as placing key strategic spots labelled with variable qualities, such as ones likely to be targeted by stealth or open combat playstyles. This was called the Post System. Naughty Dog Game Programmer Allen Chou shared one such application of this (Chou 2016). In more open areas, the positions likely to be taken by the avatar were colour-coded depending on which playstyle they would support: stealth or open combat. Programmers could then tell non-player character AI to read these variables and adjust their behaviour accordingly.

This is combined with other additions to enemy AI behaviour, which add further textures to game mechanics requiring time-critical action. As per default, each enemy has a set variable in their behaviour, such as inclination to flank, taking cover, or their commitment to chasing the avatar (Sinclair 2016). When on the lookout, mercenaries have three distinct states: perceived threat, investigate threat, and confirm threat. Should the enemy AI enter any of these states, they light up in white, yellow, and red, respectively, with a deltoid icon hanging over their head, to indicate to the player the change in their state, which is also accompanied by a sound effect for accent. This is particularly useful in stealth playstyles. When investigating, enemy AI is likely to do it in pairs, with one non-player character investigating, while the other keeps watch. These mechanics further challenge the player to either perform a stealthy take-down, or go into further hiding. All things considered, the most notable way *Uncharted 4* expands the possibility space for avatar action in the temporal-ergodic dimension when compared to previous instalments of the franchise is in wide-linear levels, where level design and non-player character behaviour are deployed in tandem to give more control to the player over the pace of gameplay. However, in all other types of gameplay sections, avatar action is restrained in this dimension in order to adhere to the pace and structure that is not to discrepant with that of a film, as authored by the designers.

Narrative-Dramatic Agency in **Uncharted 4**

Since the game's narrative structure is largely linear in its delivery, it does not afford many possibilities for the player to meaningfully intervene in its development. Nevertheless, there are a few branching pints in the narrative, even if regardless of player choice the story returns to its main trajectory. Notably, certain cut-scenes offer dialogue options for the player/avatar to choose from. While these gameplay situations do offer slightly different responses to non-player characters' questions, and as such they invite the player to construct slightly different interpretations of storyworld events, the player's choices here do not actually result in any alteration of the major plot as designed to be delivered. In a cut-scene from early in the game, for example, Elena catches Nathan Drake wandering off in thought while she tells him about her day, and tests whether he paid attention with a question the player/avatar has to answer. None of the answers provided are actually correct, and there is no way the player could answer them correctly as Elena's voice was muffled for the majority of her monologue. All three lead to her reacting the same way—sarcastically smirking.

As such, we can argue that a very low degree of narrative agency is being afforded through sections such as this. Besides a few more instances like this, most other cut-scenes are more traditional, although Naughty Dog disposed of the black letterbox framing that used to appear in previous instalments. Such framing, remediating filmic traditions of maintaining aspect ratios when transferring widescreen footage to be displayed on screens with different aspect ratios, such as TV, has been typically used in videogames to distinguish cut-scenes from playable sequences in games. *Uncharted 4*'s disposal of this tradition makes transitions between cut-scene and gameplay even more seamless, blurring the boundary between film-y and game-y sections. The fluency of the resulting gameplay experience is, in a way, more reminiscent of a film-viewing experience.

Besides recalling the 'familiar voice of a genre' (Klevjer 2013: 305), cut-scenes in *Uncharted 4* make use of further cinematic storytelling tools: acting, mise-en-scene, and cinematography. An example that is rich with such devices appears about halfway through the game, when Nathan Drake's wife Elena tracks him down to confront him about a lie. The function of this cut-scene is to convey character emotions and trace changes in relationships, as well as to inform on where each character is heading next. The scene begins with the camera panning out in a long aerial shot of a construction site, which was the scene of the previous gameplay section. This is followed by a wipe scene transition, *Star Wars* style, to a hotel, which is where the rest of the cut-scene takes place. Here, Nathan Drake and his brother Sam quickly brief their mentor Sully (and with that, the player) on the next mission objective. As the three walk in the hotel room, they find Elena there, standing by the desk, looking at maps and holding letters, which indicates that she discovered the lie, albeit not yet in all its details.

The scene then continues with an alternation of close ups and medium shots of the couple, as they argue. They are framed together again when Elena prompts Drake to be honest with her, and he begins by introducing his brother Sam as the camera blurs the two and sharpens focus on Sam's figure.

It then cuts to Elena as she walks slowly backwards in disbelief, and stumbles as she tries to grab hold of a chair, her body language and empty gaze reflecting the emotional state her husband's betrayal left her in. As she is listening to his excuses, she plays with her wedding ring, which suggests that she is now questioning the very vows they made to each other. Their argument concludes with a tense instrumental score playing as Elena walks out in anger.

This cut-scene is a perfect example of how more advanced technology has allowed videogame characters to be created with increasing correspondence to a naturalistic acting style,[19] as opposed to the highly stylised, over-the-top acting designed to get an absolutely necessary amount of information across that was typical of videogames in the decades preceding. However, as Wolf (2003: 57) points out, just because digital performance is further removed from real human acting, it is not of a lower quality. Indeed, this cut-scene in *Uncharted 4* makes use of filmic tools such as framing, body language, and score to portray character emotions and changes in relationships. In doing so, it constrains avatar action and thus agency in all dimensions, as it is a crucial moment in the linear story that cannot accommodate player intervention. As such, cut-scenes like the above work towards facilitating a cinematic experience by remediating filmic storytelling devices, all the while constraining agency across dimensions.

While the player/avatar's narrative agency is considerably constrained, we can still identify means to expand the possibility space for dramatic agency to be realised in the design of *Uncharted 4*. The PlayStation 4 did not only allow for complex game systems to be implemented, but, as discussed in the paratextual analysis, extremely detailed audiovisual representation, and consequently, believability. Looking at *Uncharted 4*'s design reveals that this aspect of the communicated design intention was very much adhered to. As far as audiovisual richness is concerned, there are an exceptionally large number of animations for Drake's traversal which are triggered by the same button press, but which all depend on the terrain and surrounding objects: momentary stumbles, pushing non-player characters out of his way, or turning left or right by an object and putting his arm up. Climbing also has a similarly diverse set of animations, depending on the angle of reach and direction of movement. In combat, one melee button press may result in left or right punch to head, stomach, legs, or a kick, or even jump kick, depending on the enemy AI's movements. In-game objects will also react dynamically: the sausages at the marketplace will sway as bullets hit them, leaves will react to a character traversing through the jungle, mud will spray where the jeep traverses wet terrain. Moreover, contextual sounds adapt to what terrain the avatar is moving through, or what objects they impact with their movement: there are distinct running sounds for different terrains such as pebble, concrete, or mud; distinct ambient sounds for the Scottish Highlands, Madagascan cities, or the jungle; different sounds for a variety of surfaces and materials the avatar grabs when climbing, such as pipes, or ledges; the list goes on.

108 An 'Active Cinematic Experience'

These contextual animations and sound effects are not predetermined in occurrence but emerge dynamically from play. However, due to *Uncharted 4*'s constraints to core mechanics, many of these happen as a result of one button press. As such, the diversity of avatar action does not match that of player action, that is, the player does not have to deploy different combinations of buttons to better traverse sticky mud for example. *Uncharted 4*'s detailed audiovisual content can thus be used to expand our catalogue of how dramatic agency can be afforded by game design. Girina makes this connection between detailed animation and potential for narratively charged, but not predeterminedly occurring, gameplay events when he discusses typical differences between physics and animation engines:

> Contrary to physics engines, animation engines generally do not substantially affect the gameplay, but rather *enrich* the quality of the staging by enhancing its level of 'realism' and the amount of interaction available . . . the implementation of physics engines in contemporary productions *generates the proliferation of micro-procedural*[20] *narratives* that allow the player to experiment with the game environment creating events resulting from the procedurally calculated effects of the player's action in the game world.
>
> (Girina 2015: 85–86, my emphasis)

In other words, Girina argues that animation can enrich the narrativity of videogames by allowing for the inhabitants of game spaces, humanoid or else, to be represented audiovisually as reacting to moment-to-moment player/avatar action, thereby creating what Girina above calls 'micro-procedural narratives', which are, in the terms used in this book, player stories. As such, highly detailed and diverse audiovisual representation can be seen to enrich the player story, and thus contributes to the amplification of dramatic agency, all the while constraining avatar actions to core mechanics.

In light of the above, as comparatively restricted as they may be, *Uncharted* 4 affords agency in the spatial-explorative and temporal-ergodic dimension via gameplay in wide linear levels, which then in turn enables dramatic agency to emerge. This, then, is further amplified by the high quality and detail in audiovisual presentation. Therefore it is not only the predetermined cut-scenes and other such events that evoke a 'cinematic feel' in the game, but also the sections that allow more player freedom. Indeed, as Veale (2012) argues when discussing 'interactive cinema', such modes of entertainment have less to do with visual aesthetics, more with the interactive object evoking a feeling the like of which is elicited by film.

This chapter set out to explore player agency as conceived and communicated by Naughty Dog, and as enabled by design in their most prevalent franchise, *Uncharted*. It showed that the studio's design ethos crystallised into one that is concerned with cinematic quality in design with the *Uncharted* franchise. After a brief look at the early history of the studio, using the example of the fourth game, *Uncharted 4: A Thief's End*, the paratextual analysis of developer interviews, postmortems, and other texts produced during the press cycle identified three main themes regarding design intention: a cinematic feel, the reduction of possibility space for player action to core mechanics, and a dedication to high audiovisual detail. All three were regarded by Naughty Dog's developers as means to the end of facilitating a 'cinematic feel'. Against this background, the textual analysis examined in how far design intention matched the final outcome by deploying the multidimensional heuristic framework for analysing player agency. Cinematic quality was found to be inherent to the *Uncharted* series, and was achieved by restrictions to avatar action in the spatial-explorative, temporal-ergodic, and configurative-constructive dimension in order to regulate the pace of gameplay so as to make it more akin to action-adventure films. By doing so, this case study showed that despite the restriction to core mechanics, the rich audiovisual detail amplified the narrative quality of mundane moment-to-moment events, therefore expanding the possibility space for dramatic agency to manifest, regardless of the constraints on avatar action in other dimensions. The analysis concluded that these design affordances contribute towards a 'cinematic feel' by remediating the film-viewing experience, relying largely on cinematic devices throughout the game's design, as was aspired for by developers, and therefore that design intention was met. This aspiration fits within the broader strategy seemingly pursued by Naughty Dog parent company Sony's recent launch of video production studio PlayStation Productions, which is said to adapt proprietary videogame content to the screen (BBC 2019), and of course as demonstrated by the recent release of the film adaptation *Uncharted* (2022). This branching out carries on the intention of creating bridges between the two media.

Notes

1 The process of remediation, they argue, is determined by what they call the logic of immediacy and the logic of hypermediacy, where the former is a desire to make new media be like our real world surroundings in terms of ease and transparency, 'natural' in a way (Bolter and Grusin 2000: 23) which would eventually lead to the erasure of the fact that the artifact is a representation; and the latter 'acknowledges multiple acts of representation and makes them visible' (ibid. 34).
2 Another context-sensitive connotation of a cinematic quality in videogames appears in discussions about adaptation of IPs from other media such as film and TV, and convergence in film and game production (see, e.g., Brookey 2010). However, since Naughty Dog's games are all original IP, this is not relevant to this chapter.
3 Known in Europe as *Lylat Wars*.
4 See Gershon and Kanayama 2002; Alvisi et al. 2003 on Sony's position in the interactive media market in those years.

5   In the context of 3D animation, texturing is the process of applying layers with a certain quality, such as light reflection, colour, or ruggedness, to objects and environments. For more on this, see Bogost 2008.
6   I will discuss in more detail the history of the 'open world' descriptor in the last chapter, when juxtaposed with the similarly often-used moniker of 'sandbox'. For now, let it suffice that I use 'open world' to refer to the arrangement of game goals within the game spaces, and 'sandbox' to refer to the nature of said game goals in the first place.
7   For what *Ratchet and Clank* got right from a designer perspective, see Heir 2008.
8   It is becoming increasingly apparent that the work culture at Naughty Dog is unsustainable. Although the studio tried to dismiss these as a necessary evil on the route to true excellence (Reiner 2015c), numerous Naughty Dog developers have spoken up about unsustainable working conditions (Schreier 2020). On game industry labour more broadly, and how game workers regard their own situation, see, e.g., Chia 2019; Deuze et al. 2007; Dyer-Witheford and de Peuter 2005, 2006; Schumacher 2006, and the section on independent games in Chapter 5 of this book.
9   For how influential melodrama is in contemporary entertainment media, see Mittell 2015: 233–260.
10 This changed with the latest instalment, *Uncharted: Lost Legacy*, where the studio experimented with open world design.
11 A particularly interesting example illustrating just how difficult it is to create a moving train sequence is what happened with *Fallout 3* DLC *Broken Steel*, where developers created the illusion of train travel by attaching the train carriage to the avatar as equipment, while an animation plays to create the surrounding environment (Grayson 2015).
12 For more on how videogames remediate how colour is used in cinematography to convey basic spatio-temporal information (e.g., time of day), mood and atmosphere of a scene, and characterisation, see, e.g., Calahan 2000, Girina 2015: 104; Niedenthal 2013; or Seifi et al. 2012.
13 See Hunicke and Chapman 2004; Adams 2008 on DDA in general, and Silva et al. 2016; Baldwin 2016 on DDA in multiplayer specifically.
14 Fans were very enthusiastic about this release as shown by Twitter activity (Kim and Chandler 2018).
15 Theorycrafting refers to the process when, especially in online multiplayer games, 'expert players reverse engineer the game and use its underlying algorithms to calculate maximized play strategies' (Ask 2016: 190). See also Paul 2011. Straley here uses it in the broader sense of 'analyzing theoretical scenarios, speculating possibilities, performing statistical reports, planning strategies for unexpected events, or simply "connecting the dots."' (Vu 2017: n.p.).
16 Core mechanics of a videogame are those that the player uses repeatedly to achieve the game goal. Important to note however that repeatedly performed actions, such as running, may be core mechanics in a platformer game for example, but may not necessarily be considered as such in a videogame with more complex mechanics, such as a stealth game. For more on hierarchies of game mechanics, see Salen and Zimmerman 2004: 316–318; Sicart 2008; Wardrip-Fruin (2020).
17 See Andrew Maximov 2016; Foundry 2014; GDC 2016b, 2017b, 2018; Gnomon 2015; Minotti 2018; Pixologic ZBrush 2016; PlayStation 2014c; Substance 2016.
18 For more on videogame audio, see, e.g., Collins 2007; Zehnder and Lipscomb 2004; or contributions in the recently launched *Journal of Sound and Music in Videogames*.

19 As drawn on the late 19th-early 20th century theatrical tradition popularised by Stanislavski. More on types of acting styles in film and tv, see, e.g., Baron 2016; Pearson 1992; and parts Three and Four in Wojck 2004.
20 I will discuss the aesthetics of procedural content generation in more detail in Chapter 5. For now, I will just say that 'procedural' in this quote is used to refer to something that's brought to life on the go, as it were, as opposed to activating something manually placed.

References

Adams, E. (2008). The Designer's Notebook: Difficulty Modes and Dynamic Difficulty Adjustment. *Gamasutra*, 14 May. Available at: www.gamasutra.com/view/feature/132061/the_designers_notebook_.php?page=3

Alvisi, A.; Narduzzo, A.; Zamarian, M. (2003). Playstation and the Power of Unexpected Consequences. *Information, Communication & Society* 6 (4): 608–627. https://doi.org/10.1080/1369118032000163286

Andersen, A. (2016). Designing the Sound for Critically-Acclaimed Uncharted 4—with Senior Sound Designer Jeremy Rogers. *A Sound Effect*, 7 June. Available at: www.asoundeffect.com/uncharted-4-sound/

Andrew Maximov. (2016). *Uncharted 4 General-Purpose Vertex Processing—Naughty Dog*. Available at: www.youtube.com/watch?v=LjCjXFmkX-4

Ask, K. (2016). The Value of Calculations: The Coproduction of Theorycraft and Player Practices. *Bulletin of Science, Technology & Society* 36 (3): 190–200. https://doi.org/10.1177/0270467617690058

Baldwin, A. (2016). *Balancing Act: The Effect of Dynamic Difficulty Adjustment in Competitive Multiplayer Video Games*. PhD Thesis, Queensland University of Technology. Available at: https://eprints.qut.edu.au/102669/1/Alexander_Baldwin_Thesis.pdf

Baron, C. (2016). *Modern Acting: The Lost Chapter of American Film and Theatre*. London: Palgrave Macmillan.

Barton, M. (2008). How's the Weather: Simulating Weather in Virtual Environments. *Game Studies* 8 (1). Available at: http://gamestudies.org/0801/articles/barton

Batchelor, J. (2017). *Uncharted* Series Sales Pass 41 Million. *Gamesindustry*, 11 December. Available at: www.gamesindustry.biz/articles/2017-12-11-uncharted-series-sales-passes-41-million

BBC. (2019). PlayStation Productions: Sony Studio Turning Games into Films. *BBC* [Online]. Available at: https://www.bbc.co.uk/news/newsbeat-48347581

BluRay Trailers. (2009). *Uncharted 2: Among Thieves LIVE DEMO E3 2009*. Available at: www.youtube.com/watch?v=I6R7dtiwneI

Bogost, I. (2008). Persuasive Games: Texture. *Gamasutra*, 7 May. Available at: www.gamasutra.com/view/feature/132053/persuasive_games_texture.php?page=2

Bolter, J. D.; Grusin, R. (2000). *Remediation*. Cambridge, MA: MIT Press.

Bordwell, D.; Thompson, K. (2004). *Film Art: An Introduction*. 7th ed. New York: McGraw-Hill.

Bramwell, T. (2013). Why *The Last of Us* is the Opposite of *Uncharted*. *Eurogamer*, 14 June. Available at: www.eurogamer.net/articles/2013-06-14-why-the-last-of-us-is-the-opposite-of-uncharted

Brookey, R. A. (2007). The Format Wars. Drawing the Battle Lines for the Next DVD. *Convergence* 13 (2): 199–211.

Brookey, R. A. (2010). *Hollywood Gamers: Digital Convergence in the Film and Video Game Industries*. Bloomington, IN: Indiana University Press.
Bungie. (2001). *Halo: Combat Evolved* [Xbox]. Microsoft Game Studios.
Bungie. (2004). *Halo 2* [Xbox]. Microsoft Game Studios.
Bungie. (2007). *Halo 3* [Xbox 360]. Microsoft Game Studios.
Calahan, S. (2000). Storytelling Through Lighting: A Computer Graphics Perspective. In A. A. Apodaca and L. Gritz, eds. *Advanced RenderMan: Creating CGI for Motion Pictures*. San Francisco, CA: Morgan Kaufmann Publishers, pp. 337–382.
Calleja, G. (2011). *In-Game: From Immersion to Incorporation*. Cambridge, MA: MIT Press.
Caron, F. (2007). Getting Technical with Naughty Dog Co-President Christophe Balestra. *Ars Technica*, 31 October. Available at: https://arstechnica.com/gaming/2007/10/getting-technical-with-naughty-dog-co-president-christophe-balestra/
Chang, Y.-C.; Hsieh, C.-M. (2018). Filmic Framing in Video Games: A Comparative Analysis of Screen Space Design. *Multimedia Tools and Applications* 77 (6): 6531–6554. https://doi.org/10.1007/s11042-017-4564-6
Chia, A. (2019). The Moral Calculus of Vocational Passion in Digital Gaming. *Television and New Media* 20 (8): 767–777. https://doi.org/10.1177/1527476419851079
Chou, A. (2016). A Brain Dump of What I Worked on for Uncharted 4. *Allenchou.net*. Available from: https://allenchou.net/2016/05/a-brain-dump-of-what-i-worked-on-for-uncharted-4/
Collins, K. (2007). An Introduction to the Participatory and Non-Linear Aspects of Video Games Audio. In S. Hawkins and J. Richardson, eds. *Essays on Sound and Vision*. Helsinki: Helsinki University Press, pp. 236–298.
Core Design. (1996). *Tomb Raider* [PlayStation]. Eidos Interactive.
Crossley, R. (2015). *Uncharted 4*'s Neil Druckmann: "We Are Bringing Closure to Drake's Journey". *Gamespot*, 17 June. Available at: www.gamespot.com/articles/uncharted-4-s-neil-druckmann-we-are-bringing-closu/1100-6428273/
Deuze, M.; Martin, C.; Allen, C. (2007). The Professional Identity of Gameworkers. *Convergence* 13 (4): 335–353. https://doi.org/10.1177/1354856507081947
Digital Dragons. (2018). *DD2018: Andrew Maximov—On Cultures of Shared Creative Ownership*. Available at: www.youtube.com/watch?time_continue=603&v=zO9vPHcpfT0
DMA Design. (2001). *Grand Theft Auto III* [PlayStation 2]. Rockstar Games.
Dyer-Witheford, N.; de Peuter, G. (2005). A Playful Multitude? Mobilising and Countermobilising Immaterial Game Labour. *The Fibreculture Journal* 5. Available at http://five.fibreculturejournal.org/fcj-024-a-playful-multitude-mobilising-and-counter-mobilising-immaterial-game-labour/
Dyer-Witheford, N.; de Peuter, G. (2006). "EA Spouse" and the Crisis of Video Game Labour: Enjoyment, Exclusion, Exploitation, Exodus. *Canadian Journal of Communication* 31: 559–917. https://doi.org/10.22230/cjc.2006v31n3a1771
El-Nasr, M. S.; Niedenthal, S.; Knez, I.; Almeida, P.; Zupko, J. (2007). Dynamic Lighting for Tension in Games. *Game Studies* 7 (1). Available at: http://gamestudies.org/0701/articles/elnasr_niedenthal_knez_almeida_zupko
Farokhmanesh, M. (2015). How *Uncharted 4* Will Give You the Freedom to Explore Nathan Drake's Final Journey. *Polygon*, 23 June. Available at: www.polygon.com/2015/6/23/8832707/uncharted-4-e3-2015-preview
Foundry. (2014). *MODO Pre—Viz for Games—Naughty Dog at SIGGRAPH 2014*. Available at: www.youtube.com/watch?v=yrL4Qr64xog

Gamespot. (2015). *What Makes Naughty Dog Great? (Part 1)—Kinda Funny Stage Show E3 2015*. Available at: www.youtube.com/watch?v=KUGL1w2_L4w

Gavin, A. (2011). Making *Crash Bandicoot*—part 6. *All Things Andy Gavin*, 7 February. Available at: https://all-things-andy-gavin.com/2011/02/07/making-crash-bandicoot-part-6/

GDC. (2016a). *Uncharted 2: Creating an Active Cinematic Experience*. Available at: www.youtube.com/watch?v=lXxP6qN39wI&t=173s

GDC. (2016b). *Uncharted 4's Technical Art Culture*. Available at: www.youtube.com/watch?v=aZJQuHZQakQ&t=1086s

GDC. (2017a). *Among Friends—An Uncharted 2: Among Thieves Post-Mortem*. Available at: www.youtube.com/watch?v=ovJ_LC_HtZE

GDC. (2017b). *Texturing Uncharted 4: A Matter of Substance (Presented by Allegorithmic)*. Available at: www.youtube.com/watch?v=UNxOxiR5T_M

GDC. (2018). *Physics Animation in Uncharted 4: A Thief's End*. Available at: www.youtube.com/watch?v=7S—_vuoKgR4

Gershon, R. A.; Kanayama, T. (2002). The Sony Corporation: A Case Study in Transnational Media Management. *International Journal on Media Management* 4 (2): 105–117. https://doi.org/10.1080/14241270209389987

Girina, I. (2013). Video Game Mise-En-Scene Remediation of Cinematic Codes in Video Games. *ICIDS'13—Proceedings of the Interactive Storytelling 6th International Conference*, 6–9 November, Istanbul, pp. 45–54.

Girina, I. (2015). *Cinematic Games: The Aesthetic Influence of Cinema on Video Games*. PhD Thesis, University of Warwick. Available at: http://wrap.warwick.ac.uk/74038/

Gnomon. (2015). *Game Character Creation with Naughty Dog—Pt.1*. Available at: www.youtube.com/watch?v=R6uAOmH0QsE&t=2093s

Grayson, N. (2015). Years Later, Fans Discover the Strange Truth about Fallout 3's Trains. *Kotaku AU*, 22 July. Available at: https://kotaku.com/turns-out-fallout-3s-trains-were-actually-equipped-to-1719572837

Gregory, J. (2010). *Multiprocessor Game Loops: Lessons from Uncharted 2: Among Thieves*. Game Forum Germany. Available at: www.gameenginebook.com/resources/gfg2010-final.pdf

Hamilton, K. (2013). Why It Matters That PS4 Games Are Higher-Resolution Than Xbox One. *Kotaku*, 3 December. Available at: https://kotaku.com/why-it-matters-that-ps4-games-are-higher-resolution-th-1475165066

Hanson, B. (2015a). Comparing Uncharted 4's Story and Gameplay to *The Last Of Us*. *Game Informer*, 9 January. Available at: www.gameinformer.com/b/features/archive/2015/01/09/comparing-uncharted-4s-story-and-gameplay-to-the-last-of-us.aspx

Heir, M. (2008). Design Lesson 101—*Ratchet & Clank*. *Gamasutra*. i, 2 July. Available at: www.gamasutra.com/view/news/110193/Design_Lesson_101__Ratchet__Clank.php

Hunicke, R.; Chapman, V. (2004). AI for Dynamic Difficulty Adjustment in Games. *Challenges in Game Artificial Intelligence AAAI Workshop*. Available at: http://users.cs.northwestern.edu/~hunicke/pubs/Hamlet.pdf

id Software. (1992). *Wolfenstein 3D* [PC]. Apogee Software.

id Software. (1993). *Doom* [PC]. GT Interactive Software.

IGN. (2014). *Uncharted 4: A Thief's End—Gameplay Trailer—PSX 2014*. Available at: www.youtube.com/watch?v=I3SH—g8ykw4

IGN Staff. (2011). IGN Pitches *Uncharted 4*. *IGN*, 16 December. Available at: https://uk.ign.com/articles/2011/12/16/ign-pitches-uncharted-4

Indiana Jones and the Raiders of the Lost Ark. (1981). Directed by Steven Spielberg. Lucasfilm Ltd.

Infinity Ward. (2013). *Call of Duty: Ghosts* [PlayStation 4]. Activision.

Insomniac Games. (1998). *Spyro the Dragon* [PlayStation]. Sony Computer Entertainment.

Insomniac Games. (2002). *Ratchet & Clank* [PlayStation 2]. Sony Computer Entertainment.

Kim, Y.; Chandler, J. D. (2018). How Social Community and Social Publishing Influence New Product Launch: The Case of Twitter During the PlayStation 4 and Xbox One Launches. *Journal of Marketing Theory and Practice* 26 (1–2): 144–157. https://doi.org/10.1080/10696679.2017.1389238

King, G.; Krzywinska, T. (eds.). (2002). *ScreenPlay: Cinema/Videogames/Interfaces*. London: Wallflower Press.

Klevjer, R. (2013). Cut-Scenes. In M. J. P. Wolf and B Perron, eds. *The Routledge Companion to Video Game Studies*. New York: Routledge, pp. 301–309.

Konami Computer Entertainment Japan. (2001). *Metal Gear Solid 2: Sons of Liberty*. [PlayStation 2]. Konami.

Krohgie. (2016). *Making the Sound of Uncharted 4: A Thief's End*. Available at: www.youtube.com/watch?v=Ii7gMr_N910

Labbe, M. (2015). Druckmann and Straley Changed *Uncharted 4*'s Story Shortly after Becoming Co-Directors. *PlayStation Lifestyle*, 19 October. Available at: www.playstationlifestyle.net/2015/10/19/druckmann-and-straley-changed-uncharted-4-story-after-becoming-co-directors/

Leadbetter, R. (2013). Inside PlayStation 4: What Sony Told Game Developers at GDC. *Eurogamer*, 28 March. Available at: www.eurogamer.net/articles/digitalfoundry-inside-playstation-4

Lemarchand, R.; Druckmann, N. (2008). Postmortem: Naughty Dog's *Uncharted: Drake's Fortune*. *Gamasutra*, 8 October. Available at: www.gamasutra.com/view/feature/132203/postmortem_naughty_dogs_.php

Miller, G.; Altano, B. (2012). *Uncharted 4* Pitches from the IGN Readers. *IGN*, 20 January. Available at: https://uk.ign.com/articles/2012/01/20/uncharted-4-pitches-from-the-ign-readers

Minotti, M. (2018). How Planning and Technology Helped Naughty Dog Animate *Uncharted 4: A Thief's End*. *Venturebeat*, 28 February. Available at: https://venturebeat.com/2017/02/28/how-planning-and-technology-helped-naughty-dog-animate-uncharted-4-a-thiefs-end/

Mittell, J. (2015). *Complex TV: The Poetics of Contemporary Television Storytelling*. New York and London: New York University Press.

Mobygames. (2002a). Wolfenstein 3D Covers. *Mobygames*. Available at: www.mobygames.com/game/dos/wolfenstein-3d/cover-art/gameCoverId,12673/

Mobygames. (2002b). Tomb Raider Covers. *Mobygames*. Available at: www.mobygames.com/game/tomb-raider/cover-art/gameCoverId,471681/

Monaghan, D. (2013). Just hangin. #naughtydog #becurious http://instagram.com/p/e_NC08mplx/Tweeted at 6:55 PM, 2 October. Available at: https://twitter.com/DomsWildThings/status/385583951546712065

National Treasure. (2004). Directed by Jon Turtelaub. Walt Disney Pictures; Jerry Bruckenheimer Films; Junction Entertainment; Saturn Films.

Naughty Dog. (1996). *Crash Bandicoot* [PlayStation]. Sony Computer Entertainment.
Naughty Dog. (2001). *Jak and Daxter: The Precursor Legacy* [PlayStation 2]. Sony Computer Entertainment.
Naughty Dog. (2003). *Jak II* [PlayStation 2]. Sony Computer Entertainment.
Naughty Dog. (2007). *Uncharted: Drake's Fortune* [PlayStation 3]. Sony Computer Entertainment.
Naughty Dog. (2009). *Uncharted 2: Among Thieves* [PlayStation 3]. Sony Computer Entertainment.
Naughty Dog. (2011). *Uncharted 3: Drake's Deception.* [PlayStation 3] Sony Computer Entertainment.
Naughty Dog. (2013). *The Last of Us* [PlayStation 3]. Sony Computer Entertainment.
Naughty Dog. (2016). *Uncharted 4: A Thief's End* [PlayStation 4]. Sony Computer Entertainment.
Naughty Dog. (2017). *Uncharted: Lost Legacy* [PlayStation 4]. Sony Computer Entertainment.
Naughty Dog. (2019). Timeline. *Naughty Dog.* Available at: https://web.archive.org/web/20170728200647/www.naughtydog.com/timeline/
Newman, J. (2002). The Myth of the Ergodic Videogame: Some Thoughts on Player-Character Relationships in Videogames. *Game Studies* 1 (2). Available at: www.gamestudies.org/0102/newman/
Nguyen, T. (2011). Mapping the Development of *Uncharted 3: Drake's Deception. 1up,* 21 October. Available at: www.1up.com/features/mapping-uncharted-3-drake-deception.html
Niedenthal. S. (2013). Color. In M. J. P. Wolf and B. Perron, eds. *The Routledge Companion to Video Game Studies.* New York: Routledge, pp. 67–73.
Nintendo EAD. (1985). *Super Mario Bros* [Nintendo Entertainment System]. Nintendo.
Nintendo EAD. (1994). *Star Fox/Lylat Wars* [Nintendo Entertainment System]. Nintendo.
Nishita, L. (2017). *Crash Bandicoot*: An Oral History. *Kotaku,* 22 June. Available at: www.polygon.com/2017/6/22/15820540/crash-bandicoot-an-oral-history
Orland, K. (2015). Alan Tudyk: I Left *Uncharted 4* Over "Weird Changes" to Script. *Ars Technica,* 20 October. Available at: https://arstechnica.com/gaming/2015/10/alan-tudyk-i-left-uncharted-4-over-weird-changes-to-script/
Otana. (2009). *Making of Jak II.* Available at: www.youtube.com/watch?v=Ljkk94nedTs
Paquette, A. (2013). *An Introduction to Computer Graphics for Artists.* 2nd ed. London: Springer London.
Paul, C. A. (2011). Optimizing Play: How Theorycraft Changes Gameplay and Design. *Game Studies* 11 (2). Available at: http://gamestudies.org/1102/articles/paul
Pearce, C. (2008). Spatial Literacy: Reading (and Writing) Game Space. *Proceedings of Future and Reality of Gaming (FROG),* 17–19 October, Vienna. Available at: http://citeseerx.ist.psu.edu/viewdoc/download?doi=10.1.1.401.606&rep=rep1&type=pdf
Pearson, R. (1992). *Eloquent Gestures: The Transformation of Performance Style in the Griffith Biograph Films.* Berkeley, CA: University of California Press.
Pixologic ZBrush. (2016). *Official ZBrush Summit 2016 Presentation—Naughty Dog.* Available at: www.youtube.com/watch?v=aHmWZey9r9g

PlayStation. (2009a). *UNCHARTED 2: Among Thieves™—Technology and Gameplay (BTS #1)*. Available at: www.youtube.com/watch?v=D_p58o6RJ88
PlayStation. (2009b). *UNCHARTED 2: Among Thieves™—Making of the Cinematics (BTS #3)*. Available at: www.youtube.com/watch?v=tzkYa44ral8
PlayStation. (2009c). *UNCHARTED 2: Among Thieves™—Rehearsals BTS #10*. Available at: www.youtube.com/watch?v=GInXXexuhLg&index=10&list=PL60AFC03761820B74
PlayStation. (2012). *Jak and Daxter Collection™ Behind the Scenes*. Available at: www.youtube.com/watch?v=GT4Ppbg257g
PlayStation. (2013). *PlayStation 4 Launch | PS4 All Access: Greatness Awaits Live Stream*. Available at: www.youtube.com/watch?v=DIRfRPTGBgE
PlayStation. (2014a). *Uncharted 4: A Thief's End E3 2014 Trailer (PS4)* [Online video]. Available at: www.youtube.com/watch?v=y1Rx—Bbht5E
PlayStation. (2014b). *PlayStation E3 2014 | Naughty Dog Interview | Live Coverage (PS4)*. Available at: www.youtube.com/watch?v=k8Yi—9ZqSls
PlayStation. (2014c). *PlayStation Experience | Modeling Nathan Drake: Bringing an Iconic Character to PS4 Panel*. Available at: www.youtube.com/watch?v=70jVUBnp6lQ
PlayStation. (2015a). *UNCHARTED 4: A Thief's End—E3 2015—Sam Pursuit Gameplay | PS4*. Available at: www.youtube.com/watch?v=sB0xy74Zrj8&t=422s
PlayStation. (2015b). *Conversations with Creators with Wil Wheaton | S01, E02: Naughty Dog*. Available at: www.youtube.com/watch?v=SFxSz8Yqy9w&t=205s
PlayStation. (2015c). *PlayStation Experience 2015: Uncharted 4: Stories from the Performance Capture Set Panel*. Available at: www.youtube.com/watch?v=z_KFAbDgJkY
PlayStation. (2016a). *The Making of UNCHARTED 4: A Thief's End—The Evolution of a Franchise | PS4*. Available at: www.youtube.com/watch?v=aGihxo9afQQ
PlayStation. (2016b). *Making of Uncharted 4: A Thief's End—Pushing Technical Boundaries Part 1 | PS4*. Available at: www.youtube.com/watch?v=3uKia6kb1fk
PlayStation. (2016c). *The Making of Uncharted 4: A Thief's End: Pushing Technical Boundaries Part 2*. Available at: www.youtube.com/watch?v=P4wWMe85Dgo
PlayStation Europe. (2014). *Naughty Dog 30th Anniversary Video in FULL*. Available at: www.youtube.com/watch?v=KICy8_tbkDY
Rare. (2001). *Banjo-Tooie* [Nintendo 64]. Nintendo.
Reeves, B. (2011). Naughty Dog's *Uncharted* Could Have Been A Fantasy Game. *Game Informer*, 22 September. Available at: www.gameinformer.com/b/news/archive/2011/09/22/naughty-dog-s-uncharted-could-have-been-a-fantasy-game.aspx
Rehak, B. (2003). Playing at Being: Psychoanalysis and the Avatar. In M. J. P. Wolf and B. Perron, eds. *The Video Game Theory Reader*. New York: Routledge, pp. 103–127.
Reilly, L. (2011). Naughty Dog: "No Producers, No Management, Just Us Working as a Team" *IGN*, 2 November. Available at: www.ign.com/articles/2011/11/02/naughty-dog-no-producers-no-management-just-us-working-as-a-team
Reiner, A. (2015a). The Secret Depth of *Uncharted 4*'s Art Design. *Game Informer*, 21 January. Available at: www.gameinformer.com/b/features/archive/2015/01/21/the-secret-depth-of-uncharted-4-s-art-design.aspx
Reiner, A. (2015b). How *Uncharted 4* Is Taking Game Technology To The Next Level. *Game Informer*, 23 January. Available at: www.gameinformer.com/b/

features/archive/2015/01/23/how-uncharted-4-is-taking-game-technology-to-the-next-level.aspx

Reiner, A. (2015c). Naughty Dog Presidents Discuss the 'Messy Process' of Success. *Game Informer*, 28 January. Available at: www.gameinformer.com/b/features/archive/2015/01/28/naughty-dog-presidents-discuss-the-messy-process-of-success.aspx

Rogers, S. (2014). *Level Up! the Guide to Great Video Game Design*. Chichester: John Wiley & Sons.

Salen, K.; Zimmerman, E. (2004). *Rules of Play: Game Design Fundamentals*. Cambridge, MA: MIT Press.

Satterfield, S. (2001). Next to *Rayman 2*, *Jak and Daxter* is the best 3D platformer available for the PlayStation 2. *Gamespot*, 1 December. Available at: www.gamespot.com/reviews/jak-and-daxter-the-precursor-legacy-review/1900-2829768/

Schreier, J. (2017). *Blood, Sweat and Pixels: The Triumphant, Turbulent Stories behind How Video Games Are Made*. New York: Harper Collins.

Schreier, J. (2020). As Naughty Dog Crunches on *The Last Of Us II*, Developers Wonder How Much Longer This Approach Can Last. *Kotaku*, 12 March. Available at: https://kotaku.com/as-naughty-dog-crunches-on-the-last-of-us-ii-developer-1842289962

Schumacher, L. (2006). Immaterial Fordism: The Paradox of Game Industry Labour. *Work Organisation, Labour & Globalisation* 1 (1): 144–155. https://doi.org/10.13169/workorgalaboglob.1.1.0144

Seifi, H.; DiPaola, S.; Enns, J. T. (2012). Exploring the Effect of Color Palette in Painterly Rendered Character Sequences. *CAe'12—Proceedings of the Eighth Annual Symposium on Computational Aesthetics in Graphics, Visualization, and Imaging*, 4–6 June, Annecy, France, pp. 89–97.

Sicart, M. (2008). Defining Game Mechanics. *Game Studies* 8 (2). Available at: http://gamestudies.org/0802/articles/sicart

Silva, M. P.; Silva, V. N.; Chaimowicz, L. (2016). Dynamic Difficulty Adjustment through an Adaptive AI. *SBC—Proceedings of SBGames 2015. Brazilian Symposium on Games and Digital Entertainment*, 11–13 November 2015, Teresina, Piauí, Brazil, pp. 52–59.

Sinclair, B. (2016). *Uncharted 4* Is Not As Scripted As You Might Think. *Gamesindustry*, 4 November. Available at: www.gamesindustry.biz/articles/2016-11-04-uncharted-4-not-as-scripted-as-you-might-think

Sinclair, B. (2017). Was PS3 Hard to Develop for? *Gamesindustry*, 1 August. Available at: www.gamesindustry.biz/articles/2017-08-01-was-ps3-hard-to-develop-for

Sonic Team. (1991). *Sonic the Hedgehog* [Mega Drive]. SEGA.

Spottingames. (2017). UNCHARTED 10th Anniversary Cast Interview—PSX 2017 HD. Available at: www.youtube.com/watch?v=luYOGZYuypo

Square. (1999). *Final Fantasy VIII* [PC]. Square.

Staff, E. (2015). *Uncharted 4: A Thief's End*—The Story Behind the Biggest Game of the Year. *Gamesradar*, 24 February. Available at: www.gamesradar.com/uk/uncharted-4-a-thiefs-end-preview/

Stashwick, T. (2013). The Guts the Glamour the Glory That Is #uncharted #ps4 #whosthisguy? Tweeted at 2:31 PM, 22 November. Available at: https://twitter.com/ToddStashwick/status/404014375247179776

Stenson, R.; Ho, C. (2013). PlayStation® Shader Language for PlayStation®4. *GDC Europe*. Available at: http://twvideo01.ubm—us.net/o1/vault/gdceurope2013/Presentations/825424RichardStenson.pdf

Substance. (2016). *GDC 2016: Naughty Dog's Substance Pipeline In-Depth by Bradford Smith*. Available at: www.youtube.com/watch?v=r_yi537h9HQ

TheDarkStation88. (2011). *The Naughty Dog Story, Crash Bandicoot, Jak & Daxter & more*. Available at: www.youtube.com/watch?v=yRlBOgFAeHA&t=153s

Tretton, J. (2013). PlayStation Meeting 2013: PlayStation 4 Is The Future of Gaming. *PlayStation Blog*, 20 February. Available at: https://blog.playstation.com/2013/02/20/playstation-meeting-2013-the-future-of-gaming-is-here-with-playstation-4/

Ubisoft Montreal. (2002). *Tom Clancy's Splinter Cell*. [Xbox] Ubisoft.

Ubisoft Montreal. (2003). *Prince of Persia: The Sands of Time* [PlayStation 2]. Ubisoft.

Ubisoft Montreal. (2013). *Assassin's Creed IV: Black Flag* [PlayStation 4]. Ubisoft.

Uncharted. (2022). Directed by Ruben Fleischer. Columbia Pictures.

Veale, K. (2012). "Interactive Cinema" Is an Oxymoron, But May Not Always Be. *Game Studies* 12 (1). Available at: http://gamestudies.org/1201/articles/veale

Vicarious Visions. (2017). *Crash Bandicoot N. Sane Trilogy* [PlayStation 4]. Activision.

Vu, A. (2017). Design for Theorycrafting. *Gamasutra*, 31 October. Available at: www.gamasutra.com/blogs/AlexVu/20171031/308568/Design_for_Theorycrafting.php

Wardrip-Fruin, N. (2020). *How Pac-Man Eats*. Cambridge, MA: MIT Press.

Wells, E. (2014). Statement from Co-Presidents Evan Wells and Christophe Balestra. *Naughty Dog Blog*, 6 March. Available at: www.naughtydog.com/blog/statement_from_the_co_presidents1

Wojck, P. R. (ed.). (2004). *Movie Acting: The Film Reader*. New York: Routledge.

Wolf, M. J. P. (2003). The Technological Construction of Performance. *Convergence* 9 (4): 48–59. https://doi.org/10.1177/135485650300900405

XoZen. (2007). *Uncharted: Drake's Fortune—Behind-The-Scenes—PART 1*. Available at: www.youtube.com/watch?v=MlN2vJXuqMM

Yin-Poole, W. (2018). The Secrets of *Uncharted 2*'s Superb Train Level Revealed. *Eurogamer*, 12 May. Available at: www.eurogamer.net/articles/2018-05-12-the-secrets-of-uncharted-2s-superb-train-level-revealed

Zdyrko, D. (2001). *Jak and Daxter: The Precursor Legacy*. IGN, 5 December. Available at: www.ign.com/articles/2001/12/05/jak-and-daxter-the-precursor-legacy

Zehnder, S. M.; Lipscomb, S. D. (2004). The Role of Music in Video Games. In P. Vordererand and J. Bryant, eds. *Playing Computer Games: Motives, Responses, and Consequences*. Mahwah, NJ: Lawrence Erlbaum Associates, pp. 241–258.

4 'A Compelling Story with Choices That Matter'

BioWare's *Mass Effect* Series

The first case study looked at Naughty Dog, a studio with a long history in action-adventure games, and their game *Uncharted 4: A Thief's End* (2016), which exemplified how a high degree of designer control on player progression does restrain agency across a number of dimensions, but some can still emerge. This second case study focuses on the similarly established studio of BioWare, whose design history is in making role-playing videogames; and their game *Mass Effect: Andromeda* (BioWare 2017), whose design is steeped in the same heritage but is also merging with other generic design features, primarily from the shooter genre. In science-fiction action role-playing game *Mass Effect: Andromeda* (henceforth referred to as *Andromeda*), the player/avatar, aided by their motley crew of squad mates, is tasked with finding a new home for humanity in the Andromeda galaxy through space operatic adventures not at all dissimilar to those depicted by the *Star Wars* franchise. Player progress is not as highly authored as in *Uncharted 4*, but there are still plenty restrictions on avatar action that constrict the possibility space for agency to manifest. Furthermore, the game marks an important milestone in the transformation of BioWare's design ethos. Compared to the consistency seen in the previous case study, both the design ethos of BioWare and the brand identity of the *Mass Effect* franchise changed over the years, with a particularly salient shift in how agency was conceptualised. As such, this case study will complement the previous one in terms of how differently design can enable agency to manifest.

The chapter first examines the studio history of BioWare, the kinds of games they are known for, and how that forms the foundation of a particular style of game design, with recurrent themes and features. It will then briefly discuss how the *Mass Effect* franchise came to be, and how its identity was shaped by each instalment. This will provide an outline of the franchise's brand identity in terms of how they afford or limit player action, which can then be used as a basis of comparison when looking at *Andromeda* as a text. The chapter's main argument is that due to open world game design allowing more opportunity for combat encounters, which are also more diverse compared to the original trilogy, the previously central importance assigned to traditional role-playing mechanics affording narrative and

DOI: 10.4324/9781003298786-5

configurative agency in BioWare games changed, prioritising agency in the temporal-ergodic and spatial-explorative dimension. However, while this shift would in theory support the expression of dramatic agency, the textual analysis will show that *Andromeda* struggles to attach what narratologists call a quality of 'eventfulness' to these emergent player stories, and therefore ultimately fails to truly afford a high degree of dramatic agency.

BioWare and the *Mass Effect* Franchise

BioWare: The Beginnings

Three Canadian doctors, Ray Muzyka, Greg Zeschuk, and Augustine Yip, formed BioWare in 1995 during their student years. Going from programming medical software to making games under the BioWare name, their first successful games on PC were *Baldur's Gate* (BioWare 1998), and its sequel *Baldur's Gate II* (BioWare 2000a). These were based on medieval fantasy themed tabletop role-playing game *Dungeons & Dragons* license, and that *Baldur's Gate II* still ranked at 6th place on Metacritic's list of the best PC games of all times is indictive of BioWare's reputation in this genre. Player progression in these games was structured nonlinearly, with plenty side quests and branching options in the main quest, which is why the game has been analysed in studies on narrative agency (see, e.g., Carr et al. 2006: 22–24; Jørgensen 2003). The following will look at the evolution of BioWare within an ecology of studios, consumer trends, and technological possibilities, particularly from the time when they began expanding the boundaries of the role-playing genre.

The early 2000s saw a shift in game development trends, leaving behind an era dominated by neatly clustered genre masterpieces like the first-person shooter *Doom* (id Software 1993), point-and-click adventure *Myst* (Cyan, Inc. 1993) or massively multiplayer online games like *Ultima Online* (Origin Systems 1997). Technological advancement had an impact on PC performance, and, as already discussed in the previous chapter, new games consoles PlayStation 2 and Xbox were launched, joining what is known today as the 'console wars' between Nintendo and Sega (Blake 2014). While their respective consoles, the SNES and the Mega Drive, had enjoyed popularity in the market up to this point,[1] Sony and Microsoft proved to be fierce competition, with PlayStation 2 sales in particular skyrocketing. As Kerr (2006: 67) observed, 'Sony's installed [hardware] base of PS2s at over 100 million dwar[ved] Nintendo's 8 million and Microsoft's 6 million'. While PC game sales were negatively impacted by the console competition, the platform retained relevance due to the player bases of MMO and strategy games. This is noteworthy because many games in these genres share game mechanics with role-playing games, securing the continuation of this model of game design across platforms. From this we can see that there were two tendencies amongst game studios in this hardware environment: either focusing on building games which could make use of the advance graphics cards and CPUs of computers, or have the certainty of a uniform hardware architecture of consoles.

The first-person shooter genre grew in popularity with *Halo* (Bungie 2001) being an Xbox launch title. A more significant momentum in this period, however, was the release of *Grand Theft Auto: Vice City* (Rockstar North 2002). The game received critical acclaim, while quickly becoming synonymous with controversies and lawsuits over its depiction of violence and sexually explicit content (Anon 2003; Thorsen 2007).[2] Nevertheless, with this game Rockstar revolutionised open world gameplay. While horror titles like the *Resident Evil* series already offered open world experiences around this time, *GTA: Vice City* contained thus far unseen numbers of in-game objects available for interaction (Egenfeldt-Nielsen et al. 2016: 105). First-person shooters like *Far Cry* (Crytek 2004) drew on this development, but also added more destructible environments, resulting in a virtual world that felt, overall, more alive. Given that in videogames genre is determined not only by narrative tradition like in other audiovisual media such as film, but also by gameplay mechanics, the growing technological affordances allowed for the design of bigger, more complex games, with powerful graphics, simultaneously loosening genre boundaries.

In the early 2000s, BioWare's traditional role-playing games were competing against such mixed genre games. Blizzard's role-playing hack-and-slash hit *Diablo II* (2000) was so popular it was featured in the 2000 edition of the Guinness Book of World Records for being the fastest selling PC game ever sold, while Ion Storm's first-person shooter with stealth and role-playing game elements, *Deus Ex* (2000) rose to a cult status. Alongside the popularity of these two titles, BioWare carved out a space for themselves in the market by polishing the core mechanics of the role-playing genre: configuration of avatars via classes and skill trees; turn-based combat (typically realised via the ability to pause the combat to make strategic decisions and assign commands to both the avatar and their squad mates); and conversations with non-player characters. These mechanics primarily create a possibility space for player action in three dimensions. First, character classes and skill-trees that determine, for instance, attack strength statistics or available special powers, afford configurative agency. Second, turn-based combat enables temporal-ergodic agency within which temporal constraints determine the pace of combat and the window for non-trivial effort is also predetermined. Last, but not least, non-player characters tend to provide details of the overarching storyworld and game lore, or offer quests, and as such can be considered a narrative-dramatic agency affordance.

These three mechanics were central to early BioWare games, polished further with *Neverwinter Nights* (2002), another *Dungeons & Dragons* inspired title. This was the first BioWare game to afford online multiplayer gameplay, previously only available via local area network (LAN) cable connections. Besides the *D&D* style role-playing games, the studio expanded their portfolio with *MDK 2* (BioWare 2000b), a game which critics around the time approached with caution as it introduced an entirely new mechanic to BioWare's repertoire: '[w]hile BioWare had become known for its high-quality role-playing game *Baldur's Gate*, it wasn't exactly known for its quirky 3D shooters' (Wolpaw 2000: n.p.). *MDK2* featured three playable characters, each with specific design affordances: one focused on shooting, one on puzzles, and one on exploration. BioWare founder Zeschuk said in an interview that their 'aim with *MDK2* [was] to explore new directions and expand beyond the constrictive environments established in other 3D games' (IGN 1998: n.p.). However, this expansion only began with *MDK2*. BioWare continued to work on medieval fantasy style role-playing games with their first original IP, *Dragon Age* in development from 2004 onwards, but two other games were released before *Mass Effect* which both laid down the foundations for the quintessentially BioWare formula of game design.

In 2000 BioWare announced that they were working on a *Star Wars* game for LucasArts, to be released in conjunction with the film *Star Wars: Episode II—Attack of the Clones* (BioWare 2002). *Star Wars: Knights of the Old Republic* (BioWare 2003, from here on referred to as *KOTOR*) was developed for the Xbox, thus allowing BioWare to take advantage of a single uniform hardware architecture. Working with this certainty allowed them to polish how avatars moved in a 3D environment, a feature the studio had already experimented with in *MDK2*, while incorporating more typical role-playing mechanics. The two key aspects of BioWare's vision for *KOTOR* according to its creators were a 'choreographed combat system' and a 'cinematic storytelling camera' (Bertz 2016: n.p.). The game sold out within days of its release, and won 48 'Game of the Year', 33 'RPG of the Year', and numerous other awards. *KOTOR* is repeatedly cited amongst the best videogames ever made throughout the years (IGN 2007; Polygon 2017).

Regarding the genre and game mechanics, *KOTOR*'s combat was still a kind of turn-based d20 system[3] in the vein of traditional role-playing games. In spectacle however the combat sequences were more dynamic and cinematic. The game retained other typical role-playing game elements like tiered class and skill management, and featured conversations with non-player characters, though the main character was not voice-acted. These fairly typical genre mechanics aside, *KOTOR* also introduced what was called an 'alignment system', which kept track of how the player/avatar's actions were perceived by non-player characters, and turned the consequences into rewards or penalties of sorts. This 'alignment system' was the precursor to the morality system in the *Mass Effect* franchise.[4] The alignment system in *KOTOR* kept track of certain decisions and actions undertaken at key moments to determine whether the player character aligns with the good or evil side. Correspondence with either determined the avatar's visual appearance, unlocked special powers, or changed behaviours and reactions of party members and other non-player characters. This mechanic emphasised the importance of player choice, and subsequently, agency, to BioWare's design in many ways.[5] For instance, it framed choice according to the epic warring sides of the *Star Wars* universe, affording narrative agency. Not only that, but repeatedly choosing an inconsiderate or aggressive conversation option would take the player character closer to the Dark side, which then in turn would unlock special Dark-side-only powers, thereby linking narratively meaningful choice to other agency dimensions. *Mass Effect* games would further develop this feature, affording avatar action in even more complex ways.

While *KOTOR* still featured a combat system that allowed the player to pause time and assign commands as opposed to real-time action, BioWare's first original IP released introduced a more complex combat system. With *Dragon Age* still in development, the action role-playing game *Jade Empire* (BioWare 2005) moved away from turn-based action completely and featured real-time combat while keeping the by then characteristic BioWare formula: an ensemble of characters on a grandiose quest. As Zeschuk said in an interview: 'In the case of *Jade Empire*, we're really trying to pursue a goal of carefully matching a fully interactive real-time combat system with sublime story and character elements' (Tuttle 2004: n.p.). As such, although the game was one of BioWare's minor achievements, it still managed to evolve the studio's design ethos as it was a clear demonstration that BioWare was indeed capable of producing original content that is also keeping up with the technological developments in gaming. With *Jade Empire*, BioWare moved away from licensed content, developing an original game mixing genre mechanics, which also corresponded to market trends demanding dynamic combat in 3D environments.

Looking at BioWare's early games reveals not only the foundations of the studio's design ethos, but also what agency dimensions were becoming increasingly emphasised in design. Traditional role-playing games like the *Baldur's Gate* series or *KOTOR* predominantly afforded narrative agency through choices made in the branching narratives, and configurative agency through the management of avatar and party member skills, gear, and other resources. With combat in earlier BioWare games being designed in the turn-based d20-style rooted in tabletop role-playing games (meaning time is either stopped regularly or could be paused mid-combat to plan attacks and defences), temporal-ergodic and spatial-explorative dimensions of agency were quite different, if not limited, compared to live action games. However, the studio experimented with three different modes of play in *MDK2*, and *Jade Empire* developed real-time 3D combat. As such, early BioWare games have a lot in common with the current landscape of videogames, where there are no longer pure genres like those of the 1990s, but instead games tend to combine a variety of genre-typical mechanics. This shows that since their formation in the mid-1990s, BioWare laid down the foundations for a design ethos as one rooted in role-playing traditions with a taste for generic hybridisation. This eventually crystallised with the *Mass Effect* trilogy.

124   *'A Compelling Story with Choices That Matter'*

The Mass Effect *Franchise*

The success of *Baldur's Gate* and *KOTOR* showed that BioWare could develop intricately designed role-playing games. With *MDK2*, the studio experimented with incorporating exploration and shooting as core mechanics into their repertoire. Last but not least, *Jade Empire* was proof that BioWare could create original IP and could reinvent their approach to combat. With the *Mass Effect* trilogy, the studio condensed all these features into one brand. The IP was intended to be a trilogy from the early stages of development, with complex cause-and-effect relations designed into the branching story of each game, their availability depending on the choices players made at critical moments. The games could be played in isolation, but the player was given a choice at the beginning of each game to import the saved character they built from the previous instalment, alongside with the main decisions made, and squad members who are still alive. This conditional structure of predetermined story elements afforded a thus far unseen degree of complexity in the possibility space for narrative agency. At the time of the third game's release, its Lead Writer Mac Walters reminisced:

> [w]e had a paragraph written on what would happen in ME3 when finishing up ME1; the story was straightforward, in a sense. But still, this game took months of planning to get a handle on every different permutation.
>
> (qtd. in Diver 2012: n.p.)

The three games in the trilogy are *Mass Effect* (BioWare 2007), *Mass Effect 2* (BioWare 2010b), and *Mass Effect 3* (BioWare 2012a). The games' premise is that humanity discovered new alien cultures with the development of high-speed space travel, which brought war to Earth's doorstep. The player character is Commander Shepard, who can be played as male or female, who leads a battle against the looming threat. Throughout the three instalments, Shepard develops as a soldier and as a person, builds and manages a reliable squad, fights enemy forces, explores alien planets, forms interplanetary alliances, and negotiates galactic diplomacy. Casey Hudson, credited for a variety of design and lead roles throughout the trilogy and for *Andromeda*, recalled the circumstances of the franchise's inception as follows:

> [w]e wanted to make a console RPG on the PC, on the console, and we wanted it to be a little bit more accessible in terms of action that people understand, versus a kind of D20 turn-based thing. And there was another challenge out there, which is 'What if we could create our own universe for this?' That was really the genesis.
>
> (qtd. in Game Informer 2011: n.p.)

Hudson identified three main trajectories for design intention: a role-playing game; with less time-pausing and more live action in combat; set in a wholly original world. But what did this mean in terms of game mechanics? BioWare studio founder Ray Muzyka summarised what he calls the 'activity pillars' of all BioWare games, and specifically *Mass Effect*:

> At BioWare, we see the types of character and story-driven games we make as having four key activity pillars. There's story and characters, there's exploration, there's combat/conflict/action, and there's customization/progression. All of our games have those, to some extent.
> (qtd. in Tuttle 2007: n.p.)

With the phrase 'activity pillar', Muzyka anchored the identity of the *Mass Effect* brand not so much in its genre or game feel, like Hudson did, but in its defining game mechanics. The four activity pillars are the foundations of the BioWare brand of games as far as design is concerned, however, it is important to note that they do not map directly onto the four heuristic dimensions they seem to have similarities with. The difference become apparent in a close examination of how *Mass Effect* revolutionised conversation with non-player characters in avatar-based games, a predominantly narrative agency affordance, and the implications this had for player agency.

The *Mass Effect* trilogy placed considerable emphasis on affording narrative agency with an intricate structure of predetermined story permutations that carried over each instalment. The narrative building blocks of this structure were typically delivered via interaction with non-player characters. Such design was not uncommon for role-playing games, however, it was novel when comparing it to shooters—a genre the *Mass Effect* franchise increasingly moved towards with each instalment, especially with the introduction of the multiplayer mode in *Mass Effect 3*. As Mac Walters, *Andromeda*'s Creative Director, reminisced:

> I think the multiplayer was probably easily the single most thing that moved our gameplay forward. Obviously, I think the switch from more of a role-based sort of gameplay system in *Mass Effect 1* to more of a twitch-based in *Mass Effect 2*, that was a big shift.
> (qtd. in Hussain and James 2017a: n.p.)

Indeed, the shift was eminent; the trilogy was a 'cool shooter-RPG hybrid', as described by *Andromeda* Producer and long-time BioWare developer Mike Gamble (Hussain and James 2017h: n.p.). All three games were developed in the Unreal engine, which is a game engine that has typically been used for first-person shooter games, but in recent years is increasingly used in projects of diverse team sizes, genres, and platforms (Toftedahl and Engström 2019). Generally speaking, Unreal is optimised to afford game design specific to this genre, such as complex navigable environments, destructible objects, collision detection, and live-action combat (Unreal n.d.). This change had a major impact on how the games afforded avatar action in a temporal-ergodic dimension, because it facilitated a completely different way of challenging players to the previously typically BioWare design of turn-based action, increasing the possibility space for player/avatar action in this dimension. Configurative agency affordances, such as character and squad member skill trees, profiles, gear, and power management were carried on from previous BioWare games, and conversation with non-player characters also saw a major revamp with the first *Mass Effect* game.

In *KOTOR* and *Jade Empire*, BioWare's activity pillar of 'story and characters' manifested primarily in cut-scenes, and conversation with non-player characters. Dialogue was presented as alternating shots of the participants, capturing their figures in cinematically arranged, but relatively static frames. Only non-player characters were voice acted, the protagonist remained silent. Overall, the flow of conversation was quite fragmented, rendered in cut-scenes rather than in engine.

Mass Effect introduced a more cinematic way of presenting conversation, with more emphasis on camera movement and atmospheric lighting. BioWare hired voice actors to breathe life into Commander Shepard, which could be seen as an explicit effort to augment and legitimise the dramatic scope of the characters. But more importantly, conversation happened in-game through a tool called the dialogue wheel, which revolutionised how interaction between the player's character and non-player characters is modulated in videogames. BioWare was very aware of the value of this solution, so much so that they patented it to the very last detail, and indeed, most AAA games today use some form of the tool.[6]

The dialogue wheel enabled narrative agency to be realised, but it also afforded agency in other dimensions due to *Mass Effect*'s morality system. *KOTOR*'s alignment system already did this to some degree, but the dialogue wheel in *Mass Effect* was a more complex tool enabling the morality system to have wider implications for agency. In *KOTOR*, the nature of responses given would contribute towards a path of the avatar, leading to the good or evil side. This alignment to either sides would change character appearance, unlock special powers and bonuses, and may result in non-player characters intervening with certain acts they do not share an alignment with. In *Mass Effect*, BioWare expanded the effect these paths taken (called Paragon and Renegade) have on the unfolding of the overall narrative, accessibility of character skill bonuses, and non-player character reactions, making the player's choice feel even more impactful.

Seemingly, BioWare's activity pillars of story and character translate directly onto the narrative agency. However, a closer look at the dialogue wheel shows this is not the case. While the wheel is the primary vessel for delivering narratively relevant content, what also happens simultaneously is that the game keeps track of decisions made, contributing to Paragon or Renegade points. Going down either path makes certain narrative arcs available, affording agency in a narrative dimension as the two paths become branches of the skill tree, making certain conversation shortcuts available depending on Paragon or Renegade points accrued. Moreover, the path chosen could give the avatar stats bonuses, for instance, the ability to run faster or jump higher, a shorter power cool-down, more health, or more damage points. Thus, through choices made in the dialogue wheel, which is framed by developers as primarily a story and character affordance that enables narrative choice (Hussain and James 2017h), the *Mass Effect* trilogy afforded agency in other dimensions: in the spatial-explorative, as well as temporal-ergodic and configurative-constructive.

By the time the second and third instalments of the trilogy were released, BioWare as a studio had gone through a lot of change in management and in production strategies. Most importantly, it was subsidised by publisher Electronic Arts, or EA for short, and soon after, the founders left the studio to pursue different projects. Greg Zeschuk called this change 'an EA bear hug . . . well-meaning, but vigorous' (Crecente 2013: n.p.). Despite these significant changes, the brand pillars of the franchise were well-established and stable. Muzyka's vision of BioWare's design ethos grounded in the four activity pillars was manifest to various degrees in each instalment of the trilogy. *Mass Effect* featured planetary exploration and hub-worlds with less predetermined spatial progression design, as well as plenty options for customising playstyles; *Mass Effect 2* focused on story and character with tweaks to combat; and *Mass Effect 3* perfected combat mechanics, while keeping a tight grip on the story and with that, spatial progression. This franchise therefore could be seen as the one which represents a crystallised design ethos.

While the *Mass Effect* trilogy is heralded as one of the best franchises of the previous console generation (Albert 2013), fan reactions to the third instalment were overwhelmingly negative, primarily due to how its ending apparently deprived players of a sense of agency. There was an inconsistency between how the game was marketed (as one where all decisions made throughout the trilogy would impact the ending) versus how it actually ended (with a decision to be made between three only mildly differing outcomes, available irrespective of previous choices). Some fan groups sued (Thier 2012a), others turned to more unconventional ways of protesting, such as sending the studio cupcakes with icing in three colours (representing the three final choices in *Mass Effect 3*) that all tasted the same (Thier 2012b). As a result of this failure to please fans, the trilogy's conclusion became one of the most controversial endings in the history of gaming (Clarkson 2013; Thier 2012c). Narrative agency was at the heart of the franchise's brand identity, but the ending did not fit this. In an attempt to remedy the situation, BioWare released an *Extended Cut* as downloadable content (DLC), free of charge, to offer something in lieu of a conclusion. After this debacle, BioWare did everything to distance the new *Mass Effect* game from the trilogy. 'You tend to think of the next [game in the series] as the next step, but really, we are taking a leap' wrote Chris Wynn, then-Senior Development Director in a BioWare blogpost early in pre-production (Pierse 2014: n.p.). Indeed, *Andromeda* marks a major shift in what is understood as a typical

BioWare game. While the dialogue wheel and the connected morality system was central to the franchise, *Andromeda* would take a slightly different approach, which is but one of many departures from the franchise's identity.

Developing *Mass Effect: Andromeda*

A salient indicator of the shift in the franchise's brand identity was how BioWare's design philosophy changed with *Mass Effect 3*'s release. It was the first game in the trilogy that allowed a lower degree of narrative agency than previous instalments, with a greater focus on combat. This was of course especially true in the game's multiplayer mode, where players fought in an enclosed space against timed hordes of enemies.[7] Before *Mass Effect 3*'s release, BioWare's design philosophy was summed up on their website's 'About' section with a quote from founders Zeschuk and Muzyka, in a manner that suggests a focus on narratively rich design: 'BioWare's vision is to deliver the best story-driven games in the world' (BioWare 2010a: n.p.). Sometime later in 2013, the section began with a different quote: 'BioWare's vision is to Create, Deliver, and Evolve the Most Emotionally Engaging Games in the World' (BioWare 2013: n.p.). Story-driven-ness is removed from the design philosophy, and replaced with the broader idea of engaging players emotionally—which, as Perron (2005) argued, is not necessarily connected to experiencing a story, but could also be elicited by gameplay ('gameplay emotions'), or the qualities of the game as an object ('artifact emotions'). As such, this change of communicated design philosophy on the studio's website is a notable sign that there is a corresponding change in how BioWare games post-*Mass Effect 3* afford agency.

The following paratextual analysis will unpack this change in design philosophy, as communicated during *Andromeda*'s development, examining how the four activity pillars of 'story and characters', 'exploration', 'combat/conflict/action', and 'customization/progression' were discussed by developers in *Andromeda*'s promotional discourse during production; and what implications these discussions have for design intention regarding agency in *Andromeda*. The analysis will identify themes emerging from early materials as well as how these themes were expanded towards the end of the press cycle. The focus will be on how developers discuss what the player's avatar would and would not be able to do, and how that relates to the four dimensions of agency afforded and limited via game design.

One final note is due in order to contextualise the following analysis of the promotional surrounds. *Andromeda*'s development was riddled with increasingly conflicted studio politics and key staff departures, which enhanced the veil of secrecy surrounding its production, unusually so even for such a highly secretive industry. According to Aaryn Flynn, BioWare's

General Manager during *Andromeda*'s development, this increased secrecy was due to a desire to feel more confident when eventually sharing details:

> sometimes those things shift and adjust, or maybe we cut a follower because we can't get it done to quality, and then we feel like argh, we feel bad now because we mentioned that kinda thing.
> (qtd. in Hanson 2016a: n.p.)

However, there is quite possibly another reason for it. *Andromeda* was received terribly (though critics were generally mixed in their reviews, it is at 5.0/10 User score on Metacritic at the time of writing), with most commenters criticizing its animation and writing. From this climate, post-release interviews and reports emerged, revealing the circumstances of production, with sources ranging from anonymous developers who were bound by non-disclosure agreements to departed staff members (Schreier 2017a, 2017b). These sources helped contextualise promotional material, adding an additional layer of caution to the already critical reading of the promotional surrounds.

General Themes in Design Intention

Andromeda's development began immediately after *Mass Effect 3*'s release in 2012. The game was announced by Yannick Roy, then-head of BioWare Montreal (now closed). This was the studio that worked on *Mass Effect 3*'s multiplayer, and developed the combat-focused DLC *Mass Effect 3: Omega* (BioWare 2012c). In a dev blog post, Roy shared that BioWare Montreal was taking over as the main studio developing the new game. Besides a short introduction to the team, Roy revealed two noteworthy things about the forthcoming game that have implications regarding player agency. The first one concerned the choice of game engine:

> [the game] will be built with the amazing technology of Frostbite as its foundation, enhanced by many of the systems that the *Dragon Age III* team has already spent a lot of time building.
> (BioWare 2012b: n.p.)

'Dragon Age III' refers to *Dragon Age: Inquisition* (BioWare 2014), the third instalment of BioWare's original IP that carries forward the traditions of *Dungeons & Dragons* style traditional role-playing games. It was the first BioWare game to be developed in Frostbite, EA's proprietary in-house engine. Choosing this engine for *Andromeda* carried meaning regarding design intention, for it marked a shift away from what had previously been a typical BioWare game. The Frostbite engine was first built for open world first-person shooter *Battlefield: Bad Company* (EA DICE 2008). It is optimised for 'large scale multiplayer interactions in dynamic destructible environments' with 'changing weather, adaptable cities, landscapes and complex events', 'ultra-realistic animation', and 'stunning visual effects' (EA 2017: n.p.). While these features support largely predetermined progression design the like of which is often found in shooter and sports games (which both happen to be EA's flagship genres), they are not very accommodating of more typical role-playing game mechanics, such as managing avatar and party member skill trees, which is a game mechanic affording configurative agency.

Much like tech trees in strategy games, which are 'a rule set of certain premises that have to be fulfilled to unlock a technology, which then has certain consequences, often including unlocking the path to newer technologies' (Ghys 2012: n.p.), skill trees in role-playing games are branching structures of object properties assigned to the character/s. Each skill's availability is conditioned by progression in the game, measured by the accumulation of an in-game currency (most typically, Experience Points, or XP). Compared to typical first-person shooter games, such as the *Call of Duty* series, where the player controls one avatar whose most prominent statistical variable (determining attack or shield strength) tends to be their weapon and armour, skill trees in role-playing games are highly complex relations. While, as we have seen, the *Mass Effect* trilogy was leaning towards the shooter genre in its mechanics, which typically does not have the same degree of configurability of avatar as role-playing games do, it still retained a fairly complex interfacing and implementation of this mechanic.[8] Using Frostbite for *Dragon Age: Inquisition* meant that the game looked even flashier than *Mass Effect* did in Unreal, and so the decision to develop *Andromeda* in Frostbite signalled the importance of this priority for the new *Mass Effect* game too.

Opting for Frostbite to be the new game's engine guaranteed extensive software engineer support and shared workload with EA's other studios, but it also meant that every tool had to be completely redesigned to fit role-playing mechanics and character animation, which resulted in a long crunch period and the final release being postponed numerous times, according to developers (Schreier 2017a). This decision suggests that at this time in production, how player action was historically afforded in BioWare games would change with *Andromeda*. Avatar configuration and player choice-triggered branches in the plot would become increasingly difficult to implement, as there are only so many tasks a game engine can simultaneously process. At the same time, the possibility space for action in the form of 'combat/conflict/action' and 'exploration' pillars would grow, due to the engine's optimization, which suggests a drawth towards temporal-ergodic and spatial-explorative agency as centre of the designed gameplay experience. Indeed, as *Andromeda*'s development carried on, the two pillars of 'exploration' and 'combat/conflict/action' in particular were repeatedly emphasised, while the others took a backseat.

In June 2014, two years into development, following relative radio silence (with minor exceptions of concept art of vehicle and environment design published), BioWare screened a developer diary-style video featuring key *Mass Effect* personnel at E3. The video was a standard talking head format, with behind-the-scenes footage and concept art from previous *Mass Effect* games, the then-forthcoming *Andromeda*, and the studio's new, at the time not yet revealed IP which now we know to be *Anthem* (BioWare 2019). The background music was one of the most popular tracks from the original soundtrack of *Mass Effect*, 'Uncharted Worlds'. This track was used in the game while players navigated the Galaxy Map and explored planets. Its usage in promotional material is arguably quite suggestive of the theme of the forthcoming game: exploration. This thematic focus becomes even more evident when looking at Casey Hudson's words on what the player would be able to do in the new *Mass Effect* game. Several of the verbs used are connected to movement:

> One of the things that fans have told us most about what they want for the next *Mass Effect* game is to go somewhere new and to move forward . . . we're taking you to a whole new region of space. This world is so vast you can just kinda continue on with the horizon, and there's more and more experience for the player to enjoy. Pick a planet, across the other side of the galaxy, and fly there and see what you'll discover.
> (GameTrailers 2014: n.p.)

As I discussed in Chapter 1, actions are the verbs of game mechanics (Järvinen 2008: 139–143; Schell 2015 [2008]: 130–144). Through this lens, Hudson's words can be seen as indicative of agency affordances. 'Continue on', 'fly', and 'discover' suggest the theme of exploration, while another salient theme is volume: 'vast worlds', 'horizon', galaxy' and 'more and more experience for the player to enjoy' all evoke a sense of grandeur in the viewer.

Despite the sense of unity displayed at E3, 2014 saw a major change: several members of staff, including *Mass Effect*'s Creative Director Hudson and then-game director of *Andromeda* Gérard Lehiany, left BioWare. In response to worrying fans, and possibly to even more concerned stakeholders, BioWare General Manager Aaron Flynn published a dev blog post towards the end of the year, introducing development team leads (Pierse 2014). In his introduction Flynn mentioned Frostbite being a challenge, and the new console cycle being an exciting factor, but concluded that 'no matter what changes, stories are timeless, and a great story needs to be at the heart of the next Mass Effect game' (ibid. n.p.). While he did point to 'a great story' being 'at the heart' of the new game, there seems to have been a shift in how this story was planned to be delivered to players via game design. As discussed earlier in this chapter, each game in the previous trilogy focused on one or two of the four BioWare activity pillars: the first game attempted to innovate in all four but premiered exploration of uncharted planets, while *Mass Effect 2* focused on characters, and the third perfected combat mechanics. Creative Director Mac Walters wrote in the same post that they were 'working to bring back some of that wonder and sense of exploration that [they] had in the original trilogy', with 'deep characters and compelling story with choices that matter' (ibid. n.p.). However, few details were offered beyond this vague aim, and those that were had to do with means of affording exploration.

For instance, Producer Fabrice Condominas' duties in bringing back 'the original *Mass Effect* feel' were anchored in 'evaluating the features that players have fond memories of, such as the Mako, and finding ways to integrate them into gameplay in a better and more versatile way' (Pierse 2014: n.p.). The Mako was *Mass Effect*'s vehicle for planetary exploration that became memorable amongst fans for its clunky controls, simultaneously frustrating and endearing. No other iconic element of the trilogy, such as its alien races, was mentioned specifically in the dev blog post, which really draws attention to exploration. Beyond revisiting previous mechanics affording agency in this dimension, the building of worlds available for exploration was also discussed. Art Director Joel MacMillan and his team

> are creating immersive worlds that interact with the player. Using set pieces, lighting, and environmental weathering, his team is building lived-in worlds that tell their own stories. And whether it's shattered doorways and the scars of battle, or overgrown with moss, he says the environments can convey stories about what's happened and what may be yet to come.
>
> (qtd. in Pierse 2014: n.p.)

Despite Walters' reference to narrative affordances as characters and 'choices that matter', the details provided about environment design suggest that there is a reliance on these environments in providing the foundations of the possibility space for agency in the narrative-dramatic dimension, as opposed to characters or quests. This makes sense when taking into account the studio's choice of technology, as the Frostbite engine is rich in world-building tools. The focus on environment and vehicle design is also evidenced by concept art BioWare shared on their dev blog and Facebook page around the same time, all promoting environments and vehicles (Mass Effect 2014).

Schreier's (2017b) investigative report into the production of *Andromeda* provides context for the above identified focus of design intention to afford a high degree of spatial-explorative agency. According to Schreier, by 2015, the game was nowhere near where it should have been. The plan was to make procedurally generated planets, like those of *No Man's Sky* (Hello Games 2016),[9] but technological limitations stood in the way of implementing such a resource-heavy design challenge. As two developers told Schreier separately:

> In an ideal world you'd have one of those [planets] proven out so the process is repeatable. But we were still answering those questions of if we could do that type of thing.
> (qtd. in Schreier 2017b: n.p.)

> We started to realize by summer 2015 that we had great technological prototypes, but we had doubts they would make it into the game.
> (qtd. in Schreier 2017b: n.p.)

With development dedicated solely to realising procedurally generated planets, it makes sense that most of the paratextual surrounds thus far had focused on the creation of worlds and exploring them. Without these foundations, other teams, such as writing, art, or indeed, game design, could not begin developing those mechanics that afford player agency in other dimensions, such as conversation, or time-critical challenges. This contextual information points towards a sense that design intention mid-stage was more focused on affording player action in a spatial-explorative dimension, building the very spaces, both in a ludic and a representational sense, that the avatar would be able to traverse, as well as the means of traversal.

While *Andromeda*'s development underwent rescaling, and the idea of procedurally generated planets was slowly abandoned (Schreier 2017b: n.p.), another design priority started to emerge. The activity pillar of 'combat/conflict/action' was increasingly emphasised from 2015 onwards, which suggests that affording agency in the temporal-ergodic dimension by creating plenty opportunity for time critical challenge was a theme very much present in design intention. This assumption gains further credibility when looking at a marketing survey allegedly circulated by the studio, asking participants to express their opinions on gameplay and story details, leaked by a (since then deleted) user on *Mass Effect*'s Reddit forum (Anon 2015). In this enumeration of potential game mechanics that decision makers were considering including, each BioWare activity pillar was discussed, albeit in various degrees of detail. In the 'context' section, a look at the verbs used to describe the playable character's activity affordances reveals that most activity pillars were touched upon, with 'exploration' being slightly more prominent. Besides the main character being described as a 'combat-trained but untested explorer', and the actions available being described with verbs such as 'lead an expedition', 'survive and colonize', or 'explore [a] sprawling series of solar systems', the sheer volume of the space available for players was repeatedly underscored throughout the text. 'A cluster of 100s of solar systems' was mentioned numerous times, and the promised game claimed to be 'over 4x times the size of *Mass Effect 3*'.

Typical BioWare design features, such as resource management, avatar and team skill trees, and dialogue and action-based choices were also mentioned, but there was also significant time spent detailing features that are slightly less characteristic of the franchise. The inclusion of mechanics such as deploying strike teams, participating actively in strike team missions, vault raids and elite vault raids, and enemy outpost occupation suggested by the survey would result in increased gameplay time dedicated to combat to such a degree that it is indicative of a shift in emphasis in between activity pillars. Combat situations primarily consist of affording avatar action in a possibility space restricted in space (predominantly ludic and locally represented space in particular) and time (by temporal structures such as powers cooling down dictating the pace of combat), with configurative agency affordances enabling the customization of the combat experience. Furthermore, as opposed to narrative agency afforded by predetermined story elements such as interactions with no-player characters, combat scenarios create space for dramatic agency to emerge, whereby they create the possibility space for less predetermined narratives to emerge from play, such as the use of an epic combo.

Indeed, the emphasis of design intention on combat, alongside exploration, is prominent when looking at the different trailers released during the last few years of *Andromeda*'s development. The *Announcement Trailer* showed at E3 2015 featured a character standing at the helm of a space shuttle, scrolling through planet surface vistas, then landing on one, driving a six-wheel-drive vehicle, making use of a jetpack, and engaging in combat. The sequence hints at four game mechanics affording agency, out of which one is particularly noteworthy. Interplanetary travel, vehicle driving, and combat were present in the original trilogy, but there was a new feature: the avatar's mobility was promised to be enhanced by a jetpack, which would introduce new axes of movement. Although this was not a gameplay trailer but a cinematic one, meaning it was pre-rendered rather than a collage of captured actual gameplay, it is nonetheless suggestive of the general direction of design intention behind *Andromeda* being exploration and combat. The E3 2016 trailer, in turn, featured behind-the-scenes footage of developers creating design affordances enabling the avatar's traversal of space. Ever so slightly more specific than previous year's trailer, this one revealed more concrete details about how avatar movement in the game's space was being developed.

From the above we can conclude that the change of engine was a significant circumstance, as due to its optimisation serving open world shooter mechanics better than role-playing ones, it marked a shift in what a typical BioWare game was considered to look and feel like. Based on a based on paratextual analysis of early dev blog posts, trailers, forum posts, and news coverage, the two general themes in design intention emerging were exploration and combat. Decisions like procedurally generated planets that have a larger number of combat encounters have potential implications regarding

'A Compelling Story with Choices That Matter' 135

the possibility for player agency to manifest, whereby they allow for avatar action in the spatial-explorative and temporal-ergodic dimension, while somewhat marginalising configurative and narrative agency, which were central to the franchise's brand identity up to that point.

Developers on Game Mechanics

Game Informer writers were invited by BioWare to interview department leads and play the game itself at BioWare Montreal, for a special cover story and a month-long online coverage published shortly before the release of *Andromeda* in March 2017. *GameSpot* produced a two-episode documentary on the *Mass Effect* franchise based on extensive interviews with the same department leads and producers, and a few new faces, transcripts of which were simultaneously published on the website. Due to the nature of the press cycle, developers spoke more freely of the design features and intentions behind them. Examining these in more detail will help unpack the themes of exploration and combat in terms of game mechanics.

Andromeda's designers discussed creating mechanics to offer player freedom in an open world-like environment in terms of letting the player go wherever they want, and interact with whomever they want. Early trailers and blog posts suggested design intent emphasising exploration as one of the main activities. The central role of this activity throughout production was further confirmed by a variety of developers and producers. BioWare Montreal studio lead Yannick Roy said they 'wanted to reinvest heavily in exploration' (Hussain and James 2017b: n.p.). Level designer and Space Lead Jessica Campbell said about what motivated design: 'I think the legacy of what *Mass Effect* was trying to do . . . coming back to exploration, returning to the uncharted worlds was kind of that dream' (Hussain and James 2017c: n.p.). Producer Fabrice Condominas said exploration is 'at the centre of this game' (Hussain and James 2017d: n.p.), and level designer Chris Corfe hoped 'fans take away their [sense of] exploration and discovery' (Hussain and James 2017e: n.p.). What game mechanics were mentioned in the promotional surrounds of late production that would afford spatial-explorative agency? The four design elements (as, arguably, they are too complex to be reduced to mere game mechanics) mentioned which were designed with the intention to afford exploration are the Nomad (planetary vehicle), the planets themselves, the Tempest (space shuttle), and the map interface. In all four cases, what is emphasised most is volume: actual volume, as well as the illusion of it.

Andromeda Space Lead Jessica Campbell said she 'gets a kick out of' how much bigger the Tempest feels due to putting up windows' (Hussain and James 2017c: n.p.), while Creative Director Mac Walters said building the levels with the Nomad's horsepower in mind meant they scaled up the size of levels, as well as 'the way how we approach things like density, and the types of gameplay we put on levels' (Hanson 2016b: n.p.). In terms of how this change in level size and structure related to the design of the original trilogy, Producer Mike Gamble said:

> There are so many different elements we can bring in by putting it on those planets with exploration areas. It makes the number and the type of side quests that we can do that much more interesting, whereas before if you're on the hub you're kind of limited to a fetch quest type of thing. . . . This is the biggest we've ever gone, in terms of number pieces of content.
>
> (qtd. in Wallace 2016: n.p.)

A fetch quest is a typical role-playing game mechanic with a somewhat derogatory reputation due to its over-use in recent role-playing games, such as BioWare's very own *Dragon Age: Inquisition*. It is often used to incentivise exploration, and begins with the player's avatar interacting with a non-player character, who delivers a short narrative, which calls the player to action in the form of going to another place in the storyworld and retrieving an item. Some scholars classified quests as primarily narrative vehicles (Juul 2001; Ryan 2015; and specifically with regard to *Mass Effect 2*, Jørgensen 2010). Indeed, the mechanic of interacting with the non-player character is a narrative affordance whereby it delivers a predetermined story element. As we have seen with other *Mass Effect* games, this interaction happened in the dialogue wheel, the real-time paraphrasing-based conversation tool contributing to a Paragon/Renegade metre. There, selecting certain conversation options resulted in skill bonuses and other modifiers. Therefore, depending on whether the fetch quest, or side quest, is on the main path of progression set so by developers or not, or the kinds of challenges posed, it has a rather complex impact on the manifestation of agency, with all dimensions supported to varying degrees.

Andromeda was not to feature the Paragon/Renegade mechanic, and instead would introduce a system of expressing opinion that had no impact on the game beyond affording role-play, according to Creative Director Mac Walters:

> So, Paragon and Renegade is gone. . . . With agree and disagree it changes by the circumstance and it changes by the character you're talking to, so you have to actually be more engaged in what's going on, to know if you're going to do that.
>
> (qtd. in Prell 2017: n.p.)

The available choices were no longer promised to be strung along a morality metre like in previous *Mass Effect* games, but rather, the player/avatar could choose whether they 'agree' or 'disagree' with what is being said, which Walters argued would lead to more engaging conversation scenes. While the decision may have been motivated to get players 'more engaged', and Gamble's words above suggest 'more interesting' side quests, removing the morality mechanic from the dialogue wheel, and with that, from the game as a whole, foreshadows the opposite effect on player agency in all dimensions—a reduction of the ludic impact of decisions made in dialogue. Furthermore, interesting-ness seems to have been measured in quantity of quests available, despite Creative Director Mac Walters' insistence that as large as the game may seem, they 'continued to restrain the scope as much as possible so that [they could] bring quality to each of these areas and make each one memorable' (Wallace 2016: n.p.).

But instead of promoting these 'more interesting', primarily narrative, affordances, developers emphasised the size of the world, and locomotion. Indeed, getting planetary navigation right was a central concern. As Producer Mike Gamble explained:

> a big focus for us is making sure that the Nomad handles better, drives better, cascades better—that it has all the nimbleness that the original Mako did without any of the frustrations.
>
> (qtd. in Wallace 2016: n.p.)

Arguably, developers wanted to avoid spoiling content for fans and therefore withheld crucial details of the plot, but even with that in mind, as the evidence shows, design intention placed emphasis on designing means of exploration, rendering everything from level design through mechanics delivering narratives to fit this objective.

An important contextual influence behind this decision was, as implied by early dev blog posts, the move to a more powerful game engine. As then-General Manager Aaryn Flynn's words show, getting into gear with the new development tool was a challenge, especially with regards to how it relates to the franchise's identity:

> With *Andromeda*, we had more confidence, but we switched to Frostbite, and we spent a lot of time lifting every rock and going back to the original vision document for *Mass Effect* saying 'what did we really want to achieve with this original game, or even the trilogy, that we didn't, because of time or budget constraints, or the technology, because we couldn't do it on that generation of hardware'. That created ambiguity for sure.
>
> (qtd. in Hanson 2016a: n.p.)

Reconciling this ambiguity was a central concern throughout development. Developers wanted to 'do more open world things with the game, you know, give people more planets to explore, as opposed to straight up linear missions' (Hanson 2016a: n.p.); and maintain what they identify as their goal, which is 'telling stories, and we love doing it in these amazing universes' (Hanson 2016a: n.p.). But what did 'telling stories' mean to BioWare at this point?

In the very few instances of story elements discussed in the paratext, while the characteristically BioWare loyalty missions and romances were occasionally mentioned, even Lead Writer Cathleen Rootsaeert said very little beyond stating that yes, characterisation and story are 'core of what BioWare does' (Hussain and James 2017f). Of course, discussing narrative affordances could spoil key moments, so it is only logical that these were not talked about. The predetermined mechanics of interacting with non-player characters, which would afford narrative agency (such as *Mass Effect*'s characteristic romances and loyalty missions), were also not discussed and promoted as much as other features affording spatial-explorative were. What did appear, however, was a strong intention to distance the gaming experience offered by the new game from the lengthy, complex, yet in a way still one-directional path of progression in the original trilogy; and a decision to do away with the morality system, a mechanic which translates choices made in conversations into power bonuses and other ludic functions.

One of the most prominent reasons for this can be deduced from interviews contextualising production. As disclosed anonymously by developers after the game's release, there was a severe delay in development due to the difficulties of the engine, and badly managed production (Schreier 2017b). With development still focusing on actualising the idea of procedurally generated planets mid-way through production, work was stalling in several departments—most crucially, writing. As one developer disclosed:

> What you see [in the final game] is writing that has been done in the past two years rather than the full five years of writing. . . . The writing team—writing the characters and everything—was unleashed too late, just because of too many discussions about the high-level direction.
> (qtd. in Schreier 2017b: n.p.)

Therefore, due to the combination of market pressures to reinvent the franchise as an open world game, and difficulties in production, it would seem that BioWare's design ethos founded on a specific kind of storytelling that gives the player agency over how the designer story develops was changing with *Andromeda*. This begs the question: how would stories be told in *Andromeda*?

The conceptualisation of narrative-dramatic dimension of agency offered in Chapter 2 is built around the distinction between designer story and player story. Thus far, we have seen how creating a series of openly navigable worlds (planets), *Andromeda*'s developers endeavoured to afford what they conceptualised as player freedom, in a desire to move away from the more critical-path-focused trilogy. An illustrative example of various game mechanics in tandem affording dramatic agency is that of combat scenarios. In these, coherent chains of events connected by cause-and-effect relations, such as tales of heroic escapes and epic combo moves, also have a narrative quality to them, but in a very different way to, say, a cut-scene.

'A Compelling Story with Choices That Matter'   139

Besides exploration, the other salient theme in the focus of design intention as implied by early trailers, and the growth in the amount of time dedicated to fighting as suggested by the leaked survey questions, was that of combat. Trailers released throughout 2017 showcased high-octane fights, with developers proudly detailing how certain weapons, powers, level design, or the quality of graphics would enable this experience (Mass Effect 2016).

According to then-Montreal Studio Lead Yannick Roy, they were 'going to stick with what we have with combat' from *Mass Effect 3*, but eventually 'ended up, actually, progressing that action quite a bit far' (Hussain and James 2017b: n.p.). In a similar vein, Level Designer Ian Frazier opined 'I think we are, as you say, more of a shooter, more of an action game than any previous *Mass Effect* games' (qtd. in Hussain and James 2017g: n.p.). Producer Fabrice Condominas described the general motivation: 'We can summarise the overall idea by saying we want to get back to the depth of *Mass Effect*, with the action of *Mass Effect 3*' (qtd. in Hanson 2016c: n.p.). He promoted fluidity, increase in pace, more responsive controls, and less predictable layouts as facilitators of the 'sheer fun' *Mass Effect 3*'s multiplayer offered players (Hanson 2016c). On how they captured that in terms of mechanics in the single player experience, Condominas said:

> The most obvious one will rightaway be the jump. It's not a permanent rocket that you will have and you can fly around with, there is a beginning and an end to it, there's really a curve, a momentum curve that is based on when you do your input. Is it after a sprint? Walk, Etc. Yes, you can hover, so for example if you jump and hover, it gives you time to see the combat layout, even shoot at enemies.
>
> (qtd. in Hanson 2016c: n.p.)

This expansion of the avatar's core move set predominantly would increase the possibility space for spatial agency, primarily in the game's ludic and locally represented spaces. In previous instalments of *Mass Effect*, vaulting over covers was an automated mechanic, which could be activated when pressing a directional button while sprinting towards cover. The introduction of a jumping mechanic in *Andromeda* enables player agency to manifest in another dimension, beyond spatial, and that is temporal-ergodic. On the one hand, it introduces an ability that the player develops by spending skill points earned, afforded by configurative agency mechanics, which allow for longer hover time and more precision. On the other, Condominas details how this addition of verticality changes their attitude to level design:

> [Y]ou can jump above cover, you can have different stages of cover on a single layout, and for multiplayer, we also took the idea that enemies can spawn in different places in the layout not necessarily facing you. Again, the challenge will remain the tactical aspect that the player loves . . . it is

obviously a challenge when you can go up, down, sideways, people can spawn behind you, enemies can spawn on the side, etc.

(qtd. in Hanson 2016c: n.p.)

The timing of jumping, and the end to which this means is used, creates challenge for the player. In this sense, the jump mechanic itself affords not only spatial or configurative, but also temporal agency. The fact that these features were discussed in such detail, that they were given this degree of visibility before the game's launch suggest that they were deemed a selling point of the game. Moreover, with the contextual knowledge revealed by Schreier's interviewees referred to earlier, combat was the only thing that was more or less finalised early in development, which further reinforces that design intention was pre-occupied with game mechanics affording agency in the spatial-explorative and temporal-ergodic dimensions. This observation is also supported by Lead Designer Ian Frazier, who located the overall design intention in creating a, compared to the previous trilogy, scaled up 'sense of freedom' (qtd. in Hussain and James 2017h: n.p.), where freedom was predominantly understood as the freedom to move.

Not only does the plan to enhance mobility in combat has the potential to expand the possibility space for agency in the spatial-explorative and temporal-ergodic dimensions, it also promises to impact configurative agency positively by enabling more complex and diverse styles in combat was also given increased consideration by designers. According to Frazier:

> Why not let players, instead of just having that class choice in the beginning, you're going to be a Sentinel for 60 hours or whatever, just say, no, you're going to get to decide a thing and then morph and change and expand that over the course of the experience, and it ended up fitting really, really well.
>
> (qtd. in Hussain and James 2017g: n.p.)

'Sentinel' refers to one of the many classes players could play in previous instalments, with locked in buffs and debuffs, that is, temporary enhancements or diminutions on different abilities. This feature afforded configurative agency whereby players could spend experience points earned in specialised skill trees as well as the readily available ones. Once committed, players could not change these classes. What was the intention behind changing this to allow more flexibility? Frazier argued that the change to redistributable class points and changeable profiles, affording more configurative agency, was motivated by creating a more diverse and customisable combat experience

> We've tried to do more moment to moment before, with the jump, with locomotion in general, how you get around the world, with some of the

gunplay, and the powers and the way that you remix them. In that way, it is more of a shooter than it used to be.

(qtd. in Hussain and James 2017g: n.p.)

As to the broader motivations for such changes, Producer Fabrice Condominas stressed the importance industry trends played in this decision:

But obviously, it's been five years, you know, the industry has changed, and I think the stop-and-go aspect of the third person shooter will not remain for long. There's still games doing that and that's great. But we are responsive, *Overwatch, Halo, Destiny*, all that, you see that idea that we want a more responsive, more fast-paced thing. The key thing here is to balance between the accessibility, the sheer fun of the action, and the depth of RPG systems.

(qtd. in Hanson 2016c: n.p.)

All the games listed by Condominas were best-seller shooter titles, single player as well as multiplayer, and they each tick the same boxes in terms of game mechanics. This alone would afford a broader possibility space for emergent player stories, and through that, dramatic agency. However, especially when reading it in conjuncture with the observations made so far regarding agency in the spatial-explorative and temporal-ergodic dimensions also being prioritised by developers, it becomes even clearer that the story told with *Andromeda*, and the methods of its telling no longer correspond to BioWare's historic design ethos and the *Mass Effect* brand's identity. While this is, of course, entirely normal, and could be considered a mundane observation even (after all, the studio and the franchise are old and change is inevitable), the textual analysis below will explore in more detail the consequences these design decisions had on player agency.

In summary, the following points need stressing. The observations regarding design intention during early- to mid-production reveal that the two emergent themes were that of exploration and combat. Dev blog posts stressed the technological affordances of the new Frostbite engine; announcements, trailers, and concept art published revealed environments and vehicle design; and the leaked survey suggested there would be more time dedicated to combat. Looking at in-depth interviews solidified the hypothesis that these foci were partly selected due to a desire to respond to industry trends of creating more open world games with more free movement afforded to players, and more dynamic, customisable combat encounters. As to how this freedom was conceptualised by *Andromeda*'s designers, the heuristic framework helped to identify how designers intended to realise agency across dimensions. It proved especially productive when looking at the detail regarding intentionality behind certain game mechanics offered by paratextual evidence from the end of the press cycle. Having surveyed *Andromeda*'s paratext, we can now conclude that as far as design intention is concerned, the meaning of 'compelling stories where your choices matter', as per Creative Director Mac Walters' words, changed with *Andromeda*. Although designers still claim to have maintained *Mass Effect*'s brand identity and upheld the importance of 'story and character' as one of the four BioWare activity pillars, there seems to be a move away from how these stories are designed to be told: less through an elaborate, but nonetheless predetermined structure of branching options, more via creating opportunities for individual and diverse player stories to be realised. A critical examination of the game-text itself through the analytical lens of the heuristic framework will shed some light on whether the final product matches design intention. By doing so, we will find more clarity as to how the way agency is discussed could translate into how agency is afforded in a typical avatar-based videogame.

Narrativity, Eventfulness, and Agency

The *Mass Effect* trilogy is widely discussed in game studies. Some scholars examine narrative characteristics (Jørgensen 2010) and narrative agency ('bounded agency' in Bizzocchi and Tanenbaum 2012), while others concentrate on the representation of morality (Patterson 2014), religion (Irizarry and Irizarry 2014) colonialism (Fuchs et al. 2018), community management (Reardon et al. 2017), and gender and sexuality (Adams and Rambukkana 2018; Condis 2015; Gallagher 2012; Krampe 2018) in the franchise. That said, not many studies distinguish in much detail between more specific dimensions in which not only narrative representation, but other aspects of the gameplay experience occur. Applying the heuristic framework to *Andromeda* will unpack these more specific dimensions. The first goal of the textual analysis is therefore a general appropriation of how the game's design affords and limits avatar action, as observed through the analytical lenses of the multidimensional heuristic framework.

Second, and perhaps more interestingly, the textual analysis of *Andromeda* will reveal not only how game design allows for the different dimensions of agency to manifest and support each other, but also how these dimensions can break down if not integrated in a meaningful way. The paratextual analysis revealed that *Andromeda*'s developers intended to make a game which afforded freedom of exploration and combat in abundance, while also adhering to BioWare's design ethos of telling 'compelling stories where your choices matter', as per Creative Director Mac Walters' words. It was clear that, while BioWare development leads extensively discussed realizing spatial-explorative and temporal-ergodic agency affordances, the studio was aiming to continue privileging narrative agency with this new addition to the *Mass Effect* franchise. The following textual analysis will show that within the game, the other agency dimensions cannot only struggle to support that privileging, they can also undermine it.

Regarding *Andromeda*'s design in general, the keyword is volume. There are numerous explorable planets, thousands of lines of dialogue were written, and the combat situations are more dynamic than they were in the original trilogy. Apart from the small and contained scenes of key plot moments, each star system and planet offers a large number of side quests and minigames, making up for 130+ hours of gameplay. This is significantly more than the average offered by competing open world titles for the same retail price: *Far Cry Primal* (Ubisoft Montreal 2016) contains 55+ hours of content, while newcomer studio Guerilla Games' *Horizon Zero Dawn* (2017) offers just under 100 hours of play, all included.[10] Keeping this in mind, the following analysis will show that the delivery of a predetermined branching plot affording narrative agency took the backseat amongst other design priorities, in particular, the large volume of spatial-explorative, temporal-ergodic, and configurative (but not constructive) dimensions of agency affordances.

Earlier dramatic agency was conceptualised as one emerging from play, creating the 'player story', as opposed to the 'designer story' (Rouse 2005: 203). Hence, logic would dictate that the more opportunities there are to, say, flaunt special combo moves in the many combat situations stumbled upon in the vast explorable space of *Andromeda*, the larger the possibility space for dramatic agency to manifest is. However, I will argue that these encounters become gradually less meaningful, whereby their abundance decreases what narratologists call a quality of 'eventfulness' (Hühn 2010, 2011; Schmid 2003). Therefore, the following will unpack how the potential for dramatic agency is devalued by the plenitude of other agency affordances enabling exploration and combat in *Andromeda*, with the argument being that *Andromeda*'s text does not quite match the design intention of 'telling compelling stories with choices that matter'.

Spatial-Explorative Agency in Andromeda

In terms of an overview of game spaces, there are seven main planets of which five are explorable both on foot and by the in-game six-wheel-drive vehicle called 'Nomad', one is only traversable on foot only, and one is the tutorial and as such cannot be revisited. There is also a self-contained hub-world (a space station called 'Nexus') which serves as a sort of centre of operations (similar to the 'Citadel' in previous instalments), and numerous smaller similarly self-contained spaces (such as asteroids or space debris) which typically can only be visited once for events relevant to the overarching plot of the game, or that contain smaller optional missions (like squad member loyalty missions). In terms of how these game spaces can be navigated, we can draw on Bizzocchi and Tanenbaum's (2012) 'graduation of storyworld scale' in *Mass Effect 2* to better understand how each game space affords agency. Bizzocchi and Tanenbaum (ibid. 399–400) distinguish between 'the Milky Way galaxy, star regions, individual stars, solar systems, individual planets, space stations, multiple locations within each planet or space station'. Applying a similar filter to *Andromeda* yields the following list: Heleus cluster of the *Andromeda* galaxy, star systems, individual units within that system (for instance planets, comets, or debris), surface of these units, and if available, multiple locations within some of these units.

While Bizzocchi and Tanenbaum's graduations are a productive way of scaling the game's space, they still leave some stones unturned. First, they conceptualise the game's space as storyworld. While they do acknowledge this space is characterised by 'ludic challenge and narrative enrichment' (ibid. 399), little is said in terms of the specificities of how the storyworld offers these, and consequently, what 'storyworld' means in each regard. Second, their analysis does not distinguish between the different perspectives afforded by the game's design, and its various effects on player action. The three levels, for lack of a better term, of game spaces discussed in Chapter 2, namely that of ludic, locally represented, and storyworld space, will help us better identify how agency in this dimension is afforded by *Andromeda*'s design.

For example, as direct control of the avatar's spaceship in the ludic and locally represented spaces is not available, designers endeavoured to enhance the feeling of traversing the storyworld through audiovisual means and pacing. Every time the player/avatar decides to travel to a different planet, an unusually long medley of scripted scenes plays out. It features interactable cluster and galaxy maps, info sheets of celestial objects, and cut-scenes of take-off, acceleration, deceleration, and landing, which all contribute to recreating the laboriousness of navigating the vastness of space. Space Lead Jessica Campbell said they 'wanted [the player] to be able to fly around the system so you could see the movement' (Hussain and James 2017c: n.p.). Indeed, with this sequence of events, the space of the storyworld in *Andromeda* seems larger, and traversal of it slower.

Things change when the player/avatar decides to land. Here, the possibility space for player action manifests not just in the storyworld space, but in ludic and locally represented space as well. On most planets, space stations, and other game spaces, a new set of avatar actions afford spatial agency such as walking, running, taking cover, and vaulting medium-height objects. In addition, there are movements afforded by the newly introduced jetpack, such as jumping, hovering, and evading attacks mid-air. If the 'Nomad' is available, then further spatial affordances are offered in acceleration, brakes, handbrake, steering, thrusters, boosts, and a change to four-wheel drive for better traction uphill. Some planets, such as 'Eos', offer complete free movement on foot and via the Nomad, with a superimposed interface showing prioritised quest markers and nearby points of interest, and a button-activated map of the whole area featuring all points of interest and fast travel mechanics is also accessible. On these planets and such spaces, ludic and representational spaces align as closely as is typical of similarly designed games, and the player has spatial and explorative agency to move

'A Compelling Story with Choices That Matter' 145

around relatively freely. The background vista is not merely a 2D backdrop, every boulder, desert, and cliff seen is directly accessible, and offers game content in quests and other challenges.

Such extensive freedom of movement is regulated by level design features such as the occasional terrain and environmental hazards. Radiation or extreme temperatures can render certain areas difficult to navigate, or entirely inaccessible, which, again, is a rather common means to counter more practical issues like how much of the planet is actually rendered at any given time, or which areas designers would rather the player/avatar avoids for storytelling and pacing purposes. For example, an orange meter in the bottom left corner of the screen signifies radiation exposure. If the avatar or their vehicle remains exposed to radiation, their shield capacity eventually reduces, resulting in eventual death.

That being said, although such areas temporarily limit spatial-explorative agency, as the player progresses in the game, quests for removing some of these hazards are gradually made available.

The above enumeration of design elements and game mechanics shows clearly that the player has considerable spatial-explorative agency afforded by *Andromeda*'s design, as intended by BioWare's developers. This scaling up is especially salient when compared to the mostly linear space and level design of the previous *Mass Effect* trilogy. Those three games featured a largely predetermined order of progression in the narrative and cover-based combat, or as Producer Fabrice Condominas referred to it, 'stop-and-go aspect of third-person shooters' (Hanson 2016c: n.p.). Both of these changed with *Andromeda* by the expansion of game spaces, and the simultaneous loosening of designer control on how the player/avatar progresses through them. What follows looks at what there is to do in the space or, in other words, the gameplay affordances that the spatial design and basic movement-related game mechanics provide in the temporal-ergodic dimension of agency.

Temporal-Ergodic Agency in Andromeda

Temporality in the *Mass Effect* series was mostly examined as an aspect of narrative representation (Carvalho 2014; Zakowski 2014). There are, however other ways in which temporal structures in *Andromeda* impact the possibility space for player action. As mentioned in the paratextual analysis, *Andromeda*'s design headquarters were BioWare Montreal, the studio previously responsible for *Mass Effect 3*'s combat and multiplayer development. It also emerged from the analysis that besides exploration, combat was another dominant theme in design intention—something the Montreal studio already knew how to design well. Developers also spoke about the avatar's jetpack, which introduced verticality to movement that is especially useful in combat, expanding the possibility space for spatial agency to manifest. Since reacting to enemies suddenly spawning behind the avatar is time-critical, we can say that spatial affordances support agency to be realised in the temporal-ergodic dimension.

Andromeda's most prominent means of affording agency in this dimension are time-critical challenges during enemy encounters. As customary for third-person shooter games, but quite unlike the turn-taking fights in BioWare's earlier games, combat in *Andromeda* is live-action and real-time, meaning player actions tend to trigger near-immediate feedback from the objects in the game system: pressing the appropriate buttons will result in near-instant evasion of attacks, firing of a gun, or the usage of powers. Besides the fights connected to the predetermined narrative of the game, Ryder can randomly encounter troops of AI-controlled enemies at almost any point in the game, whom they would fight off with the help of squad mates. During combat, a superimposed interface displays squad member status, health bar, shield charge level, power cool-downs, and ammunition left.

The most basic challenge in combat scenarios is staying alive and killing all enemies. This can be achieved with proficient navigation of, predominantly, time-critical game mechanics. In *Andromeda*, evading enemies, melee or range attacking moving targets, or combining the avatar's powers with those of the squad members, are all manifestations of temporal-ergodic agency. Furthermore, the player can customise the level of challenge presented by adjusting the difficulty level (Narrative, Casual, Normal, Hardcore, or Insanity).[11] The four design elements that seem to be impacted most by difficulty settings, which influence player agency in a temporal-ergodic dimension, are: aim assistance; enemy stats and AI; shields; and environmental conditions. The level of difficulty changes the degree of aim assistance, for example, meaning that the time available for taking a shot varies: the lower the difficulty, the longer the window is. This is achieved by, for instance, a slower enemy AI, or by the centre of the aiming reticule being drawn towards the target for the player. Enemies' health, damage and accuracy statistics determine the length of combat encounters, while enemy AI may react differently, faster or slower to avatar action.

Certain enemies, such as the Cardinal, an enemy type belonging to the class of 'Ascendants', regenerate their shield on a regular loop, therefore determining the size of the window in time available to deal damage to them. Last but not least, some levels where combat scenarios take place feature areas where environmental hazards drain the avatar's health—the higher the difficulty, the faster the drain, the greater the challenge. Particularly in this last case, spatial agency afforded by level design supports the challenge constructed via temporal-ergodic agency affordances.

Besides these, there are four sets of design affordances that dictate the pace of combat regardless of difficulty settings, thereby facilitating or restricting non-trivial effort in time: combos, reloading weapons, reviving squad members, and power cool-down times. In other words, detonation of squad members' previously planted attacks to get an advantage in damage output is time-critical; reload rates and reviving fallen squad members impact the time/frequency of being disengaged from every other action, therefore exposing the avatar to damage; and finally, powers are not available for a certain amount of time after having been used. Most of these features were present in the previous trilogy, though those games allowed greater control over squad mates, a feat reminiscent of BioWare's turn-taking role-playing games.

What is different in *Andromeda*, however, is the frequency of gameplay sequences regulated by these temporal structures, or in other words, combat encounters. Accordingly, with the considerable increase of spatial and explorative agency affordances in the game (in the form of a more diverse avatar move set, and a large number of navigable planets), the amount of time spent overcoming challenges set by agency affordances in the temporal-ergodic dimension increases as well. As a result, while there is not much innovation or expansion regarding how agency in the temporal-ergodic agency is afforded by time-critical challenge in *Andromeda*, there is definitely a growth in the frequency of such events. However, there is another dimension, that of configurative-constructive agency, that contributes to this growth.

Configurative-Constructive Agency in Andromeda

In *Andromeda*. almost every single design affordance listed above as creating possibility space for agency in the spatial-explorative dimension and the temporal-ergodic dimension is open to configuration via resource management. For example, the 'Nomad' can be upgraded to go faster, or the player's avatar can develop new skills, and improve existing ones. While most of these configurative and constructive agency affordances are represented either on a local level, on that of the storyworld, or both (for example, the avatar's chosen gear is displayed both during gameplay and in cut-scenes), configuration is even more impactful in a ludic sense. Indeed, managing the in-game economy of resources, items, and other such things is an integral part of role-playing games' challenge (Picard 2013). As we have seen in the overview of the studio's previous games, BioWare established their reputation with role-playing games, and the *Mass Effect* trilogy thus far contained role-playing mechanics of various complexity. This continues to be the case in *Andromeda*, where all of the powers and skills, as well as avatar and squad member health, damage, accuracy, and other stats affording or limiting avatar action in combat are modifiable by investing in skill trees and upgrading tools.

The acquisition and development of weapons, armour, and other useful items is made possible by resource gathering. This game mechanic thus not only affords configurative agency but also further incentivises explorative agency in *Andromeda*. With the help of tools like the scanner, the mining drone, or the mundane act of looting, the player can gather natural resources, collect items used for crafting, or trade goods to accumulate wealth. These objects can also be scanned to earn research points, which can be invested in researching and developing 'Blueprints' for weaponry and armour, 'Augmentations' for these, and other special items. These assign additional bonuses to the already determined stats of the item, such as headshot bonus for range weapons, or longer shield endurance when the avatar's health is low. This shows just how much configurative agency players are afforded by the game's design to experiment with the different combination of gear for their avatar. Such agency affordances thus open up additional avenues for personalising combat, supporting agency in the spatial-explorative as well as the temporal-ergodic dimension.

As typical of similar role-playing/shooter hybrids, the player/avatar's progress through the game is measured and communicated by a variety of currencies. 'Experience Points' (XP) are earned in bulks after certain actions. Once enough XP is accumulated, the avatar levels up, earning them skill points that can be invested in skill trees for both the avatar and their squad members, thereby affording configurative agency. Not only can the player spend the skill points earned to level up their avatar, but they can also fully re-specify (or re-spec, in gaming lingo) the avatar. This means that all skill points spent can be redistributed at any point in the game. This game mechanic expands the possibility space for temporal-ergodic agency within the game, as by being able to completely change the strengths and weaknesses, special powers, and other such skills mid-game, the player is incentivised by design to seek out more and more combat encounters where they can try out the different specifications. At the same time, it creates a disconnect between the avatar as fictional character and as game piece, which, in turn, is at odds with the delivery of a highly authored designer story, previously important to BioWare's design ethos.

The three main skill groups are 'Combat', 'Biotics' (similar to magic), and 'Tech', each containing skills and powers specific to the group. For example, an avatar specialising in 'Tech' skills and powers can focus on perfecting the 'Invasion' skill, which shoots nano-projectiles towards enemies to disable their shields. Each power and skill can be developed further by the investment of skill points, with options available to pursue slightly different trajectories of the skill, such as deciding whether to improve how far the projectiles reach or how broad an area they cover. It is also possible to zigzag between branches, giving the player even more freedom in configuring their avatar and their abilities on the battlefield.

With enough skill points invested in certain skill trees, new profiles become available for the avatar, which determine pre-set configurations of strengths and weaknesses on the battlefield. In previous *Mass Effect* games, the avatar could specialise in, and from there onwards was limited to, one profile. *Andromeda* has a similar feature also, but it also expands upon it, thereby broadening the possibility space for configurative agency in two respects. First, it allows the player to combine profiles. For example, the

'Tactical Assassin' profile is a combination of the 'Soldier' and 'Engineer' profiles, specialising in 'Combat' and 'Tech' skills. Second, not only can the player combine profiles, they can also alternate between other unlocked profiles, such as the 'Adept', which focuses on 'Biotic' powers. Each profile offers a plethora of specific bonuses and other such things. For instance, assigning the 'Tactical Assassin' profile grants a profile-specific tool (the 'Tactical Cloak'), and skills ('Combat Fitness' and 'Tactical Cloak'), as well as a variety of bonuses to avatar stats.

In terms of constructive agency, there is but one prominent feature of design that facilitates its realisation albeit to a rather low degree: colony building. Notably, 'Andromeda Viability Points' (AVP) are accumulated by completing planet-specific missions—the more there is, the more colonists the player/avatar can send out to establish 'Science', 'Military', or 'Commerce' colonies. These colonies only exist in the game's storyworld space, and although are not represented locally, only as a catalogue of still images in a menu, they do have ludic functions, such as regular access to resources, or additional weapon slots on the avatar's holster. As such, they unlock rewards that impact the avatar's attributes, thereby contributing to further expansion of configurative agency affordances.

In summary, the large variety of resources, items, and currencies enable configurative agency to a degree none of the previous *Mass Effect* games did. This richness in features recalls the early years of BioWare's games, when in *Baldur's Gate* or *KOTOR*, hours could be spent contemplating the best weapon, armour, and power configuration for each member of the player character and their party. While constructive agency is rather limited, such a sizeable possibility space for configurative agency to manifest supports agency in the spatial-explorative and temporal-ergodic dimension, due to the various options and systems designed to encourage the player to tailor when, where, and how they face the time-critical challenges posed by combat situations. What does this mean for *Andromeda*'s narrativity and agency? This is what the next and final section of this chapter will explore.

Narrative-Dramatic Agency in Andromeda

As demonstrated in the first section of this chapter, BioWare's design ethos has been historically centred on weaving elaborate branching plots that demand limited spatial freedom and a more or less straight-forward ushering of the player along the game. In this way, games in the *Mass Effect* franchise afford a high degree of narrative agency, which is in line with the philosophy of BioWare summed up by Walters as 'telling stories'. But do these stories feature 'choices that matter'? As a first step towards answering this question, the following will review how agency is afforded by design features that contribute to the narrative structures within *Andromeda*.

The game was intended to contain a comparatively complex variety of narrative agency affordances. As Creative Director Mac Walters said, quite a large number of assets were created to contribute to the creation of *Andromeda*'s vast storyworld:

> *Mass Effect 3* had something like 670 characters in it and *Andromeda* has over 1200. The dialogue lines [are] basically *Mass Effect 2* plus *Mass Effect 3*. We've doubled down on characters, and yet our story isn't necessarily, like the critical path story, I would say, isn't necessarily that much longer.
>
> (Hussain and James 2017a: n.p.)

Characters could afford agency in the narrative-dramatic dimension to various degrees, which we can scale according to the degree to which encountering them is accidental or predetermined. On one end of the spectrum, there are the quests, or missions. First, there is what Walters above called the 'critical path', or in other words, the predetermined plot afforded by 'Priority Ops'. These consist of 18 missions that are gradually added to the 'Mission Journal' as the player progresses in the game, and take roughly 19 to 25 hours to complete, depending on difficulty level. While 'Priority Ops' afford some forking paths for completion thereby granting the player/avatar some flexibility when it comes to the order of completion, they all lead to the same final mission regardless of which route the player went down on. This makes *Andromeda*'s narrative structure nonlinear, albeit not to the same degree as previous *Mass Effect* games have been. For example, there are multiple 'Priority Ops' available for pursuit, such as 'Hunting the Archon' which directs the player to the next mission in the main plot centred around the antagonist figure called the 'Archon', while 'Elaaden: A New World' leads to a newly discovered planet, where additional quests are available to support the odds of success in the war.

Additionally, there is a large number of different side missions, some of which are connected to allies, some to planets or other locations, and which can take 100+ hours to complete, depending on difficulty, pace, and other variables.

These missions are also predetermined in that the dialogue, scripted events, cut-scenes, and environmental objects delivering elements of the designer story are, of course, designed. However, they are also optional, that is, not necessarily crucial in order to successfully complete the critical path of the game, and as such can be considered further narrative agency affordances. This is a major step away from previous *Mass Effect* games, where quests connected to allies and relationships were more strictly conditional to overall success. Some of these side missions are relatively closely tied to the 'critical path', in that their completion could have some impact on its development, as they yield rewards that can be used to improve the variables of other agency affordances, such as stats, items, or XP.

For example, the 42 conditionally structured (i.e., they are only unlockable in a certain order) 'Allies and Relationships' missions strengthen relationships with allies which in turn brings rewards like new powers, increasing squad members' combat competency, while also affording configurative agency in newly unlocked skills and powers. Other mission groups, named after locations like the planets 'Aya' or 'Elaaden', are structured similarly, and are targeted at increasing a planet's viability for colonisation. They usually involve undoing environmental hazards, or pacifying local armed forces, predominantly affording agency in the spatial-explorative and temporal-ergodic dimensions. On top of these, there are an additional, 80+ set of miscellaneous missions acquired most typically by talking to non-player characters scattered across the open worlds. The completion of these is largely inconsequential regarding the critical path. These side missions, listed under 'Additional Tasks', can be classified according to the three commands, or calls to action they present: go somewhere, shoot something, or push a button.

Before the game's release, developers spoke about how they were working on 'side quests that we can do that are much more interesting', as opposed to repetitive ones like fetch quests (Wallace 2016: n.p.). However, *Andromeda*'s side quests fail to actualise this design intention. For example, the missions 'Better Crafting', 'Roekaar Manifestos', and 'Unearthed' can be acquired by talking to a non-player character (barman/alien scientist/sage respectively), who asks the player/avatar to visit different spots, interact with a certain number of game-objects (beer ingredients/datapads/alien devices), and they all yield XP and some inconsequential information about the non-player character never to be seen again, as they disappear after the task's completion.

In comparison, previous *Mass Effect* games offer similarly structured optional quests, but they have a more textured impact on player agency. For instance, *Mass Effect* sets a task of scanning the 'Keepers', the mysterious alien caretakers of the galactic capitol called the 'Citadel'. This task can be acquired via one of two missions, each presenting different sides of a quarrel between two scientists. 'Citadel: Scan the Keepers' and 'Citadel: Jahleed's Fears' provides different contexts for the same act of scanning. These two missions in *Mass Effect* offer further opportunities for the player to characterise their Shepard (*Mass Effect*'s player character) through actions and choices.

In terms of the conveyed narrative, these two missions illustrate that rarely is anything black and white in the first *Mass Effect* game, and as such, scientists are neither completely innocent nor transparent about their motivations for asking the player/avatar this favour. This way the game provides opportunity for dramatic agency to emerge: the player/avatar has to decide whether to take the scientist's life, spare him, or spare him and carry out the immoral work of scanning 'Keepers' for him. Thus far, this seems to have a lot in common with *Andromeda*'s repetitive missions. However, besides incentivising the exploration of the hub-world, the missions in *Mass Effect* yield more than just XP and money. If the player/avatar decides to not scan all 'Keepers', they earned 'Paragon' points (as scanning 'Keepers' is not an ethical thing to do in the game's storyworld), which, as the overview of earlier BioWare games showed, have implications for agency in the configurative-constructive and temporal-ergodic dimensions. This way, the player/avatar's interaction with the game as a ludic system gains relevance within the storyworld. Should the player/avatar decide to ignore this ethical principle, they would get levelled XP for each scan, appropriately reflecting the avatar's development in the progression system, and by extension, the player's decisions, leading up to this point. In this sense, the decision about whether to scan 'Keepers' and the implications it has on the avatar's development is unlikely to happen in exactly the same way in different gameplay sessions. Such design adds a distinct quality to dramatic agency that is not present in *Andromeda*. Narratologists refer to this quality as 'eventfulness'.

When discussing eventfulness, Hühn distinguishes between two types of events in narratives. He argues that while any change of state can be classified as a type I event, type II events acquire significance from contextual factors, implying 'change of a special kind' (Hühn 2011: n. p.) Type II events must

> be brought into being and related to its surroundings by an entity (character, narrator, or reader) that comprehends and interprets the change of state involved.
>
> (Hühn 2011: n.p.)

In other words, eventfulness is a quality of change where significance is attributed to the event based on a contextual factor. Furthermore, as Schmid (2003) argues, eventfulness could be regarded as not a binary, but a matter of degrees, depending on how events adhere to different qualities they ought to possess, such as 'relevance', 'unpredictability', 'persistence', 'irreversibility', and 'non-iterative-ness' (Schmid 2003: 26–29).

In this vein, the inconsequentiality of *Andromeda*'s repetitive side quests leads to a low degree of eventfulness, as they fail to be relevant to the storyworld. The exceptionally large number of miscellaneous missions feature calls to action that are barely more than the above mentioned 'go somewhere', 'shoot something', or 'push a button'. Because they are exactly that, miscellaneous and additional, no 'entity' in the game attributes significance to them. They are not 'comprehended' or 'interpreted' in any way, besides being a mindless grind with little in-game consequence. The most salient characteristic of this content is, alas, volume. *Andromeda*'s side missions eat up more than two-thirds of playable content. Even reviewers pointed it out that the game 'works better as a management simulator':

> People bumbling around futuristic IKEA colony outposts tell you about their friend who got lost, or the medical supplies that got stolen, or the data samples they always need help collecting. . . . You then add it to

your quest list, a log that by the end of the game has more in common with Microsoft Outlook than a readable plot summary.

(Gach 2018: n.p.)

The proportion of hours invested in the main plot events versus all the 'management' done in side missions that afford predominantly spatial, temporal, and configurative agency means that narrative agency affordances are outweighed by the 100+ hours spent roaming the many planets and other celestial bodies, encountering all kinds of enemy troops in between quest locations. Agency affordances in the spatial-explorative and temporal-ergodic dimensions enable player stories to emerge from the gameplay, which is further supported by the wide range of options for configuring the avatar to perform better in combat. This should create a possibility space for dramatic agency to emerge. However, the game-text fails to integrate the design features to afford dramatic agency in a compelling way. The sheer volume of inconsequential tasks results in dramatic agency losing its value. In the paratextual analysis, 'interesting'-ness of side quests was qualified not in terms of complexity, depth, or socio-cultural relevance. Since they are inconsequential in the game-text, 'interesting'-ness is also not manifest when we define it according to BioWare's design ethos of 'compelling stories where the player's choice matters'. For the vast majority of the game, the player's choices do not really matter. *Andromeda*'s text therefore seems to reinforce not only the assumption that BioWare's design priorities in terms of player agency shifted, but also that the game-text does not match design intention.

This case study chapter turned to *Mass Effect: Andromeda* to show how different ways of affording or limiting player action have been both at the forefront of developer discourse surrounding production and within the game's design. *Andromeda* was developed across numerous studios of BioWare (and by extension, EA), a studio known for designing role playing games where the player has a real sense of import in shaping their characters and stories. During the development of the original *Mass Effect* trilogy, which played a significant part in the formation of the franchise brand and studio's authorial identity, BioWare was subsidised by EA, an industry giant with uniform production tools. This move brought about significant changes not only in staff and production cultures, but in the general direction of the studio's authorial trademark style as well—most notably, due to the shift to Frostbite. While the *Mass Effect* trilogy stepped away from BioWare's signature combat system allowing the player/avatar to manipulate time and allow for strategic decision making rather than the success rate of trigger-reflexes deciding the outcome as typical of role-playing games, and *Mass Effect 3* in particular foreshadowed some of the major implications of this change in the increased effort put towards perfecting single-player and multiplayer combat, it was with *Andromeda* that this shift in focus became most evident. In the game's paratextual surrounds we saw that developers acknowledged the shift, but they attempted to reconcile the tension between this newfound direction and BioWare's ethos.

In turn, while the analysis of the game-text revealed a correspondence to the paratextually communicated design intent regarding the focus on exploration and combat, it also revealed that there was, indeed, a disconnect between how BioWare's developers conceptualised their design ethos versus how *Andromeda*'s features relate to this ethos as defined across the two decades of BioWare's works. The main disconnect was between BioWare's intention to continue to prioritise the narrative-dramatic dimension of agency, and the game's design being unable to deliver due to the lack of eventfulness in the abundance of side quests. Previously, BioWare games, and the *Mass Effect* franchise in particular, placed significant emphasis on delivering 'compelling stories with choices that matter'. This meant that the player could shape the development of the main plot, typically by making non-reversible decisions concerning politics or a non-player character's fate, through tools like the dialogue wheel. However, *Andromeda* features a significantly larger game space, populated with, predominantly, combat encounters, which this chapter has shown make use of spatial-explorative, temporal-ergodic, and configurative-constructive agency affordances. Such disconnect between what kind of player experience designers intend the game to offer (and so how it is marketed), and how the game is actually designed, draws attention to both the accuracy of promotional paratexts and conflicts in what different parts of the industry perceive as important to players/about games.

This case study, along with the first one, illustrated how agency is discussed and designed in different contexts, yes, but still within the AAA segment of the videogame landscape, with its characteristic production cycles and preferences of gameplay features. As such, they raise the question of what similarities and differences we could find when looking at the discourses surrounding agency in yet unexplored (within this book, that is) production contexts, as well as how agency is afforded by game design fitting into a game design lineage tapping into different models of game design. This is what the final case study chapter will demonstrate.

Notes

1 For overviews of the Japanese game industry, see Consalvo 2016; DeWinter 2015.
2 See Part One in Garrelts 2006 for more on the relationship between the game, its violent content, the reputation it generated over the years.
3 D20 is a tabletop role-playing game mechanic which got adopted by computer games. The name refers to a 20-sided dice. In essence, players would roll a 20-sided dice in response to an event in the game that required player/avatar action, and then modify the number according to their character's stats (such as strength or stamina). If the end result meets or is above the target number (Difficulty Number) set by the Dungeon Master (person/system upholding game rules), the action was successful.

4   See Zagal and Altizer 2014 on reputation systems in role-playing games, Sicart 2009: 207–212 for a detailed analysis of alignment systems and its limitations, Wardrip-Fruin 2009: 59–69 on the strengths and weaknesses of the dialogue tree and the quest system in *KOTOR* specifically.
5   Although some would argue the opposite, see, e.g., Mejeur 2018: 208.
6   Excerpt from the patent: 'A system and method for creating conversation in a computer program such as a videogame. A plurality of classes of dialog is provided and a conversation segment is assigned to each class. A graphical interface is displayed during operation of the program that provides a choice indicator, wherein the choice indicator has a plurality of selectable slots, each associated with a dialog class. The graphical interface is consistent as to the position of dialog classes throughout at least a segment of the program' (Sinclair 2012: n.p.).
7   Also known as 'horde mode'.
8   Interestingly, while shooting was a central activity in the *Mass Effect* trilogy, the first instalment was more a 'hard-core RPG dressed as a shooter', according to game designer Christina Norman, who worked on all three games (Fullerton 2014 [2004]: 25). She said '[w]hether you hit enemies or not was determined by an invisible die roll. This meant that even if you aimed perfectly, you could miss, so guns felt weak and unreliable' (ibid.). *Mass Effect 2* and *3* however, feature more traditional shooter mechanics.
9   I will discuss *No Man's Sky* and procedural planet generation in more detail in Chapter 5.
10 All statistics are from howlongtobeat.com, a website processing player-submitted data.
11 There is a possibility that the game's AI can also scale enemies according to the avatar's level in a certain encounter, despite difficulty setting being pre-set. It seems only minor adjustments are made to accuracy and damage output in *Andromeda*, whereas other studios in the same genre, like Bethesda, do this to a larger degree. This question is extensively debated on several forums (see, e.g., Muzle84 2017).

References

Adams, M. B.; Rambukkana, N. (2018). "Why Do I Have to Make a Choice? Maybe the Three of Us Could, uh . . .": Non-Monogamy in Videogame Narratives. *Game Studies* 18 (2). Available at: http://gamestudies.org/1802/articles/adams_rambukkana

Albert, B. (2013). The Top 25 Xbox 360 Games. *IGN*, 21 September. Available at: https://uk.ign.com/articles/the-top-25-xbox-360-games-4?page=3

Anon. (2003). Vice City 'Racism' Sparks Protests. *Eurogamer*, 26 November. Available at: www.eurogamer.net/articles/news261103vicecityracism

Anon. (2015). Last Month I Took a Random Survey about Mass Effect 4. Here Is What I Found Out. *Reddit*, 17 April. Available at: www.reddit.com/r/masseffect/comments/32yzxf/last_month_i_took_a_random_survey_about_mass/

Bertz, M. (2016). Doctors & Dragons. The History of the RPG Powerhouse BioWare as Told by the Dungeon Masters Who Wrote It. *Game Informer* 284: 20–35.

BioWare. (1998). *Baldur's Gate* [PC]. Interplay Entertainment.

BioWare. (2000a). *Baldur's Gate II: Shadows of Amn* [PC]. Interplay Entertainment.

BioWare. (2000b). *MDK2* [PC]. Interplay Entertainment.

BioWare. (2002). *Neverwinter Nights* [PC]. Infogrames.

BioWare. (2003). *Star Wars: Knights of the Old Republic* [PC]. LucasArts.

BioWare. (2005). *Jade Empire* [PC]. Microsoft Game Studios.

BioWare. (2007). *Mass Effect* [PC]. Microsoft Game Studios.
BioWare. (2010a). About BioWare. *BioWare*. Available at: https://web.archive.org/web/20101006091642/www.bioware.com:80/bioware_info/about
BioWare. (2010b). *Mass Effect 2* [PC]. Electronic Arts.
BioWare. (2012a). *Mass Effect 3* [PC]. Electronic Arts.
BioWare. (2012b). An Update from BioWare Montreal. *BioWare Blog*, 12 November. Available at: http://blog.bioware.com/2012/11/12/an-update-from-bioware-montreal/
BioWare. (2012c). *Mass Effect 3: Omega* [PC]. Electronic Arts.
BioWare. (2013). *About BioWare*. Available at: https://web.archive.org/web/20130115052802/www.bioware.com/about
BioWare. (2014). *Dragon Age: Inquisition* [PC]. Electronic Arts.
BioWare. (2017) *Mass Effect: Andromeda* [PlayStation 4]. Electronic Arts.
BioWare. (2019). *Anthem* [PlayStation 4]. Electronic Arts.
Bizzocchi, J.; Tanenbaum, T. J. (2012). *Mass Effect 2*: A Case Study in the Design of Game Narrative. *Bulletin of Science, Technology & Society* 32 (5): 393–404. https://doi.org/10.1177/0270467612463796
Blake, H. J. (2014). *Console Wars: Sega, Nintendo, and the Battle That Defined a Generation*. New York: itbooks.
Blizzard North. (2000). *Diablo II* [PC]. Blizzard Entertainment.
Bungie. (2001). *Halo: Combat Evolved* [Xbox]. Microsoft Game Studios.
Carr, D.; Buckingham, D.; Burn, A.; Schott, G. (eds.). (2006). *Computer Games: Text, Narrative, Play*. Cambridge: Polity Press.
Carvalho, V. M. (2014). Leaving Earth, Preserving History: Uses of the Future in the *Mass Effect* Series. *Games and Culture* 10 (2): 127–147. https://doi.org/10.1177/1555412014545085
Clarkson, S. (2013). *Mass Effect 3*'s Ending Disrespects Its Most Invested Players. *Kotaku*, 12 April. Available at: https://kotaku.com/5898743/mass-effect-3s-ending-disrespects-its-most-invested-players
Condis, M. (2015). No Homosexuals in *Star Wars*? BioWare, 'Gamer' Identity, and the Politics of Privilege in a Convergence Culture. *Convergence* 21 (2): 198–212. https://doi.org/10.1177/1354856514527205
Consalvo, M. (2016). *Atari to Zelda. Japan's Videogames in Global Contexts*. Cambridge, MA: MIT Press.
Crecente, B. (2013). The Long, Strange Journey of BioWare's Doctor, Developer, Beer Enthusiast. *Polygon*, 28 January. Available at: www.polygon.com/2013/1/28/3924078/bioware-greg-zeschuk-beer-diaries
Crytek. (2004). *Far Cry* [Xbox]. Ubisoft.
Cyan, Inc. (1993). *Myst* [PC]. Brøderbund.
DeWinter, J. (2015). Japan. In M. J. P. Wolf, ed. *Video Games around the World*. Cambridge, MA: MIT Press, pp. 319–344.
Diver, M. (2012). *Mass Effect* Is to Videogames What *Battlestar Galactica*'s Reboot Was to TV. *The Guardian*, 3 March. Available at: www.theguardian.com/technology/2012/mar/03/mass-effect-three
EA. (2017). Frostbite: the Engine. *EA*, Available at: www.ea.com/frostbite/engine
EA DICE. (2008). *Battlefield: Bad Company* [PlayStation 3]. Electronic Arts.
Egenfeldt-Nielsen, S.; Smith, J. H.; Tosca, S. P. (2016). *Understanding Video Games. The Essential Introduction*. 3rd ed. New York: Routledge.

Fuchs, M.; Erat, V.; Rabitsch, S. (2018). Playing Serial Imperialists: The Failed Promises of BioWare's Video Game Adventures. *The Journal of Popular Culture* 51 (6): 1476–1499. https://doi.org/10.1111/jpcu.12736

Fullerton, T. (2014 [2004]). *Game Design Workshop: A Playcentric Approach to Creating Innovative Games*. 3rd ed. Boca Raton, FL: CRC Press

Gach, E. (2018). *Mass Effect: Andromeda* Works Way Better as a Management Sim. *Kotaku*, 9 January. Available at: https://kotaku.com/mass-effect-andromeda-works-much-better-as-a-managemen-1821929025

Gallagher, R. (2012). No Sex Please, We Are Finite State Machines: On the Melancholy Sexlessness of the Video Game. *Games and Culture* 7 (6): 399–418. https://doi.org/10.1177/1555412012466287

Game Informer. (2011). *Casey Hudson Interview—How Mass Effect Began*. Available at: www.youtube.com/watch?v=Zi0EvhiDPUQ

GameTrailers. (2014). *E3 2014 Bioware Studio Announcement*. Available at: www.youtube.com/watch?v=epRIxX7kr—k

Garrelts, N. (ed.). (2006). *Meaning and Culture of Grand Theft Auto: Critical Essays*. Jefferson, NC: McFarland & Co.

Ghys, T. (2012). Technology Trees: Freedom and Determinism in Historical Strategy Games. *Game Studies* 12 (1). Available at: www.gamestudies.org/1201/articles/tuur_ghys

Guerrilla Games. (2017). *Horizon: Zero Dawn* [Play Station]. Sony Interactive Entertainment.

Hanson, B. (2016a). BioWare's New Horizon: *Andromeda, Star Wars*, and The New IP. *Game Informer*, 28 November. Available at: www.gameinformer.com/b/features/archive/2016/11/28/biowares-new-horizon-inside-andromedas-challenges-star-wars-future-and-the-new-ip.aspx

Hanson, B. (2016b). Answering *Mass Effect Andromeda*'s Lingering Questions. *Game Informer*, 9 December. Available at: www.gameinformer.com/index.php/b/podcasts/archive/2016/12/09/answering-mass-effect-andromedas-lingering-questions.aspx

Hanson, B. (2016c). How *Mass Effect 3*'s Multiplayer Influenced *Andromeda*'s Gameplay. *Game Informer*, 16 November. Available at: www.gameinformer.com/b/features/archive/2016/11/16/what-mass-effect-andromedas-gameplay-takes-from-mass-effect-3s-multiplayer.aspx

Hello Games. (2016). *No Man's Sky* [PlayStation 4]. Hello Games.

Hussain, T.; James, L. (2017a). *Mass Effect: Andromeda* Mac Walters Interview. *Gamespot*, 20 March. Available at: www.gamespot.com/articles/mass-effect-andromeda-mac-walters-interview/1100-6448749/

Hussain, T.; James, L. (2017b). *Mass Effect: Andromeda* Yannick Roy Interview. *Gamespot*, 20 March. Available at: www.gamespot.com/articles/mass-effect-andromeda-yanick-roy-interview/1100-6448762/

Hussain, T.; James, L. (2017c). *Mass Effect: Andromeda* Jessica Campbell Interview. *Gamespot*, 20 March. Available at: www.gamespot.com/articles/mass-effect-andromeda-jessica-campbell-interview/1100-6448767/

Hussain, T.; James, L. (2017d). *Mass Effect: Andromeda* Fabrice Condominas Interview. *Gamespot*, 20 March. Available at: www.gamespot.com/articles/mass-effect-andromeda-fabrice-condominas-interview/1100-6448750/

Hussain, T.; James, L. (2017e). *Mass Effect: Andromeda* Chris Corfe Interview. *Gamespot*, 28 March. Available at: www.gamespot.com/articles/mass-effect-andromeda-chris-corfe-interview/1100-6448789/

Hussain, T.; James, L. (2017f). *Mass Effect: Andromeda* Cathleen Rootsaert Interview. *Gamespot*, 20 March. Available at: www.gamespot.com/articles/mass-effect-andromeda-cathleen-rootsaert-interview/1100-6448782/

Hussain, T.; James, L. (2017g). *Mass Effect: Andromeda* Ian Frazier Interview. *Gamespot*, 20 March. Available at: www.gamespot.com/articles/mass-effect-andromeda-ian-frazier-interview/1100-6448748/

Hussain, T.; James, L. (2017h). *Mass Effect: Andromeda* Michael Gamble Interview. *Gamespot*, 20 March. Available at: www.gamespot.com/articles/mass-effect-andromeda-michael-gamble-interview/1100-6448739/

Hühn, P. (2010). Introduction. In: P. Hühn et al., eds. *Eventfulness in British Fiction: Historical, Cultural and Social Aspects of the Tellability of Stories*. New York: De Gruyter, pp. 1–16.

Hühn, P. (2011). Event and Eventfulness. In P. Hühn et al., eds. *The Living Handbook of Narratology*. Hamburg: Hamburg University Press. Available at: https://wikis.sub.uni-hamburg.de/lhn/index.php/Event_and_Eventfulness

id Software. (1993). *Doom* [PC]. GT Interactive Software.

IGN. (1998). BioWare Developing *MDK2* for PC, Dreamcast. *IGN*, 20 October. Available at: https://uk.ign.com/articles/1998/10/20/bioware-developing-mdk-2-for-pc-dreamcast

IGN. (2007). Top 100 Games of All Time! *IGN*. Available at: https://web.archive.org/web/20071203021612/http://top100.ign.com/2007/

Ion Storm. (2000). *Deus Ex* [PC]. Eidos Interactive.

Irizarry, J. A.; Irizarry, I. T. (2014). The Lord Is My Shepard: Confronting Religion in the Mass Effect Trilogy. *Heidelberg Journal of Religions on the Internet* 5: 224–248. https://doi.org/10.11588/rel.2014.0.12168

Järvinen, A. (2008). *Games without Frontiers: Theories and Methods for Game Studies and Design*. PhD Thesis, Tampere University.

Jørgensen, K. (2003). *Aporia & Epiphany in Context: Computer Game Agency in Baldur's Gate II & Heroes of Might & Magic IV*. Hovedfag (MA) Dissertation. Department of Media Studies, University of Bergen.

Jørgensen, K. (2010). Game Characters as Narrative Devices. A Comparative Analysis of Dragon Age: Origins and Mass Effect 2. *Eludamos: Journal for Computer Game Culture* 4 (2): 315–331. https://doi.org/10.7557/23.6051

Juul, J. (2001). Games Telling Stories? A Brief Note on Games and Narratives. *Game Studies* 1 (1). Available at: www.gamestudies.org/0101/juul-gts/

Kerr, A. (2006). *The Business and Culture of Digital Games. Gamework/Gameplay*. London: SAGE Publications.

Krampe, T. (2018). No Straight Answers: Queering Hegemonic Masculinity in BioWare's Mass Effect. *Game Studies* 18 (2). Available at: http://gamestudies.org/1802/articles/krampe

Mass Effect. (2014). Happy N7 Day, Everyone! We Look Forward to the Future . . . *Facebook*, 7 November. Available at: www.facebook.com/masseffect/posts/732704220138297

Mass Effect. (2016). *MASS EFFECT: ANDROMEDA—Official Gameplay Trailer—4K*. Available at: www.youtube.com/watch?v=NOIzH6UcoW4

Mejeur, C. (2018). Chasing Wild Space Narrative Outsides and World-Building Frontiers in Knights of the Old Republic and The Old Republic. In S. Guynes and D. Hassler-Forest, eds. *Star Wars and the History of Transmedia Storytelling*. Amsterdam: Amsterdam University Press, pp. 199–209.

Muzle84. (2017). Differences between Difficulty Levels? *Reddit*, 24 April. Available at: www.reddit.com/r/MassEffectAndromeda/comments/677wfi/differences_between_difficulty_levels/

Naughty Dog. (2016). *Uncharted 4: A Thief's End* [PlayStation 4]. Sony Computer Entertainment.

Origin Systems. (1997). *Ultima Online* [PC]. Electronic Arts.

Patterson, C. B. (2014). Role-Playing the Multiculturalist Umpire: Loyalty and War in BioWare's *Mass Effect* Series. *Games and Culture* 10 (3): 207–228. https://doi.org/10.1177/1555412014551050

Perron, B. (2005). A Cognitive Psychological Approach to Gameplay Emotions. *DiGRA'05—Proceedings of the 2005 DiGRA International Conference: Changing Views: Worlds in Play*. Available at: www.digra.org/digital-library/publications/a-cognitive-psychological-approach-to-gameplay-emotions/

Picard, M. (2013). Levels. In M. J. P. Wolf and B. Perron, eds. *The Routledge Companion to Video Games*. Abingdon: Routledge, pp. 99–106.

Pierse, C. (2014). Introducing Some Dev Team Leads for the Next *Mass Effect*. *BioWare Blog*, 7 November. Available at: https://blog.bioware.com/2014/11/07/introducing-some-dev-team-leads-for-the-next-mass-effect/

Polygon. (2017). The 500 Best Games of All Time. *Polygon*, 27 November. Available at: www.polygon.com/features/2017/11/27/16158276/polygon-500-best-games-of-all-time-500-401

Prell, S. (2017). *Mass Effect: Andromeda* director Mac Walters explains the dialogue system replacing Paragon/Renegade. *Gamesradar*, 8 February. Available at: www.gamesradar.com/uk/mass-effect-andromeda-director-mac-walters-explains-the-dialogue-system-replacing-paragon-renegade/

Reardon, D. C.; Wright, D.; Malone, E. A. (2017). Quest for the Happy Ending to Mass Effect 3: The Challenges of Cocreation with Consumers in a Post-Certeauian Age. *Technical Communication Quarterly* 26 (1): 42–58. https://doi.org/10.1080/10572252.2016.1257742

Rockstar North. (2002). *Grand Theft Auto: Vice City* [PC]. Rockstar Games.

Rouse III, R. (2005): *Game Design: Theory & Practice*. 2nd ed. Plano, TX: Wordware.

Ryan, M.-L. (2015). *Narrative as Virtual Reality 2*. Baltimore, MD: Johns Hopkins University Press.

Schell, J. (2015 [2008]). *The Art of Game Design: A Book of Lenses*. Burlington, MA: Morgan Kaufmann.

Schmid, W. (2003). Narrativity and Eventfulness. In T. Kindt and H.-H. Müller, eds. *What Is Narratology? Questions and Answers Regarding the Status of a Theory*. Berlin: De Gruyter, pp. 17–33.

Schreier, J. (2017a). *Blood, Sweat and Pixels: The Triumphant, Turbulent Stories Behind How Video Games Are Made*. New York: Harper Collins.

Schreier, J. (2017b). The Story behind *Mass Effect: Andromeda*'s Troubled Five-Year Development. *Kotaku*, 7 June. Available at: https://kotaku.com/the-story-behind-mass-effect-andromedas-troubled-five-1795886428

Sicart, M. (2009). *The Ethics of Computer Games*. Cambridge, MA: MIT Press.
Sinclair, B. (2012). Patented Game Mechanics That Might Surprise You. *Gamespot*, 2 April. Available at: www.gamespot.com/articles/patented-game-mechanics-that-might-surprise-you/1100-6369027/
Star Wars: Episode II—Attack of the Clones. (2002). Directed by George Lucas. Lucasfilm Ltd.
Toftedahl, M.; Engström, H. (2019). A Taxonomy of Game Engines and the Tools That Drive the Industry. *DiGRA'19—Proceedings of the 2019 DiGRA International Conference: Game, Play and the Emerging Ludo-Mix*. Available at: www.digra.org/digital-library/publications/a-taxonomy-of-game-engines-and-the-tools-that-drive-the-industry/
Thier, D. (2012a). Fan Makes FTC Complaint Over *Mass Effect 3* Ending, But It Won't Hold Water. *Forbes*, 19 March. Available at: www.forbes.com/sites/davidthier/2012/03/19/fan-makes-ftc-complaint-over-mass-effect-3-ending-but-it-wont-hold-water/
Thier, D. (2012b). *Mass Effect 3* Protesters Sending Cupcakes to Bioware. *Forbes*, 27 March. Available at: www.cinemablend.com/games/Mass-Effect-3-Fans-Sending-BioWare-Cupcakes-Protest-40864.html
Thier, D. (2012c). Why Fans Are So Angry About the *Mass Effect 3* Ending. *Forbes*, 14 March. Available at: www.forbes.com/sites/davidthier/2012/03/14/why-fans-are-so-angry-about-the-mass-effect-3-ending/#9b31313775f0
Thorsen, T. (2007). *Grand Theft Auto* Sparks Another Lawsuit. *Gamespot*, 3 October. Available at: www.gamespot.com/articles/grand-theft-auto-sparks-another-lawsuit/1100-6118699/
Tuttle, W. (2004). *Jade Empire* Q&A with Dr. Ray Muzyka and Dr. Greg Zeschuk. *Xbox/GameSpy*. Available at: http://xbox.gamespy.com/xbox/jade-empire/572980 p1.html
Tuttle, W. (2007). BioWare Talks *Mass Effect*: Part 2. *Team Xbox*, 12 February. Available at: https://web.archive.org/web/20080322070522/http://interviews.teamxbox.com:80/xbox/1890/BioWare-Talks-Mass-Effect-Part-2/p1/
Ubisoft Montreal. (2016). *Far Cry Primal* [PlayStation4]. Ubisoft.
Unreal. (n.d.). Features. *Unreal Engine*. Available at: www.unrealengine.com/en-US/features
Wallace, K. (2016). Six Fun Activities to Pursue in *Mass Effect: Andromeda*. *Game Informer*, 23 November. Available at: www.gameinformer.com/b/features/archive/2016/11/23/six-fun-activities-to-pursue-in-mass-effect-andromeda.aspx
Wardrip-Fruin, N. (2009). *Expressive Processing: Digital Fictions, Computer Games, and Software Studies*. Cambridge, MA: MIT Press.
Wolpaw, E. (2000). *MDK2* Review. *Gamespot*, 12 June. Available at: www.gamespot.com/reviews/mdk2-review/1900-2586155/
Zagal, J. P.; Altizer, R. (2014). Examining 'RPG Elements': Systems of Character Progression. *FDG'14—Proceedings of the 9th International Conference on the Foundations of Digital Games*. Available at: https://my.eng.utah.edu/~zagal/Papers/Zagal_Altizer_RPG_Elements_Progression.pdf
Zakowski, S. (2014). Time and Temporality in the *Mass Effect* Series: A Narratological Approach. *Games and Culture* 9 (1): 58–79. https://doi.org/10.1177/1555412013512421

5 'The World Is Your Play-Doh'
System Era Softworks and *Astroneer*

While the previously discussed case studies were produced from budgets rivalling those of Hollywood blockbusters with team members often in the hundreds, such games are, of course, not the only ones on the market. It is therefore worthwhile to include a case study from a different production context, especially one where both design intention and the possibility space for player action are articulated and realised in ways that the previous two case studies did not account for. By doing so, we can not only demonstrate the diverse applicability of the framework to a variety of production contexts and game design models, but also add to it whatever findings emerge from this particular analysis. The aerospace-themed, procedurally generated survival-crafting game *Astroneer* (2019) by System Era Softworks (henceforth referred to as System Era) is one of many such videogames released over the past decade, since the success of *Minecraft* demonstrated audiences' desire for this model of game design. *Astroneer*'s premise is that the player/avatar crash-lands on a desolate planet and needs to survive until reinforcements arrive. The game's audiovisual aesthetics are cartoonish and non-threatening, tapping into joyful and exciting space exploration fantasies. The core mechanic of the game revolves around the 'Terrain Tool', which is an upgradeable object somewhere between a gun and a vacuum cleaner. *Astroneer* is exemplifies several characteristics of a specific path in independent game design, characterised by less direct designer control on moment-to-moment gameplay, and a more direct relationship with the player base that informs the design of the game. As such, it is an illuminating case study for demonstrating the applicability of the heuristic framework to a broader spectrum of game production and game design.

Since System Era is a new studio and *Astroneer* is their first game, there is no historical design ethos to speak of. Nonetheless, its developers all came from some of the biggest AAA studios, and were outspoken about what this move toward independent production meant to their professional identity, their work ethic, and the kind of game they wanted to make. Therefore, in lieu of a historical reconstruction of the studio's design ethos, this chapter will survey what connotations the labels 'independent' and 'indie' have,

DOI: 10.4324/9781003298786-6

and what game design model milestones there have been over the years. In light of such a tradition, the chapter will then interrogate the promotional paratexts of *Astroneer* for a founding ethos—namely how the independent tradition influenced the formation of the studio and aspects of game production. I will then expand this discussion into an analysis of design intention as communicated via the promotional surrounds, particularly zooming in on how developers conceptualised player agency, and what implications design decisions can have on how avatar action would be afforded or limited in *Astroneer*'s design. The argument is that the design intention was to afford free, experimentational, creative, i.e., 'paidic' (Caillois 1961) play which will be attached to the notion of 'playfulness' (Huizinga 2009 [1949]; Millar 1968; Sicart 2014; Stenros 2015). Finally, in the last third of the chapter, *Astroneer*'s design will be more closely examined via the heuristic framework, to identify how agency is afforded by game mechanics across dimensions; and more specifically, how *Astroneer*'s design affords playfulness. Thus, this case study will not only engage with a tradition of making videogames that showcases many typical features of the independent sector, it will also examine the role of player agency in an approach to game design that is rather different from the previous two case studies: one less preoccupied with storytelling or role play, and more focused on affording play for play's sake. As the first step towards this, we need to ask: what makes a game independent? What separates this sector of videogames from the broader gaming landscape?

Independent Games: Definitions and Trends

Defining Independence

The term 'indiepocalypse' is now used in the gaming community to refer to an overabundance of a certain subset of videogames, which makes the market of these games so saturated that it is difficult for developers to reach their audience (GDC 2016; Lipkin 2019). But what exactly is an independent game, and is it the same as an indie game?[1] Generally speaking, these qualifiers are used inconsistently, and interchangeably, in discourses surrounding videogames. For instance, 'indie games', 'indies', 'independent developers', 'indie sector', or 'indie sphere' are phrases often used by journalists without any comment as to which aspects of the mainstream videogame industry there is an independence from (see, e.g., Diver 2016: 8). There has been ample debate around the decoding of 'independent' and 'indie' labels both in journalistic and developer discourse (Antropy 2011; Gnade 2010) as well as in academia (Garda and Grabarczyk 2016; Juul 2014, 2019; Lipkin 2013; Ruffino 2013, 2021; Simon 2013; Thon 2019; Wilson 2005; Zimmerman 2002) What these approaches have in common is that they emphasise the importance of context—technological, industrial, socio-economic and political—when attributing the 'independent' label and its different variations and iterations. Garda and Grabarczyk (2016) identify three main ways in which a game can be 'independent', each determined by what it is that the game is independent from:

(A) financial independence (constituted by the developer—investor relation), (B) creative independence (developer—intended audience) and (C) publishing independence (developer—publisher).
(Garda and Grabarczyk 2016: n.p.)

An important result of this distinction is that games can be considered independent so long as they tick at least one of the three above specified criteria. A somewhat similar list of conditions is provided by Juul (2019), who draws on three types of independence in American cinema identified by King (2005):

1. Financially independent in terms of its 'industrial location'.
2. Aesthetically independent . . . in its 'formal/aesthetic strategies'.
3. Culturally independent . . . in its 'relationship to the broad social, cultural, political or ideological landscape'.
(Juul 2019: 12)

Juul also adds that these three types of independence each tend to dominate discourse at different points in time, meaning that how independence is understood tends to pivot around what is at the focus of broader socio-cultural discourses in any given decade: the power dynamics between various stakeholders within the specific landscape of videogame production and distribution, as well as within the entertainment media industries as a whole; broader socio-cultural issues such as gender or diversity both on and off screen; or corporate work ethics.[2] Considering all this we, can conclude that independence in the context of videogames should always be understood according to context-specific terms.[3]

Upon first look, a salient difference in the two aforementioned approaches is that Juul argues independence can be better understood as a matter of rhetoric rather than a property of an object or quality of the circumstances of production. Ruffino (2013) makes a similar point when he underscores that independence in the video game industry is a discursive construct, and as such, 'narratives of production' (Ruffino 2013: 106) should be studied and historicised accordingly. That being said, Garda and Grabarczyk's typology does account for this in type (B) creative independence, which they argue is supposed to capture how developers assign themselves the label 'in direct developer's quotes describing the game in promotional materials, interviews, product description and other paratexts' (Garda and Grabarczyk 2016: n.p.). In this way, while the lists do not necessarily align, they both address the same issues at least to a certain degree. What we can draw from this is that independence in the context of videogames is discussed as a means to locate and/or position both product and producer within the landscape governed by cultural politics and production logics.

The second main difference is the extent to which the two typologies include ludo-aesthetic associations attributed to the independent label by participants of the discourse. On an overall level, Garda and Grabarczyk's typology does not account for what Juul calls 'cultural independence', which is supposed to capture how games are promoted to be about culturally, politically, and morally diverse topics, and are also made by culturally and politically diverse teams who work under, as Juul points out, better conditions than their corporate counterparts who often face extended periods of crunch in order to meet deadlines. On a more specific level, while Juul specifically argues against drawing terminological distinctions, Garda and Grabarczyk distinguish 'indie' from 'independent', where the former refers to videogames coming out in the mid-2000s with a certain 'indie look' and 'indie feel' to them. These, they argue, are characterised by digital distribution, experimental aesthetics, a smaller budget and lower retail price, smaller team size, a retro style looking back at early videogames with nostalgia, coming from a certain scene (such as the Independent Game Festival in a North American context), or using similar development tools (Garda and Grabarczyk 2016: n.p.). This historical approach, though productive in a way, only applies to a specific group of videogames made around this time period. A more nuanced description is offered by Juul (2014, 2019), who argues for there being a certain 'independent style' which

> is a representation of a representation. It uses contemporary technology to emulate low-tech and usually cheap graphical materials and visual styles, signalling that a game with this style is more immediate, authentic, and honest than are big-budget titles with high-end, three-dimensional graphics.
>
> (Juul 2019: 38)

Juul argues that games employing an 'independent style' claim authenticity by mimicking the aesthetics of older game styles which could be considered more authentic as they tap into romanticised values such as individual artisanship, small-scale production, and more direct relationship between producer and consumer. This, in turn, Juul links to the Arts and Crafts movement of the 19th century, which emerged as a counter-effort to robust change brought about by the industrial revolution (ibid. 34–37). As such, we can talk about independence not only in the sense outlined above with regards to the (cultural) politics of production and distribution, but also with regards to aesthetics.[4] Regarding System Era and *Astroneer*, we will see both a discourse of independence woven by developers, as well as design features that could be seen as belonging to Juul's 'independent style'. For terminological simplicity, I will use 'independent' throughout, to encapsulate all the complexities discussed above.

Independent Games: A Brief History

In doing so, in lieu of a founding ethos for the studio, we can reconstruct the environment and tradition in which System Era began working on *Astroneer*. While the previous chapters focused on the console market, here the focus is more oriented towards the PC market. As Kevin Toms, developer of the original *Football Manager* series (Toms 1982–1992) said, '[w]hen I released *Football Manager* it was January 1982, and at that time, all of the games developers were indies' (Baker 2018: n.p.). However, if everyone was independent, then in a sense nobody was, because the industrial structures had not yet formalised yet, so there was nothing to be independent from (as also pointed out by Garda and Grabarczyk 2016: n.p.). That said, lines of division started to appear with the growth of big game publishers, as discussed in the previous case study chapters. In the 1990s, budgets grew and teams multiplied, which marginalised many developers who did not want to join the increasingly corporatised production culture that gradually chipped at the authorial power of the individual designer (i.e., a proper industry) that had begun to emerge (see, e.g., Keogh 2015: 155; Kerr 2017: 34; Nichols 2014; O'Donnell 2012). Still wanting to produce games and find a way to distribute them without relying on established channels of retail typically controlled by corporate entities (which, at the time, mostly meant buying copies off the shelf), many developers opted for shareware. Designers with visions who were marginalised by the growing publisher and retailer dominance could reach out to players through what were called bulletin board systems, or BBS, a pre-internet dial-up modem that facilitated networked communication (Camper 2007: 155). Back then, developers could share parts of their games for free, and then if players liked it, they could purchase the whole version as a physical copy, directly from the developer. As developer David Braben said, then, 'games were distributed by stuffing envelopes from home with cassettes you duplicated yourself and photocopies of instructions that you folded up and put into the cassette box' (Diver 2016: 13). This approach to distribution, namely fewer middlemen and a resultant reduced distance between those who make games and those who play them, continues to distinguish independent game production from AAA today.

An important turning point in this came with growing support for players to modify contents of released games in the 1990s. Games like *Doom* (id Software 1993) or *Quake* (id Software 1996) allowed for player-generated maps, while Valve released an official modding kit in tandem with their game *Half-Life* (1998) called Worldcraft. Better known today as the Valve Hammer Editor, this modding kit was a training ground for many young game enthusiasts interested in developing (Laukkanen 2005: 18–63). This established a tradition of game developers handing over their means of creation to their player base, thus involving potential audiences in production. This tradition, although not atypical of the practices of AAA studios (think Bethesda, at least for a time), is certainly more prevalent in independent production. In the early 2000s, besides events and trade shows dedicated to videogames gradually opening up their floor to non-corporate affiliated productions (Parker et al. 2018), as well as festivals being dedicated to promoting and awarding independent games (Juul 2019: 57–124), Valve opened an online videogame distribution platform called Steam. It was set up in 2003 to connect developers and customers, thereby cutting out the publisher. From the store, games can be downloaded directly onto PC. While the field of rivals grew with time, with powerful contenders such as EA's Origin or the Epic Store offering similar services, Steam, at the time of writing, is the most popular online store for PC games (Wilde 2019). The launch of Steam spawned an era often referred to as the 'indie boom', from the mid-2000s onwards.[5] It was within this general production and distribution landscape that System Era was founded and created their first, and to this day only, game, *Astroneer*.

In terms of the aesthetics of independent games, considering at their core is a DIY attitude to creativity (Guevara-Villalobos 2015; Juul 2019: 34–38; Westecott 2013), it should not come as a surprise that they come in many shapes. Still, it is possible to identify some typical patterns without risking oversimplification. In terms of visual aesthetics, the games of the 'indie boom' of the mid-2000s, such as *Braid* (Number One 2008), *Super Meat Boy* (Team Meat 2010), *Limbo* (Playdead 2010), and *Fez* (Polytron Corporation 2012) popularised the low-key, underscored, often pixelated visuals typically associated with independent games, and had similar game mechanics centred around puzzle-solving and platforming. At the same time, there has also been a boom in narrative-driven games with simple mechanics, also called walking simulators, such as *Dear Esther* (The Chinese Room 2012) and *Gone Home* (The Fullbright Company 2013).[6] Independent production and distribution models also helped the proliferation of horror games like *Amnesia: The Dark Descent* (Frictional Games 2010)[7] or *Five Nights at Freddy's* (Cawthon 2014), as well as experimentational art games like *Kentucky Route Zero* (Cardboard Computer 2013)[8] or *Untitled Goose Game* (House House 2019). No less importantly, so-called roguelike games, that is, procedurally generated top-down dungeon crawlers such as *Spelunky* (Mossmouth, LLC 2008), *The Binding of Isaac* (McMillen 2011), or *Enter the Gungeon* (Dodge Roll 2017) are also critically acclaimed and boast sizeable fan bases (Bailes and Shaw 2018).[9] There is one further genre often associated with independent game design which form the background against which System Era developers refined the directions their studio in general, and their game in particular, would take. This is the genre of sandbox games, of which *Minecraft* in particular stands out as an exemplary case.

Minecraft redefined the videogame landscape, changing the way games are perceived, made, and played. Its creator, Notch, was heralded as a poster boy for independent games, and *Minecraft* has been one of the most popular streamed games on Twitch (Gandolfi 2016).[10] It was hugely relevant to the development of *Astroneer* not only because the game greatly inspired System Era's developers (System Era 2016c, 2016e), but also because former Lead Artist on *Minecraft* Spencer Kern joined the studio as *Astroneer*'s Art Director (Noclip 2019). In the simplest of words, *Minecraft* is a 3D survival-crafting sandbox game with blocky visuals, and procedurally generated game spaces. Its appeal lies in that it can be enjoyed by players of various abilities and backgrounds: the average player can mine, build, and fight whatever and whomever they please; more tech-savvy gamers can mod freely, creating entire games within the game; and packages like the *Minecraft: Education Edition* (Mojang 2016) offer educational resources and facilitate interactive in-game classrooms, accompanied with websites and learning materials. *Minecraft* is an 'editor game' (Abend and Beil 2015), a kind of 'virtual LEGO' (Schutz 2014: 237), where the main goal is less to win, more to play:

> These play- or sandboxes pose new questions regarding the player's motivation(s) and the appeal of a gameplay that consists of building a game world rather than playing within one—thus, the material agency of the game (which usually becomes visible via the rule set, the game world, or the narration) seems to dissolve.
>
> (Abend and Beil 2015: 2)

While Abend and Beil's argument that sandbox games' design 'dissolves' agency is perhaps not the most fortunate way to describe the relationship between such design and the player's expression of meaningful action (as *Minecraft* affords a high degree of agency in the constructive-configurative dimension), their point about games facilitating a somewhat different possibility space for player action compared to games with more direct designer direction is nonetheless a valid one. How this plays out in *Astroneer* will be explored in the textual analysis part of this chapter, but in order to do that, we first need to take a closer look at what sandbox design is, and how it differs from open world design, like that of *Mass Effect: Andromeda* discussed in the previous chapter.

The two terms 'sandbox' and 'open world' refer to a similar concept: that of design that lets the player roam around freely and decide what goals to pursue. As such, they are often used interchangeably (see, e.g., Deen 2011; Gazzard 2011; Sites and Potter 2018). However, a subtle difference can be drawn between the two when looking at their usage through a historical lens. With the release of *The Sims* (2000) and *Grand Theft Auto III* (DMA Design 2001), 'sandbox' and 'open world' entered gaming vernacular (Breslin 2009). At the heart of such design, according to *The Sims* creator Will Wright, is a 'metrics of progression, but it's not mission based' (Smith 2011: n.p.). Indeed, this design model 'gives players latitude in experimentation or in devising their own game tactics and goals' (Giddings 2014: 259). Such games are often without goals, or incentivise the player to shape their own goals, tailor their playstyle (Juul 2007: 191). Accordingly, both descriptors refer to a game's level design and degree of predetermined-ness in progression. There was, however, a paradigm-shift in how sandbox and open world design was understood as triggered by *Garry's Mod* (Facepunch Studios 2004), a player-created mod of Valve's *Half Life 2* (2004) (where there are no set goals, only a gameworld and objects that can be spawned and manipulated) and subsequently, *Minecraft*.

With *Minecraft* thrown into the mix, the heavily predetermined encounter types of most games previously described as open world or sandbox appear rather less unconstrained. There is a difference in the degree of constraint levied on avatar action, in, say, *Grand Theft Auto* games' open playable cityscapes and the construction blocks of *Minecraft*, as the verbs determining these tend to be broader: the interaction verb 'shoot' in *Grand Theft Auto* games is slightly less versatile in its implementation than 'break' or 'shovel' which can be applied to a plethora of things in *Minecraft*.[11] Nitsche points out that while the term 'sandbox' emphasises the 'placeness of game worlds', it 'focus[es] on their use, which is very different' (Nitsche 2008: 171). In this vein, we can argue that 'open world' describes a more limited possibility space for action, whereas 'sandbox', with its reference to children moulding the sand into whatever shapes they want at playgrounds, implies that there is a broader possibility space for the player to do whatever they like, particularly in the configurative-constructive dimension. In this sense, we can describe *Minecraft* and games in its wake, such as *Astroneer*, as sandbox rather than open world.

Developing *Astroneer*

As mentioned in the introduction to this chapter, System Era is a new studio, and *Astroneer* is their debut, and to date only, game. It therefore makes more sense to establish a founding ethos, rather than a historically developed design ethos the like of which was reconstructed in the previous two case study chapters. Albeit not as cemented as an ethos formulated over decades, the following analysis will show how the founding ethos influenced decisions about development nonetheless, which then, in turn, impacted how player action was to be enabled or constrained by the game's design. The following will first explore what going independent meant for System Era's founders, and what implications this move had for future design decisions. It will then look at two games regularly occurring in the early paratext as sources of inspiration, and highlight two features in particular that they have in common, a sandbox design and procedurally generated content, which represent the general design direction System Era was heading towards. Doing so will identify what general direction *Astroneer*'s design would take with regards to affording agency.

Independent Studio, Independent Audience

Five game developers, all of whom had several years of experience working on AAA videogames, founded System Era around 2015, 'to see how much we can get done entirely ourselves' (Microsoft Developer 2018: n.p.). They set out to make a game about 'wonder, discovery, power, greed, mystery, and grand endeavour in a new age of expansion on the fringes of humanity' (admin 2015: n.p.).[12] The team was inspired 'less by *Star Wars* and more by *Cosmos*, the Space Race, the Apollo program, and SpaceX' (ibid.). Adam Bromell was Lead Artist and Art Director on Ubisoft games *Assassin's Creed: Unity* (2014) and *Watch Dogs* (2014); Jacob Liechty, Brendan Wilson, and Paul Pepera worked at 343 Industries' take on the *Halo* franchise (Bungie 2001–) as Graphics Engineer, Software Development Engineer, and Art Lead, respectively; and Riley Gravatt spent years working on *The Sims 4* (2014) as Audio Asset Manager at Electronic Arts, and as Sound Designer at Disney Interactive. The initiative to leave the big budget world stemmed from a desire to make a game that they have 'wanted to play for a very long time' (System Era 2016a: n.p.). Yet, developing independently from corporate structures was a steep learning curve for the team. As to what unforeseen consequences going independent had in store for the team, Jacob Liechty said:

> We spent the first year of that learning hard lessons, and the next year doing something better. We're all triple-A developers so we think we know how to make games. But it's completely different, making your own game. . . . Because you jump into [indie development] and you think you're working on the right thing, and then actually no, you aren't, and you realize six months later you could have been making a lot more progress. My own failures are all tied to having this overly triple-A mindset about what you're working on. . . . Coming from triple-A, you kind of feel like . . . at a distance from indie devs. They seem like these super-spry, almost crazy kind of people who think they can do anything, Triple-A people also feel like they can do anything, but they have this chip on their shoulder that like . . . they're the pros, you know? That they're the real pros.
>
> (Wawro 2015: n.p.)

Not only did they have to reconsider workflow and priorities, but also reconcile the changes in their professional identities. Brendan Wilson further underscored how difficult it was not having someone calling the shots for them:

> When you work at a big company, there's still so much that is, sort of taken care of for you. Leaving the walled garden of the corporate culture, in America . . . that's when you're really on your own, and you feel how difficult that is.
>
> (Tirado 2016: n.p.)

While it was stressful to not be produced in this way, it did come with its benefits, notably an increased authority over all aspects of game-making. Adam Bromell said he was much more attached to the game, whereas in AAA it was more common to experience a detachment from work, which altered their attitude to work:

> I'm never not working basically. And I think that's the same for everybody. But we could do all these things ourselves in our spare time. . . . We work 8 hours as developers, and then we spend our extra time doing marketing and things like that. We don't work with any third parties and stuff, it's all handled [by] ourselves.
>
> (System Era 2016a: n.p.)

While not in line with how the notion is conceptualised in the heuristic framework presented in this book, it is nonetheless evident that agency lies at the heart of the studio's ethos—that of the individual developers to be making their own, independent decisions over all aspects of their work, from content production through management all the way to promotion. A crucial step in accomplishing this was the decision to release the game in Early Access, which is a distribution plan Steam offers where developers can release unfinished versions of their games which players purchase for a reduced price.[13] It is different from pre-purchasing a game (a format often offered by AAA publishers) for two main reasons. First, once the consumer buys the game in Early Access, they will likely have continued free access to all upcoming content, including a final, release version, and beyond. Second, players are often given means to report bugs and provide feedback. This strategy promotes not only more direct engagement between game-makers and consumers, but also advocates players' involvement in the game's production.

System Era's reasons to follow this path were numerous, as co-founder Brendan Wilson recalled:

> There were sort of three options. Get a publisher, do Kickstarter, or do Early Access and self-fund. The publishing side was difficult. We were kind of being presented with two options. One was either maintain more the level of control that we wanted to have over the title, but

for the cost of a very low budget, while still being under the pressure of publishing milestones and things like that; or, accept a much higher budget, but really give up most of the effective ownership of the title. There were deals that were, there were publisher around who would say things like 'Yeah, you know, you're gonna keep all of your IP, but we're gonna take what they call exploitation rights' which sort of like effectively gives them the IP without giving them the IP. It was important to us to be in control, that was why we wanted to be independent.

(Noclip 2019: n.p.)

Not only did the decision to release via Steam's Early Access enable System Era to maintain creative independence, it also enabled them to have their audiences more involved in production. Arguably, there is a less romantic aspect to this: quality assurance testing is very time- and resource-expensive, and while System Era did outsource some testing to a small company, it was never going to be enough for such an ambitious project. By releasing the game in Early Access, the studio, in their own words, benefited from the community in that they could 'basically have every single CPU, GPU on the market testing the game . . . and solving those issues' (System Era 2017a: n.p.). In addition, Steam Early Access enabled the studio to build a strong, direct relationship with their audiences. As Artist Adam Bromell said:

It's really liberating to work on a thing where you kinda don't care about the problems, cause it' just so fucking fun. It's just this thing like, people will get it. If we talk about it honestly, they'll understand what we're doing. We'll tell you not to buy it if you don't want to buy a broken thing. We'll be as honest about this thing as we can.

(Noclip 2019: n.p.)

The studio's founding ethos was thus centred around the notion of independence, and agency—for themselves, as well as for their audiences. But what is the kind of game they wanted to develop, the one they felt like they did not have the space to pitch in a AAA environment?

Games That Inspired

'[T]he four of us started the company [and] we just sort of had a desire to play a game like this' said Adam Bromell in a Twitch live development stream (System Era 2016a: n.p.). What overall aesthetics were they going for, and more specifically, what mechanics did they say they felt were missing from games they worked on before, like the photorealistic sci-fi shooter *Halo* or historical action-adventure *Assassin's Creed*? 'This game wasn't made in a vacuum' disclaimed Adam Bromell (System Era 2017a: n.p.). Indeed, survival-themed fiction is not new—think *Robinson Crusoe* (Defoe 1994 [1971]), *Lord of the Flies* (Golding 2009 [1954]), or *The Road*

(McCarthy 2006) in literature. Popular culture is also increasingly saturated with survival-themed content, such as TV shows like Channel 4's *Man vs Wild* (2006–2011), or ITV's *I'm a Celebrity, Get Me Out of Here* (2002—), and better not get started on zombies. The popularity of survival games also exploded recently, and *Astroneer*'s developers name-check numerous influential survival-crafting titles across the paratextual surrounds. *Factorio* (Wube Software Ltd 2012) is cited for its ingenious approach to automatization (System Era 2016a, 2017a), the chaotic, goal-less freeplay in the early months of *DayZ* (Bohemia Interactive 2018) is thought of fondly (System Era 2016a), but it is three games— *Minecraft* (Mojang Studios 2009), *Space Engineers* (Keen Software House 2013), and *Subnautica* (Unknown Worlds Entertainment 2017)—that are repeatedly mentioned during the first few years of development as sources of inspiration for the broader strokes of the game in the making (System Era 2016a, 2016b, 2017a). As such, interrogating how they afford and constrain avatar action reveals general directions regarding how System Era's developers thought about designing agency in *Astroneer*. Arguably, this is a slightly less direct way of distilling design intention from promotional paratext than done in the previous two chapters, but since System Era is a studio with effectively no credibility they could use as promotional advantage, it makes sense for them to cite popular games they are inspired by as a means of appealing to audiences, as opposed to promoting the game with grandiose statements about authorial intention, at least pre-Early Access.[14] Looking at how the sandbox worlds of these games were designed with the help of procedural generation can shed light on what implications such design has for how agency would be afforded in *Astroneer*.

All three games mentioned above are voxel-based[15] survival-crafting games featuring an avatar, and are built on similar foundations. They are all sandbox games (or at least offer a sandbox mode); and they all contain some degree of procedural content generation. *Astroneer*'s developers consistently described the game as sandbox[16]; and, at least in the first two years of development before the launch of *No Man's Sky*, also highlighted procedurally generated worlds as a key feature while promoting the game (DevGAMM 2017). As stated earlier, *Minecraft* was a game-changer in many ways. Not only were the original founders of System Era 'huge fan[s]' of the game (System Era 2016e: n.p.), they also sketched *Astroneer* as a 'very *Minecraft*-like' game (System Era 2016c: n.p.) in terms of open-world design and lack of linear narrative content. They also hired Spencer Kern, former Lead Artist on *Minecraft* (post-Microsoft acquisition), as the new Art Director on *Astroneer*.[17] Space exploration-themed *Space Engineers* offered NASA-like space exploration fantasies System Era also wanted to tap into (System Era 2016a), while they saw *Subnautica* as one of those 'cool game[s]' that 'shipped very non-assuming releases, and then been out for some time and they just keep making the thing better' (System Era 2016b: n.p.), which made it 'massively inspirational' (System Era 2017a:

n.p.). As far as their setting were concerned, they all were space-themed games less in the vein of alien shooting or intergalactic politics defining the sci-fi genre in videogames, and more emphasising the joy of exploring and leaving a mark on the world discovered. They were also regularly mentioned together, with *Minecraft*, in gaming-related discourses (see, e.g., Birnbaum 2015; Hayward 2014). In true crafting-survival game fashion, the avatar typically started from scratch with a rudimentary toolkit, only to slowly work their way towards crafting more and more complex gear that help their avatar stay alive and thrive in the world they found themselves in.

As previously discussed, the open world label has implications for level design, while sandbox foreshadows more about the game goals. We can think of distinguishing sandbox games from open world games historically, i.e., in the post-*Minecraft* era, sandbox games acquired a very specific meaning. Both *Space Engineers* and *Subnautica* followed in the same vein of sandbox design as understood post-*Minecraft*. This understanding of sandbox connotes a preoccupation with game goals, and with implications to level design, but is increasingly geared towards a specific model of gameplay determined by the actions of crafting and building, with the aim to survive and reach whatever goal, if any, provided by the game.

The design of these two games was primarily geared towards affording avatar action in the spatial-explorative and configurative-constructive dimension, as to thrive, the player had to constantly explore new territories for valuable resources, and work towards establishing and expanding a secure base. In *Space Engineers*, this was done on the variety of customisable maps the player can set up for themselves using 'World Settings' and selecting 'Scenarios', which then in turn determine sometimes hard, sometimes soft goals for players within the sandbox itself. *Subnautica* also has various modes, such as 'Survival' or 'Creativity', which affect variables like hunger or thirst, as well as optional permadeath.

The keyword is optionality: both these games offered the player choice over how difficult they wanted to make their experience by allowing them to set challenge levels. In neither case was there a breakdown of predetermined checkpoints in progression that all have to happen in a certain sequence, at certain times. *Astroneer* developers being inspired by these games foreshadows intention behind theme, things to do, and general world design of the game.

Another thing *Minecraft*, *Space Engineers*, and *Subnautica* had in common was how the sandboxes were brought to life: they made use of a method called procedural content generation either to generate terrain, resources, or both.[18] 'Procedurality' is an important quality of the digital to Janet Murray (1997: 71), who defines it as a device's 'defining ability to execute a series of rules'. In Ian Bogost's words: '[t]o write procedurally, one authors code that enforces rules to generate [some kind of representation, rather than authoring the representation itself (Bogost 2007: 4). Such design is interesting with regard to designing agency, because it is a different way of exerting authorial control over the game's affordances to what was discussed in the previous two case studies. Procedural content generation in the context of videogames means that, as opposed to hand-crafting every single detail, the system (semi-)randomly arranges things like level layout, or location of resources, according to rules predetermined by the designer.

While Bogost is concerned with the rhetoric of representation, computer science provides more practical definitions of procedural content generation which are more relevant for an investigation concerned with how player action is afforded by a game's design, it not being concerned with the intricate processes of meaning-making. In the context of computer science, procedural content generation is generally understood to mean 'the algorithmic creation of game content with limited or indirect user input' (Togelius et al. 2016: 1), where content is understood as everything contained in a game, bar non-player character behaviour, and the engine itself: 'levels, maps, game rules, textures, stories, items, quests, music, weapons, vehicles, characters, etc.' (ibid.).[19] System Era's developers decided early on to pursue a mixed approach regarding how much content would be pre-designed and how much would be generated on the go. This intention was further signposted by the studio switching engines. They started prototyping using Unity, an engine favoured by independents for its accessible user interface and its versatility regarding implementation of other software (Nicoll and Keogh 2019), but upon the release of the Unreal Engine 4 in 2014, System Era quickly changed tools. They relayed several reasons for this in vlogs and interviews, the most prominent of which was that having come from AAA, they all had more experience working with this engine, and it was also the 'definition of out of the box' with plenty tools already implemented (System Era 2016d: n.p.). Besides the software being more familiar than Unity, and Unreal 4's then-newly introduced 'Blueprint' feature, which visualises code in a way that allows non-programming developers to work on the logic of the game, it was really in the procedural content generation that this change in technology helped.

While the below excerpt is from Unreal's own website and therefore a promotional motivation is undeniably present, Jacob Liecthy's list of reasons for using Unreal is noteworthy nonetheless:

> With procedural generation, you really have to make sure that the 'randomization knobs' have the right range. If you give up too many parameters to the generator, you're going to get a lot of noise that isn't fun or interesting to the player. We've solved this issue by introducing artist-designed biomes.[20] These biomes are picked semi-randomly and distributed on our planets, and the placements of all the plants, minerals, and features are fully random. But, at the end of the day, each environment is one that we know is going to be fun and play well each time we hit the 'generate' button. . . . We've ended up coupling many of Unreal

Engine's features deeply into the terrain engine, especially from Unreal's Actor system. Each biome is an Actor, which lets us easily create variations that share certain parameters without having to create them from scratch. We can also add Components to decorators that can be read by the generation algorithm to customize their placement criteria. By fully embracing the modular nature of the engine, we've been able to spend a lot more development time designing our biomes instead of writing the code to generate them.

(qtd. in Rowe 2016: n.p.)

Specifically, it was *Minecraft* developer Markus 'Notch' Persson who based terrain generation on what is known amongst 3D animators and programmers as Perlin noise (Notch 2011). Noise-based generation is a technique often used in this approach to terrain creation in videogames. It was created as a solution for 'develop[ing] naturalistic looking textures' (Perlin 1985: 287) in computer-generated imagery for Disney, and today has many variants. In general, it is most useful 'whenever small variations need to be added to a surface (or something that can be seen as a surface)' (Shaker et al. 2016: 58). System Era artist Adam Bromell explained noise-based generation in *Astroneer* as:

> the simplest way to think about it is random frequency that we represent by waves, and those waves you can think of as mountain peaks and valleys, and we manipulate them to make terrain.
>
> (System Era 2018a: n.p.)

This manipulation is typically done by setting variables such as 'amplitude' determining maximum value output, or 'persistence' that refers to the time amplitudes are applied (Libnoise). Bromell further explained what this looked like in practice, and what it meant for design authority over the game:

> So it is literally different every time we do it, within a set of rules that we apply. As an example, the exotic moon is made up of three different biomes . . . so we can do things like flat terrain . . . versus the dips down into the crater system, and then out into a mountain. . . . It's not just terrain that we get the benefit from, it's the control over the assets.
>
> (System Era 2018a: n.p.)

In *Astroneer*, developers worked towards combining procedural content generation with hand-crafted assets, as a means to achieve balance between overly resource-expensive detail and procedurally generated chaos. Engineer Zabir Hoque said

> The goal with procedural content is to provide novelty, but we want some level of familiarity, so the player isn't just experiencing chaos. . . . From a technical side I think the most important thing to consider when

building procedural systems is how to allow for artistic control at various authoring levels. You want to allow for authoring a rule set for general use cases, and then provide enough vectors of configuration so users can exercise artistic control when needed. . . . With our terrain system, we could just use Perlin noise everywhere in the terrain with random values and say 'Look! It's different every time!' but this is what leads to the feeling of bland repetition. Instead, we try to think of how the player will play the game and when they'll seek out novelty, and that is where we try to introduce variation.

(qtd. in Bradley 2018: n.p.)

The kind of gameplay afforded by a game design so devoid of designer control is one that gives more freedom to the player to exercise their creativity. Deciding on making a sandbox game with procedural content generation, where the levels and goals are not as defined as they tend to be in games such as the two discussed in previous case studies here, signals that design intention is less to restrict avatar action and therefore agency across dimensions, and more to enable exploration, experimentation, and a broad possibility space for avatar action in general.

From early 2017, the studio's means of engaging with their audiences changed markedly. This was due to numerous reasons: the explosive success of the game's launching into Early Access in December 2016, in contrast to thought-to-be competitor *No Man's Sky*'s fall from grace earlier that year; Lead Designer Jacob Liecthy leaving the studio; and most importantly, and indeed, most tragically, the passing away of Lead Artist Paul Pepera (Noclip 2019). Following a few silent months in early 2017, while the remaining developers began their journey towards recovery from this loss, the studio's promotional methods as well as the game's branding changed. Procedurally generated worlds were no longer at the heart of their marketing efforts and were replaced by something new. The next section will examine what newly hired designers said about how they think about game mechanics. Diegetic user interface and modularity were introduced as the pillars of design, which I will argue allow for more direct interaction with the gameworld and more freedom to act. These characteristics will be framed according to paidic play, and the notion of playfulness.

Designing Playfulness

In early 2017, soon after entering Early Access on Steam and Game Preview on Xbox, *Astroneer* developers were astonished by the explosive success of the game. 'Watching dozens of simultaneous gameplay streams at once was a surreal experience that I'll never forget' wrote System Era co-founder Brendan Wilson in a blog post (admin 2017b). Soon after, a lot would change for the studio. In order to tackle increasing demand for updates as well as to stay on top of performance and quality of life issues in the game, System Era made several new hires, which became ever so important as game designer Jacob

Liechty left the company, and artist Paul Pepera passed away. These events led to a few months of radio silence as the studio scrambled to meet game patch demands. In time, however, and with the help of new members of staff, development got back on track. In particular, the hiring of community manager[21] Joe Tirado streamlined studio communication to the player base, and two game designers, Aaron Biddlecom and Samantha Kalman had very specific ideas for how they imagined the future for *Astoneer*'s gameplay and were quite vocal about it too. Biddlecom outlined the design objective as follows:

> One of our primary goals with *Astroneer* is to provide an open-ended gameplay experience that incentivises creative problem solving.
> (admin 2017a: n.p.)

This design intention can be qualified with the help of the distinction between two types of play proposed by anthropologist Roger Caillois in the 1960s. He posited that on one end of the spectrum there is rule-regulated play, which he called 'ludus', while on the other is free, unconstrained, creative play, which he referred to as 'paidia'. Paidia is an 'an almost indivisible principle, common to diversion, turbulence, free improvisation, and carefree gaiety', an 'uncontrolled fantasy'; a 'frolicsome and impulsive exuberance' (Caillois 1961: 13). Ludus, the other end of the spectrum, restricts paidia by 'arbitrary, imperative, and purposely tedious conventions' (Caillois 1961: 13). Now, it is important to keep in mind that while paidic play is free play, it is still constrained by rules, as all play is 'free movement within a more rigid structure' (Salen and Zimmerman 2004: 304). As Frasca (2003: 230) points out, 'a child who pretends to be a soldier is following the rule of behaving like a soldier and not as a doctor'. Frasca calls such rules in videogames, for example those governing the behaviour of in-game objects, 'paidia rules' (2007: 116). Keeping this caveat of sorts in mind, Biddlecom's 'open ended gameplay' incentivising 'creative problem solving' would then fall into paidic territory, whereby there are ample possibilities for player agency to be realised via avatar action.

When reviewing Caillois' discussions of ludus and paidia, Frasca argues that paidia is typically the form of play children enjoy, using 'construction kits, games of make-believe, kinetic play)' (Frasca 2003: 229). Interestingly, *Astroneer*'s elevator pitch[22] was that '*Astroneer* to Play-Doh is what *Minecraft* is to LEGO' (DevGAMM 2017; Microsoft Developer 2018), and both Play-Doh and LEGO can be described according to Frasca's examples. While some argue that LEGO's potential supersedes that of modelling clay whereby it 'empower[s] people to build' (Gauntlett 2014: 191), the LEGO ethos of Systematic Creativity, which 'is about using logic and reasoning along with playfulness and imagination, to generate ideas or artifacts that are new, surprising and valuable' (Ackermann et al. 2009: 4) rings true for Play-Doh. As anyone who has ever touched a LEGO brick of a blob of

Play-Doh can attest, such activities do not have a winner or a loser in the strict sense, no game goals to speak of, as opposed to ludus, which inevitably results in a win or lose state. As System Era Game Designer Aaron Biddlecom puts it elsewhere, the main design decisions align with a logic of paidia in that the aim is less to create a winning situation, more to facilitate creative problem-solving:

> We see ourselves as a puzzle-based survival game in the sense of, you're this stranded engineer kinda McGuiver-ing your way to success. The obstacles that we wanna introduce are obstacles that you can solve, rather than defeat.
>
> (System Era 2017d: n.p.)

This attitude is echoed by fellow game designer Samantha Kalman, who described the design process as following a template commonly found in the 'open world survival crafting' genre:

> It's a script that has emerged with sort of more open world survival crafting games, which *Astroneer* is that. There's a lot of like, open ended gameplay, and you can make up your own goals, and so like we're trying to more, like give you toys to play with. Do you wanna play with this? No? Okay there's like 30 other things over here, maybe you like one of those.
>
> (Giant Bomb 2018: n.p.)

Kalman's words reinforce the idea that the studio's design intention was less to create a game where the player's path is guided, more to provide tools for the player to do as they please. As such, the intention seemed more to be about creating a game still constrained by rules (primarily in a way all games are by definition), but were also increasingly about incentivising experimentation and tailoring the play experience to player preference. Generally speaking, this would mean that the player has a large degree of agency across all dimensions. This incentive aligns with the general principle of designing paidic games, according to game developer and theorist Chris Bateman: 'to support paidia we need to encourage and allow for the player's capacity to experiment freely, and assist the player to express the most obvious implied actions for each game element' (Bateman 2005: np). There were two topics recurrent in the paratextual surrounds of *Astroneer*'s development that relayed how designers thought about enabling creative experimentation and playfulness. One is the notion of 'diegetic interface', and the other is 'player archetypes'.

Although it could be argued that distinguishing between diegetic v. non-diegetic elements of game design presupposes the presence of fictionality (see, e.g., Jørgensen 2013: 66), System Era developers find it a productive term to describe their approach to interface design nonetheless. 'Diegetic'-ness appears repeatedly throughout the corpus of paratexts surveyed (System Era 2016a; DevGAMM 2017). What this term, borrowed from Aristotelian scholarship popularised in literary studies by Genette (1983), means to *Astroneer*'s developers was most neatly summarised by Brendan Wilson at a GDC talk:

> The biggest standout feature in *Astroneer* is diegetic interaction. 'Diegetic' refers to elements that are rendered in the world in a way that the characters would be able to see and interact with them. A HUD overlay with a health metre is non-diegetic, but, like, a readout on an oxygen tank rendered in the world, that would be diegetic [pause for video demonstration]. This direction emerged from the desire of clever improvisation to be part of the gameplay, we wanted *Apollo 13*, we wanted Mark Watney,[23] tinkering and jury rigging, we wanted that process to feel alive and deeply interactive. . . . it brings out that sort of tactile joy that you get from physical toys.
> (Microsoft Developer 2018: n.p.)

Minimising the overcast user interfaces on *Astroneer*'s gameworld was thus a step towards wanting to facilitate playful, experimentational interaction in the game by removing obstacles which phase said interaction with said gameworld. Wilson furthermore adds the notion of 'tactile joy' as a desired impact, the like of which is elicited by playing with physical toys. This aspiration is also mentioned elsewhere by game designer Samantha Kalman:

> [T]he other designer Aaron and I did this analysis of what are all the sort of emotional aesthetics of the game. And we found that tactility is one of our key aesthetics. When I played the game with controller, the sort of [brief pause] metaphor that arrived in my mind was that, like, I used to play with action figures, where you like squeeze the legs and you punch or something like that, so to me it was like, the controller becomes some sort of action figure. I feel like when I'm playing *Astroneer*, I'm playing with action figures.
> (System Era 2017e: n.p.)

It is this almost visceral feeling of playing with actual toys that the diegetic implementation of research logs, craft menus, backpack management, and other features normally relayed by superimposition, was working towards.

System Era developers conceptualised this free experimentation along two strands of player archetypes, which then informed the design decisions made. The studio internally referred to these as the 'pioneer' and the 'engineer' player, as game designer Samantha Kalman recalled in a documentary:

> We identified pretty early on that there are a couple of different archetypes for players. We talked a lot internally about the pioneer who

wants to focus on exploring, and the engineer player that wants to focus on building. Because the game requires both exploring and building, that sort of evolved into 'well, the pioneer must do a little engineering to be able to explore and vice versa" . . . We spent some time trying to design two different games, like, 'let's have *Astroneer*: the pioneer game and *Astroneer*: the engineer game' and then sort of, after some time and encountering difficulties with that approach, we did come to the conclusion that the real *Astroneer* experience is sort of wavering back and forth.

(Noclip 2019: n.p.)

On the one hand, '*Astroneer:* the pioneer game' forecast a theme of exploration, which would potentially translate into spatial-explorative agency affordances. On the other hand, designing '*Astroneer:* the engineer game', as per Kalman's words, would concentrate on affording agency in the configurative-constructive dimension, by means of research and base building.[24] However, Kalman also acknowledged that there would be a flux in between the two, and certain goals players would set for themselves require alternating between these two archetypical modes of playing the game. Fellow game designer Aaron Biddlecom's words suggest this was because they wanted to give as much agency to the player as possible:

We think the game is most interesting when the player has as much agency as possible over how they tackle a given challenge. And so as much as possible we don't wanna give you pre-baked solutions to things. We wanna give you the pieces and the tools so that you can build up your toolbox and use those tools dynamically as you encounter a problem, in a different way each time.

(System Era 2017d: n.p.)

Wanting to design a game where the player can set their own goals would contribute to a fluidity in difficulty levels, which would then alleviate constraint on avatar action in the temporal-ergodic dimension by giving the player/avatar the power to tweak how long they take to perform certain tasks, and also selectively choose which challenges they want to engage with. Although it is not discussed in terms of this terminology specifically, with such freedom, the possibility space for dramatic agency to be realised could also be significant: by creating such a ludic environment, there would be plenty of opportunity for player stories to be realised that are highly unique to the individual gameplay session. In summary, we can say that System Era's developers seemed to have conceptualised agency as a synonym for creative freedom, playful experimentation reminiscent of child's play and physical toys, and the power to tailor the level of challenge to their preference. Such design intention revolving around the notion of playfulness

'The World Is Your Play-Doh' 181

therefore implies that player agency would be afforded to a high degree across all dimensions.

These themes in design priorities were also interlaced in the way the studio promoted the game. System Era developers attended numerous expos and conventions where they made playable demo version available to anyone who walked by, which generated hype for the experience of playing the game. They also used trailers, many of which turned out to be award-winning. Typically, as we have also seen in the previous two case study chapters, videogames, especially AAA ones, have cinematic trailers edited and presented in a way similar to those of the film trailers. They tend to include storylines and spoken dialogue, possibly using footage captured in-engine, but not quite showing what the actual gameplay would look like (Cassidy 2011: 298). *Astroneer* trailers are a different story. They feature gameplay footage captured by developers, and in some instances, by players themselves who sent in footage they had recorded during the lengthy Early Access period of the game. The resultant trailers all had a humorous, self-referential, and often self-deprecating tone; were accompanied by endearing, cartoon-like sound design and soundtracks bringing space fantasy nostalgia to mind; and featured tiny astroneers gleefully running around exploring, slotting together base-building units, and reacting to all sorts of situations via emotes often based on internet memes and pop culture references. The 'Basebuilding Update Trailer' (System Era 2018b) for example introduced the new modular base building mechanics and a new UI for the research catalogue in the form of a supercut of gameplay footage. The trailer features a song-like rhythm and melody created from the in-game sound effects of clicking, snapping, and plonking, as several astroneers assembled various platforms and modules, and browsed the research database. This made the whole process of unpacking and assembling units seem like a musical performance and dance of some sort.

Vollans, drawing on Hesford (2013), argues that videogame trailers 'perform the experience of their products rather than presenting that experience' (Vollans 2017: 124). In this vein, *Astroneer*'s trailers perform the experience of playfulness afforded by the game's design. They still contain narratives—such as an astroneer reminiscing about all the ways the rover used to be buggy before sitting in the new rover for the first time in the rover update trailer, or the astroneers controlling each other through a mock screen with a controller in the PlayStation 4 announcement trailer (System Era 2019). The trailers placed less emphasis on a compelling designer story or photorealistic visuals often presented by AAA counterparts, and more on the myriad ways in which the design affordances of each update package further facilitate playfulness.

So far, this chapter has looked at what independence could mean in the context of videogames and outlined the main characteristics of independent design by focusing on recurrent trends since the mid-2000s, when the label re-emerged. It then discussed how System Era positioned themselves against the background and history of independent games. By looking at three games System Era developers named as inspiration, I showed that part of design intention was to design a procedurally generated sandbox game, which has implications for how player action would be afforded in the spatial-explorative and configurative-constructive dimension. As development progressed and the game launched in Early Access, with monthly updates being published for nearly two years, the theme of playfulness emerged as a dominant direction in design intention. Developers aimed to facilitate this by the introduction of features such as LEGO-like modularity and a diegetic interface. The game was designed with two player archetypes in mind: the game for pioneer players would emphasise and incentivise exploration thereby enabling spatial-explorative agency to manifest, while the game for engineer players would afford player action in terms of crafting and building, opening up the possibility space for configurative-constructive agency. Following System Era developers' discussions of their work, it was argued that such conceptualisation would not hold up in practice, only if they also allowed for the two ways of playing the game to be intertwined, thereby enabling the realisation of dramatic agency. Developers saw this as enabling the player to tailor challenge levels to their preference, thus creating a different experience of agency afforded by temporal-ergodic agency mechanics. Textual analysis below will interrogate *Astroneer*'s game text to explore how playful design was achieved, and what that meant for player agency as afforded by the game's design.

Agency and Playfulness

Before we get started it needs acknowledging that the following analysis focuses on the launch version of the game, released January 2019, titled *Astroneer 1.0*. Since then, several content updates and patches have been released, and are planned to be released in the future. Some of these introduce new objects, like storage units or lights in the 'Summer Update'; time-sensitive events, such as a temporarily discoverable model of the Eagle on in-game moons in celebration of the Apollo anniversary; or new game mechanics, such as flying with jetpacks, or the ability to capture in-game photos in the 'Exploration Update' (see SES_dev 2019). Making critical observations about a subject in such flux raises the challenge of what Elizabeth Evans calls 'instant history', or 'the value of charting a moment within a period of change' (Evans 2011: 79). While these updates add a great deal to the playing experience, they do not fundamentally change the game's core gameplay, which is why the analysis below focuses on the *Astroneer 1.0* release alone.

The textual analysis is split into three sections according to how developers conceptualised the types of engagement preferred by player archetypes, as conceptualised by System Era's designers. As previously stated, dimensions of agency can hardly be identified in complete isolation. In practice, there is always some degree of interrelation between mechanics. For example, in *Astroneer*, the various suits available to dress the avatar in enable agency both in the spatial-explorative and configurative-constructive dimension, due to the fact that their availability depends on how much of planets' surfaces have been explored, and what achievements have been unlocked. Similarly, on the avatar, there are two tools that enable agency to manifest in both the spatial-explorative and configurative-constructive dimension. These are the multifunctional terraforming tool called 'Terrain Tool', and the avatar's inventory in the 'Backpack'. The 'Terrain Tool' is based on a simple idea: it can hoover up or flatten terrain, and provided the avatar has a canister, it can spew out the soil thus collected. It can then further be configured with the addition of modifications, or 'Mods' for short (which is a game mechanic intrinsic to the game, not a player-added modification), which either improve its hoovering function, or introduce further functions. Some Mods impact the scope of terraforming ('Narrow' and 'Wide Mods'), others improve speed and efficiency ('Boost Mod'), and there are also drills of different strength that enable the avatar to dig through harder terrain ('Drill Mods 1, 2, and 3'). On the one hand, the 'Terrain Tool' affords spatial-explorative agency: once equipped with a 'Canister', it allows the player to hoover up terrain which it can then spew back out, thus allowing the player to alter the level layout. From makeshift paths and bridges over ravines to laboriously perfected underground ramp systems, it puts up no boundaries to the player's desire to mould their terrain, much like Play-Doh. On the other hand, the 'Terrain Tool' is the key to unlocking the possibility space to crafting and base building, thereby supporting agency in the configurative-constructive dimension. It is with the 'Terrain Tool' that the player can mine resources, which is the first step towards progress.

While the examples above clearly demonstrate a cooperation between agency dimensions, it is nonetheless productive to sift the game's design features and mechanics through the sieve of the heuristic framework, as by doing so we can get closer to understanding how free, creative play can be facilitated by a game's design.

Spatial-Explorative Agency in Astroneer

As discussed earlier, System Era's designers approached their task by theorising different player types to enjoy different gameplay experiences. The first one they called the 'pioneer', whose primary activities would be connected to exploration. Filtering game mechanics according to this player archetype we can look at how avatar action is afforded in the game in the spatial-explorative dimension. Compared to *Uncharted 4*'s Nathan Drake and *Andromeda*'s Ryder, the movement affordances of *Astroneer*'s avatars are comparatively limited. First off, all avatar movement depends upon a steady access to 'Oxygen'. *Astroneer*'s planets are all hostile, meaning the avatar must always be connected to an oxygen generator, or 'Oxygenator', for short. Tethers help build networks with oxygen access, while 'Oxygen Tanks' on the avatar supply a limited amount of oxygen, thus allowing some brief excursions into areas with no tethers. There is no crouching, climbing ledges, dodging bullets, or stealth. The avatar can move forwards, backwards, left, and right in the 3D space, as well as walk, sprint, jump, slide down slopes, and eventually, drive vehicles.

Exploration was one of the main features the developers focused on, and indeed, there are many ways in which the game's design not only enables, but incentivises this activity. There are altogether seven planet types created by System Era: 'Terran', 'Terran Moon', 'Arid', 'Exotic', 'Exotic Moon', 'Tundra', and 'Radiated'. In *Astroneer*, each planet type generates one particular planet at the beginning of a new game: 'Sylva', 'Desolo', 'Calidor', 'Vesania', 'Novus', 'Glacio', and 'Atrox', respectively. Besides differing widely in visual terms, with surface and underground colour palettes ranging from serene pastels to popping primaries, certain other properties of each planet type are also determined by designers prior to procedural generation. For example, on medium difficulty planet 'Vesania', the availability of resources, general features like atmosphere or terrain, and options for harvesting power are locked in in every round of generation. These variables allow the player/avatar to tailor their exploration efforts to their preference, balancing the need for a certain resource, the likelihood of finding that resource, and the difficulty of terrain. It is perfectly feasible to stay on one planet for quite a long time. Interplanetary travel becomes necessary only when certain planet-specific resources need to be acquired, such as 'Helium' from the very hard planet 'Atrox', which is needed to craft a late game energy generator device called 'Radioisotope Thermoelectric Generator'.

Astroneer's planets are in part procedurally generated, which means that they will always be built from scratch at the launch of a new game, with the abovementioned initial properties definitely making an appearance on each generation. While there is a strong procedural element to level design, planet generation is also predetermined insofar as the planet-specific details are concerned. As Engineer Zafir Hoque explained:

> On the technical side we take two general rules of Perlin & Billow noise and blend them using artistic discretion based on play-tests. When the player has explored for a bit and has enough experience to leave the home planet, other planets then use these noise functions in different ways to create more difficult and varied terrain. In this way, we are combining simpler general rules to provide a more tuned experience.
>
> (qtd. in Bradley 2018: n.p.)

For instance, on the starting planet 'Sylva', surface biomes include purple forests, mountains, ravines and green plains, while underground there are rock formations, different looking flora and giant mushroom forests.

Not only are planet surfaces generated procedurally, but the underground layers as well. All planets and moons have similarly structured terrain in that they are divided into drillable layers from mantle to core, and each have different values for, amongst others, colour, thickness, scarcity of resources (to be discussed in the next sub-section), biomes, hazards, and gravitational force. These values have various degrees of influence on how player agency as expressed via avatar action is afforded or limited in the spatial-explorative dimension (System Era 2018a). It is easier to dig terrain closer to the surface, but the resources are more valuable the deeper astroneers venture. The deeper the astroneer digs into a planet's core, the lower gravitational force is, meaning that what were simple hops on a planet's surface turn into extended periods of floating mid-air near-uncontrollably. Biomes and hazards are either targets, thus enabling, or obstacles, thus constraining, avatar action. Such diverse level design incentivises the player to move further out from a given planet's starting base, as well as to dig deep in the ground, to seek out new areas with discoverable items and resources, thereby providing a broad possibility space for spatial-explorative agency to emerge. Planets being procedurally generated in this manner increases the game's replayability, as besides presence and likelihood of appearance, the exact location of resources, hazards, landing zones, and other such things are not designed to be present at the same location, in the same size, or in the same quantity for each generated planet. There is always going to be forests on 'Sylva', forests will always have purple and blue terrain, and there will always be a possibility for 'Ammonium' to be found in those forests, but the exact nature of where and how to find 'Ammonium' changes with each planet generation.

There is more than harvestable resources and interesting flora that can be found in the game spaces. While there is no fauna to speak of, no aliens to shoot, there are hostile plants who attack in defence if the avatar is within a set proximity. All bearing quirky names like 'Spinelilies', 'Bouncevines', or 'Thistlewhips', they will snap, spew poison fluid, or emit toxic clouds in the avatar's general direction, should they venture too close. These attacks can be tackled less in the vein of the sci-fi shooter tradition of laser guns, more driven by the pacifist attitude of scientists: by digging them out, and then replanting the seeds for decoration purposes, or researching them. Should the avatar find themselves too close to such flora, they could get hurt in the shockwave triggered by the plants defence mechanism. The element of randomisation in the location of these environmental hazards has a twofold impact on the player's explorative agency: they may incentivise it (for example, if the goal is to harvest seeds and plant a garden nearer to base), or they may hamstring the desire to wander off (for example, they may be present in such high concentration around a singular path across a ravine that they cannot be dug up one at a time, therefore presenting a genuine risk to the avatar's health).

There are also collectibles and other discoveries that provide ample reason to explore *Astroneer*'s planets. For example, research items can be found both above and underground, either lying around as carriable rock-like or organic formations, or locked in triangular pods called 'EXO Dynamics Research Aid', which require the player to insert a specific resource into it before they can open. Furthermore, there are small salvageable objects like a solar array, damaged base building items like platforms, broken down rovers, or as large as a crashed satellite. These can be transported back to the base to be turned into 'Scrap'. They also tend to contain consumable resources like 'Oxygen Filters' or 'Power Cells'. There are also a few extra rare items hidden on planets, which players can only find out from forums and hype that the developers themselves lean into. One such item is the mythical 'Zebra Ball', a geometrically perfect globe that does not have much function besides emitting a faint glow.[25] Much like the various types of terrains, biomes, and hazards, these discoverables are also procedurally generated, and as such, they each serve to incentivise exploration of game spaces both above and below the planets' surfaces.

In terms of navigating the game's spaces, the primary affordance at the player/avatar's disposal is the network of 'Tether' lines that can be crafted and laid down to provide steady access to oxygen wherever the astroneer wanders. These serve like trails of crumbs scattered in a labyrinth, eventually leading back to the starting base or oxygen source placed on the planet by the player, thereby supporting free-roaming within the game spaces. Besides this tool, while there is no map or HUD overlay to speak of, there are other, more traditional means of navigational functions offered by the game's design. Looking up from every planet's surface, all other celestial bodies are visible in the sky, quite like they would be looking up at the night sky on Earth. If the mouse hovers over the avatar, a compass reticle pops up, further assisting with navigation. The player/avatar can also collect soil and erect artificial towers as pointers, or research the 'Beacon' to use as means of navigation. These all facilitate a submersion in the joy of exploration in beautifully designed landscapes, but the main reason for exploring *Astroneer*'s vast lands is to find resources.

Configurative-Constructive Agency in Astroneer

Besides exploration, the other game model System Era developers kept in mind was base building and crafting, which was theorised with the 'engineer' player archetype. As mentioned earlier, the main function of the 'Terrain Tool' is to terraform, which is a means of exercising agency in the spatial-explorative dimension, but it also is a means to gather raw, unrefined resources. When supplied with a 'Canister', the 'Terrain Tool' stores hoovered up soil, which then can be put through the 'Soil Centrifuge' as a means of refining for finer resources available on the planet. There are raw minerals that can be mined freely above or over ground, some of which can be further refined by smelting. There are naturally occurring gases that can be harvested from the atmosphere, and last but not least these raw and refined resources can be combined with gases to make even more refined materials. Besides the 'Terrain Tool', resources can be mined with the 'Rover' and its attachable 'Drills', as well as the 'Crane'. Some resources collected thus are useful in and of themselves, such as 'Compound' or 'Resin' to make basic items like 'Oxygen Filters' or 'Canister', while others can be refined by the Smelter, the 'Atmospheric Condenser' and the 'Chemistry Lab'.

Altogether there are 42 resources that can be gathered, refined, and combined in *Astroneer*. Of these, the ones that can be mined on every planet type are, in no particular order: 'Compound', 'Resin', 'Organic', 'Ammonium', 'Quartz', 'Graphite', 'Clay', 'Laterite', and 'Astronium'. Using these, most items required to set up a base as well as venture out to look for further resources can be crafted from the 'Backpack', as well as the two things required to take off from any planet: a 'Small Shuttle', and a disposable 'Solid-Fuel Thruster'. Once the avatar leaves the starting planet to explore other ones, rarer resources are made available, which enable more complex recipes to be created. Each planet type has further resources which are either specific to them, or occur on multiple planets. For instance, 'Tungsten', a smelted refinement of 'Wolframite' found on 'Desolo' and 'Calidor', is necessary for the printing of the 'Chemistry Lab' and the 'Medium Solar' panel, which are mid-game items, whereas 'Hematite' from 'Novus' and 'Glacio' yields 'Iron' after smelting, which is the basic component, amongst many other things, of the 'Atmospheric Condenser', which is a top tier object capable of harvesting gases from a planet's atmosphere. As a last resort of resource accumulation, for it is rather energy expensive, discoverables can be dragged back to the base to be put through 'Scrappers', which break them down into 'Scrap', to be traded at the 'Trade Station' for a resource of choice.

While such listing of most (not even all) things consumable may offer a dry reading, it is nonetheless essential to give a glimpse into the detail-richness and complexity of *Astroneer*'s resource bank. Resource management is one of the core mechanics of *Astroneer*, one which affords agency in the configurative-constructive dimension by incentivising the player to transform the game's terrain not only for traversal reasons, but also to mine resources. In the process of mining, the avatar deforms terrain, thereby effectively changing the very matter of the game spaces. There being so many resources and so many mechanics for combining them further expands the possibility space for agency to manifest in this dimension. While in survival games, the mere repetition of tasks such as chopping wood contributes to a mesmerising game-feel facilitated by rhythmic interactions (Costello 2018), and even though *Astroneer*'s sound design does reward such actions with a satisfying beep-boop, the mere gathering of resources would not make for particularly engaging gameplay, unless the player in question has a fascination with accumulating things. Indeed, in *Astroneer*, resources serve a variety of purposes that in general, and rather simple terms, could be described as building things: small, portable objects, means of transport, platforms, machinery, all of which ultimately make up bases. The construction of all these happens not via manual labour, but by using 3D printers, thereby affording constructive agency.

One of *Astroneer*'s key features relevant to agency in the configurative-constructive dimension is modularity: platforms, devices, and other machinery can be assembled, disassembled, stacked, and dragged in any shape the player desires it to be done, such as a circular layout of platforms and devices, with a power system built on an overhanging cliff. As long as there are cables connected to plugs ensuring a secure flow of power from generator to device, the opportunities are near-endless.

All in-game objects, including printable base-building components, are split into four tiers, depending on how many slots they take up, and whether they can be carried by hand, or require other modes of transport. The four tiers are, rather self-explanatorily, 'Small', 'Medium', 'Large', and 'Extra Large'. Some, like the 'Beacon' mentioned above, are small objects: they require one ingredient to print, take up one slot, and they fit into, and can be printed from, the 'Backpack'. 'Medium' tier objects, such as 'Medium Storage', require two ingredients, can be carried by hand, and can be printed from the 'Small Printer'. 'Large' objects require three ingredients, cannot be carried by hand, and so on. *Astroneer* does not have buildings per se, but instead the avatar can print Platforms of various shapes and sizes, arrange them in whatever formation they desire, and place functional objects like the 'Smelter' or the 'Chemistry Lab' on them.

However, not all such objects are available to print from the start, and they do not work immediately upon having been placed on the platforms. While the game does not pressure players to follow any specific path or pace, there is progression available to those who choose to pursue it, and it hinges on two currencies: 'Bytes' and 'Power'. 'Bytes' are the research currency, which can be accumulated by scanning a variety of different medium-sized objects called 'Research Items' in the 'Research Chamber', yielding varying amounts of 'Bytes' depending on where they were found. Those lying around the surface would have lower 'Byte' counts attached to them, while the deeper underground the avatar goes, the more the 'Byte' count rises. Thus, reward scales with level of challenge. With enough bytes, recipes can be unlocked in the 'Research Catalog' attached to the 'Backpack'. The higher tier the researchable object is, the more 'Byte'-expensive it will be. Thus, resource gathering enables crafting and building, which then in turn adds further layers to how *Astroneer*'s design affords agency in the configurative-constructive dimension.

What 'Oxygen' is to spatial-explorative agency, 'Power' is to configurative-constructive. Besides the 'Backpack' and the 'Shelter' which have their own steady supply of power, everything else in *Astroneer* requires power. Much like 'Oxygen', it cannot be scooped up with the 'Terrain Tool' or dragged back to the base, it has to be generated. There are many ways power can be harnessed and managed: it can be fossil fuel-like (burning 'Organic' on the 'Small Generator', or using 'Carbon' on the 'Medium Generator'), or renewable-like (solar and wind panels and turbines), and eventually, endlessly supplied (from the 'Radioisotope Thermoelectric Generator'). It can also be stored in consumables of various sizes. Base building modules need to be powered to be operational, objects must be placed on 'Platforms' in order to connect to power, and 'Platforms' need to be connected to a power source (generator or storage), in order to power the modules placed on them. Each power generator and storage item have a set amount of 'Power' it can produce, measured in 'Units' and represented by yellow bars, and thus power management becomes the absolute necessary requisite of configurative-constructive agency: without 'Power', there is no mining, no building, and no operating of anything. Further complexity is introduced by the possibility to build power networks, using directional cables, extenders, splitters, and the like. 'Bytes' and 'Power' are two currencies that enable avatar action indirectly. They enable the option to tailor circumstances for avatar action to the player's preference, such as different base layouts and functions. Base size and efficiency depend on careful management of these currencies, and so does its profile. It could focus on mining operations near a resource deposit, could be a research outpost in the wilderness, or could be dedicated to refinement and manufacturing. Thus, these two currencies indirectly support the manifestation of agency in the configurative-constructive dimension. But the freedom granted by *Astroneer*'s design certainly does not stop here.

The fact that there is no single 'right' way of building a base enables the creative freedom required for the playful experience that 'throw[s] off constraint' (Millar 1968: 21) to be realised. As long as modules are on powered platforms, they will work. There are no limitations to how bases should look, no preferred paths in crafting or power management, and the modularity of building allows for the LEGO-like assembly of base and vehicle modules. This, complimented with the terraforming ability of the 'Terrain Tool', really means no boundaries to both the aesthetic and functional construction of bases, whether they be stationary, or moving. An aerial megabase can be constructed by simply erecting towers from hoovered up soil, then using some more soil to make a flat platform on top, and set up all equipment there (u/luckyluuk28 2019). Similarly, to make a sinister underground mining station one need only pick a cave, flatten its floor, set up storage and printing facilities, power up with 'Large Batteries' or a 'Radioisotope Thermoelectric Generator', and get working. Whatever the player builds does not even have to be strictly-speaking functional, because the game allows them to simply build—thus affording agency in the configurative-constructive dimension.

Temporal-Ergodic and Narrative-Dramatic Agency in Astroneer

In games where some, if not all, goals are not clearly defined and the player can set them for themselves, a playful attitude is required. This can be described in terms of Bernard Suits' concept of a 'lusory attitude', which is when players willingly accept the unnecessariness of constraints on their ability to achieve the goals, and also accept that the act of playing is as much of a goal as winning is (Suits 1990: 38–40). Drawing on Suits, amongst others, Salen and Zimmerman (2004: 304) conceptualise three levels of playful activity, and their relation to each other. They argue that 'gameplay' is the most narrow kind of activity where the players adhere to the clearly set rules of a game, 'ludic activities' they define as those that may not necessarily take place within the confines of a clearly defined game, such as animals playing with toys, and 'being playful' is the broadest category that encompasses not only the activity of play, but also the attitude, or 'spirit' of play (Salen and Zimmerman 2004: 303). Miguel Sicart (2014: 21) complicates this observation further when, pointing to the ubiquity of 'emotional design' (Blijlevens et al. 2009) in marketing and design of technology, he argues that playfulness is not restricted to the context of games, or even play, but is a more generalizable attitude that many designers actively rely on to generate our interest in, and foster our engagement with, technologies, services, and other designed artifacts. The distinction that Salen and Zimmerman as well as Sicart make between play as an activity and playfulness as a state of mind (which is observed by many others, see, e.g. Bateson and Martin 2013; Malaby 2007; Schechner 2013; Stenros 2015) is an important one to make. It is easy to take it for granted that playing with video games automatically means that we have a playful attitude towards the experience, which is not necessarily the case—or at least not exclusively. Video games can enable, and often encourage, a variety of different emotions: the footsteps of lurking threat Mr X in horror game *Resident Evil 2* (Capcom 2019) can induce sheer panic, whereas repeatedly trying and (inevitably) failing to defeat notoriously difficult bosses Ornstein and Smough in *Dark Souls* (FromSoftware 2011), a fantasy role-playing game known for its high skill ceiling, will make anyone's blood boil.[26] It is important to note that these emotions do not necessarily make it impossible for a degree of playfulness to also be facilitated by games, it just might not be the dominant affect video games can trigger. Even something as seemingly contradictory as seriousness can not only coexist with playfulness but is a necessary component to it (Jørgensen 2014).

Playfulness is perhaps even more comprehensively theorised by Jaakko Stenros (2015) who defines it as a

> metamotivational state, or an attitude. . . . It is innate to the player, and characterised as being voluntary, spontaneous, and wherein the activity itself is its primary goal. It is present in the moment and can be sparked

in an instant, change drastically at any time, and can disappear without warning. Although it is possible to foster and harness playfulness, it cannot be fully tamed.... Playfulness does not have a moral dimension; it is neither good nor bad in itself—it simply is.

(Stenros 2015: 77)

Not only does this framing of playfulness acknowledge the conceptual distinction between play as an activity and playfulness as a mindset, it also expands the definition so that it covers any activity governed by a playful attitude, regardless of duration, the confirmation of other players or spectators, or even universal values such as good or bad play. In this way, Stenros' understanding of playfulness encompasses both categories of 'ludic activities' and 'being playful' proposed by Salen and Zimmerman, and more.

There is a condition to play in *Astroneer*, namely survival, but as long as the avatar is connected to oxygen, there is no pressure imposed by the game's mechanics to do anything whatsoever. As Game Designer Samantha Kalman phrased it, the '*Astroneer* experience is sort of wavering back and forth' (Noclip 2019: n.p.) between the two player archetypes of 'pioneer' and 'engineer', depending on what specific goal the players set themselves. Accordingly, the kind of challenge posed by the game's design depends on what goal the player wishes to pursue. Such goals can be anything: gathering resource from a nearby field, finding a way to explore underground caves, or some more inventive activities that may appear less in tune with the theme of the game, such as making a chess board with harvestable minerals as figurines. As such, and in Stenros' words, *Astroneer*'s design does not aspire to tame, but instead to 'foster and harness' playfulness, and consequently, agency. We can better understand this through the analytical dimensions of temporal-ergodic and narrative-dramatic agency.

Before the 1.0 release, there were player-constructed challenges circulating on forums for anyone keen to take them on.[27] With the release of *Astroneer 1.0* came the introduction of 'Achievements', which is an optional game mechanic integrated into the distributor platform offering unlockable plaques for completing certain tasks. They are accessible not via in-game interfaces, but the player has to temporarily leave the game to view them in the distributor's superimposed menus. The game's design does not prioritise amongst the achievements. Players can either pick one and follow their chosen goal or accidentally unlock them as they play. This mechanic is very common in similarly structured survival-crafting games, such as *Don't Starve* (Klei Entertainment 2013) or *Rust* (Facepunch Studios 2013). Besides the Achievement being marked as unlocked on the player's Steam, Xbox, or PlayStation account, they do not come with any other tangible rewards. There are over 50 such challenges in *Astroneer 1.0*, and they all have quirky titles. Some are awarded for something as mundane as doing things for the first time, for instance 'One Small Step' is for visiting 'Desolo' for the first time, or 'Making a New Friend' is for planting a seed. Others are awarded for happy accidents, such as 'Where We're Going, We Don't Need Roads' for driving an airborne rover for 10 seconds, or 'Hang 10-Squared' for sliding uninterrupted for 10 seconds. Some Achievements even go meta: 'EXO Dynamics Outreach Advocate' is unlocked after the player having spent a minimum of four hours in multiplayer, or 'Research Scientist' goes to those gaining over 100,000 'Bytes' across all games played from the same account.

It is in the possibility space generated by the optionality of these achievements that *Astroneer* most saliently affords temporal-ergodic agency. They may impose time-critical challenges of various complexities onto the player, but they can just as easily be ignored. As a result, *Astroneer*'s difficulty curve is rather malleable. There is nothing in the game mechanics to limit time spent doing menial tasks such as mining or running around freely on 'Sylva'. These tasks are influenced by temporal structures in the game, such as the day-night cycle (solar power can only be harvested in the daylight), or how much power there is in the 'Terrain Tool', and how long it takes to recharge it, but they are not time-critical as such. It is entirely up to the player how much challenge they want to opt in to. That being said, there is some degree of pre-determination in how difficulty is scaled: each planet has a difficulty level associated with it, and the rarer the resources on it are, the higher this difficulty is. The more complex the recipes are, the higher tier base building items can be printed, which in turn enable the seeking out of even higher degree of challenge. Thus, in *Astroneer*, agency in the temporal-ergodic dimension is jointly supported by spatial-explorative and configurative-constructive agency mechanics, and vice versa.

The same optionality applies to whatever predetermined narrative content there is in the game.[28] At first glance, there is very little in the way of such design features. New playthroughs begin with a highly scripted sequence of events that show a landing capsule transporting an astroneer departing a space station and entering a planet's atmosphere, with the player only being capable of moving the virtual camera around before the shuttle lands and they take full control of their avatar. In addition, throughout any given playthrough, the various instances of interplanetary travel that the game mechanics allow for are relayed via similarly scripted sequences of events showing the avatar's take-off and landing. The player/avatar can also unlock cross-planetary transporter beams as part of Astroneer's endgame, which is rewarded with a more traditional filmic cut-scene.

Adopting the audiovisual vocabulary of cinema in traditional non-interactive fashion, the cut-scene shows the player's avatar at a crossroads: entering a cosmic gate into the unknown in the spirit of adventure, or awaiting a familiar space vessel, presumably a rescue ship, nearing their location. The cut-scene ends with the astroneer stepping into the unknown, which triggers another astroneer being printed aboard the spaceship, suggesting that astroneers are not humans, but artificial creations designed to pursue a corporation's objective. Finally, the player/avatar can find debris that was presumably left behind on each of the planets by previous astroneers and thus also hints at a broader backstory. Throughout the game, there are no explicit text boxes, lore menus, or databases to chronicle these adventures past. In fact, there is very little text (only in the rudimentary menu cataloguing all resources and planet descriptions), and no spoken word whatsoever, in *Astroneer*. Nothing about the reasons for the presence of monoliths, space junk, or any deeper lore is relayed in the game except that they look visually different to other in-game objects, which implies alien origin. The order and means in which astroneers unlocks these chambers is not prescribed. In other words, it is nonlinear, meaning *Astroneer* does afford some narrative agency. What is even more noteworthy however is how it affords dramatic agency.

Astroneer features a variety of animations to represent certain events that we could attribute a basic degree of eventfulness to, such as the avatar's death. The avatar grabbing their throat as they run out of oxygen allows for the attribution of at least some degree of narrativity to what would be considered primarily ludic events from a structural perspective.

More importantly, *Astroneer* affords dramatic agency on a bigger scale as well. The combination of agency affordances across dimensions can generate infinitely different emergent playthroughs, which in turn creates possibility space for a very high degree of dramatic agency to be realised—highest of the three case studies in this book. The player/avatar is almost entirely in control of creating their stories: they can set their own goals, which create narratives of different volumes and durations. If, say, they want to go to a hill on the horizon, all they need to do is mine some 'Compound', a commonly found resource, and print 'Tether Poles' from the printer in their 'Backpack', which allows them to traverse the surface with a safe supply of 'Oxygen'. But if they want to make 'Nano-Carbon Alloy', a complex chemical necessary for printing 'Radioisotope Thermoelectric Generator', the most powerful generator in the game, they are in for a longer adventure. They first need to travel to 'Astrox', the highest difficulty level planet and the only planet with 'Helium' in its atmosphere, which is the necessary fuel for creating 'NanoCarbon Alloy'. In order to be able to condense 'Helium' from 'Astrox', the player must build the biggest available shuttle, which would be able to carry a packaged up 'Atmospheric Condenser'. The machine then would need to be supplied with sufficient energy, and 'Astrox' is very low in solar and wind power. In order to overcome this problem, large batteries must be printed, which require 'Lithium', available to mine on 'Vesania' or 'Novus'. And the story goes on. The 'Radioisotope Thermoelectric Generator' is not a necessary and unavoidable obstacle to progress in the game. It is not even necessary for the game's endgame, as there are many other ways to generate energy. It is an option. An expensive, slightly more efficient, but ultimately non-crucial option. Therefore, while the production chains are predetermined, their optionality affords emergent gameplay, and subsequently, dramatic agency.

When looking at the player community, one can easily find a variety of creative base camp building solutions that make rather ambitious use of the terrain tool, for example, tower bases or sky bases are common (see, e.g., Tactile Object 2019). Some players create intermedial references, such as the magical gauntlet of Thanos from the Marvel Cinematic Universe (see Man in a Van with a Plan 2019), while others create games within the game, such as an oversized chess board with various platforms and organic materials and minerals as pieces (see u65535 2019). Arguably, these kinds of player practices shift the focus from narrativity to creativity. In other words, *Astroneer*'s gameplay could be described as predominantly paidic (Caillois 1961) play. As long as the avatar is connected to oxygen, there is no pressure imposed by the game's mechanics to do anything whatsoever. The playful wavering back and forth between exploration and crafting, and the flexibility to set their own goals, facilitates player stories to emerge. It is because of the procedurally generated environment that creates a new and unique possibility space for exploration and a varied landscape of resources that each *Astroneer* playthrough is unique, and unlikely to be repeated. And it is because of this ability to pursue whatever goals the player sets themselves that *Astroneer*'s design makes possible the emergence of narratively meaningful content, which then, in turn, affords dramatic agency. While there is some predetermined 'designer story' in the 'Achievements' and some hints at lore with the endgame cut-scene, the large majority of *Astroneer* is all about the 'player story' emerging from the procedurally generated assets. In summary, *Astroneer* affords a low degree of narrative agency by nonlinear branching structures of the discoverable alien sites that can unlock interplanetary travel, and more importantly, affords a high degree of dramatic agency by encouraging playfulness.

This final case study chapter expanded the scope of the inquiry at the heart of this book by applying the heuristic framework to a very different production context and game design model when compared to the previous two chapters. System Era being an independent studio and *Astroneer* exemplifying a model of game design commonly referred to as survival crafting sandbox, this chapter complemented the previous two in both aspects, thereby strengthening the analytical power of the multidimensional heuristic framework. The chapter first surveyed common connotations of the 'independent' label, and provided a brief history of milestone games standing out for their design innovations over the decades. This was done to sketch a background against which System Era, a new studio lacking a historical design ethos like Naughty Dog or BioWare, positioned themselves. Having identified inspirations for their game in the early years of development, the analysis then moved on to interrogate post-Early Access-launch paratext in a quest to identify a more crystallised design intention, which was revealed to be focusing on facilitating paidic play, and consequently, playfulness. The textual analysis then connected this notion to agency being afforded in the spatial-explorative, configurative-constructive, and temporal-ergodic dimensions through mechanics facilitating free, unconstrained, experimentational, creative play. While these agency dimensions enable player stories to emerge, the analysis showed that *Astroneer*'s design incentivises less a 'write your own story' kind of game, as there is not even a semblance of pressure to narrativise the experience. Instead, *Astroneer*'s overall design and its specific game mechanics enable, and more importantly, encourage a state of creative experimentation, curiosity, and playfulness. While there is an argument to be made for how playfulness seemingly inherently affords dramatic agency, precisely because of the high levels of other agency forms, the point I want to emphasise is that it is in the spatial-explorative and configurative-constructive dimensions that *Astroneer*'s design predominantly affords agency.

Notes

1. I will not discuss mobile games, as my focus is on console and PC games. For more on how mobile games fit into the broader landscape of independent games, see, e.g., Juul 2009.
2. See, e.g., Deuze et al. 2007; Dyer-Witheford and de Peuter 2009: 3–93, Johns 2005, or Ruffino 2013 on the politics of labour and capitalist mechanics of videogame production; Harvey and Fisher 2015 on women in independent game production; Kennedy 2018 on women in game jams; and Gallagher 2017 or Guevara-Villalobos 2015 on identity politics in and around independent games.
3. A good example illustrating the complexity of independence is the studio Bungie. They bought themselves out of Microsoft's corporate ownership in 2009 and thereby asserted themselves as an 'independent studio' (Destiny Dev Team 2019) after having developed the Xbox's flagship shooter franchise *Halo* (Bungie 2001, 2004, 2007). Shortly after in 2010, they signed a deal with publishing giant Activision to develop another highly successful AAA shooter franchise *Destiny* (Bungie 2014–), only to part ways in 2019 and take over its publishing, thereby regaining their independence. See Martin and Deuze 2009 for an analysis of the first buy-out.
4. Notably, as Juul argues, big-budget games could also be of an 'independent style': for example, LEGO games tend to present blocky versions of franchises such as Star Wars (Juul 2019: 56). The contrary is also true: multiplayer online shooter *PlayerUnknown's Battlegrounds* (PUBG Corporation 2017), or survival-horror game *The Forest* (Endnight Games 2014), although could be considered independent from a production perspective, very much showcase efforts towards realistic-looking animation, typically seen in bigger budget productions.
5. See Lipkin 2019 for a detailed analysis on how Steam contributed to an oversaturated market of independent games from the mid-2010s onwards, referred to as the 'indiepocalypse'.
6. For more on this genre, see, e.g., Kagen 2018; Muscat et al. 2016; Zimmerman and Huberts 2019 and the rest of the articles in a recent special issue of *Press Start* 5(2) on walking simulators.
7. See Thon 2019.

8 See Mitchell 2014.
9 For more on roguelikes, see Craddock 2015 or Ross 2020 for a historical overview; Harris 2011 or Nutt 2014 for main design principles; and Smith and Bryson 2014 for the role of procedural content generation in dungeon design.
10 Interestingly, *Minecraft* was purchased by Microsoft, which muddles the discourse establishing its independent status.
11 These are much more permitting than some mechanics found in AAA games. It is enough to think of the infamous moment (now meme) from *Call of Duty: Advanced Warfare* (Sledgehammer Games 2014), where the player attends a fellow soldier's funeral, and a prompt appears on the screen after the cut-scene that reads 'Press F to pay respects'.
12 On the *Astroneer* developer blog, poster identity is indicated inconsistently throughout the years. I will cite the username who is shown to have posted the article, rather than the signature, if there is one.
13 The game is now also available on Xbox and PlayStation 4.
14 A fourth game that needs acknowledging is *No Man's Sky*. It was developed for a while in parallel with *Astroneer*, but was released earlier, to dreadful reception. Early on during production System Era developers often received questions about their relationship to the game. They acknowledged shared traits (System Era 2016c), but saw difference in their audience management and marketing strategies, with *No Man's Sky* being solely backed by Sony, a corporate giant (System Era 2016b; DevGAMM 2017).
15 Voxels are in a 3D grid what pixels are in 2D.
16 See, e.g., Microsoft Developer 2018; System Era 2016a, 2016b, 2017b, 2017c, 2018a.
17 This was not an entirely conscious decision. Kern, a self-professed fan of the game, posted a self-made astroneer model and sample merchandise on social media, as well as physical copies to the studio, which sparked conversation. This is how the team found out about Kern's previous role in *Minecraft* and proceeded to interview him for the role of Art Director at System Era (Noclip 2019).
18 Not to be confused with story generator algorithms, which focus on language-based content generation. See, e.g., Gervás 2012; Koenitz et al. 2015; Rishes et al. 2013.
19 Though some contest the ubiquity of this term due to the overly generalised and restrictive nature of 'content' in videogames. See 'generative methods' in Compton et al. 2013.
20 Biologists would use 'biome' to refer to a group of flora and fauna that live in a specific area due to having similar needs. In procedural content generation, biomes are a (not necessarily organic) group of pre-set objects and associated values or properties that have the possibility to occur within a given gameworld.
21 For more on the role and impact of community managers in the videogame industry, see, e.g., deWinter et al. 2017; Zimmerman 2019.
22 A short summative description used by the team for reference during development as well as for promotional purposes.
23 Wilson is referring to the film *Apollo 13* and the book/film *The Martian*.
24 They also mention a third one, the socialeer, seeking social and co-operative play, but in later interviews this boils down to the engineer and pioneer types.
25 Since the Summer Update, they also have a hitbox registered by an in-game printable object called 'Recreational Canopy', which functions as a football goal.
26 For more on gameplay and emotions, see, e.g., Csíkszentmihályi 1975 on flow, Mäyrä and Ermi 2005, or Ryan 2015: 85–114 on typologies of immersion; Järvinen 2008 or Perron 2005 on classifying emotions elicited by game design;

Perron 2018: 66–127 and Thon 2019 on fear specifically; Swink 2008 or Isbister 2016: 1–42 for designer perspectives on emotion and games; Grodal 2009: 158–181 on agency and emotions during gameplay; Gregersen and Grodal 2009: 66–69 or Keogh 2018 on agency and embodiment; or the essays on cognition, affect, and emotion and video games in Perron and Schröter 2016.
27 See the 'Smelt Me Not' challenge (ApoNono 2017), or the Solar System Challenge (Marck 2017).
28 This has changed somewhat with the 'Wanderer Update', but it is still not to the same degree as *No Man's Sky*'s similarly narrative update packs.

References

Abend, P.; Beil, B. (2015). Editors of Play. The Scripts and Practices of Co-creativity in *Minecraft* and *LittleBigPlanet*. *DiGRA'15—Proceedings of the 2015 DiGRA International Conference: Diversity of Play: Games—Cultures—Identities*. Vol. 12, pp. 1–15. Available at: www.digra.org/wp-content/uploads/digital-library/37_AbendBeil_Editors-of-Play.pdf

Ackermann, E.; Gauntlett, D.; Weckstrom, C. (2009). *Defining Systemic Creativity*. Billund: LEGO Learning Institute.

admin. (2015). Hello World(S). *Astroneer News*, 15 October. Available at: https://blog.astroneer.space/p/hello-worlds/

admin. (2017a). Augments. *Astroneer News*, 21 April. Available at: https://blog.astroneer.space/p/augments/

admin. (2017b). 50 Days. *Astroneer News*, 4 February. Available at: https://blog.astroneer.space/system-era/50-days/

Antropy, A. (2011). Beyond Indie. *Auntie Pixelante*, 1 March. Available at: http://web.archive.org/web/20161228000021/http://auntiepixelante.com/?p=960

ApoNono. (2017). Challenge Series: Smelt Me Not. *System Era Forum*, 19 January. Available at: https://forum.systemera.net/topic/10198-challenge-series-smelt-me-not/

Bailes, J.; Shaw, L. (2018). Live, Die, Upgrade, Repeat: The Modern Roguelike. *Kotaku*, 9 November. Available at: www.kotaku.co.uk/2018/11/02/evolution-of-the-roguelike

Baker, T. (2018). The Complete History of Indie Games. *The Indie Game Website*, 19 October. Available at: www.indiegamewebsite.com/2018/10/19/the-complete-history-of-indie-games/

Bateman, C. (2005). The Anarchy of Paidia. *Only a Game*, 23 December. Available at: http://onlyagame.typepad.com/only_a_game/2005/12/the_anarchy_of__1.html

Bateson, P.; Martin, P. (2013). *Play, Playfulness, Creativity and Innovation*. Cambridge: Cambridge University Press.

Birnbaum, I. (2015). *Subnautica*: Early Impressions of *Minecraft* Under the Sea. *PC Gamer*, 10 January. Available at: www.pcgamer.com/subnautica-preview-impressions-early-access/

Blijlevens, J.; Creusen, M. E. H.; Schoormans, J. P. L. (2009). How Consumers Perceive Product Appearance: The Identification of Three Product Appearance Attributes. *International Journal of Design* 3 (3): 27–35.

Bogost, I. (2007). *Persuasive Games: The Expressive Power of Videogames*. Cambridge, MA: The MIT Press.

Bohemia Interactive. (2018). *DayZ* [PC]. Bohemia Interactive.

Bradley, A. (2018). Devs Weigh in on the Best Ways to Use (But Not Abuse) Procedural Generation. *Gamasutra*, 12 March. Available at: www.gamasutra.com/view/news/315400/Devs_weigh_in_on_the_best_ways_to_use_but_not_abuse_procedural_generation.php

Breslin, S. (2009). The History and Theory of Sandbox Gameplay. *Gamasutra*, 16 July. Available at: www.gamasutra.com/view/feature/132470/the_history_and_theory_of_sandbox_.php?page=3

Bungie. (2001). *Halo: Combat Evolved* [Xbox]. Microsoft Game Studios.

Bungie. (2004). *Halo 2* [Xbox]. Microsoft Game Studios.

Bungie. (2007). *Halo 3* [Xbox 360]. Microsoft Game Studios.

Bungie. (2014). *Destiny* [PlayStation 4]. Activision/Microsoft Game Studios.

Caillois, R. (1961). *Man, Play, and Games*. New York: The Free Press of Glencoe, Inc.

Camper, B. (2007). Shareware Games. Between Hobbyist and Professional. In M. J. P. Wolf, ed. *The Video Game Explosion: A History from PONG to PlayStation and Beyond*. Wesport, CT: Greenwood Press, pp. 151–158

Capcom. (2019). *Resident Evil 2* [PC]. Capcom.

Cardboard Computer. (2013). *Kentucky Route Zero* [PC]. Annapurna Interactive.

Cassidy, S. B. (2011). The Videogame as Narrative. *Quarterly Review of Film and Video* 28 (4): 292–306.

Cawthon, S. (2014). *Five Nights at Freddy's* [PC]. Cawthon.

Compton, K.; Osborn, J. C.; Mateas, M. (2013). Generative Methods. *FDG'13— Proceedings of the 4th Workshop on Procedural Content Generation in Games*. Available at: www.fdg2013.org/program/workshops/papers/PCG2013/pcg2013_6.pdf

Costello, B. M. (2018). The Rhythm of Game Interactions: Player Experience and Rhythm in *Minecraft* and *Don't Starve*'. *Games and Culture* 13 (8): 807–824. https://doi.org/10.1177/1555412016646668

Craddock, D. L. (2015), *Dungeon Hacks: How NetHack, Angband, and Other Roguelikes Changed the Course of Video Games*. Canton, OH: Press Start Press.

Csíkszentmihályi, M. (1975). *Beyond Boredom and Anxiety: The Experience of Play in Work and Games*. Washington, DC: Jossey-Bass Publishers.

Deen, P. D. (2011). Interactivity, Inhabitation and Pragmatist Aesthetics. *Game Studies* 11 (2) Available at: http://gamestudies.org/1102/articles/deen

Defoe, D. (1994 [1791]). *Robinson Crusoe*. London: Penguin.

Destiny Dev Team. (2019). Our Destiny. *Bungie.net*. Available at: https://www.bungie.net/en/News/Article/47569

Deuze, M.; Martin, C.; Allen, C. (2007). The Professional Identity of Gameworkers. *Convergence* 13 (4): 335–353. https://doi.org/10.1177/1354856507081947

DevGAMM. (2017). *Riley Gravatt (System Era Softworks)—Marketing Astroneer*. Available at: www.youtube.com/watch?v=RvsA1eF2X3U

deWinter, J.; Kocurek, C. A.; Vie, S. (2017). Managing Community Managers: Social Labor, Feminized Skills, and Professionalization. *Communication Design Quarterly* 4 (4): 36–45.

Diver, M. (2016). *Indie Games. The Complete Introduction to Indie Gaming*. London: LOM Art, Michael O'Mara Books Limited.

DMA Design. (2001). *Grand Theft Auto III* [PlayStation 2]. Rockstar Games.

Dodge Roll. (2017). *Enter the Gungeon* [PC]. Devolver Digital.

Dyer-Witheford, N.; de Peuter, G. (2009). *Games of Empire: Global Capitalism and Video Games*. Minneapolis, MI: University of Minnesota Press.
Endnight Games. (2014). *The Forest* [PC]. Endnight Games.
Evans, E. (2011). *Transmedia Television: Audiences, New Media and Daily Life*. New York: Routledge.
Facepunch Studios. (2004). *Garry's Mod* [PC]. Valve.
Facepunch Studios. (2013). *Rust* [PC]. Facepunch Studios.
Frasca, G. (2003). Simulation Versus Narrative: Introduction to Ludology. In M. J. P. Wolf and B. Perron, eds. *The Video Game Theory Reader*. New York, London: Routledge, pp. 221–235.
Frasca, G. (2007). *Play the Message. Play, Game, and Video Game Rhetoric*. PhD Dissertation, IT University Copenhagen.
Frictional Games. (2010). *Amnesia: The Dark Descent* [PC]. Frictional Games.
FromSoftware. (2011). *Dark Souls* [PC]. Namco.
Gallagher, R. (2017). *Videogames, Identity and Digital Subjectivity*. New York: Routledge.
Gandolfi, E. (2016). To Watch or to Play, It is in the Game: The Game Culture on Twitch.tv Among Performers, Plays and Audiences. *Journal of Gaming & Virtual Worlds* 8 (1): 63–82.
Garda, M. B.; Grabarczyk, P. (2016). Is Every Indie Game Independent? Towards the Concept of Independent Game. *Game Studies* 16 (1). Available at: http://gamestudies.org/1601/articles/gardagrabarczyk
Gazzard, A. (2011). Unlocking the Gameworld: The Rewards of Space and Time in Videogames. *Game Studies* 11 (1). Available at: http://gamestudies.org/1101/articles/gazzard_alison
Gauntlett, D. (2014). The LEGO System as a Tool for Thinking, Creativity, and Changing the World. In M. J. P. Wolf, ed. *LEGO Studies. Examining the Building Blocks of a Transmedial Phenomenon*. New York: Routledge, pp. 189–205.
GDC. (2016). *What Do We Mean When We Say Indiepocalypse?* Available at: www.youtube.com/watch?v=r30CIneO534
Genette, G. (1983). *Narrative Discourse: An Essay in Method*. Ithaca, NY: Cornell University Press.
Gervás, P. (2012). Story Generator Algorithms. In *Living Handbook of Narratology*. Available at: www.lhn.uni—hamburg.de/node/35.html
Giant Bomb. (2018). *Giant Bomb Presents: A GDC Interview with Samantha Kalman.* [Podcast]. 28 March. Available at: https://podbay.fm/podcast/628532858/e/1521770700
Giddings, S. (2014). Simulation. In M. J. P. Wolf and B. Perron, eds. *The Routledge Companion to Video Game Studies*. London: Routledge, pp. 259–266.
Gnade, M. (2010). What Makes an Indie Game . . . Indie? *Venturebeat*, 13 July. Available at: https://venturebeat.com/2010/07/13/what-makes-an-indie-gameindie/
Golding, W. (2009 [1954]). *Lord of the Flies*. London: Faber.
Gregersen, A.; Grodal, T. (2009). Embodiment and Interface. In B. Perron and M. J. P. Wolf, eds. *The Video Game Theory Reader 2*. New York: Routledge, pp. 65–84.
Grodal, T. (2009). *Embodied Visions: Evolution, Emotion, Culture, and Film*. New York: Oxford University Press.
Guevara-Villalobos, O. (2015). Independent Gamework and Identity: Problems and Subjective Nuances. *DiGRA'15—Proceedings of the 2015 DiGRA*

International Conference. Available at: www.digra.org/digital-library/publications/independent-gamework-and-identity-problems-and-subjective-nuances/

Harris, J. (2011). Analysis: The Eight Rules of Roguelike Design. *Gamasutra*, 30 December. Available at: www.gamasutra.com/view/news/123031/Analysis_The_Eight_Rules_Of_Roguelike_Design.php

Harvey, A.; Fisher, S. (2015). "Everyone Can Make Games!": The post-feminist context of women in digital game production. *Feminist Media Studies* 15 (4): 576–592. https://doi.org/10.1080/14680777.2014.958867

Hayward, A. (2014). *Space Engineers: Minecraft Amidst the Stars? IGN*, 8 May. Available at: www.ign.com/articles/2014/05/08/space-engineers-minecraft-amidst-the-stars

Hesford, D. (2013). 'Action . . . Suspense . . . Emotion!': The Trailer as Cinematic Performance. *Frames Cinema Journal* (3). Available at: http://framescinemajournal.com/article/action-suspense-emotion-the-trailer-as-cinematic-performance/

House House. (2019). *Untitled Goose Game* [Nintendo Switch]. Panic.

Huizinga, J. (2009 [1949]). *Homo Ludens: A Study of the Play-Element in Culture*. Abingdon, Oxon: Routledge.

id Software. (1993). *Doom* [PC]. GT Interactive Software.

id Software. (1996). *Quake* [PC]. GT Interactive.

I'm a Celebrity, Get Me Out of Here (2002–). ITV.

Isbister, K. (2016). *How Games Move Us. Emotion by Design*. Cambridge, MA: MIT Press.

Järvinen, A. (2008). Understanding Video Games as Emotional Experiences. In B. Perron and M. J. P. Wolf, eds. *The Video Game Theory Reader 2*. New York: Routledge, pp. 85–108.

Johns, J. (2005). Video Games Production Networks: Value Capture, Power Relations and Embeddedness. *Journal of Economic Geography* 6 (2): 151–180.

Jørgensen, K. (2013). *Gameworld Interfaces*. Cambridge, MA: MIT Press.

Jørgensen, K. (2014). Devil's Plaything: On the Boundary between Playful and Serious. *Proceedings of Nordic DiGRA 2014 Conference*, 29–30 May, Uppsala, Sweden. Available from: http://www.digra.org/digital-library/publications/devils-plaything-on-the-boundary-between-playful-and-serious/

Juul, J. (2007). Without a Goal: On Open and Expressive Games. In B. Atkins and T. Krzywinska, eds. *Videogame, Player, Text*. Manchester: Manchester University Press, pp. 191–203.

Juul, J. (2009). *A Casual Revolution: Reinventing Games and Their Players*. Cambridge, MA: MIT Press.

Juul, J. (2014). High-Tech Low-Tech Authenticity: The Creation of Independent Style at the Independent Games Festival. *Proceedings of the 9th International Conference on the Foundations of Digital Games*. Available at: www.jesperjuul.net/text/independentstyle/.

Juul, J. (2019). *Handmade Pixels. Independent Video Games and the Quest for Authenticity*. Cambridge, MA: MIT Press.

Kagen, M. (2018). Walking, Talking and Playing with Masculinities in Firewatch. *Game Studies* 18 (2). Available at: http://gamestudies.org/1802/articles/kagen

Keen Software House. (2013). *Space Engineers* [Microsoft Windows]. Keen Software House.

Kennedy, H. W. (2018). Game Jam as Feminist Methodology: The Affective Labors of Intervention in the Ludic Economy. *Games and Culture* 13 (7): 708–727.

Keogh, B. (2015). Between Triple-A, Indie, Casual, and DIY: Sites of Tension in the Videogames Cultural Industries. In K. Oakley and J. O'Connor, eds.

The Routledge Companion to the Cultural Industries. New York: Routledge, pp. 152–162.
Keogh, B. (2018). *A Play of Bodies: How We Perceive Videogames*. Boston, MA: MIT Press.
Kerr, A. (2017). *Global Games. Production, Circulation and Policy in the Networked Era*. New York: Routledge.
King, G. (2005). *American Independent Cinema*. Bloomington, IN: Indiana University Press.
Klei Entertainment. (2013). *Don't Starve* [PC]. 505 Games.
Koenitz, H.; Ferri, G.; Haahr, M.; Sezen, D.; Sezen, T. I. (eds.). (2015). *Interactive Digital Narrative. History, Theory and Practice*. New York: Routledge.
Laukkanen, T. (2005). *Modding Scenes. Introduction to User-Created Content in Computer Gaming*. University of Tampere Hypermedia Laboratory Net Series 9. Available at: https://trepo.tuni.fi/bitstream/handle/10024/65431/951-44-6448-6.pdf?sequence=1&isAllowed=y
Libnoise. 'Amplitude'; 'Persistence'. *Libnoise. A portable, open-source, coherent noise-generating library for C++*. Available at: http://libnoise.sourceforge.net/glossary/
Lipkin, N. D. (2013). Examining Indie's Independence: The Meaning of "Indie" Games, the Politics of Production, and Mainstream Cooptation. *Loading . . . The Journal of the Canadian Game Studies Association* 7 (11). Available at: https://journals.sfu.ca/loading/index.php/loading/article/view/122
Lipkin, N. D. (2019). The Indiepocalypse: The Political-Economy of Independent Game Development Labor in Contemporary Indie Markets. *Game Studies* 19 (2). Available at: http://gamestudies.org/1902/articles/lipkin
Malaby, T. (2007). Beyond Play: A New Approach to Games. *Games and Culture* 2 (2): 95–113. https://doi.org/10.1177/1555412007299434
Man in a Van With a Plan. (2019). Close Enough. *Steam*, 1 March. Available at: https://steamcommunity.com/sharedfiles/filedetails/?id=1670418195
Man vs Wild. (2006–2011). Channel 4.
Marck. (2017). Solar System Challenge. *System Era Forum*, 3 January. Available at: https://forum.systemera.net/topic/7668-solar-system-challenge/
Martin, C. B.; Deuze, M. (2009). The Independent Production of Culture: A Digital Games Case Study. *Games and Culture* 4 (3): 276–295. https://doi.org/10.1177/1555412009339732
Maxis. (2000). *The Sims* [PC]. Electronic Arts.
Maxis. (2014). *The Sims 4* [PC]. Electronic Arts.
Mäyrä, F.; Ermi, L. (2005). Fundamental Components of Gameplay Experience: Analysing Immersion. *DiGRA'05—Proceedings of the 2005 DiGRA International Conference: Changing Views: World in Play*. Available at: www.digra.org/digital-library/publications/fundamental-components-of-the-gameplay-experience-analysing-immersion/
McCarthy, C. (2006). *The Road*. New York: A. A. Knopf.
McMillen, E. (2011). *The Binding of Isaac* [PC]. Edmund McMillan.
Microsoft Developer. (2018). *Building Astroneer: Charting New and Challenging Courses*. Available at: www.youtube.com/watch?v=oUkDSHnnFsI
Millar, S. (1968.) *The Psychology of Play*. Harmondsworth: Penguin.
Mitchell, A. (2014). Defamiliarization and Poetic Interaction in Kentucky Route Zero. *Well Played* 3 (2): 161–178.
Mojang. (2016). *Minecraft: Education Edition* [PC]. Microsoft.
Mojang Studios. (2009). *Minecraft* [PC]. Mojang Studios.

Mossmouth, LLC. (2008). *Spelunky* [PC]. Mossmouth, LLC.
Murray, J. (1997). *Hamlet on the Holodeck*. Cambridge, MA: MIT Press.
Muscat, A.; Goddard, W.; Duckworth, J.; Holopainen, J. (2016). First-Person Walkers: Understanding the Walker Experience through Four Design Themes. *DiGRA/ FDG'16—Proceedings of the First International Joint Conference of DiGRA and FDG Dundee, Scotland: Digital Games Research Association and Society for the Advancement of the Science of Digital Games*. Available at: www.digra.org/ digital-library/publications/first-person-walkers-the-walker-experience-u-tnhdroerusgtha-nfdoiunrg-design-themes/
Nichols, R. (2014). *The Video Game Industry*. London: British Film Institute.
Nicoll, B.; Keogh, B. (2019). *The Unity Game Engine and the Circuits of Cultural Software*. Cham: Springer International.
Nitsche, M. (2008). *Video Game Spaces: Image, Play, and Structure in 3D Worlds*. Cambridge, MA: MIT Press.
Noclip. (2019). *The Untold Story Behind Astroneer's Difficult Development*. Available at: www.youtube.com/watch?v=tfUjl4owxTQ
Notch. (2011). Terrain generation, Part 1. *The Word of Notch*, 9 March. Available at: https://notch.tumblr.com/post/3746989361/terrain-generation-part-1
Number One. (2008). *Braid* [PC]. Number One.
Nutt, C. (2014). 'Roguelikes': Getting to the Heart of the It-Genre. *Gamasutra*, 21 May. Available at: www.gamasutra.com/view/feature/218178/roguelikes_getting_ to_the_heart_.php
O'Donnell, C. (2012). This Is Not a Software Industry. In P. Zackariasson and T. Wilson, eds. *The Video Game Industry: Formation, Present State, and Future*. London: Routledge, pp. 17–33.
Parker, F.; Whitson, J.; Simon, B. (2018). Megabooth: The Cultural Intermediation of Indie Games. *New Media & Society* 20 (5): 1953–1972.
Perlin, K. (1985). An Image Synthesizer. *ACM SIGGRAPH Computer Graphics* 19 (3): 287–296. Available at: https://dl.acm.org/doi/10.1145/325165.325247
Perron, B. (2005). A Cognitive Psychological Approach to Gameplay Emotions. *DiGRA'05—Proceedings of the 2005 DiGRA International Conference: Changing Views: Worlds in Play*. Available at: www.digra.org/digital-library/ publications/a-cognitive-psychological-approach-to-gameplay-emotions/
Perron, B. (2018). *The World of Scary Video Games: A Study in Videoludic Horror*. New York: Bloomsbury.
Perron, B.; Schröter, F. (eds.). (2016). *Video Games and the Mind: Essays on Cognition, Affect and Emotion*. Jefferson, NC: MacFarland & Co.
Playdead. (2010). *Limbo* [Xbox 360]. Playdead.
Polytron Corporation. (2012). *Fez* [Xbox 360]. Trapdoor.
PUBG Corporation. (2017). *PlayerUnknown's Battlegrounds* [PC]. PUBG Corporation.
Rishes, E.; Lukin, S. M.; Elson, D. K.; Walker, M. A. (2013). Generating Different Story Tellings from Semantic Representations of Narrative. In H. Koenitz et al., eds. *Interactive Storytelling. ICIDS 2013. Lecture Notes in Computer Science* 8230. Cham, Switzerland: Springer, pp. 1–12.
Ross, R. C. (2020). ASCII Art + Permadeath: The History of Roguelike Games. *Ars Technica*, 19 March. Available at: https://arstechnica.com/gaming/2020/03/ ascii-art-permadeath-the-history-of-roguelike-games/

Rowe, B. (2016). Inspired Space: Inside the Development of *Astroneer*. *Unreal Engine*, 28 May. Available at: www.unrealengine.com/en-US/developer-interviews/inspired-space-inside-the-development-of-astroneer

Ruffino, P. (2013). Narratives of Independent Production in Video Game Culture. *Loading: Journal of the Canadian Game Studies Association* 7 (11): 106–121.

Ruffino, P. (ed.). (2021). *Independent Videogames: Cultures, Networks, Techniques and Politics*. London: Routledge.

Ryan, M.-L. (2015). *Narrative as Virtual Reality 2*. Baltimore, MD: Johns Hopkins University Press.

Salen, K.; Zimmerman, E. (2004). *Rules of Play: Game Design Fundamentals*. Cambridge, MA: MIT Press.

Schechner, R. (2013 [2006]). *Performance Studies: An Introduction*. 3rd ed. New York: Routledge.

Schutz, K. (2014). The Virtualization of LEGO. In M. J. P. Wolf, ed. *Lego Studies. Examining the Building Blocks of a Transmedial Phenomenon*. New York: Routledge, pp. 227–240.

SES_dev. (2019). *We Launched an Xbox into Space*. Available at: www.twitch.tv/videos/485972110

Shaker, N.; Togelius, J.; Nelson, M. J. (2016). *Procedural Content Generation*. Cham: Springer International Publishing.

Sicart, M. (2014). *Play Matters*. Cambridge, MA: MIT Press.

Simon, B. (2013). Indie Eh? Some Kind of Game Studies. *Loading . . . The Journal of the Canadian Game Studies Association* 7 (11): 1–7.

Sites, J. D.; Potter, R. F. (2018). Everything Merges with the Game: A Generative Music System Embedded in a Videogame Increases Flow. *Game Studies* 18 (2). Available at: http://gamestudies.org/1802/articles/sites_potter

Sledgehammer Games. (2014). *Call of Duty: Advanced Warfar* [PC]. Activision.

Smith, A. J.; Bryson, J. J. (2014). A Logical Approach to Building Dungeons: Answer Set Programming for Hierarchical Procedural Content Generation in Roguelike Games. *Proceedings of the 50th Annual Convention of the AISB*. Available at: https://pdfs.semanticscholar.org/f69b/f76b77da89bfd7135b9c60d2b9b10fc1ac20.pdf

Smith, G. (2011). Will Wright at BAFTA: The Creator of *The Sims* on His Influences and Hints to His Next Game. *PC Gamer*, 6 June. Available at: www.pcgamer.com/will-wright-at-bafta-the-creator-of-the-sims-on-his-influences-and-hints-to-his-next-game/

Stenros, J. (2015). *Playfulness, Play, and Games. A Constructionist Ludology Approach*. PhD Thesis, Tampere University.

Suits, B. (1990). *Grasshopper: Games, Life, and Utopia*. Boston, MA: David R. Godine.

Swink, S. (2008). *Game Feel: A Game Designer's Guide to Virtual Sensation*. Burlington, MA: Morgan Kaufman.

System Era. (2016a). *Developer Let's Play #2 (Live from TWITCH!)*. Available at: www.youtube.com/watch?v=QhXFm—idxSU&t=25s

System Era. (2016b). *Astroneer—Developer Let's Play #3 (Live from TWITCH!)*. Available at: www.youtube.com/watch?v=6lhWJH6mOM0

System Era. (2016c). *Live Dev: Let's Prototype Discoveries!* Available at: www.youtube.com/watch?v=—WZXzI2OCH4

System Era. (2016d). *Live Dev: Let's Build a Planet!* Available at: www.youtube.com/watch?v=g71TcfoMeaI

System Era. (2016e). *Let's Build a MOON!* Available at: www.youtube.com/watch?v=bs—7ii_ODpQ&t=973s

System Era. (2017a). *Live Dev: 3D Modeling w/Riley & Adam!* Available at: www.youtube.com/watch?v=SFYl06k—954

System Era. (2017b). *LIVE Podcast*: Astroneer *dev team talks current pre—alpha bugs! #creative #gamedev.* Available at: www.youtube.com/watch?v=QcXoPD7Tkn0

System Era. (2017c). *Friday Q&A: Base Interiors, Challenge, Caravans.* Available at: www.youtube.com/watch?v=G88IfaAzcOA

System Era. (2017d). *Stream Replay: Experimental Test 002—Terrain As A Resource.* Available at: www.youtube.com/watch?v=jQS42QEvZK0

System Era. (2017e). *SES Vlog 010: Space Woodchippers, Storms, Controls, & Experimental.* Available at: https://www.youtube.com/watch?v=VvAJcZzIYJo

System Era. (2018a). *Half of a Planet, New Minerals, The Goonies—SES Vlog 032.* Available at: www.youtube.com/watch?v=3qwptlfZTes

System Era. (2018b). *Astroneer—Basebuilding Update Trailer.* Available at: www.youtube.com/watch?v=GCA80QgMTNU

System Era. (2019). Astroneer—*Announce Trailer | PS4.* Available at: www.youtube.com/watch?v=SpsTt2MMaas

System Era Softworks. (2019). *Astroneer* [PC]. System Era Softworks.

Tactile Object. (2019). The Sky Base Isn't That Convenient for Grabbing Soil, But the View Makes It Worth It Haha, 5 August. Available at: www.reddit.com/r/Astroneer/comments/cmajlg/the_sky_base_isnt_that_convenient_for_grabbing/

Team Meat. (2010). *Super Meat Boy* [Xbox 360]. Team Meat.

The Chinese Room. (2012). *Dear Esther* [PC]. The Chinese Room.

The Fullbright Company. (2013). *Gone Home* [PC]. The Fullbright Company.

Thon, J.-N. (2019). Playing with Fear: The Aesthetics of Horror in Recent Indie Games. *Eludamos: Journal for Computer Game Culture* 10 (1): 197–231.

Tirado, J. (2016). IO IN_DEPTH: System Era Softworks. *Indie Obscura*, 23 September. Available at: https://ag.hyperxgaming.com/article/1926/io-indepth-system-era-softworks

Togelius, J.; Shaker, N.; Nelson, M. J. (2016). Introduction. In N. Shaker et al., eds. *Procedural Content Generation.* Cham: Springer International Publishing, pp. 1–15.

Toms, K. (1982). *Football Manager* [Sinclair ZX80]. Addictive Games.

u65535. (2019). Astroneer Biological Chessboard. *Reddit*, 25 July. Available at: www.reddit.com/r/Astroneer/comments/chfomv/astroneer_biological_chess_board/

Ubisoft Montreal. (2014a). *Assassin's Creed Unity* [PlayStation 4]. Ubisoft.

Ubisoft Montreal. (2014b). *Watch Dogs* [PlayStation 4]. Ubisoft.

u/luckyluuk28. (2019). Rate my base. *Reddit*, 16th February. Available from: https://www.reddit.com/r/Astroneer/comments/arcvf8/rate_my_base/

Unknown Worlds Entertainment. (2017). *Subnautica* [Microsoft Windors]. San Francisco, CA: Unknown Worlds Entertainment.

Valve. (1998). *Half Life* [PC]. Sierra Studios.

Valve. (2004). *Half-Life 2* [PC]. Valve.

Vollans, E. (2017). The Most Cinematic Game Yet. *Kinephanos: Journal of Media Studies and Popular Culture* 7(1): 106–130.

Wawro, A. (2015). *Astroneer*'s Ex-AAA Devs Explore a Strange New World of Indie Life. *Gamasutra*, 30 October. Available at: www.gamasutra.com/view/news/257267/Astroneers_exAAA_devs_explore_a_strange_new_world_of_indie_life.php

Westecott, E. (2013). Independent Game Development as Craft. *Loading . . . The Journal of the Canadian Game Studies Association* 7 (11): 78–91. Available at: https://journals.sfu.ca/loading/index.php/loading/article/view/124/153

Wilde, T. (2019). How the Epic Games Store Compares to Steam Right Now. *PC Gamer*, 18 January. Available at: www.pcgamer.com/uk/how-the-epic-games-store-compares-to-steam-right-now/

Wilson, J. (2005). Indie Rocks! Mapping Independent Video Game Design. *Media International Australia Incorporating Culture and Policy* 115 (1): 109–122.

Wube Software Ltd. (2012). *Factorio* [Microsoft Windows]. Prague: Wube Software Ltd.

Zimmerman, E. (2002). Do Independent Games Exist? *Game On*. Available at: https://static1.squarespace.com/static/579b8aa26b8f5b8f49605c96/t/59924e1337c581f4bdf9a38a/1502760467970/indiegames.pdf

Zimmermann, F.; Huberts, C. (2019). From Walking Simulator to Ambience Action Game: A Philosophical Approach to a Misunderstood Genre. *Press Start* 5 (2): 29–50.

Zimmermann, J. J. (2019). Computer Game Fan Communities, Community Management, and Structures of Membership. *Games and Culture* 14 (7–8): 896–916. https://doi.org/10.1177/1555412017742308

Conclusion

Videogames have come far from merely being considered a more interactive version of films, and with the relentless march of technological advancement, the ways in which videogames engage their players in interaction will only become more complex. At the same time, the videogame market has also become increasingly saturated over the past decades, and so the marketing of videogames has simultaneously become more centred on highlighting how the given product will offer a player experience that grants even higher volumes, or even more distinct kinds, of player freedom. It is therefore important to examine not just how the games themselves can afford agency, but also how those who make them think about the issues around player freedom and facilitation or restriction thereof. The heuristic framework proposed in this book, and the subsequent case studies, addressed this dual perspective, and by doing so, demonstrated the complexity of agency within the current videogame landscape. The research questions targeted how agency can be conceptualised in a way that is informed not only by scholarship but also by game design; what can be understood about agency design intention through observing the way videogame developers talk about their games; and how avatar-based games' design affords and constrains player action.

Whether the player is escorted along a linear path of progression signposted by level design and scripted events or is free to engage with the gameplay mechanics offered by the game in a chosen order has an impact on how their agency manifests. Equally, configurability of character appearance and skillset, as well as the gameworld affects the player's possibility of exerting agency, whereby these features allow the player various degrees of designing the challenge, tailoring it to their preference. As a means of addressing these variables, this book framed agency as an affordance of game design. It examined how agency is conceptualised in different discourses surrounding videogames, as discussed in game studies, and as theorised by game design discourse. The findings in these parts were synthesised to create a multidimensional heuristic framework for conceptualising agency in avatar-based games. Game studios with a particular design focus that draw on 'game design lineages' (Bateman and Zagal

2018) were selected as case studies to demonstrate the analytical power of this framework, examining how agency is designed (textual analysis) and how designers discuss how it is designed (paratextual analysis). Such an approach facilitated a way of looking at game design which is informed by the vocabularies of theoretical and academic discussions concerning videogames, as well as the language used to refer to these phenomena by industry practitioners, therefore grounding abstract theory in production practices and discourses.

Chapters 1 and 2 drew on game design and game studies literature in order to develop a conceptualization of agency as the possibility space for avatar action, as afforded and limited by game design. It then distinguished between four dimensions in which player action can be realised, which, put simply, can be described as agency in space, in time, over customising the avatar and its surrounds, and as narratively meaningful action. The core argument was that avatar action in these dimensions can be observed according to the avatar's function in the game being ludic or representational, and proceeded to further complicate how these two functions unfold in each dimension of agency. I first unpacked what forms the interplay between game spaces affording ludic and representational functions can take, and how it can sometimes lead to interesting tensions. I called the possibility space for action determined by these interplays the spatial-explorative dimension of agency. Then, I focused on the two main ways the possibility space for action in time can be shaped. I called this the temporal-ergodic dimension, and argued that it can be shaped by game design: by discussing how avatar action afforded or constrained in time can be a means to present challenge; and how the ability to influence temporal structures can impact the possibility space for avatar action to be realised. Next, I unpacked how design features such as avatar attribute systems, in-game economies, or whether the power to alter terrain is granted can shape the possibility space for avatar action in what I called the configurative-constructive dimension. Lastly, I argued that narratively relevant content in avatar-based games can be identified according to degrees of predeterminedness. Looking at whether, and if yes how, such content is presented (such as by non-player characters or environmental storytelling) shapes the possibility space for avatar action in what I termed the narrative-dramatic dimension. Chapter 2 concluded with a reiteration that the separation into the four dimensions was done for analytical purposes, and that these dimensions can support or undermine each other in various ways. The remaining of the book was dedicated to case studies demonstrating the analytical power of this multidimensional heuristic framework, and showing how agency dimensions play out in individual cases.

The first case study in Chapter 3 was *Uncharted 4: A Thief's End* (Naughty Dog 2016), a game representing a game design model that can be traced back to the action and adventure games of the 1990s, and which is characterised by a high degree of designer control on player progression.

The chapter first traced the development of the studio's design ethos from their early games, which laid the foundations for the studio's trademark linear 3D character-based action gameplay with platforming, shooting elements, and memorable characters. Then I discussed how with the *Uncharted* games Naughty Dog left behind the world of cartoonish animation in favour of realistic rendering of human characters in recognisable environments, all the while adhering to the genre mechanics of action-adventure games. I showed that the studio's design ethos, and with that, the brand identity of the *Uncharted* franchise was interwoven with discussions of a cinematic quality in games both in terms of audiovisual aesthetics and gameplay. This, as the paratextual analysis of the promotional surrounds showed, continued to be the case with *Uncharted 4: A Thief's End*. Then, a textual analysis of the game showed that the cinematic quality of the *Uncharted* series was achieved by restrictions to avatar action in the spatial-explorative, temporal-ergodic, and configurative-constructive dimensions to regulate the pace of gameplay so as to make it more akin to action-adventure blockbuster movies. Furthermore, this case study showed that despite the restriction to core mechanics, the extremely detailed, motion-captured, and rich audiovisual detail amplified the narrative quality of gameplay sequences, and therefore afforded a degree of dramatic agency. This chapter examined the interplay between dimensions of agency and how agency is understood, sacrificed, and afforded in the development of cinematic gameplay.

Chapter 4 looked at BioWare and their game *Mass Effect: Andromeda* (2017), a game that taps into the tradition of role-playing games, but also exemplifies an adaptation to the current videogame market. The hypothesis of this chapter was twofold: that BioWare's conceptualization of player freedom, and subsequently, agency, has changed with *Andromeda*; and that the communicated design intention only partially matches the actual design of the game. The chapter began by establishing BioWare's design ethos, which I argued was based on the typical mechanics of the role-playing genre, and as such predominantly afforded configurative and narrative agency. The next section outlined the brand identity of the *Mass Effect* franchise, as shaped by its various instalments, in terms of how the games afford or limit player action, which was then used as a basis of comparison when looking at *Andromeda* as a text. The analysis revealed that open world game design allowed more opportunity for combat encounters which are also more complex when compared to the original trilogy. However, an emphasis on these gameplay features caused a shift that was not quite reconcilable with BioWare's historic design ethos. Previously, role-playing mechanics affording narrative and configurative agency were of core importance. This new focus led to the possibility space for player action to be predominantly shaped in the temporal-ergodic and spatial-explorative dimension. The chapter concluded by arguing that, although this shift would in theory support the expression of dramatic agency, in reality, *Andromeda* struggled to attach a quality of eventfulness to these emergent player stories, and therefore ultimately failed to truly afford a high degree of dramatic agency.

The final case study in Chapter 5 expanded the scope of the inquiry at the heart of this book by applying the heuristic framework to a different production context and game design model. The independent studio of System Era Softworks was chosen for two reasons. First, its founders moved away from AAA studios, and thus had articulate opinions about their past experiences in this section of the videogame industry and why they chose to abandon it. This meant the paratextual material was rich enough to be analysed in terms of design intent. Second, the game they set out to make, *Astroneer* (2019), exemplifies a specific game design model of survival crafting sandbox games. These draw on very early videogame genres, and with technologies improving, they evolved less in their visuals like AAA games did, but more in terms of their game design. The chapter began by surveying common connotations of the 'independent' label and providing a brief history of milestone games standing out for their design innovations over the decades. This was done to establish a background against which System Era, a new studio lacking a historical design ethos comparable to those of Naughty Dog or BioWare, positioned themselves, which I called their founding ethos. Having identified various inspirations for their game in the early years of development, the chapter then moved on to interrogate the paratext starting from the launch of the Early Access version of *Astroneer* paratexts in a quest to identify a more crystallised design intention. This intention, I argued, was a focus on facilitating playfulness. The textual analysis then connected the notion of playfulness to agency being afforded in the spatial-explorative, configurative-constructive, and temporal-ergodic dimensions through mechanics facilitating free, unconstrained, experimentational, creative play. I further argued that dramatic agency is inherently playful.

The case studies presented have laid the groundwork for analysing agency in a way that combines paratextual analysis and textual analysis. Such application of the multidimensional heuristic framework provided insight into not only how game designers think about agency, but also into how intentions can translate into features of the released game. The investigation mapped three ways in which communicated design intention and the final product can relate to each other as well as to the design ethos of the studio (and the brand identity of the franchise in the first two cases). Naughty Dog showed alignment, BioWare showed discord, while System Era showed fluidity. The case studies showed that circumstances of production, such as technology used and management of production and distribution, impact how player action is thought to be afforded, and is eventually afforded. The picture these case studies painted was that the fewer stakeholders are involved in negotiating a studio's design ethos, the more consistently it evolves over time; and the more transparent a studio is about their progress during development, the smaller the discrepancy between game-as-promised and game-as-released.

Generally speaking, the book offered a design-oriented approach to understanding agency, and the case studies symbolise three kinds of experiences videogames can offer: spectacle, role-play, and free play. Furthermore, they also mark a gradual relaxation of designer control on player action: from highly linear, through open world, to sandbox. *Uncharted 4* showed that despite a high degree of designer control, player agency can still manifest in multiple dimensions, and it underscored the importance of highly detailed animation in dramatic agency. *Mass Effect: Andromeda*, while maintaining the configurative freedom typical of role-playing games, served as a cautionary tale for what happens to agency when gameplay moments lack a quality of eventfulness. Lastly, *Astroneer* exemplified how a high degree of agency across all dimensions can result in paidic play. The three case study chapters showed that the multidimensional conceptualisation of agency in the heuristic framework is but the first step towards better understanding agency in videogames, and that with each example come further complexities in the way that production context and design intent shape player agency.

The conceptualisation of agency presented in this book can be further expanded in a variety of ways. It will often yield interestingly different results when used to analyse other avatar-based games and different circumstances of production. Although many potential applications may result in similar findings, there will likely be other, highly specific cases that would expand our understanding of how agency is discussed and designed across the diverse field of videogame production. It would also be worth asking how dimensions support or obstruct each other in non-avatar-based genres, such as strategy or god games. Or, as a somewhat radical departure, it would be worth exploring what further dimensions of agency can manifest in different forms of media, such as augmented and virtual reality. The heuristic framework also has the potential to be the starting point in an investigation into agency in multiplayer games. It would be interesting to observe how the infinite variable that is the other player, as well as approach to audience management in ongoing support for online games, could impact affordances and restrictions of player action both on the level of game design, but also in terms of communication and social interaction. While this book has already done substantial groundwork for this kind of expansion, producing results that are in and of themselves are interesting, such an approach would then move the focus from the game to the player. It would therefore be concerned with cultural politics as well, as in multiplayer games, besides the game rules set in place by designers, player-to-player interaction is designed to a degree as well. In this case, the multidimensional framework would be used in an audience studies project, with more empirical methodologies that examine actual player interaction. The notion of agency, and by extension, the player's ability to act is an inherent feature of the medium of videogames, and so the more the medium evolves, so will the questions around player agency.

References

Bateman, C.; Zagal, J. P. (2018). Game Design Lineages. Minecraft's Inventory. *Transactions of the Digital Games Research Association* 3 (2): 13–46.

BioWare. (2017). *Mass Effect: Andromeda* [PlayStation 4]. Electronic Arts.

Naughty Dog. (2016). *Uncharted 4: A Thief's End* [PlayStation 4]. Sony Computer Entertainment.

System Era Softworks. (2019). *Astroneer* [PC]. System Era Softworks.

Index

Aarseth, Espen 14–15, 30, 44, 49–51, 58, 60
Adams, Ernest 15, 20–21, 49, 51–52
Age of Empires II (videogame) 25, 56
Alvarez Igarzábal, Federico 49
Amnesia: The Dark Descent (videogame) 166
Animal Crossing (videogame series) 51
Anthem (videogame) 131
Antropy, Anna 162
Apollo 13 (film) 179
Aristotle 179
Arsenault, Dominic 22, 44, 49
Assassin's Creed (videogame series) 1, 57, 88, 90, 169, 171
Astroneer (videogame) 6, 161–205, 209–210
Atkins, Barry 14, 26, 58

Backe, Hans–Joachim 58
Baldur's Gate (videogame) 120, 122–124, 149
Balestra, Christophe 81, 89
Banks, John 13
Bartle, Richard 44
Bateman, Chris 3, 20, 178, 207
Batens, Diderik 43
Beil, Benjamin 4, 167
Biddlecom, Aaron 177–180
Bienia, Rafael 54
The Binding of Isaac (videogame) 62, 166
Bizzocchi, Jim 4, 142, 143–144
Björk, Staffan 18–19, 27, 49, 54
Bleszinski, Cliff 48
Blom, Joleen 25
Bogost, Ian 26, 30, 173–174
Boon, Richard 20
Boonen, Casper 2, 41
Booth, Paul 4

Bordwell, David 13, 92
Braben, David 165
Braid (videogame) 52, 166
Brock, Tom 14
Bromell, Adam 169–171, 175
Burn, Andrew 44

Caillois, Roger 162, 177, 194
Caldwell, John Thornton 4
Call of Duty (videogame series) 1, 90, 130
Calleja, Gordon 42, 49, 93
Campbell, Colin 18
Campbell, Jessica 135, 144
Carr, Diane 14
Castronova, Edward 57–58
Chandler, Rafael 61–62
Chapman, Adam 4, 53
Charles, Alec 22
Cheng, Paul 14, 59
Chou, Allen 105
Church, Doug 18–19
Condominas, Fabrice 132, 135, 139–141, 145
Consalvo, Mia 3–4
Cosmos (television series) *169*
Costikyan, Greg 18, 28, 57
Crash Bandicoot (videogame series) 76–79
Crawford, Chris 14
Creswell, John W. 43

Dahlskog, Steve 54
Dark Souls (videogame) 190
DayZ (videogame) 172
Dear Esther (videogame) 166
Debus, Michael S. 45
Detroit: Become Human (videogame) 52, 60
Deus Ex (videogame) 121

Deuze, Mark 2
Diablo (videogame series) 55, 121
Disco Elysium (videogame) 55
Domsch, Sebastian 2, 16–17
Don't Starve (videogame) 50, 191
Doom (videogame) 77, 120, 165
Dragon Age (videogame series) 122, 129–130, 136
Druckmann, Neil 83–84, 88–89, 92–93, 96–97
Dungeons and Dragons (tabletop game) 120–121

The Elder Scrolls V: Skyrim (videogame) 50
Elverdam, Christian 49
Enter the Gungeon (videogame) 62, 166
Eskelinen, Markku 14–15, 27, 49, 54
Evans, Elizabeth 182

Factorio (videogame) 172
Fallout 4 (videogame) 50, 56
Falstein, Noah 18, 59
Far Cry (videogame series) 88, 121, 143
Fernández-Vara, Clara 4–5
Fez (videogame) 166
Final Fantasy VIII (videogame) 86
Five Nights at Freddy's (videogame) 166
Flynn, Aaron 128–129, 131–132, 137
Football Manager (videogame) 165
The Forest (videogame) 56
Foucault, Michel 13
Foxman, Maxwell Henry 3
Frasca, Gonzalo 14–15, 29, 59, 177
Fraser, Emma 14
Frazier, Ian 139–140
Fullerton, Tracy 20, 58, 61

Gallagher, Rob 142
Gamble, Mike 125, 136–137
Garda, Maria B. 162–165
Garry's Mod (videogame) 168
Gavin, Andy 77
Gazzard, Alison 46, 167
Genette, Gerard 3, 179
Gibson, James J. 3, 26
Giddens, Anthony 13
Girina, Ivan 102–103, 108
Glassner, Andrew 59
Gone Home (videogame) 166
Grabarczyk, Paweł 162–165

Grainge, Paul 4
Grand Theft Auto (videogame series) 79, 121, 168
Gravatt, Riley 169
Gray, Jonathan 4
Gregersen, Andreas 28
Grodal, Torben 28, 59
Guevara-Villalobos, Orlando 166

Habel, Chad 14
Half Life (videogame series) 25, 165, 168
Halo (videogame series) 81, 121, 169, 171
Hanson, Christopher 49
Harrell, Fox D. 14, 41
Harvest Moon (videogame) 56
Hatfield, Mike 85
Heidegger, Martin 13
Hennig, Amy 83, 87, 89, 93
Holopainen, Jussi 18–19, 27, 49
Hoque, Zabir 175–176, 184
Horizon: Zero Dawn (videogame) 143
Hudson, Casey 124, 131
Hühn, Peter 143, 152–153
Huizinga, Johan 162
Hunicke, Robin 27–28, 53

I'm A Celebrity, Get Me Out of Here (television series) 172
Indiana Jones (film series) 82–83, 98
Isbister, Katherine 20, 25

Jade Empire (videogame) 121–125
Jak and Daxter (videogame) 76, 79–80, 84
Jak II (videogame) 81
Jannidis, Fotis 58
Järvinen, Aki 28–30, 131
Jenkins, Henry 13, 44, 58–59
Johnson, Catherine 4
Jørgensen, Kristine 2, 24, 44, 136, 142, 178, 190
Joseph, Daniel J. 13
Juul, Jesper 2, 15–16, 26, 44, 49, 58, 136, 162–165, 166

Kalman, Samantha 177–180, 191
Karhulahti, Veli-Matti 53
Katamari Damacy (videogame) 25
Kennedy, Helen 5
Kentucky Route Zero (videogame) 166
Keogh, Brendan 14, 165, 174
Kern, Spencer 167, 172

Kerr, Aphra 120, 165
King, Geoff 2, 41, 46, 75, 87
Klastrup, Lisbeth 14, 44
Klevjer, Rune 25–26, 44, 59, 106
Knowland, Michael 89
Knowles, Isaac 57
Kooyman, Ben 14
Koster, Raph 20, 53
Kovats, Phil 88, 99
Krampe, Theresa 142
Kremers, Rudolf 48
Krzywinska, Tanya 2, 26, 41, 46, 54, 75, 87

Lankosi, Petri 28
The Last of Us (videogame) 87–89, 104
Latour, Bruno 13
LeBlanc, Marc 18, 51, 61
The Legend of Zelda: Breath of the Wild (videogame) 1
Lemarchand, Richard 82, 84–85
Liechty, Jacob 169, 174, 176
Limbo (videogame) 166
Linderoth, Jonas 25
Lindley, Craig 49
Lipkin, Nadav D. 162–163
Lord of the Flies (novel) 171

MacCallum-Stewart, Esther 22, 54
MacMillan, Joel 132
Man Vs Wild (television series) 172
Margenau, Kurt 94
The Martian (film) 179
Mass Effect (videogame) 124–128
Mass Effect 2 (videogame) 124–128, 151–152
Mass Effect 3 (videogame) 124–129, 133, 139
Mass Effect: Andromeda (videogame) 6, 119–160, 184, 208–210
Mateas, Michael 18, 26–27, 49–50, 61
Max Payne (videogame) 52
MDK 2 (videogame) 122–124
Meretzky, Steve 25
Metal Gear Solid 2 (videogame) 79, 104
Mieritz, Daniel 2, 41
Minecraft (videogame) 54, 56, 161, 167, 172, 177
Mochoki, Michal 59
Mortal Kombat X (videogame) 47
Mukherjee, Souvik 13

Murray, Janet 2, 14–16, 23, 30, 55, 61, 173
Muzyka, Ray 120, 125, 128
Myst (videogame) 120

National Treasure (film) 83
Neitzel, Britta 58
Neverwinter Nights (videogame) 121
Newman, Anthony 94
Newman, James 4, 104
Nichols, Randy 165
Nicoll, Benjamin 174
Nieborg, David B. 3
Nitsche, Michael 24, 44, 168
No Man's Sky (videogame) 172, 176
Norman, Donald 26

O'Donnell, Casey 3, 165

Parsler, Justin 22
Pearce, Celia 14
Pepera, Paul 169, 176
Perlin, Ken 175–176
Perron, Bernard 22, 44, 48, 49, 128
Peterson, Jon 54
Poole, Don 81–82
Prince of Persia: Sands of Time (videogame) 52, 81

Quake (videogame) 165
Quantum Break (videogame) 52

Ratchet and Clank (videogame) 80
Resident Evil (videogame series) 47, 121, 190
Richmond, Justin 89
The Road (novel) 172
Robinson Crusoe (novel) 171
Rogers, Jeremy 98–99
Roller Coaster Tycoon (videogame) 56
Rootsaeert, Cathleen 138
Rouse, Richard III 20, 28, 62, 143
Roy, Yannick 129, 135, 139
Ruberg, Bonnie 13
Rubin, Jason 76–80
Ruffino, Paolo 162–163
Rust (videogame) 191
Ryan, Marie-Laure 14–15, 58–60, 136

Salen, Katie 20, 23–24, 27–30, 60, 177, 190–191
Schell, Jesse 20, 24, 29, 45, 131
Schmid, Wolf 143, 152

Schott, Gareth R. 41
Schreier, Jason 89, 129–130, 132, 138
Shaw, Adrienne 13
Sicart, Miguel 2, 28–29, 54, 162, 190
The Sims (videogame) 21, 25, 56, 168–169
Skolnick, Evan 55
Sonic the Hedgehog (videogame) 77–78
Sotamaa, Olli 13
Space Engineers (videogame) 172–173
Spelunky (videogame) 62, 166
Stang, Sara 2
Star Fox (videogame) 77
Star Wars (film series) 106, 119, 122–123, 169
Star Wars: Knights of the Old Republic (videogame) 122–126, 149
Stardew Valley (videogame) 56
Stashwick, Todd 89
Stenros, Jaakko 162, 190–191
Stern, Andrew 18, 26–27
Straley, Bruce 83–84, 88–89, 91, 93, 95
Subnautica (videogame) 172–173
Suits, Bernard 190
Super Mario Bros (videogame series) 77–78
Super Meat Boy (videogame) 166
SUPERHOT (videogame) 52
Švelch, Jan 4
Swink, Steve 20

Tanenbaum, Karen 2
Tanenbaum, Theresa Jean 2, 142–144
Theme Hospital (videogame) 56
Thomas Was Alone (videogame) 45
Thompson, Kristin 92
Thon, Jan-Noël 44–45, 47, 58–59, 162
Tirado, Joe 170, 177
Togelius, Julian 54, 174
Tomb Raider (videogame series) 46, 77
Tom Clancy's Ghost Recon Wildlands (videogame) 46–47

Tom Clancy's Splinter Cell (videogame) 81
Toms, Kevin 165
Tretton, Jack 90
Tudyk, Alan 89
Tulloch, Rowan 2, 27

Ultima Online (videogame) 120
Uncharted: Drake's Fortune (videogame) 81–83
Uncharted 2: Among Thieves (videogame) 82–83, 85–87, 94, 97
Uncharted 3: Drake's Deception (videogame) 82, 97
Uncharted 4: A Thief's End (videogame) 5, 87–109, 183, 207–210
Untitled Goose Game (videogame) 166

Vella, Daniel 25–26, 46
Vollans, Ed 4, 181

Walters, Mac 124–125, 132, 135–137, 150
Wardrip–Fruin, Noah 2, 20, 26, 43
Wells, Evan 80
Wells, Nate 89
Westecott, Emma 25, 166
Willumsen, Ea Christina 25, 54
Wilson, Brendan 169–171, 176, 179
Wolf, Mark J. P. 44, 107
Wolfenstein 3D (videogame) 77
Wright, Esther 4
Wright, Will 168

Yates, Jeremy 95, 98
Yip, Augustine 120

Zagal, Jose 3, 49–50, 54, 207
Zeschuk, Greg 120, 122–123, 127–128
Zhu, Jichen 14, 41
Zimmerman, Eric 20, 23–24, 27–30, 60, 162, 177, 190–191